Moved by Modernity

Moved by Modernity

*How Development Shapes Migration
in Rural Ethiopia*

KERILYN SCHEWEL

OXFORD
UNIVERSITY PRESS

Oxford University Press is a department of the University of Oxford.
It furthers the University's objective of excellence in research, scholarship,
and education by publishing worldwide. Oxford is a registered trade mark of
Oxford University Press in the UK and in certain other countries.

Published in the United States of America by Oxford University Press
198 Madison Avenue, New York, NY 10016, United States of America.

© Oxford University Press 2025

All rights reserved. No part of this publication may be reproduced, stored in a retrieval system, transmitted, used for text and data mining, or used for training artificial intelligence, in any form or by any means, without the prior permission in writing of Oxford University Press, or as expressly permitted by law, by license or under terms agreed with the appropriate reprographics rights organization. Inquiries concerning reproduction outside the scope of the above should be sent to the Rights Department, Oxford University Press, at the address above.

You must not circulate this work in any other form
and you must impose this same condition on any acquirer.

CIP data is on file at the Library of Congress.

ISBN 9780197680728

ISBN 9780197680711 (hbk.)

DOI: 10.1093/9780197680759.001.0001

The manufacturer's authorized representative in the EU for product safety
is Oxford University Press España S.A., Parque Empresarial San Fernando de Henares,
Avenida de Castilla, 2 – 28830 Madrid (www.oup.es/en or product.safety@oup.com).
OUP España S.A. also acts as importer into Spain of products made by the manufacturer.

For Benji

Contents

Acknowledgments	viii
Introduction	1
1. Theorizing Migration in Modernity	17
2. The Modernization of Ethiopia	37
3. The Mobility History of Wayisso	58
4. The State	75
5. The Market	102
6. Education	131
7. Foreign Investment	160
8. Land and Climate	182
9. The Good Life	201
10. Lessons from Wayisso	223
Epilogue	241
Methodological Notes	243
Notes	250
Index	272

Acknowledgments

This research would not have been possible without the support and guidance of so many. I am forever grateful to my mentors, Hein de Haas and Jørgen Carling, for their intellectual companionship throughout this long journey. Your work continues to inspire me. My deep gratitude goes to the Bahá'í community of the Adami Tulu cluster, particularly Kidanemariam, Eshetu, Solomon, Bashula, and Tahirih, for their hospitality and friendship, and to Kedir Gemechu and Tilah Alemayehu, whose dedication, skills, and humor made fieldwork a joy, even on the most challenging days. I am immensely grateful to Dr. Asmamaw Legass Bahir and the Geography Department at Addis Ababa University for facilitating my research in Ethiopia, and to the Department of Sociology at the University of Amsterdam, the Netherlands Organisation for Scientific Research, the European Research Council (ERC Grant Agreement 648496), the International Migration Institute, the Institute for Studies in Global Prosperity, Princeton University's Office of Population Research, and the Duke Center for International Development for their support at different stages of this project. I give special thanks to Michael Jauchen for his skillful editorial guidance and to James Cook and the team at Oxford University Press for guiding this book to publication. I am indebted to many friends and colleagues for their feedback on different ideas and iterations of this manuscript over the years: Simona Vezzoli, Sonja Fransen, Katharina Natter, Marina de Regt, Anja van Heelsum, Jan Willem Duyvendak, Hannah Postel, Stephen Murphy, Lee Miller, Jonathan Weiler, Eilish Zembilci, and so many others.

This book is dedicated to my husband, Ben, whose steady support and perspective sustained me over the long research and writing process. I began this book in one stage of life and ended it in quite another. I embarked on this project young, transient, driven by intellectual curiosity, and married to a remarkable man who moved countries several times to allow me to pursue new and exciting opportunities. After the birth of two children, a global pandemic, an intercontinental move, and our conscious decision to grow roots in a single place, I am concluding it in a very different stage of life—perhaps best described as a daily struggle to find coherence across what can feel like competing demands and aspirations for motherhood, academia, and community. Much like those I came to know in Wayisso, I'm striving to realize a vision of the "good life" that my society is not readily structured to support. This book is one fruit of my slow but dedicated efforts to find a way forward.

A central theme running through these pages is how our aspirations and accomplishments are never entirely our own. They are realized within wider social, economic, and cultural currents that both carry and constrain us. It is through a growing appreciation of these forces—and through the collaboration, care, and generosity of the many people who contributed to this project—that I've come to realize just how much anything we achieve as individuals relies upon community.

Introduction

This is the story of a village that may not exist in a few years. Named Wayisso, it lies in the central lowlands of the Ethiopian Rift Valley, three hours south of Addis Ababa by bus. There is nothing immediately remarkable about this place. Clusters of circular mud and thatched-roof homes huddle a few kilometers from the main road, surrounded by cornfields, cacti, and acacia trees. Cattle are commonplace, lounging behind fences in family compounds or traveling the well-worn path to a nearby river. On any given day, you might see children playing or herding cattle, stick in hand; women roasting coffee over charcoal stoves; men driving oxen in the fields or chewing *khat* leaves in the shade. There is a village primary school, a health center, a mosque, and a new well for fresh water—the latter donated by Verde Beef, a foreign-owned beef production business neighboring the village.

In the last decade, there has been a notable rise in the number of people leaving this village. Most leave for the neighboring boomtown, some land in one of Ethiopia's more distant cities, and others go as far away as Dubai to work as maids in the homes of foreign families. Regardless of the destination, the main reason people give for leaving is almost always the same: "*jiruu koo jijiruuf*" in the local language Oromiffa—"to change my life."

When I first arrived in Wayisso in 2015, I had one deceptively simple question in mind: why are people leaving? The answers I found over the course of the next three years challenged everything I previously thought about "development" and its relationship with migration.

When one imagines the drivers of migration from resource-poor, rural settings in a country like Ethiopia—one of the world's "least developed countries" according to the United Nations—ideas about poverty, climate change, or political conflict probably come to the fore. A quick perusal of news articles about migration from low-income countries almost always gives the impression that people are *forced* to leave their homes. Even in academic research on migration in Ethiopia, scholars maintain an almost myopic focus on "push factors"—population pressure and land scarcity, environmental degradation and climate change, drought and famine, conflict and political crisis.[1] With time, I began to think of these explanations as *push-factor narratives*: the stories we tell about migration that emphasize the negative forces that compel people to leave their homes. In these narratives, migration reflects a problem, and how to solve that problem has become one of the major questions of our time.

An unintended side effect of push-factor narratives is a flattening of the migration process, however. Migrants' agency, aspirations, and motivations for moving—which may be for schooling, work, love, adventure, or simply change—are de-emphasized to spotlight the structural drivers of displacement. Because push-factor narratives miss these alternative motivations for migration, they perpetuate a false assumption: if development policy and programming can alleviate the drivers of displacement—if we can help poor places develop—people will no longer *need* to migrate.

This book not only shows why that assumption is wrong but also argues precisely the opposite. Development *creates* the need to migrate, and this is particularly true in rural places. Wayisso's story is illustrative precisely because it is a poor village, and issues like climate change, land scarcity, and poverty are very real concerns of its smallholder farmers. Yet, people are not leaving Wayisso to flee these constraints on rural livelihoods. On the contrary, these constraints are what keep people in the village. Because migration requires significant resources—money, networks, and know-how—the most vulnerable and disadvantaged households cannot migrate. In other words, the families facing the strongest push factors often express feeling "trapped" in the village by their poverty. Those who do leave are those with higher levels of education, income, and social capital, and they are leaving to pursue new kinds of lives. Younger generations in Wayisso no longer want to be farmers or pastoralists. They want to become educated, to have their own business or secure salaried work, and to live in towns with urban amenities. Ethiopia's development is driving these aspirational shifts, creating new needs and desires that cannot be fulfilled in Wayisso and that require migration to achieve.

***

One rainy afternoon in London in October 2016, I met Ademtuu,[2] who at that time was the only person to have left Wayisso for Europe. Short and soft-spoken, Ademtuu is one of those quietly strong women who could easily go unnoticed as she moves through London's bustling city. I met her on her way home from work at a cosmetics store. Then in her early thirties, Ademtuu rented a small room in a five-story housing complex on an unremarkable street in central London. We sat on her bed and shared several spicy stews that she prepared the night before. She quickly apologized that she did not make the injera, the traditional Ethiopian flatbread, herself. "It's not real injera, but it's the only option we have. I bought it from a restaurant."

I lived with Ademtuu's sister while doing research in Ethiopia, and it is because of that connection that Ademtuu welcomed me. After eating, I pulled out my laptop to show her photos of her family and friends back home. But after looking at just a few, she turned away. "You don't know what it's like to be away from your family," she told me, gesturing for me to close the computer. I shared that I was also living in a country far from my home, but she objected that it is "normal" for my people. "It is not natural for mine. In Ethiopia, we live in a group. The door is always open. People come in and out. I do not like closed doors," she said, pointing toward the closed door of her room. "But here, I get up, I walk out, and I come home. I am the only one who goes in and out of this door."

Life in London is difficult, yet the money Ademtuu sends home is changing the lives of her parents, siblings, and cousins in Wayisso. Unlike many other children in the village, her younger siblings do not have to stop their schooling after they graduate from the village primary school; they can afford to rent a room in a neighboring town to attend secondary school. With a little extra cash, her cousins are emboldened to make new investments, embracing entrepreneurship as a way out of poverty. One cousin built a poultry farm, bought forty-two chickens, and runs a business selling eggs to restaurants in neighboring towns. Her mother is now the envy of her neighbors, particularly when she moves to her new home in town to rest and visit her children between planting and harvesting seasons. All of these changes come from the money Ademtuu saves and sends. "Do you think you will ever return?" I asked. "No, I don't think so," she said. "I am not happy here, but I know I couldn't be happy there anymore either."

I asked Ademtuu to tell me about Tuffaa, her great-grandfather. "Tuffaa!" she laughed. "How do you know about him?" She paused, and then her eyes grew wide: "Tuffaa lived like an animal! Tuffaa didn't have a house. There were no houses! He just hunted and lived from what he found." Ademtuu never met her great-grandfather, but she grew up hearing stories about him from her father, Hassan.

Tuffaa was born to Bariso, son of Waqoo, near Lake Langano in the late 1800s. His early life was one of hunting, foraging, and moving with the seasons through the Rift Valley's forested lowlands. He was part of the Arsi Oromo, an ethnic group that had maintained its independence from the expanding Ethiopian empire until around the time Tuffaa was born. The political backdrop to his childhood must have been tense, as the Arsi heroically fought and resisted the successive invasion campaigns of Emperor Menelik II, eventually succumbing to the European firearms of their imperial colonizers. But none of that was mentioned by his descendants. They emphasized the exceptionalism of Tuffaa's way of life. Although pastoralism, and even farming, was already practiced by many Oromo[3] peoples, Tuffaa belonged to another time. He lived from the land and "fought tigers and lions!" Things changed when he married though. He marked the moment by killing an elephant and trading the ivory for a bull at the nearest market. He began tending to a growing herd of livestock and then a growing cadre of children. His family moved and settled seasonally, traveling with their livestock between regular grazing pastures throughout the valley. Tuffaa had five sons and two daughters live to adulthood. By the time his son, Bedane, was grown, Tuffaa and his family had fully embraced pastoralism.

Bedane was, until the end of his days, a pastoralist.[4] His herd had some eighty cattle. His seasonal movements mirrored his father's: toward the lakes in the dry season and away from them in the wet, when malaria became a threat. There were boundaries to this movement—borders that marked the domains of other ethnic groups. But within the Arsi Oromo territory through the late nineteenth and early twentieth century, movement was relatively free. The Ethiopian empire that had technically claimed this territory was not yet present in any meaningful way. Those rulers were busy with their own affairs in the distant capital city or fighting off Italian invaders farther north. Bedane's family continued to linger in places for weeks or months, until eventually one location near a small mountain called Macho began to serve as a home base. Temporary shelters gradually became simple homes. When some left with the cattle, others began to stay behind, in what came to be called *ganda Bedane*, which roughly translates to "Bedane village." Bedane prospered and had three wives, seven sons, and fifteen daughters. All his daughters married and moved elsewhere. Of Bedane's seven sons, six settled in *ganda Bedane* to form large families of their own. Bedane lived to an old age—125, his children claim. He is buried in Wayisso in a small graveyard surrounded by acacia trees and his sons' family compounds.

Bedane's sons grew up shepherding cattle, but as they entered adulthood, they began to consider another livelihood prospect: growing crops. Initially, they farmed a few small plots to supplement their pastoral way of life. But with time, the political machinations of the distant empire exerted a greater effect in *ganda Bedane*. Particularly in 1974, when a military coup overthrew Emperor Haile Selassie and established a new Marxist regime, strong forces of political and economic change reached the village. *Ganda Bedane* was soon formally incorporated into the new *Waeso Qancaara kebele*, a "peasant association" where it was envisioned that pastoralists would learn to farm and become productive citizens of the new socialist nation-state. Initially resistant, many in Wayisso eventually embraced farming and other modern pursuits—entering formal schooling; learning the national language, Amharic; or assuming leadership positions in the local government. Settling into the peasant association brought significant changes to *ganda Bedane*. One of Bedane's sons, Hassan, built three homes for his three wives. Unlike the traditional mud and thatched-roof huts common in the village, Hassan's homes had multiple rooms. His wives bore him twenty-nine children.

Hassan's children grew up assisting with their family's crops and cattle, but as they entered adolescence, almost all of them turned their gaze to the city. For many, their childhood overlapped with another revolution in Ethiopia, when in 1991, the socialist regime fell and a new federal government, a self-titled developmental state, took its place. In this generation, no one wanted to be a farmer anymore. They focused on getting an education, finding urban work, and getting out of Wayisso. In fact, of Hassan's twenty-nine children, no one older than thirteen still lives in the village. None have children of their own yet—including his eldest daughter, Ademtuu, who, like her great-grandfather before her, is exceptional. She was one of the first girls in the region to go to school and the first to migrate to Europe. Her brothers and sisters are almost all urban dwellers. Most live in the district center, Ziway (recently renamed Baatuu[5]), studying, working odd jobs, or building their own businesses.

How did this come to be, that within just four generations, a single family moved through three ways of life: Tuffaa and Bedane, as pastoralists; Hassan, as a farmer; and his children, as urbanites? Each generation came of age in a very different Ethiopia, and each generation brought new ways of living and moving—from nomadism to settlement, and from settlement to rural-urban and international migration. Push-factor narratives are not sufficient to explain these transitions. The more fundamental question concerns how and why Ethiopia's pursuit of national development led to such dramatic shifts in the migration behavior of this one village.

***

In 1971, geographer Wilbur Zelinsky published an article called "The Hypothesis of the Mobility Transition." A classic example of armchair theorizing, it was nevertheless revolutionary. Zelinksy's core claim was that "there are definite, patterned regularities in the growth of personal mobility through space-time during recent history, and these regularities comprise an essential component of the modernization process."[6] His article, filled with charts and graphs, illustrated how various forms of mobility—rural-rural, rural-urban, international, circular, and frontier migration—might change at different stages of development. In short, he hypothesized a general increase in and diversification of all forms of internal and international migration as "premodern traditional societies" modernize. At later stages of modernization, international migration declines, immigration into that society increases, and "circulation"—commuting, travel, and so forth—becomes more common.

Zelinsky's article was the first to present a grand schematic for the relationship between migration and development, and at the time, the idea of a mobility transition caused quite a stir. Some regarded it as an instant classic in the field of population geography. As one reviewer wrote, the model's "broad sweep provided a useful antidote to the often myopic and sterile empiricism of contemporary work."[7] Yet, the hypothesis also had clear limitations. After all, Zelinsky's theory was not based on or supported by any rigorous empirical data. Many critiqued the model for the same reasons other grand theories of modernization were in disrepute at the time: for portraying modernization as a unilinear and uniform process and for prioritizing the experience of Western nations at a particular historical moment as the ground for universal theories.

Zelinsky's hypothesis of the mobility transition eventually fell out of favor, and—save for the work of one Scottish geographer, Ronald Skeldon[8]—it was largely forgotten by migration researchers and their textbooks for several decades. But after years of relative neglect, the mobility transition is receiving renewed attention. Equipped with new sources of increasingly reliable data on global migration and development trends, researchers are bringing added rigor to their investigation of migration-development interactions, and the idea of a mobility transition has been helpful to explain what they are finding. Multiple studies confirm one of the original patterns Zelinsky first theorized: an inverted U-shaped relationship between development and international migration, such that migration rises as countries move from low- to middle-income status and then tapers off once those countries

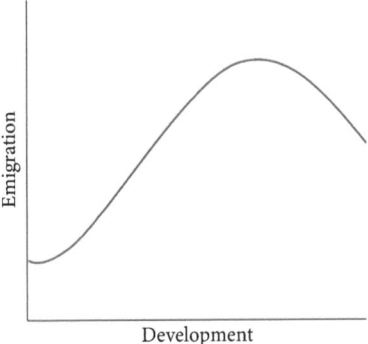

Figure 0.1 Stylized rendering of the migration transition curve

reach higher levels of economic development (Figure 0.1).[9] Whether measuring development in terms of gross domestic product (GDP) per capita or human development indicators, the trend is clear: as poorer countries develop, more people leave.

Unlike prevalent perspectives that portray migration and development as substitutes for one another,[10] there is now evidence of a patterned and potentially reinforcing relationship between migration and development as countries move from low- to middle-income status. Yet, despite growing social scientific consensus that this macro-level relationship exists, surprisingly little is known about the mechanisms driving this dynamic on the ground. An urgent puzzle remains: what is it exactly about development that drives international migration?

No single discipline has been able to provide a compelling answer. Some studies point to the loosening of financial constraints on migration as households gain access to higher incomes. Others point to education. As the proportion of college graduates in the native population increases, it is precisely this group that has the highest propensity to emigrate abroad.[11] More critical perspectives emphasize the livelihood displacement associated with capitalist development. The integration of developing regions into the global economy undermines traditional livelihoods, forcing (often rural) populations to migrate for work.[12] While each study contributes a piece to the puzzle of the mobility transition, the big picture remains fuzzy.

To better understand why development stimulates a mobility transition, more detailed case studies are needed. Existing global analyses are constrained by several factors: (1) a limited number of comparable datasets that restricts what variables can be meaningfully analyzed; (2) the related preoccupation with *international* migration, which misses important changes in how people move within their countries and how internal and international migration can complement or substitute for each other; and (3) a narrow focus on *economic* development, most often measured in GDP per capita, which misses other important political, cultural, or demographic dimensions of social change. Case studies can go deeper, drawing on a wider array of country-specific data sources to ask what the pursuit of development has practically entailed for a given country and how it affects the entire mobility complex of that society, not only volumes of international migration.

At first glance, Ethiopia does not appear to be the best candidate for a case study of the mobility transition. It remains one of the world's poorest and most rural countries, and international migration is not particularly high compared to other countries at similar levels of economic development.[13] Moreover, most accounts of Ethiopian migration still focus on the drivers of *displacement*, not development-induced migration. This is understandable, given the degree of displacement associated with the relatively rapid regime changes and protracted conflicts over the last half century.[14] The Ethiopian diaspora in the United States, for example, was first established after the bloody communist revolution in the 1970s. By 1980, over 2.5 million people (an astounding 3 percent) of Ethiopia's national population were refugees, the vast majority of whom were in neighboring countries Somalia and Sudan. Another refugee peak—which saw 1.3 million displaced abroad—occurred in 1990, just before the Ethiopian People's Revolutionary Democratic Front seized power and introduced a new government in the 1990s.[15] At the time of writing, the country is recovering from a recent civil war in Tigray, where over 2 million were displaced within and outside of Ethiopia, and regional conflicts persist. Indeed, conflict and displacement have been and remain key parts of Ethiopia's migration history.

Yet, beneath and between these peaks in violence and displacement, there are telltale signs that a mobility transition is occurring. As development indicators increased significantly in the 2000s and 2010s, volumes of international migration commensurately grew. Between 2000 and 2019, Ethiopia's Human Development Index rose by more than 60 percent, and GDP per capita tripled. Over this same period, the total number of Ethiopians residing in another country, not including refugees and asylum seekers, increased from 364,944 to 641,528, and these figures miss significant—potentially more than double—volumes of undocumented migration to the Middle East and to East and South Africa.[16] Ethiopia's rapid development over this period went hand in hand with rising international migration.

To better understand the recent rise in international migration, I conducted a study with Asmamaw Legass Bahir, a geographer at Addis Ababa University, to map migration-development interactions in Ethiopia over the last century.[17] We had several questions: What was happening to internal migration patterns as international migration rose? Had population movements changed in any meaningful way in the twentieth century before this rise in international migration? And what dimensions of development and social change—including but not limited to the country's economic growth—could help explain these shifts in migration trends?

Taking a more expansive approach to migration revealed that the relatively recent rise in international labor migration is one manifestation of a more complex shift in Ethiopia's mobility complex, taking place over the course of the last century and accelerating since the 2000s. We noticed pastoralists abandoning nomadic ways of life in growing numbers. We discovered that patterns of internal migration, which were predominantly between rural places over the twentieth century, were increasingly directed toward towns and cities in the twenty-first. Furthermore, volumes of international migration were not just increasing over the 2000s; the nature, composition, and direction of these migration flows were changing as well. More people were migrating for wage work to a growing number of destinations in Africa, the Middle East, Europe, and North America, and women made up a growing share. In short, there are signs of a deeper mobility transition unfolding in Ethiopia.

We described three core trends of this transition:

- the *sedentarization* of nomadic and seminomadic mobility,
- the *urbanization* of internal migration trajectories, and
- the *diversification* of international migration.

Taking a more expansive view of "development" similarly revealed a constellation of deep societal changes that were setting the stage for a mobility transition (Table 0.1). For example, Ethiopia is in the midst of a demographic transition. As mortality rates declined and fertility rates followed more slowly over the last four decades, a larger share of Ethiopia's population are

Table 0.1 Indicators of social transformation in Ethiopia

	1960	1970	1980	1990	2000	2010	2015	2019
Population (millions)	22.2	28.4	35.3	48.1	66.5	87.7	99.9	114.1
Fertility rate (births per woman)	6.9	7.0	7.3	7.2	6.5	5.0	4.3	4.3
Infant mortality rate (per 1,000 live births)	—	143.4	141.2	120.2	88.2	55.3	44.2	37.3
Life expectancy at birth (years)	38.4	42.9	43.7	47.1	51.9	61.6	65.0	65.8
Urban population (% of total)	6.4	8.6	10.4	12.6	14.7	17.3	19.4	21.2
Gross domestic product* (billions)	—	—	7.3$^\Delta$	12.2	8.2	30.0	64.5	95.9
Primary school enrollment (% gross)	—	15.0°	33.8	35.1	54.4	91.8	101.9	92.7
Tertiary school enrollment (% gross)	—	—	0.5	0.9	1.2	7.5	8.1†	10.4†
Air transport (passengers carried, thousands)	—	231.0	242.9	620.3	944.6	3347.0	7074.8	12,631.2

* GDP in current US$.
$^\Delta$ Data for year 1981.
° Data for year 1971.
† Data for 2014 and 2018.
Source: WDI. (2020) World Development Indicators [Data Base]. Washington DC: The World Bank.

now young adults, the cohort most prone to move for work and school. The country is also experiencing a wide-scale educational transition. Younger generations are accessing formal schooling at unprecedented rates, developing new ideas about what constitutes good work and gaining new knowledge and skills to pursue it. Ethiopia's economy is diversifying as well. Agriculture contributes a declining share to the national economy as industrial and service sectors grow. The share of the population working in the service sector more than doubled between 2000 and 2017. Relatedly, there has been a slow but steady urban transition. Ethiopia's urban population increased from less than 7 percent in 1960 to over 20 percent in 2020, a change that mirrors global trends and will likely continue in the coming decades. There are many other transitions, we realized, associated with Ethiopia's development that appear to be closely intertwined with the country's mobility transition.[18]

What we could not explain with this national-level analysis, however, is what Ethiopians themselves were thinking as they adapted their migration or staying behavior to the rapid societal changes taking place around them. When and why does a pastoralist decide to stop moving with his herds and settle in one place? How does a young man make the decision to give up on farming to drive a taxi in town? Why does one woman choose to migrate to Lebanon for domestic work while others in similar circumstances stay? To answer these questions, we need a case study within a case study, which is why this book focuses on one Ethiopian village: Wayisso.[19]

The three core trends marking Ethiopia's mobility transition are all present in Wayisso—the decline of nomadic movements, a rise in rural-urban migration, and an uptick and diversification of international migration. Because of the village's proximity to Adami Tulu, a small market town with a population of some ten thousand, and Ziway (Baatuu), the district center with fifty thousand registered inhabitants (but likely many more), it is also a rich setting to understand the dynamics and drivers of Ethiopia's urban transition (Figure 0.2). Research on urbanization in Africa often focuses on big cities, yet some of its most dramatic consequences are taking place on a smaller scale—along a continuum of rural areas, villages, towns, and smaller cities.[20] Over 50 percent of Ethiopia's urban population live in towns of fifty thousand or less, and one-quarter in towns ranging from just two thousand to ten thousand people.[21] I was continually struck by how migrating to a town just fifteen kilometers away from Wayisso is a major departure from village life. "Ziway is like the capital city!" one man told me.[22]

Several additional features of Wayisso and its surroundings offer rich and sometimes counterintuitive insights into how development reshapes migration. First, Wayisso lies near several foreign-owned corporations, which allowed me to explore the impact of these companies on local livelihoods and migration decision-making (Figure 0.2). Notably, there is Afriflora Sher, a Dutch-owned company that operates the largest rose farm in the world, and Verde Beef, a Dutch- and American-owned company that raises cattle for slaughter and export to the Middle East. Such private investments are often touted as the solution to economic and migration challenges in Ethiopia and other African countries. The expectation is that, as these companies provide more local employment, Ethiopians will not need to migrate to seek work elsewhere. I found a more complex story about how these jobs are perceived by locals, who chooses to work at these companies, and who prefers unemployment or migration instead.

Second, Wayisso is home to a community of farmers whose livelihoods depend on rainfed agriculture, making them particularly vulnerable to irregular rainfall and drought. My research coincided with the aftermath of a

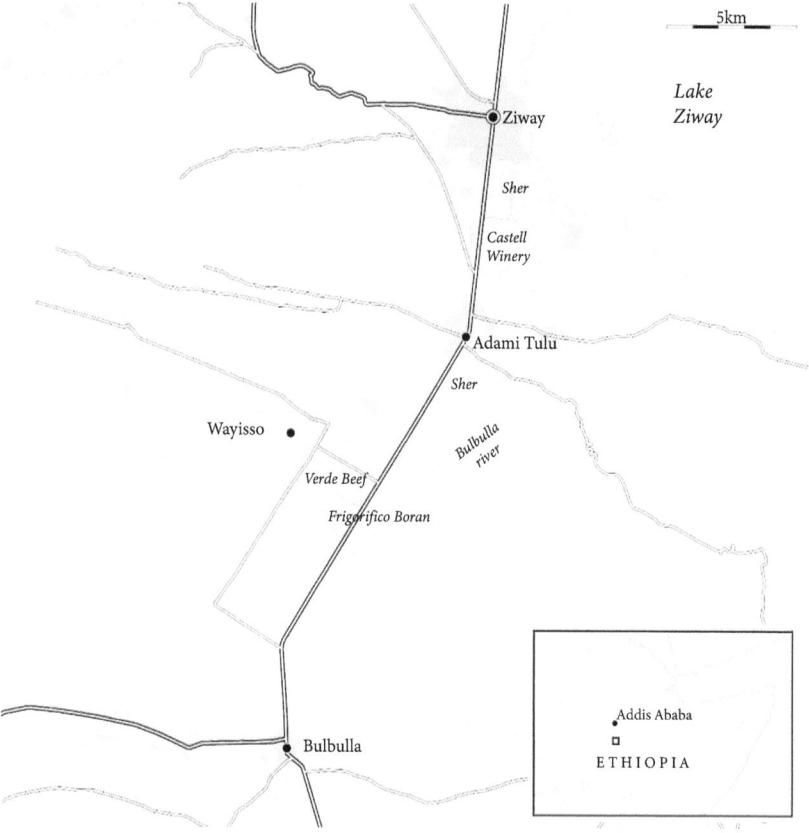

Figure 0.2 Wayisso, Adami Tulu, Ziway, and the foreign-owned companies in the district in 2018

significant drought triggered by "failed rains" in 2015, providing an opportunity to investigate how migration patterns shifted in response to this period of intensified resource scarcity. While policy discussions of climate migration—indeed, even the term "climate migration" itself—often assume a straightforward connection between environmental stress and migration or displacement, I observed a different dynamic in Wayisso: those who migrated during the drought were the least affected by it, while the most vulnerable households stayed in place, immobilized by poverty. This book argues that analyses of environmental change and migration must carefully consider existing migration systems, the conditions shaping immobility, and the social inequalities underpinning both.

Third, Wayisso's mobility history reveals the intimate connections between Ethiopia's urban transition and rising international migration. In Wayisso, migration abroad is almost always a strategy to finance a rural-urban migration project for oneself or one's family. Although one might assume that short-distance moves require fewer resources, the contradictions of globalization mean that it can be easier for a woman from Wayisso to migrate to Dubai than to Ziway. Since the 1990s, the consolidation of a migration system between Ethiopia and Middle Eastern countries—a system of brokers, agencies, and social networks—has lowered the costs of labor migration for rural women. Although labor emigration generally requires an up-front investment in a passport, health checks, and agency fees, this investment is usually paid back with a few months of work, after which women earn a salary without the expenses of food and housing. Moving to Ziway, on the other hand, requires the financial resources to buy or rent housing and pay higher prices for food, goods, and services, all without the promise of a good income from local work. A good life in the city, many explained, is only possible if you have "money in your hand." International migration for domestic work is thus a short-term, long-distance strategy to earn enough money to realize a long-term, short-distance move to town. This is the opposite of the "stepwise migration"—from villages to cities and then to international destinations—more commonly described in migration literature.[23]

Finally, there are several benefits to focusing on a single village to understand the bigger question of why development drives migration. Initially, I considered comparing how development affects migration trends in several rural and urban sites. I eventually rejected this strategy because of the pitfall common to comparative designs: painting individuals as representatives of a particular category—some rural youth quickly come to represent all rural youth; some urban youth come to represent all urban youth.[24] Rather, I found that within a single village, there was a remarkably wide range of experiences and circumstances, distinguished by age, gender, wealth, and family lineage, that influenced people's migration histories and imagined futures. Wayisso served as the linchpin around which a diversity of mobility trajectories could be explored.

***

Moved by Modernity presents a grounded and in-depth analysis of the social forces driving Ethiopia's mobility transition by examining how one rural community adapted their aspirations, livelihood strategies, and migration behavior to the transformations of modernity. Drawing on household survey data, in-depth interviews, and ethnographic fieldwork conducted in 2016 and 2018, Wayisso's story shows why push-factor narratives are inadequate to explain rural out-migration, even in resource-poor settings where constraints on rural livelihoods are pressing. It shows why "developing" these places will not stop migration. A close examination of who leaves Wayisso, and where and why they migrate, reveals how Ethiopia's development is driving rural out-migration.

When I use the term "development" throughout this book, I mean the social transformations associated with the country's pursuit of progress, including political, economic, technological, demographic, and cultural changes.[25] I aim to contribute to theory building about the relationship between migration and development while acknowledging that development is a contested concept that has been defined, pursued, and critiqued in innumerable ways. Some might argue, with good reason, that to refer to recent social changes in Ethiopia as "development" overlooks injustices inherent within Ethiopia's modernization project: the marginalization of certain ethnic groups, the neocolonial aggression of foreign capital and international development institutions, environmental degradation, political repression, and rising inequality. It is tempting to abandon the term altogether, as postdevelopment scholars advocate, and to instead analyze the drivers of migration with less value-laden or more critical terms.

And yet, as a concept, "development" remains a strong political, social, and cultural force with discursive power that continues to animate and structure the flow of capital, goods, ideas, and people around the world.[26] In Ethiopia, the concepts of development and modernization still shape the nature and substance of government policy. They also, as the anthropologist

James Ferguson argues, give form to how everyday people understand the world, "providing a set of categories and premises that continue to shape people's experiences and interpretations of their lives."[27] Thus, when I write about the consequences of Ethiopia's development on migration, I focus on what development as a social project looks like in practice—for better and for worse. Ultimately, I aim to show why changing patterns of migration reflect the changing nature, priorities, and practices of "development."

This book has three major parts. The first part (Chapters 1–3) provides the theoretical and historical context for the Wayisso case study. Chapter 1 offers a novel conceptual framework for the study of migration and development interactions, combining a social transformation perspective with the aspiration-capability framework to understand how people adapt their aspirations and behavior to social change. By drawing attention to changes in the social imaginary alongside social structures, I show why any explanation of why people migrate should consider the aspirations people hold and the capabilities they have (or lack) to achieve those aspirations. I argue that the interplay between life aspirations and local opportunity—and how different development strategies widen or lessen the gap between them—is crucial to explain variation in how the mobility transition unfolds across societies.

Chapter 2 then provides an overview of historical, national-level trends in migration patterns within and from Ethiopia, and Chapter 3 presents the migration history of Wayisso. It details how three seminomadic, pastoral families initially settled there and then analyzes subsequent patterns of out-migration. It shows where people go, how often they move, and the characteristics of those who stay, highlighting generational, gender, and family differences in migration and immobility trends.

The second part (Chapters 4–9) addresses the core question of this book: why are people leaving Wayisso? Each chapter takes one dimension of social transformation—state transformation (Chapter 4), market expansion (Chapter 5), formal education (Chapter 6), and foreign investment (Chapter 7)—and examines its impact on the changing aspirations, capabilities, and migration behavior of the local population. Chapter 8 then considers the effects of drought and environmental change. Chapter 9 culminates in a closer look at how ideas about the "good life" have changed from generation to generation. In Wayisso, the good life used to be a rural and pastoral one, and towns were widely regarded as places for the poor. Today, the opposite is true. Many now regard the village as a place of poverty, stagnation, and struggle, and the city as a place of material and social advancement. By the end of the book, it will be clear why this transformation in how rural life is perceived and valued is not a sign of development failure but an inevitable consequence of how the Ethiopian government and everyday people are pursuing "development."

This book concludes by reflecting on the lessons Wayisso offers for understanding the complex and often conflicted relationship between migration and development. It argues that Ethiopia's rapid development has cultivated a "transformation ethic"—a shared set of values that prioritize social and economic mobility over stability and social reproduction. This transformation ethic is a powerful yet underappreciated force reorienting the life aspirations of younger generations and reshaping population movements. By foregrounding the changing values, aspirations, and capabilities of this community, the stories that follow challenge conventional push-factor narratives and reveal the inadequacies of current policy responses to address the root causes of migration. Overall, this book uses migration as a lens to provoke a fundamental rethinking of how development is imagined, measured, and pursued—not only in Ethiopia but also in rural communities around the world.

1
Theorizing Migration in Modernity

In an unassuming room in the National Museum of Ethiopia lie the skeletal remains of a small, female hominin who lived 3.2 million years ago. Discovered in 1974 in a riverbed in the Awash Valley, the jubilant excavation team named her Lucy after the soundtrack to their celebrations: the Beatles' "Lucy in the Sky with Diamonds." Locally she is known as *Dinkinesh*, "you are marvelous" in Amharic. Little can be known about our early human ancestor. She was just one meter tall with a very small brain. She had long, dangling arms, but she walked upright. There were several evolutionary jumps between her species, *Australopithecus afarensis*, and our species, *Homo sapiens*, yet she is still fondly declared "the grandmother of humanity."

Ethiopia long held the claim as the birthplace of modern humans, though recent archeological discoveries in South Africa and Morocco are challenging the title. Current theories in paleoanthropology suggest the first *Homo sapiens* emerged somewhere in Africa (or potentially in several places across Africa) between three hundred thousand and two hundred thousand years ago. Distinguished from early hominins by new levels of symbolic behavior and complex technologies—what is often referred to as "behavioral modernity"—modern humans began to leave the African continent not long thereafter. The father-son McNeill historians suggest one important ingredient motivating this early expansion was the emergence of speech, which heightened levels of collective organization and introduced, perhaps for the first time, a "friction between expectation and experience" that has "never ceased to provoke efforts . . . to change behavior and compel the world to conform to human wishes, hopes, and intentions."[1] Hypotheses regarding the exact timing and motivations of our early human ancestors' great migrations—and their relationship to environmental changes—are constantly changing in light of new archeological discoveries. Yet regardless of the precise timing or trajectories taken, it is reasonable to assume that the emergence of the cognitive and behavioral foundations for complex communities spurred humankind's ability to adapt to and transform our environments—or more consciously pursue greener pastures elsewhere.

Moved by Modernity. Kerilyn Schewel, Oxford University Press. © Oxford University Press (2025).
DOI: 10.1093/9780197680759.003.0002

This expansion out of the African continent was a major turning point in humanity's migration history, arguably our first mobility transition: a transformation in our species' cognitive and collective capacities that spurred qualitatively different population movements.

A second turning point took place around 10,000 BCE. Innovations surrounding the domestication of plants and animals, combined with a more stable and warmer climate, enabled and encouraged human beings to live together in larger groups, giving rise to the first agricultural villages. This Neolithic Revolution brought profound mobility consequences: it allowed human beings to settle down, seasonally or more permanently. The very act of settling created the conditions out of which the first cities, and later civilizations, emerged. In the several thousand years thereafter, the possibility of settlement gave rise to three distinct yet interlocking ways of life: the rural agricultural, the nomadic pastoral, and the urban complex. Each played distinct and important roles in the emergence and spread of civilization throughout the centuries to come. The political strength and economic diversification possible in urban centers rested upon the acquisition and production of rural hinterlands, and pastoral communities played a crucial role in trading and raiding, twin drivers of human movement and exchange.[2] During this time, urban centers were often perceived as the seats of civilization, yet the vast majority of humanity lived in rural settings.

Over the last several centuries, another fundamental shift in humanity's collective migration history has been unfolding: urbanization, that is, the gradual displacement of rural and pastoral livelihoods by urban-centric social and economic organization. From a global perspective, urbanization has led to the mass movement of humanity from rural areas to urban centers, within their homelands or outside of them. While in 1800 only 15 to 20 percent of people lived in urban areas, this share increased to 34 percent in 1960, and by 2007, humanity reached a tipping point; the majority of people now live in towns and cities, a share that is projected to increase to 68 percent by 2050.[3] Transformations in recent international migration trends may be seen as an integral part of this global urbanization process. While a relatively high proportion of international migration in the seventeenth through nineteenth centuries was directed toward settling, conquering, and colonizing less population-dense territories—what has been described as "frontier" or "settler" migration—today, a growing share of international migration is directed toward global cities and large urban areas in wealthier countries. Humanity is thus in the midst of another mobility transition,[4] and the causes and consequences of these new population movements are what we are struggling to understand today.

The social forces driving humanity's urban transition are complex. Technological innovations in manufacturing and transport led to the wide-scale displacement of traditional systems of economic production, which often relied on producing goods by hand, with machine-based systems of production that tend to concentrate production processes in urban areas. The Industrial Revolution was intimately tied to a range of other social shifts, including new conceptions of work based on wages rather than subsistence, the expansion of formal education designed to prepare students for the specialization and division of labor in the industrial and service sectors, rising levels of and expectations for consumption, changing aspirations and notions of the good life, and investments in infrastructure to facilitate heightened levels of connectivity. As societies around the world experienced the political, economic, cultural, and technological changes associated with industrialization, more people began to leave rural ways of life to work in neighboring towns or cities elsewhere.[5] And as the world becomes increasingly connected, the destinations potential migrants consider become increasingly distant.

Globalization, what has been described as the "widening, deepening and speeding up of worldwide interconnectedness in all aspects of contemporary social life,"[6] is thus another important process of social change shaping the nature and direction of migration trends. As processes of globalization accelerate, international migration flows follow global geopolitical and economic shifts. Consider the rise of the Gulf states after the discovery of vast reservoirs of oil in the mid-twentieth century, and the 1973 oil crisis that suddenly increased the price of oil. This generated new financial resources to undertake major development projects in the region, as well as greater demand for foreign workers. While there were only some two million migrant workers in the Gulf region in 1975, some 68 percent of whom were from other Arab countries,[7] the scale of migration increased dramatically over the following decades. By 2020, Saudi Arabia alone hosted over thirteen million migrants, making it the third-largest migration destination in the world after the United States and Germany.[8] Most migrant workers now come from countries like India, Indonesia, and Pakistan. The incomes they can earn in Saudi Arabia far exceed any opportunity available to them at home, while in Saudi Arabia, the work they provide is considered cheap. Economic globalization has contributed to the emergence of new "migration systems" across long distances,[9] to such a degree that, as this book will show, a young woman in Wayisso can find it easier to migrate to Saudi Arabia as a domestic worker than to find work in the towns and cities of her home district.

Humanity's urban transition overlaps with a period in history often referred to as modernity. "Modernity" means many things, hardly agreed upon by scholars, but two dimensions of the term should be distinguished. On the one hand, it can refer to a set of structural conditions that distinguish modern societies from earlier ones—conditions that include industrialization, bureaucratization, mass education, and rapid transportation and communication technology.[10] From this perspective, modernity does not have a clear temporal demarcation but rather begins when a particular constellation of structural conditions emerges in a given society. On the other hand, the term also refers to a more ephemeral but no less powerful existential reality: the collective experience of life associated with these structural conditions. Sociologist Robert Bellah wrote that the modern should be seen not "as a form of political or economic system, but as a spiritual phenomenon or a kind of mentality."[11] Or as the philosopher Marshall Berman so aptly put it:

> *There is a mode of vital experience—experience of space and time, of the self and others, of life's possibilities and perils—that is shared by men and women all over the world today. I will call this body of experience "modernity." To be modern is to find ourselves in an environment that promises us adventure, power, joy, growth, transformation of ourselves and the world—and, at the same time, that threatens to destroy everything we have, everything we know, everything we are.*[12]

What is striking is that this "mode of vital experience," this ethic of transformation, was already present in Wayisso, a small village in Ethiopia, where education levels remain relatively low and rural livelihoods are grounded in smallholder agriculture tended with ox and plow. Nevertheless, what young people desire and pursue above all else is growth, self-development, *change*. Thus, despite living in a country categorized by the United Nations as one of the world's "least developed,"[13] the social imaginary in Wayisso is undoubtedly *modern*.

The title of this book, *Moved by Modernity*, may thus be understood from two perspectives: structural and existential. How people migrate changes over time in response to the structural transformations associated with modernity (i.e., industrialization, mechanization, mass education, bureaucratization, greater connectedness) as well as a concomitant transformation in the aspirations and expectations engendered by the experience of "modernization" or "development." There is always a twofold process at work: transformations in the structural dimensions of society and transformations in the social imaginary—both of which have implications for, among many other things, the ways in which we move and settle. The two are distinct but interlocking forces of social change.

The remainder of this chapter details my theoretical approach to exploring how the pursuit of development in Ethiopia impacted migration aspirations and behavior in Wayisso. I begin by briefly reviewing dominant theories of migration and development before introducing the social transformation framework as a more comprehensive conceptual approach to studying the relationship between migration and social change. I then introduce the aspiration-capability framework as a complementary, micro-level framework to understand everyday migration decision-making and behavior. Together, these frameworks provide conceptual tools to analyze how big social change impacts individual behavior, including but not limited to migration, over time.

***

Modernization typically refers to a society's transition from a primarily rural, agrarian society to an urban, industrial one. Inherent to that process is the movement of people from rural to urban places. Somehow this basic fact is forgotten by those who see rural out-migration from developing countries as a problem that can be solved by development. It is commonly said that to stop migration, we need to address its "root causes." But what if development *is* a root cause of rural out-migration?

A more pressing question is not whether development drives migration but rather how and why it does so—and whether alternative strategies for development might lead to different outcomes. Theories of development and its earlier incarnation, modernization, carry assumptions about the impacts of social and economic transformation on the movement of people. But they tell two very different stories about *why* development drives rural out-migration.

"Modernization" is the rigid and paternalistic parent of what we call "development" today. Modernization became a dominant paradigm in the social sciences in the 1950s and 1960s, when the international development agenda took off and development interventions were crafted and justified by theories about how societies become "modern." American economist Walt W. Rostow's "Stages of Economic Growth"[14] is one of the most well-known and influential examples of the dominant thinking at this time. Rostow's "non-communist manifesto," as he called it, presents a typology of stages delineating the conditions and economic processes that characterize the transition from a "traditional society" (e.g., a primary sector economy) through "take-off" (e.g., industrialization) to the "age of mass consumption." Such theories provided the conceptual bases for development policies often exported to developing countries in the post–World War II era.[15]

Modernization theories like Rostow's embraced the free movement of goods, capital, ideas, and, importantly, *people* as countries moved from largely agricultural economies to industrial and service-based economies. For modernization theorists, the reallocation of people (more often termed "labor") from rural, agricultural areas to urban, industrial sectors is *required* for economic growth. The urbanization of labor, goods, and capital is a taken-for-granted dimension of the development process, played out over and over again in economic history,[16] and thus considered fundamental to "balanced growth." The same logic applies to the global economy, where the free movement of people along wage and population gradients—within or across national boundaries—would lead to converging wage levels. This is the basic tenet of neoclassical migration theory. It is a hopeful vision driven by faith in the market and people's ability to respond rationally to opportunities for material betterment.

In the 1970s and 1980s, critiques of modernization began to gain influence. Immanuel Wallerstein's world systems theory is one particularly persuasive example. Wallerstein suggested that rather than leading to balanced growth, modernization processes were fueling global inequalities to serve the needs of core capitalist centers.[17] The integration of peripheral (i.e., poorer, rural, agrarian) regions into the global capitalist system undermines peasant livelihoods and uproots peasants from their rural ways of life. From this perspective, the movement of labor and capital to the city is not a rational response of free agents but a coerced displacement that serves the needs of the capitalist system more than everyday people.

The penetration of capitalism into poorer areas only furthers dependency, or as the sociologist Andre Frank famously put it, the "development of underdevelopment." As Gunnar Myrdal similarly argued in his theory of cumulative causation, economies of scale tend to deepen poverty in the periphery and accelerate the growth of core areas, furthering inequalities and driving out-migration from the periphery to the core.[18] This dynamic occurs both within countries (from rural to urban) and across them (from poor to rich countries). From this perspective, migration is driven by the livelihood displacement and deepening inequalities that come from "modernization" and "development."

These critical development theories helped disenchant the myth of modernization for many development practitioners and led to more people-centered approaches in subsequent decades. Yet, these critical perspectives also left a lasting imprint of migration as a problem, or at least a symptom of greater problems, that at times does a disservice to migrants themselves. We are still left with two very different and dissatisfying portraits of "the migrant." The first is a rational utility maximizer—a *Homo economicus*—predictably following wage and population gradients to better their economic prospects. The second is a passive pawn, as geographer Hein de Haas put it, "pushed around the globe by the macro-forces of global capitalism."[19] The former celebrates migration; the latter laments it as a sign of social stress. Neither perspective alone does justice to the reality of migration and its driving forces, nor the multifaceted human beings choosing to move or to stay as their societies transform.

Dissatisfied with prevalent framings and theories of development and of migration, a group of researchers associated with the International Migration Institute at the University of Oxford began articulating a "social transformation perspective" for the study of migration in the 2000s. This theoretical approach assumes that the ways in which people move and settle transform in patterned ways whenever social transformation occurs. Stephen Castles, an early pioneer of this approach, defines a social transformation as a "fundamental shift in the way society is organized that goes beyond the incremental processes of social change that are always at work."[20] Unlike the terms "development" or "modernization," which are inherently normative and tied to the idea of progress, "social transformation" is not inherently good or bad; it simply leads societies into new terrain for better or for worse.[21]

A core implication of a social transformation perspective is that to understand migration's underlying causes, we must look to the nature and transformation of society itself. To understand big changes, a social transformation framework directs research attention along five dimensions of inquiry:[22]

- *economic dimension* (the accumulation and use of land, labor, and capital in the production, distribution, and consumption of goods and services),
- *technological dimension* (the application of knowledge through the deployment of procedures, skills, and techniques),
- *political dimension* (the organized control over people within a given territory),
- *demographic dimension* (the structure and spatial distribution of populations), and
- *cultural dimension* (beliefs, values, norms, and customs shared by groups of people).

Taken together, these five dimensions constitute the social domain. Major processes of social change occur within each dimension. For example, the growth and spread of industrial capitalism occurs under the economic dimension, national-state formation under the political dimension, and demographic transition under the demographic dimension. Fundamental changes in one dimension will also necessarily impact others—that is, shifts in the economic or technological life of a society will have impacts on fertility and mortality, and political change can lead to cultural change and vice versa. Indeed, this is why the academic study of these dimensions falls under the umbrella of the "social" sciences.

The social transformation approach is a *framework* for studying migration, not a theory with causal claims. Alone, it does not say how different dimensions of social change impact migration behavior. Rather, it suggests that in particular settings, the timing, sequencing, and intersectionality of social change processes will stimulate particular kinds of migration or staying behavior.[23] While there can be value in focusing on the relationship between migration and one particular dimension, a social transformation perspective highlights that any comprehensive explanation for migration would need to include several (if not all) dimensions of the social realm—or at least recognize what important dimensions a more focused study might miss. This framework inspired the structure of this book, where Chapters 4 through 9 consider the drivers of migration from Wayisso through a different social lens.

The social transformation approach is a macro-level conceptual framework to orient empirical research, but it cannot tell us how people make sense of societal change or why they change their behavior as a result. For this, we need micro-level frameworks that are attentive to the interplay of structure and agency. In this light, the aspiration-capability framework is a complementary micro-level framework to explain how big social change influences individual and household-level behavior.[24]

***

In the early 2000s, the geographer Jørgen Carling proposed an "aspiration/ability model" to explain why some people migrate while others do not.[25] His model emerged out of fieldwork in Cape Verde, where he encountered widespread migration aspirations yet found many people lacked the ability to migrate. Dominant neoclassical theories, which assumed people will migrate when the benefits of migration exceed the costs, were useless to explain this reality. But what if the perceived benefits exceed the costs and people *want* to migrate but then find they lack the financial resources or a viable legal pathway to make a move?

In response to this question, Carling decided to consider the aspiration and the ability to migrate separately. Migration requires both, and immobility results from the lack of either one.[26] The resultant aspiration/ability model suggests three mobility categories: *mobility* (i.e., having both the aspiration and ability to migrate), *involuntary immobility* (i.e., having the aspiration but not the ability to migrate), and *voluntary immobility* (i.e., those without the aspiration to migrate). An important contribution of Carling's model is the ability to see, and therefore ask questions about, these distinct (im)mobility outcomes—particularly involuntary immobility.

Around the same time, Hein de Haas was studying migration and development interactions in the Todgha Valley in Morocco. De Haas focused less on immobility than Carling but encountered a similar frustration with neoclassical migration theories. "Despite significant increases in income and general living conditions over previous decades," he writes, "out-migration from the Todgha valley to big cities in Morocco and, particularly, European countries like France, the Netherlands and Spain had continued unabated."

Neoclassical economic theories and push-pull models of migration would have predicted decreased emigration as local living standards improved. This inspired de Haas to adopt the concepts of *aspirations* and *capabilities* to explain what he was observing. As he writes:

> *Although local living conditions had improved significantly in preceding decades, people's general life aspirations had increased faster, leading to growing migration aspirations. Improved education, increased media exposure alongside the regular return of the migrant "role models" and exposure to their relative wealth had all contributed to rapidly increasing material and changing social aspirations of people living in the valley. Particularly international migration had become so strongly associated with material and social success that many youngsters had become virtually obsessed with leaving. This "culture of migration" also contributed to rapidly changing ideas of the "good life" and an increasing disaffection with traditional, agrarian lifestyles. So, growing aspirations and capabilities to migrate had inspired and enabled increasing numbers of people to leave the valley despite, or paradoxically rather because of, significant improvements in local living standards, income and education.*[27]

De Haas conceptualizes migration as a function of people's aspirations and capabilities to migrate within a given set of opportunity structures and describes in detail how development increases both aspirations and capabilities to migrate while reshaping local opportunity structures.[28]

By replacing Carling's concept of "ability" with the term "capability," de Haas connects his framework with the capability approach in development thought.[29] Initially conceived by the economist Amartya Sen, the capability approach is a normative framework for assessing human well-being and orienting development practice. In contrast to mainstream development approaches that focus on maximizing income, consumption, or even happiness, the capability approach focuses on what people are effectively able to do and to be—their capabilities "to lead the lives they have reason to value," as Sen puts it.[30] Although the terms "ability" and "capability" are arguably interchangeable to speak about whether someone *can* or *cannot* migrate, the concept of capability connects this migration framework to a richer body of development thought focused on human freedoms. In this spirit, de Haas defines human mobility as people's "capability (freedom) to choose where to live, including the option to stay."[31]

Both Carling's and de Haas's work significantly influenced my own thinking about why people migrate, why others stay, and how development affects both aspirations and capabilities to migrate. However, because both frameworks initially put their emphasis on explaining migration aspirations and their realization or frustration, I remained puzzled about how to think about the category of "voluntary immobility." One might question, for example, whether the immobility of people who lack the capability to migrate is *voluntary* in the same way as someone with the ability to migrate who nevertheless aspires to stay. In other words, some may aspire to stay because they are privileged enough to realize their aspirations where they are. Theirs is a very different circumstance from others who may be poorer, undereducated, or economically frustrated yet still do not consider migrating.

To clarify this category of voluntary immobility, I added a fourth category to the aspiration-capability framework: *acquiescent immobility*, to capture those who do not aspire to migrate but also lack the ability to do so (Figure 1.1). The term "acquiescent" implies an acceptance of constraints; the Latin origins of the word mean to remain at rest. This category can be difficult to identify empirically, as it is challenging to say who has the ability to migrate if someone has never tried and does not want to. Yet the concept

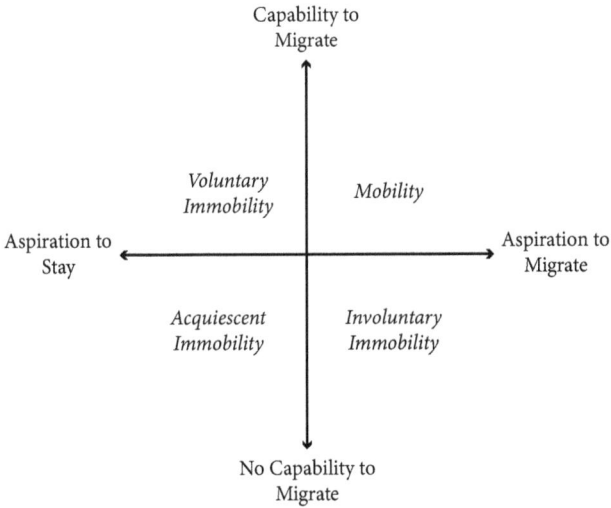

Figure 1.1 The aspiration-capability framework

Source: Kerilyn Schewel, "Understanding Immobility," *International Migration Review* 54, no. 2 (2020): 335.

has important conceptual value, if only to highlight that many people in very challenging circumstances, who would have much to gain from migration, may still prefer to stay where they are. This reality puzzles policy makers in the United States who wonder why poor people are not moving to better-paying jobs like they used to. It also puzzles researchers surveying migration intentions only to find that a respondent has never really considered the idea of leaving and thus developed a "migration intention" one way or another.

A more fundamental revision to the aspiration-capability framework is needed if it is to capture the wide range of immobility and mobility types that span the spectrum of voluntary to involuntary. Aspirations and capabilities *to migrate* need to be considered alongside aspirations and capabilities *to stay*. While de Haas's work emphasizes how development increases aspirations and capabilities to migrate, arguably bolstering an optimistic narrative of migration-development interactions, more attention needs to be given to how the social transformations associated with development may also decrease the *capability to stay*. Doing so might allow us to embrace some of the insights of more critical perspectives on development. It gives a language to explain why, in some contexts, the economic transformations made in the name of development can deprive people of the capability to realize their aspirations or the lives they value where they are. As the chapters that follow will illustrate, the same development process can enhance the aspiration and capability to migrate at the same time that it erodes the aspiration and capability to stay.

Consider one example highlighting the impact of the North American Free Trade Agreement (NAFTA) on Mexican migration to the United States. In *The Right to Stay Home*, journalist David Bacon traces the impacts of US investment in the pork industry in Veracruz, Mexico, after NAFTA. Across Mexico, the opening of concentrated animal feeding operations, more popularly known as factory farms, significantly undercut local producers. Foreign-owned factory farms imported feed from the United States, where soybeans and corn are heavily subsidized by congressional farm bills. New economies of scale, bolstered by US government subsidies favoring their own farmers, made it extremely difficult for corn farmers and small pork producers in Mexico to compete. Between 1995—the year NAFTA took effect—and 2010, pork prices received by Mexican producers dropped 56 percent and four thousand Mexican pig farms closed.[32] Many other sectors of the rural economy were similarly affected by the influx of foreign capital and competition.

Bacon traces the impacts of a massive, mechanized hog-raising facility owned by a subsidiary of Smithfield Foods in Veracruz. In addition to the economic challenges described above, he also describes environmental harms. With less regulation, the factory farms used inadequate waste management procedures, leading to the contamination of the local water table. Many people left Veracruz during this period—and a significant share were recruited by Smithfield to work at an associated slaughterhouse in Tarheel, North Carolina, thus supplying the company with an abundance of cheap labor in the United States.

Is this development? It depends on who you ask and how you measure development. In this example, US investment in Mexico helped increase national-level gross domestic product, contributing to the country's "development" from a narrow economic perspective. Yet, there were substantial local costs in places like Veracruz, including rising health problems, inequality, and unemployment. Aspirations to migrate increased, but the story Bacon presents is hardly a story of rising education, incomes, or empowerment like de Haas observed in Morocco. For rural communities in Veracruz, the consequences of this development strategy resonate more with what Andre Frank referred to as the "development of underdevelopment."

We need language to be able to describe migration-development interactions that can capture the positive narrative de Haas presents and the negative narrative Bacon describes. Development, in practice, is often Janus faced, and the mobility consequences it heralds can be a result of empowerment and disempowerment, of capability enhancement and diminishment. After all, Amartya Sen first introduced the capabilities approach as a new development paradigm to illumine what development *should* do, responding to what it was often not doing in reality. To evaluate whether rising migration reflects capabilities-enhancing development, whether it is the reluctant response to capability deprivation, or whether it is some complex combination of both, requires examining how the aspiration and capability to migrate and to stay relate to the local opportunities people have to realize their broader life aspirations.

***

To integrate the social transformation and aspiration-capability frameworks, further work is needed to clarify how macro-level social changes impact micro-level aspirations and capabilities. We need to look beyond aspirations to *migrate* or even to *stay*. Deeper questions concern how an individual's broader life aspirations change over time, the capabilities they have to achieve them, and the opportunity structures that determine *where* those aspirations may be fulfilled. It is the gap between life aspirations and the capabilities to achieve them locally that gives rise to the desire to migrate.

To date, there is not enough theoretical work in development studies on how aspirations shift as societies develop and transform. One exception is the economist Michael Piore's classic dual labor market theory, first described in *Birds of Passage*,[33] a groundbreaking work published in 1979 that explained why industrial societies experience a persistent demand for immigrant labor. A major contribution of this work was to show how the status, prestige, and expectations people attach to work impact labor market dynamics. He observed at the time that in advanced industrial economies, labor markets are bifurcated between a capital-intensive primary sector with more stable, more skilled, and better-paid jobs and a labor-intensive secondary sector where jobs are unstable, unskilled, and low wage. As countries develop, fewer natives are willing to work in jobs at the "bottom" of the secondary sector. The status and wage expectations of the native workforce contribute to the social devaluation of these difficult and precarious forms of work, thereby generating a persistent demand for immigrants who are willing to take these jobs. Immigrants are willing to do so, Piore argues, because low-wage work in a wealthy country can be a significant source of income as they remit to their home communities and a significant source of prestige and social status relative to their origin community.

In this way, Piore shows that status aspirations and the social devaluation of certain kinds of work in destination societies are crucial drivers of immigrant labor markets. One important limitation to this argument, however, is its assumption that migration is fundamentally demand driven, without giving equal attention to how aspirations and expectations also shift in the countries that "supply" migrant workers.

To theorize changing aspirations, my analysis uses three interrelated concepts: the social imaginary, the good life, and aspirations (Figure 1.2). The *social imaginary* refers to the imaginary backdrop against which all values, attitudes, ideas, and norms emerge; it is the web of conscious and unconscious assumptions about how things are and how things ought to be that give rise to particular notions of the "good life." The *good life* is one aspect of the social imaginary; it refers to imagined ideals about what an individual's life should look like—relating to work, location, family life, lifestyle,

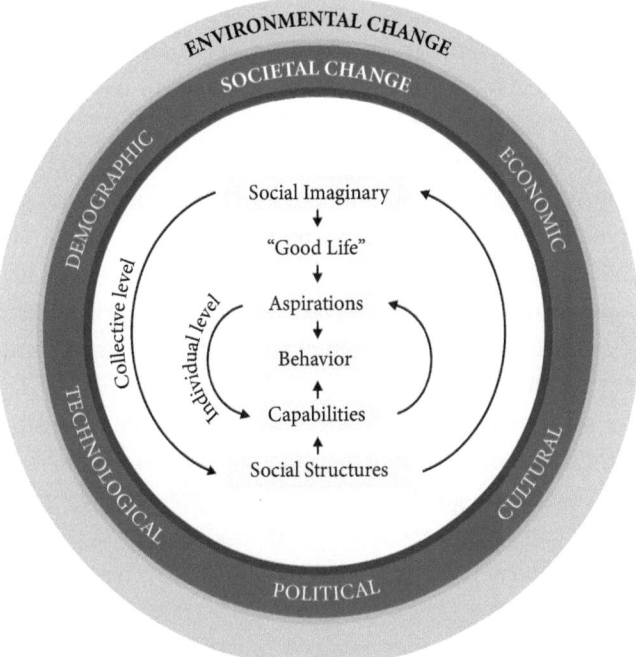

Figure 1.2 Combining the social transformation and aspiration-capability frameworks

and social position, among others. Finally, notions of the good life generate more specific *aspirations*, or desires for particular futures—toward higher levels of education, this kind of spouse, that kind of work, or, indeed, migration. Aspirations direct decision-making; they guide what factors become relevant to a cost-benefit evaluation.

The term "social imaginary" is a concept popularized by the philosopher Charles Taylor, who primarily uses it to examine the roots of Western modernity. Taylor defines the social imaginary as "the ways in which people imagine their social existence, how they fit together with others, how things go on between them and their fellows, the expectations that are normally met, and the deeper normative notions and images that underlie these expectations."[34] A social imaginary is shared by large groups of people, if not the whole society. "Our social imaginary at any given time is complex. It incorporates a sense of normal expectations that we have of one another, the kind of common understanding which enables us to carry out the collective practices the make up our social life."[35] The social imaginary, then, goes hand in hand with social structures. Social structures, as I use the term here, refer to those patterned collective practices, community relations, and institutional arrangements that structure how human beings interact and live together.

Here, I use the term "social imaginary" to capture not only the normal expectations we have of one another but also the expectations we have for the kinds of lives worth living. I am particularly interested in notions of the "good life" and understanding how conceptions of the good life impact *where* people imagine their futures. Notions of the good life and the aspirations derived therefrom emerge out of particular social imaginaries. Ideas about the good life inevitably vary across societies and social groups, even if there are some common patterns in the nature of their transformation. Whatever the exact conception of the good life, the point to emphasize here is that ideas about the good are, as the anthropologist Arjun Appadurai argues, always part of "some sort of system of ideas . . . which locates them in a large map of local ideas and beliefs about: life and death, the nature of worldly possessions, the significance of material assets over social relations, the relative illusion of social permanence for a society, the value of peace or warfare"[36]—what is here referred to as the "social imaginary." This suggests that notions of the good life are not just individually held and determined but influenced by a social imaginary that is inherently collective—indeed, *social*.

Visions of the good life animate and direct more specific aspirations. Rather than being the outcome of simple cost-benefit analyses, aspirations refer to the subjective hopes and goals that guide decision-making processes, setting the horizons within which life choices are made.[37] Thus, although aspirations are often evaluated as something individuals have, they are shaped by sociocultural norms. The links between specific aspirations and the broader social imaginary often remain vague. This is because, as Appadurai argues, the ideals that orient aspirations "often stay beneath the surface and emerge only as specific wants and choices: for this piece of land or that, for that marriage connection or another one, for this job in the bureaucracy as opposed to that job overseas, for this pair of shoes over that pair of trousers."[38] Too often, researchers focus on individual wants and preferences, neglecting the social imaginary out of which these desires emerge.[39]

Appadurai's critique is equally applicable to migration studies, particularly the growing number of surveys focused on capturing migration aspirations.[40] Analyses of migration aspiration data often retain the basic logic of rational-choice, utility-maximizing models of migration decision-making and simply use the term "aspirations" instead of, say, "preferences." When I use the term "aspirations" here—acknowledging the nuance that qualitative work affords—I am trying to get at the future-oriented goals, values, and notions of the good that orient the more specific wants and choices people make in their everyday lives. Because aspirations are socially grounded,[41] they can illuminate the value systems within which people make decisions and evaluate what constitutes a benefit, a cost, or overall utility.[42]

To theorize changing capabilities, this framework highlights that societal changes also impact the social structures that in turn affect individual-level capabilities. Capabilities—what one is effectively able to do and to be—are defined in relation to one's aspirations and "the life one has reason to value." For this reason, capabilities are highly subjective and difficult to operationalize.[43] Naiara Rodriguez Peña makes a helpful distinction between internal and external capabilities.[44] She defines internal capabilities as the resources, skills, aptitudes, and attitudes that allow one to realize one's aspirations; external capabilities refer to the external (societal and/or structural) conditions necessary to create the opportunity to realize one's aspirations.[45]

Applying this distinction to migration capability reveals the interplay between the internal and external requirements necessary for migration. What does it mean, exactly, to say someone has, or lacks, the capability to migrate? Initially, one must determine the individual's migration aspirations: Are they aiming for domestic or international migration? Do they seek a legal, documented route or plan to migrate through informal channels? These aspirations guide the assessment of an individual's capability. Consider the case of someone wishing to migrate internationally through legal means. This scenario demands specific internal capabilities, such as knowledge of visa application processes and sufficient financial resources to cover initial expenses. Additionally, it requires external capabilities, including access to legal migration pathways. The increasing complexity of global border regimes presents significant barriers for lower-skilled workers, constraining individuals' external capabilities to migrate. Similarly, aspirations for irregular migration necessitate both internal capabilities, like financial resources and knowledge, and external ones, such as access to transportation or smuggling networks. These factors together enable the individual to reach their desired destination; distinguishing between them helps to disentangle the multidimensional constraints on mobility freedom.

Returning to Figure 1.2, overall, when social transformation occurs, across any dimension of the social realm, it entails change at two levels: at the level of the social imaginary and at the level of social structures. These collective shifts have different impacts on the aspirations and capabilities of individuals, depending on, for example, their gender, age, location, wealth, or education. In this rendering, shifts in the social imaginary and social structures are more collective, while the actual aspirations and capabilities people hold are more individually specific. Further, aspirations and capabilities, at an individual level, are not just determined by the social imaginary and social structures; they also influence each other. People's aspirations may be shaped by the actual capabilities they have, for example, or the capabilities people consider relevant to their lives may depend on the aspirations they hold. They may also be shaped at the household level, where aspirations and capabilities to stay are supported by other family members' migration. Likewise, the social imaginary and social structures influence each other and change over time.

Beyond the five dimensions of the societal realm, Figure 1.2 includes an additional concentric circle highlighting the environmental realm. Societies are built upon and shaped by their environmental setting. Whether, how, and where people migrate in response to environmental change depend on the development context of a given society (i.e., its political, economic, cultural, technological, and demographic context) and the aspirations and capabilities of affected populations. In other words, the social realm mediates the impact of environmental change on individual behavior.[46] To give a rather obvious example, this is why the same degree of sea level rise in rural Bangladesh, where labor migration is already on the rise and there are limited institutional resources to enable smallholder farmers to adapt in place, will lead to very different migration outcomes than sea level rise in Amsterdam, a wealthy, population-dense destination city that already lies two meters below sea level. This environmental dimension is explored in greater depth in Chapter 8, which considers the impact of a severe drought on migration and immobility outcomes in Wayisso.

Finally, the specific combination of aspirations and capabilities can give rise to a wide range of mobility and immobility outcomes (e.g., Figure 1.1). However, one might note that instead of placing migration in the center of Figure 1.2, "behavior" appears there instead. This is to highlight that the integrated framework employed here can be applied to social phenomena beyond migration: education (aspired levels of education and the capabilities required to achieve it), work (the aspired jobs young people desire and the capabilities required to achieve them), and service (what contribution people want to make to society and what capabilities are required to do so), among others. The aspiration and capability to migrate (or to stay) are entangled within a web of other aspirations and capabilities that together make up the lives people value and ultimately live.

**

Remembering Lucy, whose skeletal remains lie in a museum in Addis Ababa, it is tempting to imagine a shared "mobility instinct" with our early human ancestors. After all, from Lucy's species, *Australopithecus afarensis*, to modern *Homo sapiens*, movement has been a fundamental part of the human story. "Ours is a migratory species," the author Mohsin Hamid reminds us.[47] Indeed, almost everyone can find some story of migration in their family history.

Yet the nature, drivers, and scale of contemporary migration patterns far exceed the wanderings of our early human ancestors, or our ancestors just a few centuries ago. Today, modern humans concentrate in cities and traverse the globe at speeds and distances unimaginable in previous centuries—facilitated by sophisticated technologies, expansive mental maps, and the aspirations to change our lives and the lives of our families in ways that extend far beyond the pursuit of survival or subsistence. Understanding these transformations requires theoretical frameworks that account for both the continuities and ruptures of the modern period. The theoretical framework outlined here—integrating social transformation and aspiration-capability frameworks—provides a set of conceptual tools to analyze these complexities. It helps us see that external "drivers" like political turmoil, climate stress, land scarcity, or a lack of jobs are alone insufficient to explain migration patterns in the modern period. The decision to move (or to stay) is shaped by the interplay of social transformation with internal factors like the life aspirations people hold and the capabilities they have (or lack) to achieve them where they are. By drawing attention to changes in the social imaginary alongside changes in social structures, this integrated framework promises a more nuanced understanding of why people migrate, why they stay, and, ultimately, the relationship between migration, development, and human flourishing.

2
The Modernization of Ethiopia

Geographically and politically, Ethiopia lies at a crossroads. For centuries, its leaders have carefully navigated the influence, advice, and assistance of Eastern and Western powers with a steadfast defensiveness of its own sovereignty. Ethiopia was never formally colonized,[1] and its history challenges the common perception that modernization is a unidirectional process, typically imposed on the "third world" by Western powers. The country's turbulent history is a story of not just one, but multiple experiments with modernity, each shaped by a complex interplay of domestic and global influences.

Many scholars mark the emergence of the "modern" Ethiopian state sometime in the second half of the nineteenth century. Some highlight the restoration of a central Ethiopian monarchy brought by Tewodros in 1853—ending decades of regional civil war known as the *Zemene Mesafint*, or "the Era of the Lords" (1769–1855)—as a key turning point.[2] Many others emphasize the modernizing efforts of Emperor Menelik II, who during the last decades of his reign focused his attention on the pursuit of technological innovation and economic development.[3] After assuming the throne in 1865, Menelik's reign primarily concentrated on managing internal and external conflicts—whether those involved his own ambitious campaign of territorial expansion within Ethiopia, particularly throughout the southern provinces (including the Lake Ziway region), or navigating precarious international relations with colonial powers, notably Italy. During this period, Menelik's ambitious pursuit of internal unification and international sovereignty distinguished him from previous *nagasts*, or kings.

After the famous Battle of Adwa in 1896, when Ethiopia defeated the invading Italian army and thwarted their colonizing ambitions for another four decades, Menelik became convinced that if the country was to maintain its independence and recognition as a sovereign state, it had to modernize.[4] This realization coincided with a period of unprecedented peace and stability in Ethiopia in the first decades of the twentieth century, a peace that enabled significant political, economic, and technological transformations.[5] Menelik established the nation's capital in Addis Ababa, where a growing population density brought innovations and economic diversification not yet seen elsewhere.[6] He laid modern roads and railways;[7] created the first national currency, taxation system, and printing press; and built the country's first modern hospital and school.

After Menelik's death in 1913, he was briefly succeeded by his grandson, Lij Iyasu (1913–1915), and then his daughter, Zewditu, who was the first and only empress regnant of the Ethiopian Empire. Empress Zewditu ruled from 1916 to 1930. Known for her conservatism and strong religious devotion, the major reforms of this period were led by her regent and eventual heir, Ras Tafari Makonnen. Upon assuming the throne in 1930, Tafari Makonnen became Emperor Haile Selassie and held modernizing ambitions as lofty as Menelik II's. The first years of Haile Selassie's reign brought many changes: an antislavery decree, the issuance of gold-backed paper money, and the country's first ministry of public works, radio station, and airports. Haile Selassie established Ethiopia's first constitution in 1931 and at that time looked to Japan as a model to emulate. Japan drew on the economic and technological advancements of the modern West while maintaining its sovereignty, traditions, and the authority of an all-powerful and sacred emperor.

But whatever progress was made, the new emperor was thwarted by a brief and contested occupation by fascist Italy from 1936 to 1941. Haile Selassie lived in exile in England for several years and used this time to galvanize global support for his country. In a famous 1936 appeal to the League of Nations, which Ethiopia had joined in 1923, Haile Selassie framed the issue not only in terms of Ethiopia's plight but also in terms of the viability of the nascent international order. The League of Nations, however, imposed only partial and ineffective sanctions on Italy. It was not until 1940, during World War II, that the British Empire—the international power with the greatest stake in East Africa—led an East African campaign to oust the Italians. They succeeded in 1941 and occupied Ethiopia until 1944, allowing Haile Selassie to return and reclaim his throne.

After this tumultuous start to his second reign, Haile Selassie ruled for over half a century. His reach extended far beyond the capital as he continued to invest in roads, railways, schools, and hospitals around the country. He oversaw Ethiopia's first electrical grid and the expansion of commercial agriculture. He cultivated international ties with countries as diverse as the United States, Iran,[8] and Japan. He welcomed the country's first foreign investors. Initially, economic development entailed the growth of light industries like cotton, sugar, cement, leather, and printing factories. Many agricultural developments were run by foreign investors—including the Dutch in sugar, the Japanese in textiles, the Greeks in shoes and beverages, and the Italians in construction, textile, and agricultural industries[9]— and Ethiopian-owned companies were dominated by the interests of large landowners with close links to Haile Selassie.[10] By the early 1970s, foreign capitalists held almost 70 percent of investments in Ethiopia, and the economy was divided between a large, traditional agricultural sector, living at the level of subsistence, and a small modern sector based on urban growth and exports.[11]

Ethiopia's development during this period widened the divide between a conspicuously rich, urban elite and the rural majority, many of whom were trapped in an unjust feudal system or who were living as they had a century ago. Discontent began to simmer. In a memorandum to US President Nixon in 1969, in preparation for his meeting with Haile Selassie, Secretary of State Henry Kissinger described the situation well:

> *The Emperor is caught, like most modernizing monarchs, in a dilemma of his own making. He has built a modern state from feudal fragments, surrendered some prerogatives to a constitution, and educated an urban elite—all in the interests of a stronger nationhood against the external danger. Now he is finding, inevitably, that these steps have only created greater political momentum—particularly among the young—toward a surrender of autocratic powers which he is determined to preserve.*[12]

Haile Selassie survived an attempted coup d'etat by the Neway brothers in 1960, but riots led by university students in Addis Ababa became more frequent in the following years. When a terrible famine struck from 1972 to 1974, hundreds of thousands of Ethiopians starved to death while Haile Selassie was said to be feeding meat to his pet lions. Discontent began to boil over.

The emperor's downfall came in 1974, which historians Gérard Prunier and Éloi Ficquet call "the year of destiny, the year when Ethiopia was suddenly thrown into the modern world."[13] All semblance of continuity with the mythic, religious past that Haile Selassie sought to balance beneath his modernization pursuits disappeared as a military junta, commonly called the Derg (meaning "committee" in Amharic), seized power and imposed an altogether different vision of modernity. This vision was inspired by Stalin and Lenin in the USSR and by Maoism in China—at the time, the alternative to capitalism for much of the world. Under the Derg, Ethiopia became one of the Soviet bloc's closest African allies.

In many ways, the Derg's plans followed classic communist prescriptions: the nationalization of land and businesses, the creation of over thirty thousand peasant associations in the countryside and urban dwellers' associations in cities, the establishment and investment in collective and state-run farms, the formation of a single Workers' Party, and controlled freedom of speech and press.[14] Most of the foreign investors that had been attracted to Ethiopia in the 1950s and 1960s fled.

In addition to its sweeping land reform, nationalization, literacy campaigns, and resettlement programs, the Derg's rule was characterized by intense political repression and violence. Several armed resistance movements arose across Ethiopia to overthrow the regime, generating conflicts that displaced local populations within Ethiopia and across its borders. At the same time, long-standing and new conflicts with outside powers exacerbated refugee movements. The Eritrean War of Independence, which began in 1961, escalated in 1967, and continued until 1991, generated significant cross-border movement from Ethiopia into Sudan. A brief border war in the Ogaden region in 1964, followed by the 1977–1978 Ethio-Somali war, displaced many more into Somalia. Refugee numbers reported by the US Committee for Refugees show an increase from 55,000 Ethiopian refugees in the Horn of Africa in 1972 to 1.1 million in 1987.[15] In 1990, during this period of political conflict and transition, over 1.68 million Ethiopians were abroad.[16]

As the government struggled against these external challenges, armed resistance movements across the country fought to overthrow the regime. The Derg and its leader, Mengistu Haile Mariam, struggled to maintain power. The Derg's capacity to govern was further tested when a famine struck in 1983 and 1984 and over a million starved.[17]

Resettlement schemes were one strategy adopted by the Derg to address food insecurity (among other issues). Resettlement had begun as a few "ad hoc initiatives" under Haile Selassie in 1966, but it became a major government strategy of the Derg in the 1970s and 1980s, culminating in the resettlement of over half a million people in 1985 and 1986.[18] Before the 1974 revolution, the imperial regime resettled some 10,000 households—constituting 0.2 percent of rural households at the time, as compared to 5 percent of rural households that migrated "spontaneously."[19] Under the

Derg, the numbers and pace of resettlement increased. From 1974 to 1983, some 46,000 households (187,000 people) were resettled in eighty-eight sites across eleven regions. In the aftermath of the 1984 famine, an "Emergency Phase" plan resettled over half a million more people between October 1984 and January 1986, constituting what Alula Pankhurst and François Piguet describe as "one of the most complex, ambitious and draconian measures ever attempted by the Ethiopian government."[20]

Both the imperial regime and the Derg justified their resettlement programs as a proactive strategy to address a wide range of perceived social ills: to help alleviate food security, redistribute populations more efficiently, develop less populated areas and increase agricultural productivity, safeguard populations against the threat of famine, provide land for the landless, establish cooperatives, lessen urban unemployment, settle pastoralists and shifting agriculturalists, and rehabilitate repatriated refugees.[21] But resettlement was never the magic bullet government planners hoped it would be. Due to inadequate planning, financial constraints, and the lack of experienced personnel to manage these projects, "the results were generally poor, the schemes tended to fail, and most settlers left the projects."[22]

The unification of several liberation forces into the Ethiopian People's Revolutionary Democratic Front (EPRDF) in 1989 and 1990 hastened the decline of the socialist regime, which could no longer rely on Soviet support at the end of the Cold War. In 1991, a three-year process began to determine what the new state would look like. This time, the writers of a new constitution looked to the West, and Ethiopian expatriates returned to help create the new charter for a democratic, ethnic federalism that privileged the rights of individuals and ethnic groups.[23] The implementation of the new state, however, spearheaded by Prime Minister Meles Zenawi, again looked to the East—to the development trajectories of South Korea and Taiwan, where the state had played a heavy-handed role in economic development with impressive results.[24]

The EPRDF coalition government initially adopted a development vision that remained, in many ways, inspired by socialist ideals. In opposition to the neoliberal Washington Consensus prevalent at the time, Prime Minister Zenawi believed that under imperfect conditions of rent seeking and patronage, development required a strong state to create the conditions under which a healthy market and democratic order could function.[25] This self-titled "developmental state" initially adopted an Agricultural Development–Led Industrialization (ADLI) model, an endogenous development strategy that embraced government control over the development process.[26] It expected that growth in agricultural productivity would create demand for basic consumer goods, leading to the emergence of simple industries. The growth of industry would then create employment opportunities for a rural labor force that would become increasingly detached from the land as productivity gains increased and fewer laborers were needed.[27]

By the early 2000s, however, it was clear the ADLI strategy was not working as hoped. Agricultural productivity stagnated, and gross domestic product (GDP) growth rates in Ethiopia were lower than at the end of the Derg. The EPRDF began to face significant disapproval in both towns and the countryside. The regime changed course and decided its new legitimacy would have to be found in "the promise of massive economic growth."[28] This led to a second stage in the regime's approach to modernization, one that was much more sympathetic to the role of private actors, foreign investment, free enterprise, and market forces.[29]

Following this shift in policy, the share of the Ethiopian population employed in agriculture dropped significantly. Although the contribution of agriculture to Ethiopia's GDP had already been declining since the 1980s, the sector remained the main occupation of more than 80 percent of the population until 2000. However, the first decades of the twenty-first century saw a steady decline in agricultural employment, from 85.8 percent in 2000 to 68.2 percent in 2017.[30] Most of those who left agriculture found work in the service sector. In Ethiopia—like many other African countries—the service sector has grown faster than manufacturing and industry. Accordingly, employment in services jumped from 10.5 percent in 2000 to 22.4 percent in 2017. Industrial jobs employ less than 10 percent of the population.[31]

Over this same period, particularly since the 1990s and 2000s, more foreign companies—from agricultural, floricultural, and meat processing enterprises to manufacturing and industrial parks—were strategically established in regions surrounding Addis Ababa or easily connected to its airport through the main railways or highway routes. As it was under Haile Selassie, these companies' proximity to the main roads accelerates the growth of neighboring towns.[32] As towns grow, so too do services like banking, insurance, restaurants and hotels, shops, and trading companies—generating new employment opportunities in the formal and informal service sector. Similarly, as the government continues to invest in road and railway infrastructure, rural-urban connectivity is increasing.[33] One study from 2010 found that the percentage of people residing in or within three hours of a city of at least fifty thousand rose from 15.5 percent in 1984 to 48.5 percent in 2007.[34]

The shift in economic strategy did indeed result in remarkable economic growth. Ethiopia was touted as an "economic miracle" in Africa and the fastest-growing economy in the world in the 2010s.[35] Yet political backlash soon followed these economic gains. Frustrations over undemocratic rule, inequality, and elite capture led to widespread protests. Some of the most significant demonstrations against the government occurred across the state of Oromia, where Ethiopia's largest ethnic group, the Oromos, have long complained of political repression and economic marginalization. The Oromo protests swept across Oromia in late 2015. They intensified and spilled over into other states until in 2018, Prime Minister Hailemariam Desalegn announced his resignation, and Abiy Ahmed, the chair of the Oromo Peoples' Democratic Organization, was elected prime minister.

Soon after his appointment, Ahmed formally ended the long-standing border conflict with Eritrea—a move that won him a Nobel Peace Prize in 2019—and merged the ethnic and region-based parties of the EPRDF into a new political coalition called the Prosperity Party. However, the Tigray People's Liberation Front (TPLF), which had long dominated Ethiopian politics, refused to join the new coalition and condemned the peace initiatives with Eritrea. The Tigray region borders Eritrea, and the TPLF viewed the peace agreements as flawed, hastily made, and without adequate consultation with their leaders.[36] Tensions between the federal government and the TPLF continued to escalate until November 2020, when conflict erupted and the country once again descended into civil war. In 2021, Ethiopia set a new record for the highest number of internal displacements in a single year; there were over 3.5 million people internally displaced by conflict, a number second only to the Democratic Republic of Congo.[37] After two years of fighting, the federal government and the TPLF signed a peace treaty in November 2022, formally ending the Tigray War. Yet, peace is on shaky foundations, with several ethnic militias continuing to cause internal strife.

Because of the relatively rapid regime changes and protracted conflicts that have characterized much of the last half century, many scholars prioritize political violence variables as the primary drivers of population movements within and from Ethiopia.[38] Clearly, conflict has been a key part of Ethiopia's migration history. These drivers of displacement also remain a part of Ethiopia's present. Yet, to reduce Ethiopia's migration history to a story of conflict and displacement obscures intergenerational shifts in the structure of Ethiopian society and in the aspirations of its peoples that are reshaping how and where people move. Here, it is important to distinguish between the deep drivers of a mobility transition—which include national state formation, the expansion of formal education, economic industrialization, infrastructure development, and cultural change—and the drivers of displacement, like conflict or resettlement programs, that can suddenly affect the movements of large segments of the population. The remainder of this chapter reviews national-level trends in migration patterns and their relationship with Ethiopia's fraught pursuit of modernization. Drawing on research published with Ethiopian geographer Asmamaw Legass Bahir,[39] it presents three core shifts in mobility trends—the *sedentarization* of traditional mobility systems, the *urbanization* of internal migration, and the *diversification* of international migration—with an emphasis on the period between 1960 and 2019 when data is more available and reliable.

Ethiopia's Mobility Transition

The structural configuration of Ethiopia's landscape, particularly a dualism between its wet highlands and dry lowlands, explains a large degree of historical differentiation in the livelihoods of Ethiopia's diverse peoples.[40] In the first half of the twentieth century, cultivation was common in the central and northern highlands, among the Agew, Amhara, and Tigrean peoples, as well as in the well-watered highlands of the south, where the Gurage, Sidama, and Omo tribes practiced ensete and other cereal grain cultivation. Nomadic and seminomadic pastoralism and agro-pastoralism characterized the livelihoods of peoples living in the more arid and semiarid lowlands: the Afar, Saho, and Somali in the east; the Oromo across the south; and the Nuer in the west.[41] Some populations resist categorization within this neat dualism, of course. The Harari peoples, for example, were the only group to have developed an early agricultural and trading tradition concentrating on a single large urban center.[42] Similarly, the Oromo, because of a long history of expansion, conquest, and adaptation, are the most widely dispersed peoples in Ethiopia and also the most diverse in livelihoods, religion, and lifestyles.

Given the historical prominence of nomadic and seminomadic peoples across Ethiopia's vast lowlands, to examine changing migration patterns requires looking beyond the typical definition of migration as a residential move across an administrative boundary; many people were not registered to residences but were nevertheless highly mobile. Because Ethiopian censuses often excluded nomadic or pastoralist areas, quantifying the prevalence of nomadic lifestyles at the national level is difficult.[43] One study from 2000 estimated that some 7,776,000 people (12 percent of the total population) were pastoralists, concentrating primarily in the Somali and Oromia states.[44] The last national census in 2007 made a greater effort to include pastoral peoples.[45] By that time, pastoralists numbered just 2.3 million (3.1 percent of the national population).[46]

A range of more qualitative work on nomadic and seminomadic populations confirms a widespread decline in nomadic lifestyles over the last century, particularly since the 1970s—from the Dasenech peoples who lived along the Omo River in southern Ethiopia to the Somali pastoralists in the east to the Afar peoples of the northeastern drylands.[47] These studies show how the rise of the modern Ethiopian state disrupted the traditional political and economic systems of pastoral or agro-pastoral communities. While many participated in barter economies well into the mid-twentieth century, today, a growing number engage in cash markets and wage labor, the latter often encouraging settlement.[48] Land seizure for development projects across Ethiopia further undermined nomadic practices, and growing participation in formal schooling further diminished aspirations for (agro-)pastoral lifestyles.[49] Thus, Ethiopia's development over the last century entailed the settlement of populations that had historically been highly mobile.

***

Alongside this sedentarization process, Ethiopia experienced slow but steady urbanization. Historically, urban growth in the country was concentrated in Addis Ababa, the capital city, first settled by Emperor Menelik II and Queen Taytu in 1886. By 1910, the population was estimated to have 70,000 permanent and 30,000 to 50,000 temporary inhabitants.[50] By the 1960s, Addis Ababa had grown to 644,190 residents, one-third (33.4 percent) of Ethiopia's total urban population at that time.[51] As small and medium-sized towns proliferated across the country in the subsequent decades (Table 2.1), the proportion of the urban population living in the capital city decreased—to 28.5 percent in 1994 and 23.6 percent in 2007—yet still remains substantial. A growing share of Ethiopia's urban population now lives in larger cities outside Addis Ababa, like Dire Dawa, Mekelle, and Adama, while one-fourth (24.9 percent) live in towns of 10,000 or less.

Table 2.1 Charting urban growth in Ethiopia by town and city size

Population size of urban centers	Number of urban centers by town and city size			Proportion of the urban population by town and city size (%)		
	1967	1984	2007	1967	1984	2007
2,000–5,000	101	186	357	16.51	13.23	10.45
5,000–10,000	36	75	245	12.92	11.79	14.45
10,000–20,000	15	38	115	10.55	11.88	13.44
20,000–50,000	8	14	61	13.97	9.36	15.86
50,000–100,000	1	10	14	2.93	15.05	8.73
100,000–500,000	1	1	10	9.20	6.31	13.47
500,000–1,000,000	1	0	0	33.93	/	/
1,000,000+	0	1	1	/	32.37	23.60
Total	163	325	803	100	100	100
Total urban population				1,917,160	4,364,140	10,769,022

Source: Data for 1967 and 1984 from Muhammad Rafiq and Assefa Hailemariam "Some Structural Aspects of Urbanization in Ethiopia," *Genus* 43 no. 3/4 (1987): 201; Data for 2007 from Central Statistical Agency *The 2007 Population and Housing Census of Ethiopia: Results for Country Level. Statistical Report Vol. I* (Central Statistical Agency 2010).

Within Ethiopia, internal labor migration historically occurred from the more highly populated northern highlands toward the less densely populated south, in the southwestern and eastern regions of the country.[52] In the early twentieth century, this "frontier migration"[53] included peasants leaving situations of land scarcity and low agricultural productivity to search for more fertile lands, and soldiers settling lands gifted as tribute by the imperial regime.[54] In the 1950s through the 1970s, movement from the highlands to the lowlands continued but began to change as Ethiopia's economy diversified under Haile Selassie. As commercial agriculture grew, internal migration was increasingly directed toward wage work at these state- or privately owned enterprises: for example, cotton and sugar plantations in the Rift Valley and Awash Valley, coffee plantations in the south and southwest, and farms harvesting sesame, beans, and oil seeds in the northwest.[55] This movement was often seasonal, but over time, it also led to the settlement of migrant laborers in these areas and the emergence of new towns.[56]

After the fall of Haile Selassie in 1974, the political and economic changes pursued by the Derg had varying impacts on population movements. On the one hand, labor migration continued, even as the Derg took over many privately and foreign-owned enterprises.[57] In fact, migration often became state sponsored: conscription, for example, was introduced by the Derg not just for military purposes but also to fill labor shortages on state farms. On the other hand, state planning under a Marxist-Leninist vision put a new emphasis on the control of population movements. Under Haile Selassie, many highland areas already had forms of land tenure that tied peasants to particular plots of land, but in other lowland and more peripheral regions of the country, the imperial regime deployed a decentralized political structure that allowed for customary land tenure systems and more mobile livelihoods (see Chapter 4).[58]

Under the Derg, the penetration of the state into these regions reached new levels, and new policies—including regulations prohibiting the sale of land, loss of land rights for those who left rural areas, and registration requirements for new internal migrants—constrained mobility. Further, peasant associations tied access to government resources to one's registered residence, often incentivizing settlement and staying put. Some suggest that internal migration rates were lower in Ethiopia than the rest of sub-Saharan Africa during this period.[59]

The rise in rural-urban migration began to increase notably after the EPRDF seized power and pursued a new economic agenda in the 2000s.

After this shift in the state's development policy, internal migration trajectories became increasingly directed toward towns and cities. One longitudinal study of twenty rural communities across Ethiopia, conducted by the WIDE project, found that rural out-migration significantly expanded in scope and complexity between 1995 and 2013.[60] Initially, seasonal and agricultural migration by men was the dominant form of out-migration, but by the 2010s, new forms of "industrial migration" to urban areas and international labor migration to the Gulf states, Sudan, and South Africa began to increase. Migrants were increasingly younger, and women made up a growing share.[61] Similarly, in a paper I coauthored with the economist Sonja Fransen, we use Labor Force Survey data on internal migration rates across zones in Ethiopia and find that only in the 2010s did rural-to-urban migration replace migration between rural areas as the most common migration trajectory for both male and female internal migrants (Table 2.2).

Rising educational attainment among young generations in Ethiopia is one important cause of the urbanization of internal migration. Generally, higher educational attainment is associated with greater spatial mobility. Internal migrants in Ethiopia tend to have higher levels of education than nonmigrants,[62] and Table 2.3 shows that certain migration trajectories are associated with more or less schooling and literacy levels. The characteristics of those who stay and of rural-rural migrants are similar: over half of this population has no formal schooling. Rural-rural migrants have completed, on average, just 2.88 years of primary education. Rural-urban migrants, in contrast, have higher levels of schooling and literacy, and urban-urban migrants have the highest levels of educational attainment. The relatively high educational attainment of urban-rural migrants reflects in part those moving as government employees, for example, as teachers or administrators assigned to work in rural areas.

As Chapter 6 details, the links between education and migration are multifaceted. For rural youth, achieving secondary and higher education often requires moving to a town or city, because schools are simply not available in rural areas.[63] Furthermore, formal education tends to teach students values, attitudes, and skills that are oriented toward professional, urban employment, which fuels the social devaluation of rural agricultural work.[64] As the Ethiopian economy grows and diversifies, labor markets concentrate skilled labor in urban areas, and higher levels of education can boost the expected economic returns of a migration project.[65] According to one World Bank study, Ethiopia has relatively high returns to schooling, an 18.5

Table 2.2 Internal migration patterns (%) by gender: 1999, 2005, and 2013

Migration patterns of recent migrants	1999			2005			2013		
	Male	Female	Total	Male	Female	Total	Male	Female	Total
Rural to rural	31.19	39.14	35.62	35.70	41.97	38.94	24.08	22.32	23.16
Rural to urban	21.79	21.58	21.67	27.60	23.91	25.69	29.42	37.26	33.52
Urban to rural	21.65	13.08	16.87	16.02	11.09	13.47	23.15	14.79	18.78
Urban to urban	24.37	25.56	25.04	17.78	20.43	19.15	23.35	25.63	24.54
Total migration	100.00	100.00	100.00	100.00	100.00	100.00	100.00	100.00	100.00

Notes: Based on Labor Force Survey data. Recent migrants are individuals who moved across zones less than five years prior to survey data collection. Based on the population aged 15 and over.
Source: Adapted from Schewel and Fransen (2018: 585).

Table 2.3 Educational characteristics of internal migrants by migration trajectory

	Nonmigrants	Rural-to-rural migrants	Rural-to-urban migrants	Urban-to-rural migrants	Urban-to-urban migrants
Literacy (1 = yes)	—	0.44	0.70	0.76	0.84
Years of schooling (mean)	—	2.88	5.77	7.14	7.82
No schooling	0.52	0.51	0.27	0.22	0.13
Primary education	0.37	0.39	0.49	0.40	0.45
Secondary education	0.09	0.08	0.23	0.34	0.34
Higher education	0.01	0.01	0.01	0.03	0.08

Notes: Based on Labor Force Survey 2013 data. Recent migrants are individuals who moved across zones less than five years prior to survey data collection. Based on the population aged 15 and over.
Source: Adapted from Schewel and Fransen (2018: 564).

percent increase in labor market earnings for each additional year of schooling completed, and the highest returns (32.7 percent) for primary school completion.[66] These factors help explain why even just primary levels of education are associated with greater migration aspirations among young people across Ethiopia and why aspirations are increasingly oriented toward *urban* futures, not rural ones.[67]

***

Most research on the mobility transition focuses on the increase in international migration that accompanies economic growth.[68] Figure 2.1 suggests a positive relationship between GDP per capita and emigration rates from Ethiopia since the 2000s. However, a longer-term perspective suggests that the more fundamental change in international migration is not in volumes or prevalence per se but a diversification in the nature, destinations, and composition of international mobility from Ethiopia.

Under Haile Selassie's rule, international migration was lower in volume, but it already showed significant diversity. Most accounts of early international migration from Ethiopia describe it as the purview of the elite, who left to pursue tertiary education in Western countries and then returned

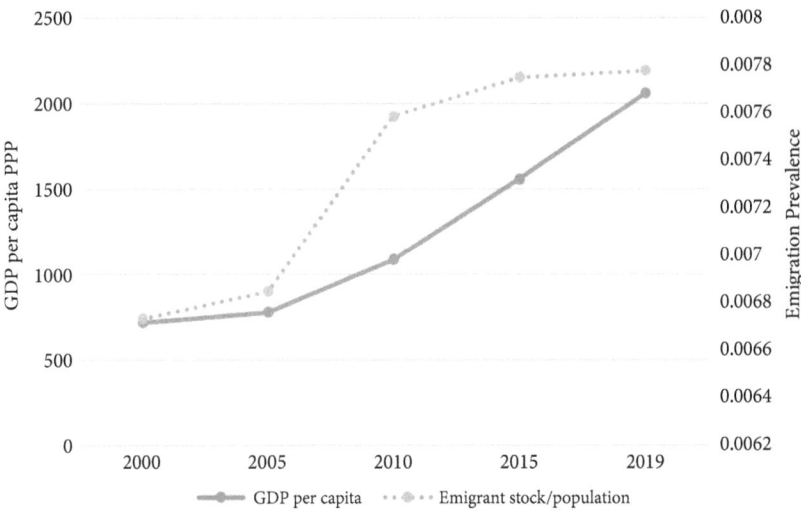

Figure 2.1 Gross domestic product (GDP) per capita, purchasing power parity (PPP) and emigration prevalence (2000–2019)

Notes: GDP per capita PPP (constant 2017 international $). Averages based on the previous five years (previous four years for 2019). Emigration prevalence refers to emigrant stock as a percentage of the total population.

Sources: United Nations. *Trends in International Migrant Stock: Migrants by Destination and Origin [Data base]* United Nations Department of Economic and Social Affairs, Population Division (2019) and WDI. *World Development Indicators [Data Base].* The World Bank (2020).

to government positions in the imperial regime.[69] Table 2.4, however, also reveals significant regional migration during this time, to Djibouti, Sudan, Kenya, Yemen, and Saudi Arabia, for example, which then accelerated under the Derg period. Because it is based on census and population register data, the figures cited in Table 2.4 likely underestimate the extent of international movement occurring over this period. Yet it highlights the already diverse and regional destinations of international migrants during the time of the imperial and socialist regimes.

After the rise of the Derg regime, another form of migration became far more prevalent: the movement of refugees fleeing political persecution, civil strife, and famine (Figure 2.2). Though the Derg formally closed Ethiopia's borders soon after seizing power, international movement significantly grew during this period. Refugee movements peaked in 1980, reaching over 2.5 million. The Ethiopian diaspora, many of whom were educated elites with some connection to the imperial regime, consolidated in countries like the United States. Most of those who left Ethiopia during the

Table 2.4 Top ten destinations of Ethiopian emigrants by decade (N)

1960		1970		1980		1990		2000	
Djibouti	3,442	Djibouti	6,273	Djibouti	12,632	United States	34,983	United States	71,578
Israel	2,736	Kenya	4,634	United States	10,583	Israel	30,337	Israel	66,967
Sudan	1,738	Canada	3,671	Saudi Arabia	7,513	Djibouti	19,811	Djibouti	25,437
United States	1,415	Israel	3,251	Canada	6,828	Saudi Arabia	19,573	Saudi Arabia	21,174
Kenya	871	United States	2,847	Kenya	6,026	Germany	9,555	Kenya	20,332
France	661	Sudan	1,658	Italy	5,820	Kenya	7,493	Canada	14,075
Canada	651	France	1,583	Israel	4,389	Sweden	7,464	United Kingdom	11,796
Yemen, Rep.	444	Saudi Arabia	1,473	Sudan	2,126	Italy	6,783	Sweden	11,776
Zimbabwe	268	Netherlands	565	Netherlands	1,563	Netherlands	4,504	Netherlands	7,455
Saudi Arabia	262	Yemen, Rep.	549	Sweden	1,426	Sudan	2,978	Italy	5,587
Total emigration	14,605		31,408		66,628		158,492		291,249

Source: Global Bilateral Migration Database World Bank Group and Özden et al. (2011).

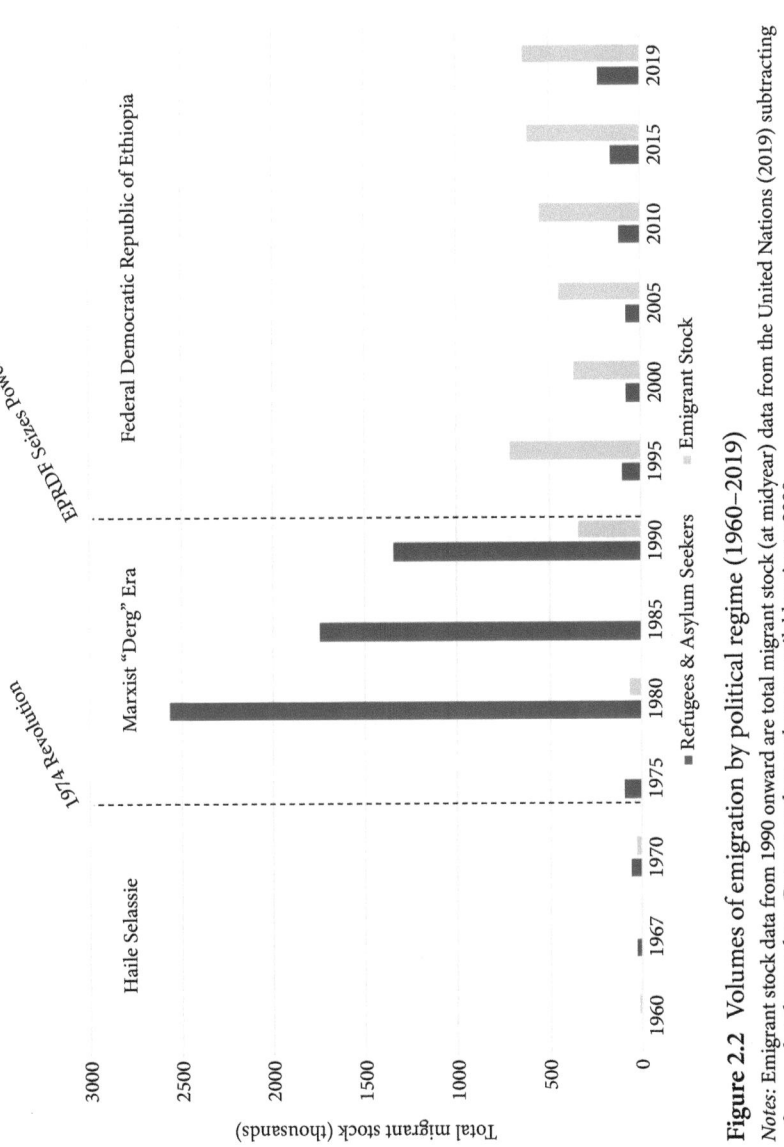

Figure 2.2 Volumes of emigration by political regime (1960–2019)

Notes: Emigrant stock data from 1990 onward are total migrant stock (at midyear) data from the United Nations (2019) subtracting refugee and asylum seekers. Data on asylum seekers unavailable prior to 2000.

Sources: Refugee and asylum seeker figures from UNHCR. *Refugee Data Finder [Data base]* The United Nations High Commissioner for Refugees (UNHCR) (2021); migrant stock data for 1960, 1970, and 1980 from the Global Bilateral Migration Database (see Özden et al. "Where on Earth is Everybody? The Evolution of Global Bilateral Migration 1960–2000," *The World Bank Economic Review* 25, no. 1 (2011): 12–56; migrant stock data for 1990–2019 from the United Nations (2019).

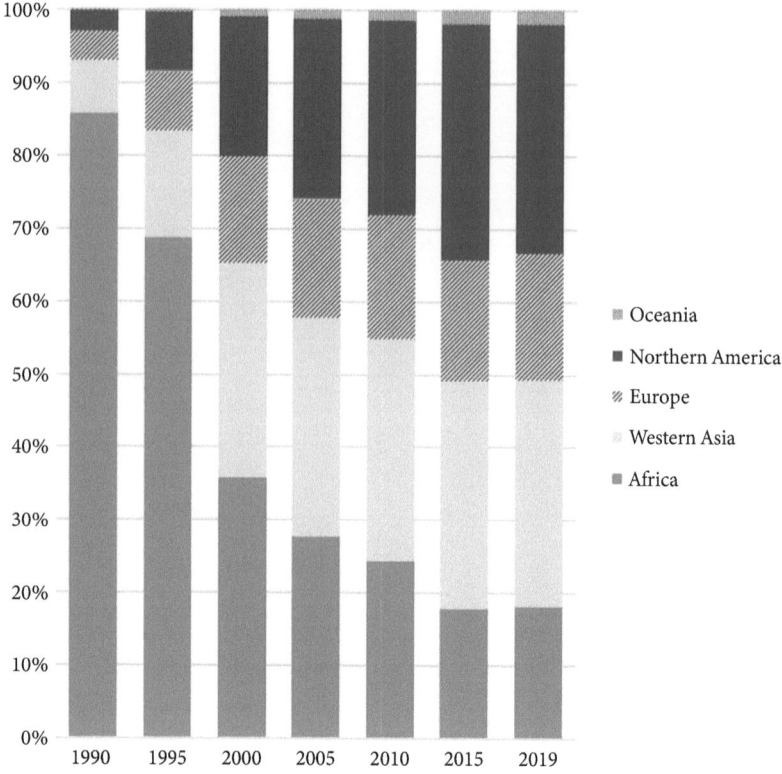

Figure 2.3 Regional destinations of international migrants from Ethiopia (1990–2019)

Note: These data include refugee figures.
Source: UN (2019).

Derg period, however, did not have the resources to move overseas. By 1990, when the EPRDF assumed power, United Nations Population Division data notes that 942,295 Ethiopians were living in Sudan, 460,000 in Somalia, 26,695 in Kenya, 13,405 in Djibouti, and 1,284 in Eritrea.[70] Most displaced Ethiopians stayed within the region; only a relatively small proportion were resettled in the United States or Europe once registered in refugee camps.[71]

After the Derg fell, refugee movements subsided, and other forms of international migration became more common (Figure 2.2). Figure 2.3 shows the growing diversity of destinations from the 1990s onward. Over this period, Ethiopians continued to flee political conflict, reunite with family, or seek educational opportunities abroad; in addition, the emigration of high- and low-skilled workers to destinations across Africa, Europe, North America, and the Middle East is increasingly common.

As Figure 2.1 suggests, there is a positive correlation between GDP growth and emigration rates as suggested in recent literature.[72] Earlier heights of emigration—the significant regional movement in 1990, for example—do not correlate with GDP growth, because this cross-border movement was largely due to displacement caused by political conflict. While displacement continues across Ethiopia, the rising levels of emigration today are increasingly associated with the pursuit of better-paying work in other countries. This rise in international labor migration appears to be driven by the economic transformations associated with rapid GDP growth and Ethiopia's growing connectivity to other countries. Labor migration that has long been directed toward destinations within Ethiopia is now extending across its borders.

The United States remains the top destination of Ethiopian emigrants, and the introduction of the Diversity Visa in 1995 contributed to the diversification of the Ethiopian diaspora there. The visa program offers 55,000 immigrant visas through an annual lottery. While applicants come from more advantaged backgrounds than nonmigrants,[73] it introduced the possibility to emigrate overseas to individuals from a wider range of socioeconomic backgrounds. Ethiopia's emigrant population in the United States grew from 66,688 in 1995 to 273,980 in 2019.[74]

The labor migration of women and men to the Middle East, through both regular and irregular channels, has grown significantly since the 1990s. Official numbers provided by the Ministry of Labor and Social Affairs chart an increase in the number of female migrants leaving for Middle Eastern countries from 1,202 in 1999 to 187,939 in 2011–2012.[75] Irregular migration is estimated to be at least double that figure.[76] A Labour Force and Migration Survey from 2021 found that more than 839,000 Ethiopians had migrated to other countries in the past five years in search of job and economic opportunities. Migrants were overwhelmingly young–78% were between the ages of 15 and 29 years old–and nearly one-third (31%) traveled to just one country: the Kingdom of Saudi Arabia.[77] A strong demand for domestic workers in Gulf countries has contributed to the "feminization" of Ethiopian labor emigration.[78]

Migration systems to the Middle East have a long history, initially emerging for religious and trade purposes.[79] One notable example is the movement of Ethiopians of Jewish descent to Israel, beginning as early as 1935. This movement increased after the newly created Israeli state offered citizenship to Jews through the Law of Return in 1950. According to Israel's Central Statistical Bureau, there were some 125,500 citizens of Ethiopian descent living in Israel in 2011. Further, Muslims make up over one-third of the Ethiopian population, and movement between Ethiopia and Saudi Arabia for pilgrimage has been ongoing for centuries.[80] These religious connections mirror economic ones; trade between Ethiopia and the Arabian Peninsula has an equally long history.[81] Still, despite these long-standing connections, the *nature* of movements within this migration system has transformed over time, such that most contemporary movement between Ethiopia and the Middle East today is labor migration—that is, migration for the purpose of wage-based employment.

***

To better understand the drivers of a migration transition in Ethiopia, it is essential to look beyond international migration alone. The relatively recent and rising trend in international labor migration, both formal and informal, is one important manifestation of a more complex shift in Ethiopian population movements taking place over the course of the last century and accelerating since the 2000s. The rise and diversification of international migration has proceeded together with the sedentarization of traditional forms of seasonal mobility and the urbanization of internal migration—all shaped by the economic and educational transformations designed to hasten Ethiopia's transition from a primarily rural, agricultural economy to one built around urban industrial and service sectors.

Across the three regimes, there has been a slow yet steady urbanization of Ethiopia's population, a trend that mirrors global experience and will likely continue in coming decades. Nevertheless, the pace and timing of this urban transition are intimately linked to the country's shifting development strategies. The Derg's focus on rural development and its more explicit ambition to control population movements helps explain why such a large share of Ethiopia's population remained in rural, agricultural livelihoods for so long. Agriculture remained the primary occupation of more than 85 percent of the population until 2000. It was only after the EPDRF's relatively abrupt shift in the economic rationale of the developmental state—notably its embrace of market forces, private entrepreneurship, foreign investment, and industrial capitalism—that the share of the population working in agriculture significantly decreased, that rural-urban migration replaced rural-rural migration as the most common type of internal migration, and that labor emigration increased.

Alongside these more structural shifts is a concomitant urbanization of the social imaginary. Young generations in Ethiopia increasingly devalue rural livelihoods, in large part because of their growing access to formal education and changing ideas about what constitutes "good work" and a "good life." As young people aspire to change their lives, most will move internally, but a growing share will consider migrating internationally. According to Gallup World Poll data from 2013, 30 percent of Ethiopians would move permanently to another country if given the opportunity, and for young people between the ages of fifteen and twenty-five, that figure rises to 42 percent.

All three signs of Ethiopia's mobility transition are present in Wayisso— the decline of nomadic movements, a rise in rural-urban migration, and an increase in and diversification of international migration. The following chapter explores how these national-level trends unfolded in this one village and shows how three family groups adapted their mobility patterns to decades of rapid societal change.

3
The Mobility History of Wayisso

In the early twentieth century, the land now called Wayisso was a comfortable place, frequented by the Oromo pastoralists who roamed the lowlands of the Ethiopian Rift Valley. It was forested with acacia trees, situated between two freshwater lakes—Lake Ziway to the north and Lake Langano to the south—and an hour or so walk west of the Awash River. Pastoralists would stay for a time, building simple shelters, only to abandon them to fall back into the earth when it was time to move on. They moved to avoid depleting grazing pastures beyond their ability to recover; they moved to trade butter and meat for grains with cultivators like the Silt'e in the western highlands; they moved for political and social gatherings with other Arsi Oromo. Their way of life was nomadic. They made a home in movement.

Over time, their simple shelters became sturdier. Some stayed long enough to grow their own crops to supplement the mainstays of a cattle-based diet: meat, milk, and blood. Then, when it was time for the herds to move on, a few family members decided to stay behind. Temporary shelters became more permanent dwellings, and the first *gandas*, or small family compounds, were established. These served as the home base around which seasonal, seminomadic movements continued.

Bedane Tuffaa was the first to construct a more permanent home in what was then informally called Wayisso Macho, named for a small hill in the area. When Bedane would leave with the cattle for weeks and months at a time, other family members stayed in what came to be known as *ganda Bedane*. A kilometer or so south, another man, Dakabo Uso, built a home for one of his three wives—the other two staying on the other side of the Awash River. This one home would in time become many, and *Ganda Dakabo Uso* was created.

Bedane Tuffaa and Dakabo Uso were both from the Habernoosa *goosii* (roughly, "tribe") of the larger Arsi Oromo ethnic group.[1] In the mid-twentieth century, a third *ganda* was formed by Dakabo Bulo from the Abayii, another *goosii* of the Arsi Oromo. Widely respected for his wealth of cattle, he gave some of his daughters in marriage to the son of another prominent Habernoosa pastoralist in the region, Dadi Tashité, and in return, Dadi gave his daughter Obse to marry Dakabo Bulo's first son, Dashi. Dashi and Obse made a home in the Wayisso Macho area, and soon, Dashi's father and others moved from the original Abayii territory, near the Aluto mountain, to join them in this comfortable place. In this way, *ganda Dakabo Bulo* was formed.

These three *gandas* represent Wayisso's first settlement. The *gandas* rooted and branched over time, and the ways in which subsequent generations lived, moved, and settled changed from generation to generation. Bedane Tuffaa, Dakabo Bulo, and Dakabo Uso were the last true pastoralists. Thereafter, Wayisso has undergone two fundamental mobility transitions: from seminomadic mobility[2] into settlement, and from settlement to migration. Before exploring the social forces that drove these mobility shifts, this chapter clarifies *how* patterns of movement changed with each generation, highlighting variations in migration and immobility outcomes across families, generations, and genders.

***

In the local language, Afaan Oromo, *godansaa* described pastoral movements, the seasonal wanderings of a people with their herds. Today, the term still carries that connotation, but it has been co-opted to describe a new reality. In the most general sense, it now means "leaving"—leaving one's home for another place, another city, another country. In English, we use the term "mobility" to refer to all kinds of human movement outside of one's direct living place and social environment; the term can refer to everything from pastoral movements to changes in residence to commuting for work. Migration is a specific kind of mobility, one that refers to a change in residence across an administrative border.

It is understandable why there is no word for "migration," as we use the term in English, in the language of the Arsi Oromo pastoralists. For them, residences were changing all the time, and *administrative* borders did not exist, even if territorial boundaries were recognized by different ethnic groups. Migration could only become a reality in life and language when people began to take up more permanent residences and as a modern state emerged that carved the land into administrative units to organize a settled populace. In short, the definition of migration assumes that people live in permanent residences and that there are administrative borders that can be crossed.[3]

In Wayisso, I primarily speak about five generations, and patterns of mobility changed significantly across them. The first generation is the generation of the founding fathers: the men who first settled Wayisso, initially using this place as a center around which seasonal pastoral movements continued. This generation remained highly mobile, but they and their wives were the first to establish dwellings that would eventually become settled residences. This first generation is now deceased.

The second generation refers to the children of these founding fathers, a generation who grew up with seminomadic pastoral movements but spearheaded the transition into more settled agricultural lives. They were Wayisso's first farmers. Today, they are the village elders, aged sixty and above.

The third generation refers to the age cohort roughly between the ages of forty and sixty (at the time of the survey and interviews), or those born between 1956 and 1976. This generation was less mobile and more rooted than previous generations. The men largely stayed in Wayisso as farmers, and most women moved to other rural areas when they married.

The fourth generation refers to the age cohort born between 1976 and 1996, between the ages of twenty and forty at the time of the survey. This generation, who largely came into adulthood after the fall of the Derg, was the first to leave Wayisso in large numbers—to take up new residences in neighboring towns, distant cities, or other countries. As growing numbers left the village, new forms of immobility also emerged among this generation, most notably the experience of involuntary immobility—aspiring to migrate but lacking the capability to do so.[4]

The fifth and youngest generation refers to those born after 1996, many of whom grow up in Wayisso but are likely, like the generation before them, to aspire to leave it.

To illustrate more clearly how mobility patterns changed across these generations, the remainder of the chapter proceeds in three parts. First, using data from a household survey, I present the family trees of Wayisso's three *gandas*. These provide a snapshot of where people born in Wayisso were living in 2016, revealing important generational, gender, and family divides in the prevalence of rural out-migration. Then, I explore where people are going, finding that most movement remains short distance, directed toward neighboring urban centers. Finally, I consider patterns of movement across the life course and across generations, showing a dramatic rise in rates of migration among younger generations. This analysis sketches the contours of a mobility transition as it unfolded at the micro-scale of a single village.

Figures 3.1, 3.2, and 3.3 show where each descendant of Bedane Tuffaa, Dakabo Bulo, and Dakabo Uso, respectively, was living in 2016. The family trees may be read from top to bottom, with cells at the top representing the oldest individuals and declining in age toward the bottom. Beneath each founding father, working downward, are the sons of these patriarchs who survived to adulthood. For example, under Lineage 1, Bedane Tuffaa has seven sons, depicted with seven white squares. Each cell is placed vertically according to their age (leftmost column)/date of birth (rightmost column) and horizontally according to birth order.[5]

Beneath each cell, a light grey line may connect a square to a circle, which designates a female family member. Each vertical line represents a marriage. Because many families are polygamous (though this trend is declining in recent years), one man may have several wives. The first son under Lineage 1, for example, has three. Beneath each wife, you find her children. All children remain in one column, according to order of birth, unless they marry and start their own family in Wayisso; in that case, they receive a new column. If an individual left and started a family elsewhere, their spouse(s) and children were not surveyed and thus are not depicted here. This chart thus gives a snapshot of the current residences of individuals who were born in Wayisso or moved to it.

Confirming qualitative histories, the family trees show that migration to urban areas (reflected in the darker shades of grey) largely concentrates in the fourth generation, with spillover into the fifth generation. With a few exceptions, men from the second and third generations have largely stayed in Wayisso.

Women, represented as circles, have historically been highly mobile—in fact, more mobile than men, as they moved households upon marriage. Women who were born in Wayisso and left for another rural area upon marriage are shown in the lightest shade of grey. I also shaded the women who moved to Wayisso upon marriage—almost all of whom came from other rural areas—to highlight the prevalence of this rural-rural marriage migration across generations. However, the kinds of migration pursued by women begin to diversify, particularly in the fourth and fifth generations, where more circles are shaded in darker shades of grey to show movement to towns and cities. Some rural-urban movement continues to be for marriage, but as

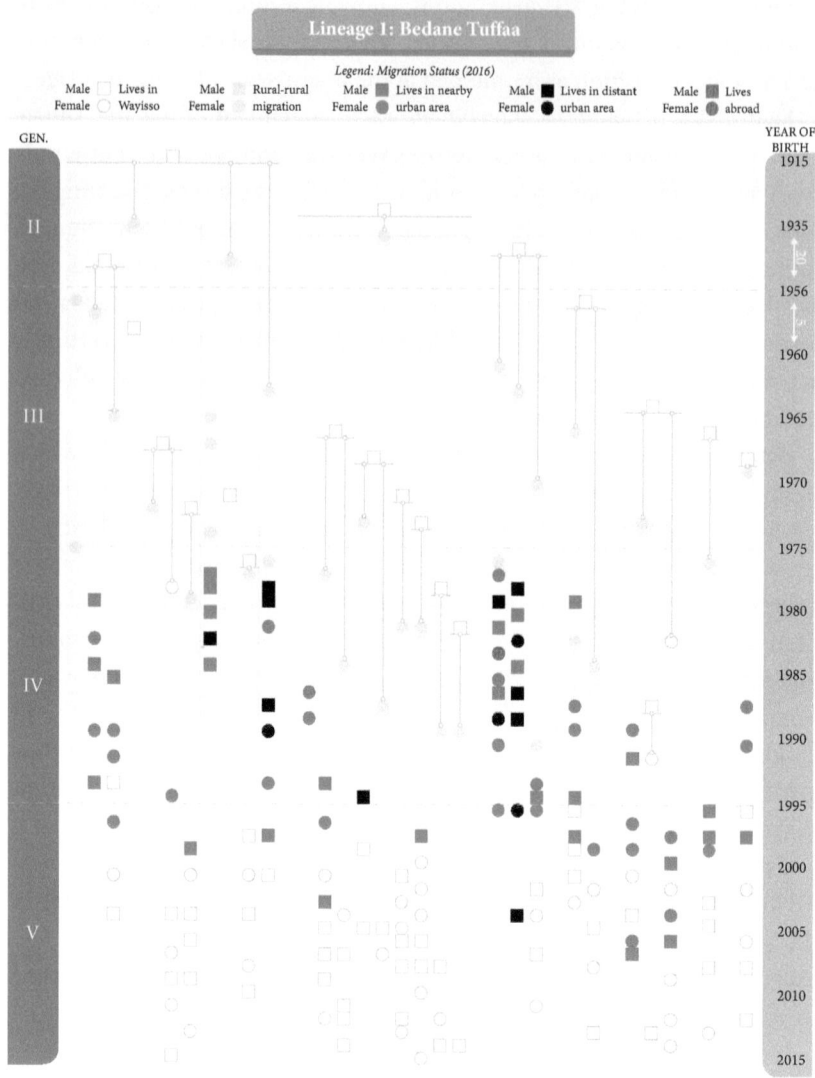

Figure 3.1 Bedane Tuffaa family tree: migration status in 2016

later chapters will show, migration for education or work is an increasingly common reason for girls' and women's out-migration.

Table 3.1 and Figures 3.4 and 3.5 then show where those who have left Wayisso were residing at the time of the survey. By far, most people move close to home: to the district's boomtown Ziway, and to a lesser

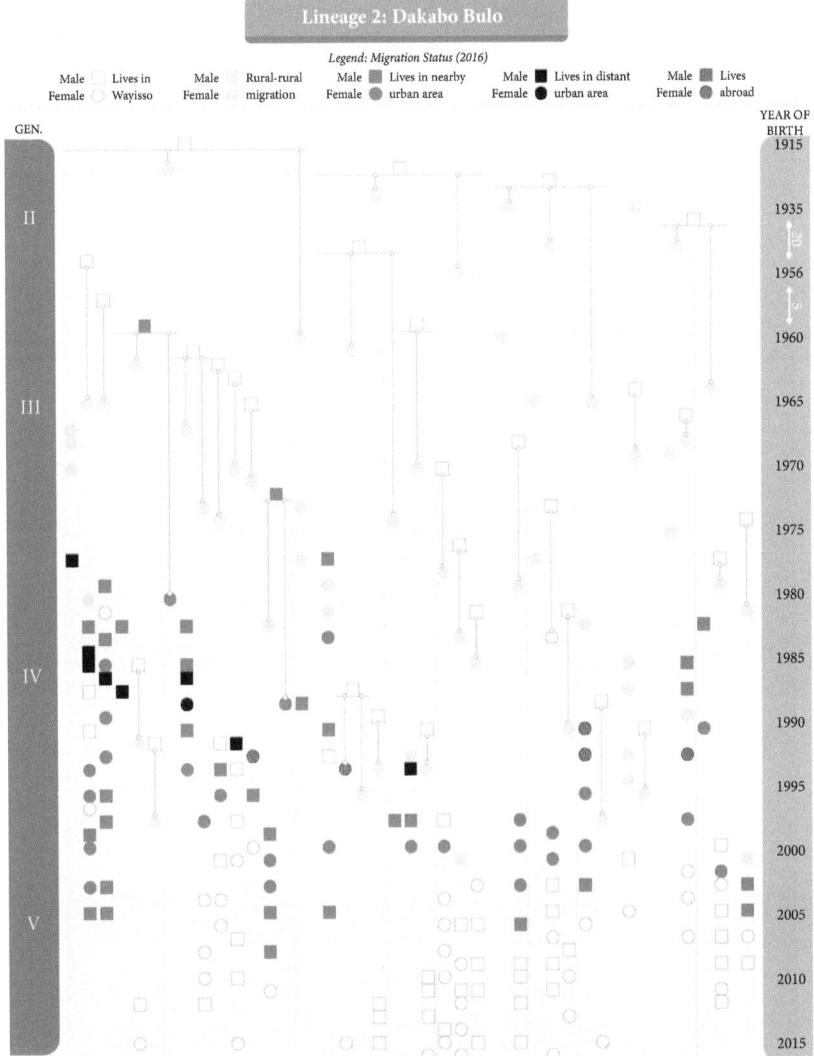

Figure 3.2 Dakabo Bulo family tree: migration status in 2016

extent, the smaller market town Adami Tulu. Migration to destinations outside the district tends to follow the main roadways toward larger urban centers like Adama, Shashemene, Hawassa, and Addis Ababa. Only three people, for example, are in the capital city, Addis Ababa. Eight individuals, less than 2 percent of those over the age of fifteen, were living abroad.

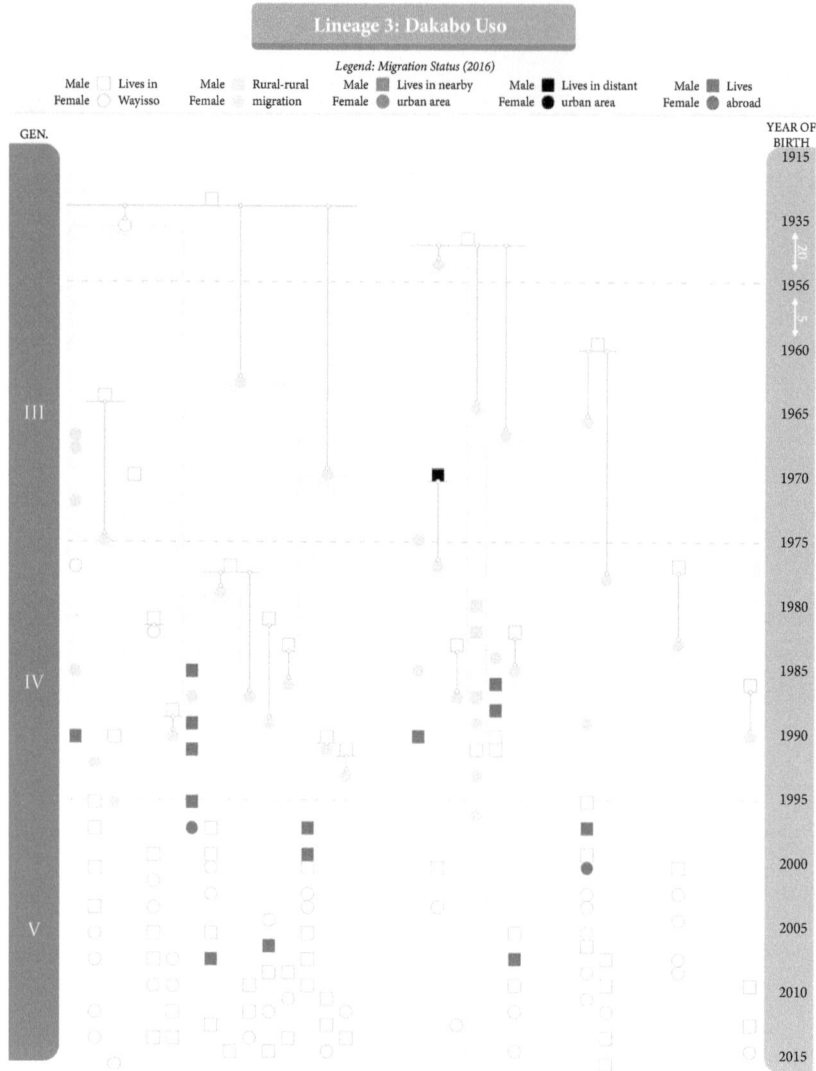

Figure 3.3 Dakabo Uso family tree: migration status in 2016

These family trees reveal clear differences in the prevalence of rural out-migration by family lineage. Bedane Tuffaa's and Dakabo Bulo's descendants are far more likely to live outside Wayisso. But even within each family lineage, migration tends to cluster within certain households. Bedane Tuffaa's granddaughter, Ademtuu, who was introduced in this book's introduction, was the only international migrant from this family group (as of the survey in 2016), represented as a circle textured with slanted lines. All her immediate

Table 3.1 Where do people go (percentages)?

Place of residence	Women (born in Wayisso)	Women (total)	Men	Total
Wayisso	16.4	47.2	57.4	51.9
Adami Tulu	7.8	4.7	7.1	5.8
Ziway	28.9	18.4	25.1	21.5
Adama	0.0	0.0	2.2	1.0
Addis Ababa	0.0	0.0	1.6	0.8
Middle East	3.9	3.3	0.0	1.8
Europe	0.8	0.5	0.0	0.3
Other: urban area (Ethiopia)	9.4	5.7	5.5	5.6
Other: rural area (Ethiopia)	32.8	20.3	1.1	11.4
Total	100.0	100.0	100.0	100.0
N	128	212	183	395

Notes: Current residences of individuals aged fifteen or older. "Women (total)" includes those born in Wayisso as well as women who moved into Wayisso most often for marriage. "Other urban area" refers to towns or cities with four or fewer people from Wayisso residing there (Bulbulla Shashemene Hawassa Borana).
Source: Household survey 2016.

brothers and sisters—the grey circles and squares immediately above and below her in the family tree—no longer live in Wayisso. The same is true for her brothers and sisters from her father Hassan's second wife, the vertical column to the right, and the children of his third wife, with the exception of a few children of Hassan's third wife who are being raised in the village. Ademtuu's cousins, however—the children of Hassan's late older brother, Dessie—are more likely to be found in Wayisso.

International migration is more common among Dakabo Bulo's descendants. Five of his granddaughters and great-granddaughters were living in the Middle East at the time of the survey.[6] None of Dakabo Uso's descendants are living abroad, and overall, this third family lineage shows much higher levels of immobility, or staying put, in Wayisso. Those who do leave only make it to nearby towns, with no one living outside of the district. Many women from this family group continue to move between rural areas for marriage, showing less diversification of female out-migration compared to the other families. However, there are a few exceptions in the fifth generation, signaling that this trend may change in the future.

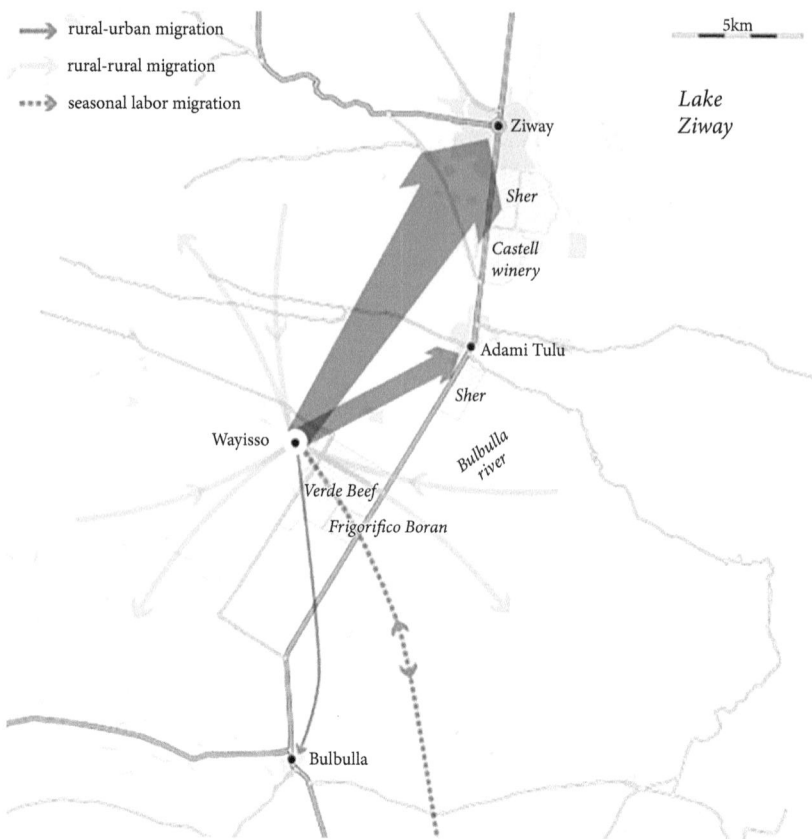

Figure 3.4 Most movement out of the Wayisso is directed toward neighboring urban areas in the Adami Tulu Jido Kombolcha (ATJK) woreda, particularly Ziway and Adami Tulu

As Table 3.2 illustrates, these family differences are further magnified when focusing on the generation in their twenties and thirties, the first generation that began to leave Wayisso in larger numbers. Just under 20 percent of young adult men from Lineage 1 (Bedane Tuffaa) remain in Wayisso, compared to 75 percent of men in Lineage 3 (Dakabo Uso). Lineage 1 sees more men moving to more distant cities outside the district as well as Ziway and Adami Tulu, and Lineage 2 shows a stronger pattern of moving to Ziway and Addis Ababa, while those who leave from Lineage 3 only go as far as Adami Tulu and Ziway.

Gender differences by family group are likewise stark. Women from Lineage 1 are far more likely to move to Ziway or other urban areas of Ethiopia

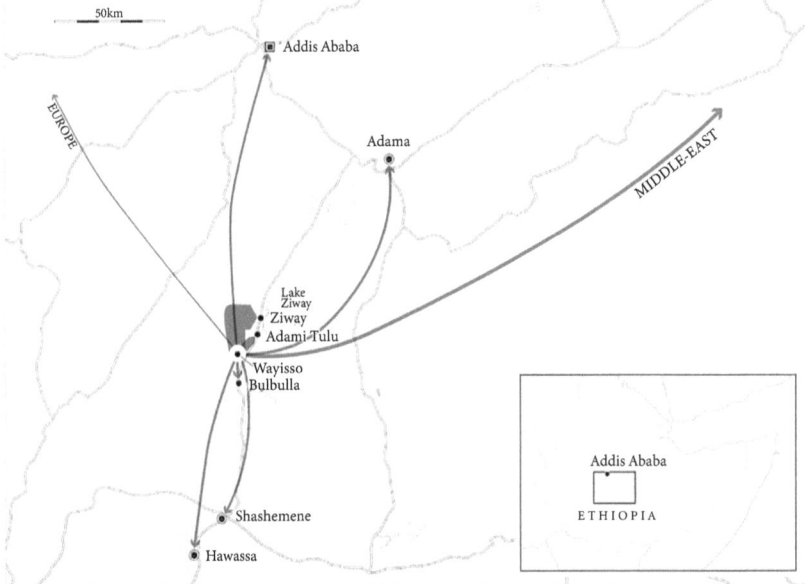

Figure 3.5 Beyond the woreda, primary destinations are large cities that lie along the main roadways and the Middle East

and far less likely to move to another rural area. Lineage 2 has a high rate of both rural-rural movement and migration to Ziway and is the only family group to send women to the Middle East. Women from Lineage 3 mostly move to other rural areas for marriage.

As the subsequent chapters will show, these family group differences in migration outcomes arise from a confluence of factors: varying levels of wealth, which shapes which families have the resources to migrate; different value systems that determine which families prioritized sending their children, particularly their girls, to school; social networks that facilitated opportunities to migrate internationally for some families and not others. Age groups determine one's place in the tide of history, but one's family provides the resources and value systems that determine how one navigates those tides.

***

The mobility patterns described above present more of a snapshot than a process. Migration is often more dynamic than the typically imagined trajectory of uprooting, moving, settling, and possibly returning. Many people move throughout their lives, from rural to urban, back to rural, out

Table 3.2 Current residence by family group in the fourth generation (ages twenty to thirty-nine, percentages)

Place of residence	Lineage 1: Bedane Tuffaa		Lineage 2: Dakabo Bulo		Lineage 3: Dakabo Uso	
	Men	Women	Men	Women	Men	Women
Wayisso	19.4	34.1	44.4	35.7	75.0	71.4
Adami Tulu	12.9	0.0	2.2	2.4	10.7	3.6
Ziway	32.3	39.0	40.0	21.4	14.3	0.0
Adama	12.9	0.0	0.0	0.0	0.0	0.0
Addis Ababa	0.0	0.0	6.7	0.0	0.0	0.0
Middle East	0.0	0.0	0.0	11.9	0.0	0.0
Europe	0.0	2.4	0.0	0.0	0.0	0.0
Other: urban area (Ethiopia)	19.4	14.6	6.7	4.8	0.0	3.6
Other: rural area (Ethiopia)	3.2	9.8	0.0	23.8	0.0	21.4
Total	100.0	100.0	100.0	100.0	100.0	100.0
N	31	41	45	42	28	28

Notes: Current residences of those surveyed between the ages of twenty and thirty-nine. "Other urban area" refers to towns or cities with four or fewer people from Wayisso residing there (Bulbulla Shashemene Hawassa Borana).
Source: Household survey 2016.

to urban again, or balancing residences in both areas. In Wayisso, it was not uncommon for some wealthier families to live in the village during the farming season and to stay in town for the winter. Likewise, for many households, the process of rural-urban migration entails straddling these two worlds first—maintaining land and relationships in rural areas while simultaneously pursuing urban-based forms of work and education—before they or future generations fully settle into urban lives.[7] The gradual nature of this transition is similar to how seminomadic ways of life transitioned into settled, agrarian ones.

Adopting a generational and life-course perspective reveals that the nature and degree of mobility experienced by different generations in Wayisso have changed over time (Table 3.3). For example, the oldest living generations, those above the age of forty, are more likely to have only settled in one place (Wayisso) if male or two places if female (most often a rural-to-rural move because of marriage migration). Only seven individuals out of the ninety-five in that age cohort had lived in three or more places (7.4 percent). This reality changes dramatically for the generation of young adults in their twenties and thirties. Over one hundred individuals (44.8 percent) have lived in three or more places. Women are slightly less mobile, with 35 percent having lived in three or more places compared to 56 percent of men. The youngest cohort, children and youth below the age of twenty, are most likely to have lived in one or two places, with only 5 percent living in three or more areas. Girls move slightly more often, with 7 percent having lived in three or more places. This may be due to moving at a young age to help with the household needs of relatives, a common practice in the area. However, for this young generation, it is likely that many more moves lie in their futures as they pursue education, work, or marriage.

To better understand the changing nature of these movements, Figures 3.6 and 3.7 illustrate the migration pathways of three generations within Lineage 1. The figures focus on migration—changes in residence—and do not address different forms of nonmigratory mobility, like pastoral movements, which occurred alongside these migratory shifts. Figure 3.6 shows the migration pathways of Bedane Tuffaa's children. In this generation, only his son Haji Tefo migrated internationally. Tefo went to Saudi Arabia for the Hajj and stayed for over a year, trying but ultimately failing to establish a new life there. His brother, Dessie, moved to Addis Ababa in his youth, initially to work for a French family who hunted in the Adami Tulu and Jido Kombolcha *woreda* and then, through their connections, for Haile

Table 3.3 Number of movements by age group (percentages)

	Age	\multicolumn{7}{c}{Number of places of residence (%)}							
		1	2	3	4	5	6	Total	N
Women	0–19	72.1	20.6	6.1	0.6	0.6	0.0	100	165
	20–39	9.6	55.2	20.8	8.0	3.2	3.2	100	125
	40–59	6.5	87.0	6.5	0.0	0.0	0.0	100	46
	60+	14.3	85.7	0.0	0.0	0.0	0.0	100	7
	Total	39.4	43.4	11.4	3.2	1.5	1.2	100	343
Men	0–19	75.8	21.0	3.2	0.0	0.0	0.0	100	157
	20–39	22.9	21.1	22.0	19.3	11.0	3.7	100	109
	40–59	62.5	25.0	3.1	6.3	0.0	3.1	100	32
	60+	80.0	20.0	0.0	0.0	0.0	0.0	100	10
	Total	55.8	21.4	9.7	7.5	3.9	1.6	100	308
Total	0–19	73.9	20.8	4.7	0.3	0.3	0.0	100	322
	20–39	15.8	39.3	21.4	13.2	6.8	3.4	100	234
	40–59	29.5	61.5	5.1	2.6	0.0	1.3	100	78
	60+	52.9	47.1	0.0	0.0	0.0	0.0	100	17
	Total	47.2	33.0	10.6	5.2	2.6	1.4	100	651

Source: Household survey 2016.

Selassie's imperial guard. Abiyo, the fourth son, was conscripted by the military under the Derg to fight in the conflict with Eritrea. All returned to Wayisso after these major long-distance movements—Tefo when he became ill in Saudi Arabia, Dessie when it was time for him to marry, and Abiyo after his period of military service ended. None ever seriously considered migrating to Adami Tulu or Ziway in their youth; at the time, these towns were not considered desirable places to live.

Figure 3.7 shows the children of Haji Tefo. Because he had three wives, Haji Tefo's children range in age from sixty, his eldest son, to fourteen, his youngest. Even within a single household—the descendants of Haji Tefo—there is a dramatic change in the degree to which migration is part of a normal life-course trajectory between the third and fourth generations. Migration becomes more complex over time, with the emergence of "stepwise" migration from smaller urban areas to larger ones—from Adami Tulu to Ziway to possibly elsewhere. While the daughters of Haji Tefo's first two wives only moved once to another rural area when they married, the last two daughters of Tayeba, his third wife, began moving to urban areas like their brothers.

***

The first international movements from this region were to Saudi Arabia for the Hajj. Over the last several centuries, many Oromo converted to Sunni Islam, integrating Islamic laws and traditions into the traditional Oromo belief system known as *Waaqeffanna* and the social-political organization known as *Sirna Gadaa*, or the Gadaa system.[8] The first two pilgrims from the Habernoosa *goosii* left in 1967, followed by another two pilgrims in 1971.[9]

This religious movement foreshadowed another form of international movement that would begin in the late 1990s. In addition to the Hajj, women began to leave for the Middle East as domestic workers. Their motivations and experiences are explored in greater depth in Chapter 5. Since 2015, a rising number of young men have begun to migrate as labor migrants to the Middle East from this district—not from Wayisso yet, but from Adami Tulu and Ziway.

Compared to national-level trends described in the previous chapter, there are clear resonances between Wayisso's migration history and Ethiopia's, notably the big-picture transformations in the decline of nomadic movements, the urbanization of internal migration, and the rise of international labor migration. However, it is important to note that patterns of

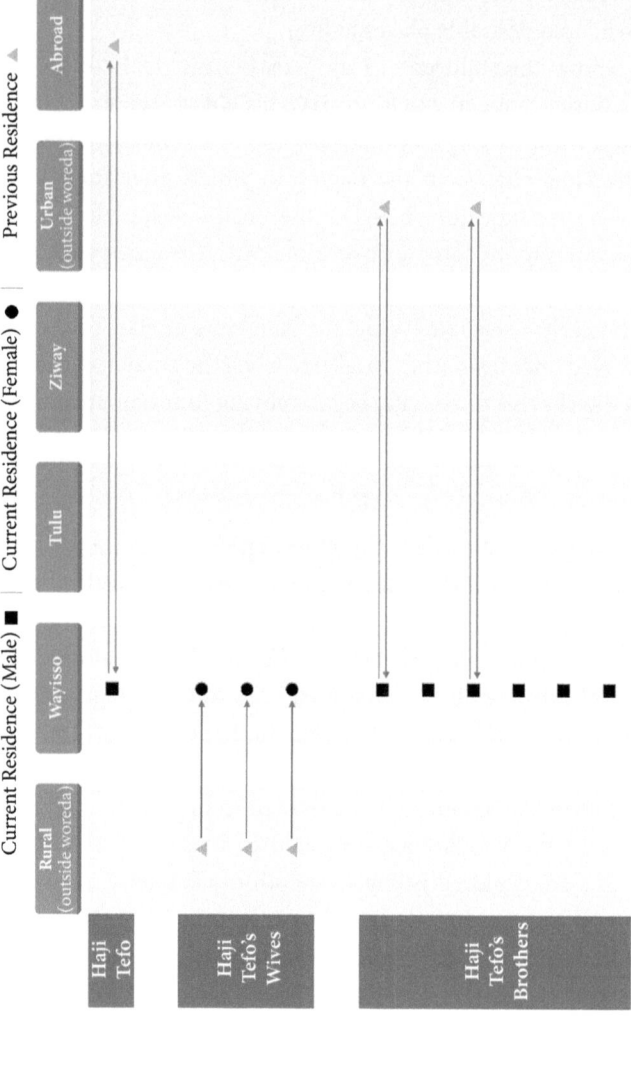

Figure 3.6 Migration pathways of the second generation after the "founding fathers"

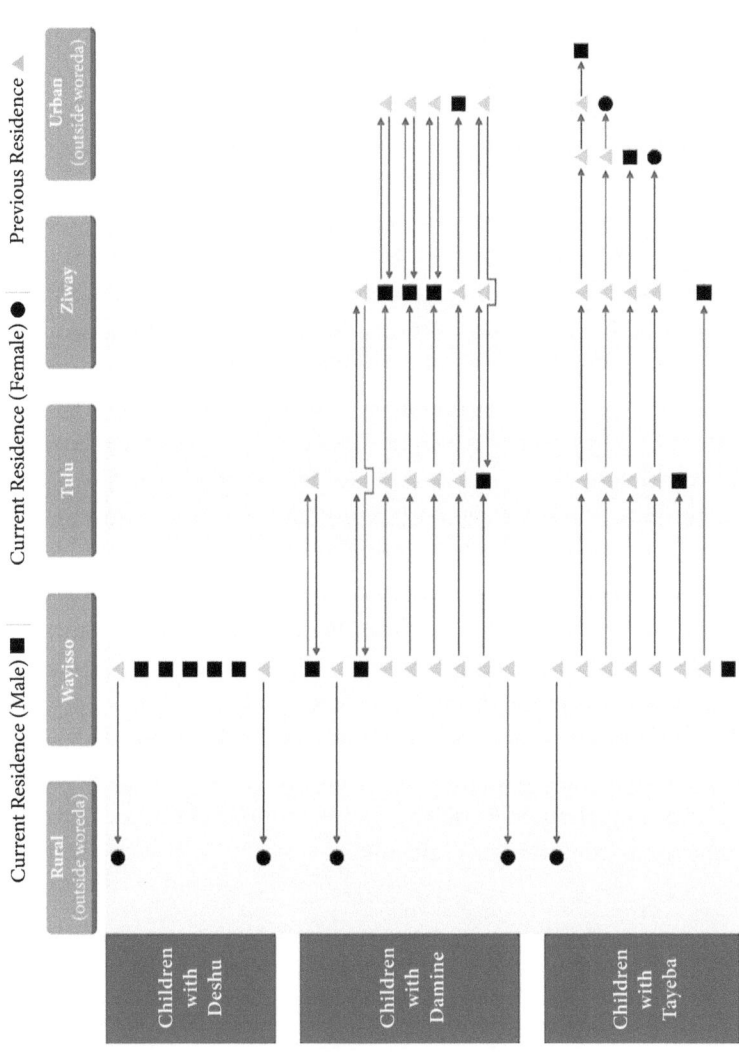

Figure 3.7 Migration pathways of the third and fourth generations: Haji Tefo's children

international migration from Wayisso are strikingly dissimilar from other regions of the country. For example, the first major international movement of Ethiopians occurred during the 1970s and 1980s, when millions fled the Derg regime, seeking asylum in other countries. The Ethiopian diaspora in the United States was established during this period, and a larger share moved to neighboring countries in the Horn of Africa. But no one from the Wayisso left during that period. Today, the Diversity Visa is common across Ethiopia, and though many young men from Wayisso living in Ziway have applied, no one has received it.

Furthermore, other regions of Ethiopia have seen a large and irregular movement of young men and women to Kenya, down to South Africa, or to Sudan, but no one from Wayisso has left in this way. In fact, the relatively small international migration that has occurred has been through relatively formal channels. I say "relatively" formal because labor migration to the Middle East was officially banned by the Ethiopian government between 2013 and 2018, meaning international labor migration from Wayisso during the time of this research was technically illegal. However, the migration of young women from this area was facilitated by migration agencies or personal connections, often with passports, a written contract, and traveling by airplane. This is very different in nature from the more dangerous routes taken by female migrants from other parts of the country—for example, from Ethiopia into Somalia and then over the Gulf of Aden into war-torn Yemen.[10]

Thus, Wayisso's migration history is not a microcosm for the migration history of Ethiopia. Yet, as the following chapters will show, the social forces driving its rapid mobility transition have much to tell us about why development drives migration. Wayisso's history is unique, but the social forces driving migration from the village are not.

4
The State

The second half of the twentieth century was a tumultuous period of rapid social change in Ethiopia. The political dramas unfolding across the country reflected upheavals occurring in many places elsewhere: the rejection of an imperial order, the rapid rise and ultimate failure of a communist revolution, and the eventual embrace of a capitalist development logic. The "state" in Ethiopia has never been one thing. It's been remade many times over as Ethiopians struggle to find a political system that reflects the aspirations of its diverse peoples. And as this chapter will show, each iteration and experimentation with a modern state reshapes how its people move and settle.

This chapter opens with an Oromo perspective on Ethiopia's nation-state building and introduces the indigenous political-social system called the *Sirna Gadaa*, or Gadaa system, that structured lives and livelihoods in the Oromo Kingdom for centuries. Notably, the Gadaa system organized society in a way that was harmonious with seminomadic pastoralism. Over the course of the early twentieth century, however, a competing political system—the Ethiopian Empire—began to encroach on traditional ways of life, and by midcentury, relationships to what was once considered communal land began to change. A few households began to claim large swaths of land, build larger homes, and experiment with growing crops. These first stirrings of settlement were then disrupted by a communist revolution in the 1970s. The Derg regime brought the state closer than ever to everyday life in Wayisso. Through sweeping land reform and the creation of peasant associations, the government effectively allocated land to the people and people to the land,[1] compelling a widespread transition into more sedentary, agricultural livelihoods. At the same time, the Derg brought access to new goods, ideas, and notions of nationhood. For the people of Wayisso, becoming part of the modern Ethiopian state required a changing relationship to land, to livelihood, to tribe, to the state—one that also required settling down. Before pastoralists became migrants, they became peasants.

Moved by Modernity. Kerilyn Schewel, Oxford University Press. © Oxford University Press (2025).
DOI: 10.1093/9780197680759.003.0005

After the socialist regime fell and the Ethiopian People's Revolutionary Democratic Front (EPRDF) took power in the 1990s, Prime Minister Meles Zenawi envisioned a state-led economy that prioritized agriculture as the cornerstone of the nation's economic growth, an approach to economic transformation described as Agricultural Development–Led Industrialization (ADLI). However, by the early 2000s, agricultural and economic productivity had stagnated. Facing significant disapproval among the Ethiopian populace and strong international pressures, the government shifted its development strategy toward one that was much more unabashedly in pursuit of economic growth and more open to privatization, market forces, foreign investment, and free enterprise.[2]

As the development thinking of the state shifted, so too did the self-development thinking of the farmers in Wayisso. They no longer believe small-scale farming is going to improve their material circumstances. They maintain this livelihood activity because for many, it is all they have, but they are now convinced that any opportunity for economic progress requires working in the industrial or service sectors. As a result, households increasingly combine rural and urban livelihoods. They maintain their farmlands as a base income but aspire toward—and if they have the means, actively pursue—alternative work in town. In this process, the "center of gravity" of rural communities, as the early migration researcher Torsten Hägerstrand once put it,[3] gradually transfers from the village to towns and cities.[4]

The Gadaa System

In narratives about Ethiopian history, the Oromo are often missing.[5] The story of Ethiopia often begins with the mythic kingdom of Abyssinia. The Abyssinians were the peoples of the Ethiopian highlands, ancestors of what are today known as the Amhara and Tigrayan ethnic groups. The Oromo were a kingdom of peoples south of Abyssinia, in what is today southern Ethiopia and northern Kenya. They begin to feature in historical accounts of the country's history when the Oromo expanded northward into the southern boundaries of Abyssinia in the sixteenth and seventeenth centuries. Thus commenced centuries of conflict between these southern and northern kingdoms. For this reason, the Oromo narrate a different history of Ethiopia. Although Ethiopia was never formally colonized by a Western power, many Oromo see their peoples as having been colonized by the Abyssinian empire. After all, Menelik II, formerly the king of Shewa in central Ethiopia, only became emperor after a series of wars that conquered lands and peoples to the south and east, including the Oromo, Kaffa, Sidama, and Wolayita.

The Oromo had their own kingdom, with a distinct indigenous democratic system of governance. The Gadaa system functioned by organizing the male members of society into a series of *luba*, or generation classes, that succeed each other every eight years. As the Ethiopian historian Mohammed Hassen details, the full cycle of the Gadaa system included ten grades, spanning eighty years, after which an individual "retired" (*gadamojjii*).[6] The first forty years, composed of five grades, were periods of preparation and educational rites of passage that trained young men in the political, economic, military, and ritual affairs of the community. Each grade served a social purpose, from boys overseeing herds as shepherds in one stage to warriors proving their military prowess through ritual warfare (*butta*) in another. After these five Gadaa grades, a *luba* graduated with a fatherhood (*dannisa*) ceremony, signaling their entrance into maturity. In the Gadaa stage, the *luba* elected a Gadaa father (*Abba Gadaa*), who would serve as the central authority and political head for the entire society. Potential candidates launched election campaigns to convince others of their strengths in the three qualities considered most important for leadership: oratorical talent, knowledge of the history and traditions of society, and past military achievements.[7] Alongside the *Abba Gadaa*, there was also a father of war (*Abba Dula*) and father of the law (*Abba Sera*). After their eight-year term, the reigning Gadaa class would transfer power to the next generation in a ceremony known as *Jarra*, with the *Abba Gadaa* handing over the *bokku*, a symbol of unity and common law of the peoples to the newly elected.

The precise origins of the Gadaa system are unknown, and its manifestations varied across different Oromo groups over time. It is commonly told that in the sixteenth century, one gadaa class governed a single Oromo nation, but as the Oromo expanded in population and space over the next three hundred years, the Gadaa system evolved into several assemblies overseeing the affairs of dispersed clans that began to show signs of differentiation in the system's everyday practice. Hassen suggests that despite this dispersion, there remained a "common political grammar" in the practice of the Gadaa system that remained relatively constant over time and distinguished what can still be described as a singular system.⁸ Other scholars contend that the distance between clans weakened the institution, and as the Oromo conquered new territories, some groups withheld wealth and power from the Indigenous populations, challenging the system's traditional egalitarian values.⁹ In some areas, the republican system was even replaced by hereditary offices and monarchical institutions.¹⁰

The Oromo who live in the Wayisso area today predominantly identify as Arsi Oromo. In the sixteenth century, Arsi arose as a separate distinct identity within the broader *Uma Orma*, or Oromo peoples.¹¹ Some eighteen generations ago, a man named Arsi had two sons, Mandoo and Sikko, from whom the Arsi lineage was born. Mandoo had seven sons and remained in their homeland of Madhagdu (Baredu) Krukuru in present-day Bale. Sikko, together with his five sons, migrated to what came to be known as Arsiland, a region roughly synonymous with the present-day Arsi district in the Oromia state.¹² Oromo conquests continued within and from Arsiland throughout the centuries to come, eventually encompassing the area that is the focus of the present study.

Lake Ziway and its surrounding territory—including what is today Wayisso—were conquered and reconquered over the centuries by the Oromo and Abyssinian empires. The Ethiopian monk Bahrey reports that conflicts were occurring as early as the reign of Emperor Sarsa Dengel (1563–1597), who conquered the Oromo forces near Lake Ziway, seizing their cattle and dispersing them southeastward toward Fatagar and Dawaro.¹³ This area was later reconquered by the Oromo, who in the process assimilated some Hadiya and Sidama groups living in the region. According to Hanumana elders in Wayisso, many of the Habernoosa *goosii* of the Arsi Oromo who live in Wayisso today were originally Hadiya who were "adopted" through the process of *mogassa* to become part of the Arsi Oromo society.

Emperor Menelik II's conquest of 1882–1886 again brought the Shewan state, and later the Ethiopian Empire, southward. Menelik, then the negus of the Shewa state, is said to have personally commanded the military forces that conquered the areas around Lake Ziway. The Arsi Oromo, particularly those in the present-day Arsi state, showed "probably the stiffest and most prolonged resistance to Menelik and his forces,"¹⁴ but they were eventually defeated, and afterward, the region remained formally within the Ethiopian Empire.

Empire

Integration into the empire introduced new political and economic realities, including new forms of land tenure, the practice of tax collection, and new positions of political power associated with the imperial regime rather than the Gadaa system. In the area where Wayisso is today, these changes came more gradually than in other areas, yet they had long-term consequences for the political, economic, and social institutions of the Oromo people who lived there.

In Oromo tradition, land was collectively held, and territorial boundaries were layered. There was the territory of the Arsi Oromo, for example, and within that, territories of various *goosii*. Boundaries could be and were contested. If the threat was external, this was often resolved through warfare; if the matter was internal, conflict mediation occurred through the Gadaa system. Land could not be sold, purchased, or inherited. According to the Ethiopian historian Ketebo Abdiyo, the idea that land could be individually held was completely foreign to the Arsi Oromo in the late nineteenth century.[15]

This changed when Menelik annexed the Arsi Oromo territories. The emperor gave large swaths of his newly conquered territories to soldiers, civil servants, clergy, or other favored individuals willing to migrate. To manage the newly acquired lands, the empire introduced a complex system of land tenure, establishing new regulations and relationships to the land that placed the state as the ultimate arbiter.[16] In some areas, transformations in land tenure were rapid and dramatic. Among the Arsi Oromo living to the northeast of Lake Ziway, for example, almost all lost their land and became tenants on the land occupied by newly arrived settlers. These new arrangements gave rise to unjust feudal systems that would galvanize political revolution in the 1970s. The southern and western Arsi, however, were allowed to retain some tracts of their former land through a land tenure system known as *sisso*, or *balabat mirt*. Much of it was kept as grazing land (*sekala*), and thus the impact of land reforms was more gradual.[17] For this reason, the Arsi Oromo in the area to the southwest of Lake Ziway, where Wayisso is today, persisted in pastoral livelihoods for much longer than Arsi Oromo elsewhere.

Nevertheless, relationships to the land began to shift. These changes were intimately tied to the new political position of the *balabat*, a state position initially conceived to facilitate a relationship between the emerging centralized state and the newly conquered peoples whose languages and customs were foreign to it.[18] The *balabat* was often a local leader,[19] whose status was already recognized by his peoples, and who took on new duties for the state, including tax collection, maintaining peace and order, and the administration of new forms of land tenure.[20] In this area, the *balabat* did not supplant the political and social organization provided through the Gadaa system in the first half of the twentieth century but rather overlaid it. Thus, the Gadaa system continued alongside the emergence of a centralized state, though it weakened as the centralized state grew stronger.[21] This political strategy was so effective that the Italians kept the position of the *balabat* during their occupation from 1936 to 1941, and it was maintained after Haile Selassie's return.

In the early and mid-twentieth century, then, the *balabat* was the primary channel through which the empire exerted an influence in Wayisso. Each *goosii* had their own *balabat*: the Habernoosa around where Wayisso is today, the Abayii near the mountains to the east of the Awash River, the Oliyee around Adami Tulu, and the Wegee near Ziway. Below each *balabat* was the *cicarsum*, an elected chief for the respective *balbaala* within a *goosii*. In the Habernoosa *goosii*, there are five *balbaala*, or "doors": Hadumana, Godemena, Alekira, Afemena, and Mujemena—divisions with the Habernoosa *goosii* who can trace their lineage to one of the five sons of Habernoosa. The *balabat* would allocate land to the *cicarsum* of each of these *balbaala*, though it was not parceled out equally. If you had a better relationship with the *balabat*, if you had connections to the government, or if you were wealthy, you tended to get more land. In the early twentieth century, the Godemana *balbaala* held the most land; it stretched from the Macho mountain down to Lake Langano.

Land was then further divided within each *balbaala* by the *cicarsum*. In Wayisso, land remained primarily for grazing, yet certain families claimed larger portions of it in the 1950s and 1960s. By paying a 20 Ethiopian birr tax, someone could claim an entire forty hectares—a *gasha* in Amharic or *wanta* in Afaan Oromo. Taxes at the time were paid by selling butter at markets in Kurkura or Borema or selling cattle at markets in Meki or Negele. However, not everyone knew the value of claiming land at that time. As pastoralists, grazing their cattle on what in practice remained collective lands, few thought to "claim" land. Those who did were mostly those in positions of political power: the *balabat*, the *cicarsum*, and their families.

There were other areas of the *woreda* that came more directly under state control during the period of Haile Selassie, which made the presence of the state more visible to local peoples. Neighboring Wayisso, for example, where Verde Beef is today, was a large area of land held by a man named Dadi Tashité. Elders remember Dadi was very wealthy, with innumerable cattle, and his land was rich and forested. At one point, a state representative arrived and announced they were going to build a fence but assured Dadi that he could stay where he was. Dadi agreed, they built the fence, and only when they were finished did they kick him off of the land. (Elders joked that Dadi couldn't find a way out; they had fenced him in!) This land became the state-run Habernoosa Cattle Ranch. In addition, administrative centers were established in Adami Tulu and Ziway, and state workers from the north moved into the area to assume their administrative positions. In this way, the presence and power of the state became more conspicuous.

According to local memory, people persisted in pastoral livelihoods well into the 1970s. It was only many years after the Derg seized power that the majority of households adopted farming as their primary livelihood. As one elder, Haji Tefo, who served as a *cicarsum* of the Hadumana in the 1960s, remembers from that time: "The government didn't look at us then.... The government allowed [the *cicarsum*] to control everyone.... At that time, the land was abundant. They even measured it by *wanta*, which is forty hectares, because we had so much. I had ten *wanta*! Four hundred hectares!" Of his four hundred hectares, Haji Tefo says he farmed three to four plots (about one hectare) to supplement his diet. "During the time of Haile Selassie, people did not like plowing the land. Most people depended on animals.... We were drinking milk and eating butter. We didn't worry about crops."

The first person of the Habernoosa clan to cultivate land for personal consumption was a man named Yaya Bude, sometime in the 1940s, in an area only a dozen or so kilometers away from Wayisso. The Silt'e people to the west were better known as farmers, and the neighboring Oromo would often trade with them. Yaya, they say, observed how the Silt'e farmed their land and started doing the same himself. The practice of small-scale seasonal farming slowly spread throughout the *woreda*.

The first profit farmer from this area was a man named Qerro, who lived south of Wayisso near a market in Jido. He was one of the few individuals in the *woreda* who, in the late 1960s, first grew soybeans for the market. A key commonality among these early cash crop farmers was that they all had some connection to the government and thus learned about a government-led initiative to grow soybeans.[22] With government support, they tried their hand at cultivation and made a significant profit. As one elder remembers, "The land was so fertile! When some people first started plowing, they really made a profit. At that time, whoever sold soybeans became very

Figure 4.1 An aerial photograph of Wayisso in 1967
Note: Land remains forested with little visible farmland.
Source: Aerial photograph provided by the Ethiopian Mapping Agency.

wealthy.... [This was] when people first started buying bicycles. Those who were wealthy bought bicycles and traveled place to place." The fruits of surplus farming became visible. Those who were benefiting, however, remained an elite few with closer connections to the state. "At the end of Haile Selassie," this elder explained, "there were only a few wealthy people. I can count them. Merchants like Bede. Farmers like Adamu, Aklilu. These were the wealthy people living at that time. They had a relationship with the government. They would get the seeds immediately, take a lot of land, and sow it." Even if some households in Wayisso did farm, they only did so on small plots of land seasonally to supplement their primarily pastoral livelihoods.

Through my interviews alone, it was difficult to discern when exactly the transition to supplementary farming occurred. Most informants described the shift to farming as taking place after the 1974 revolution, yet aerial photographs from 1967 and 1972 from the Ethiopian Mapping Agency reveal that some degree of farming became more commonplace in the latter years of Haile Selassie's reign. In a photograph of the *woreda* in 1967 (Figure 4.1), the

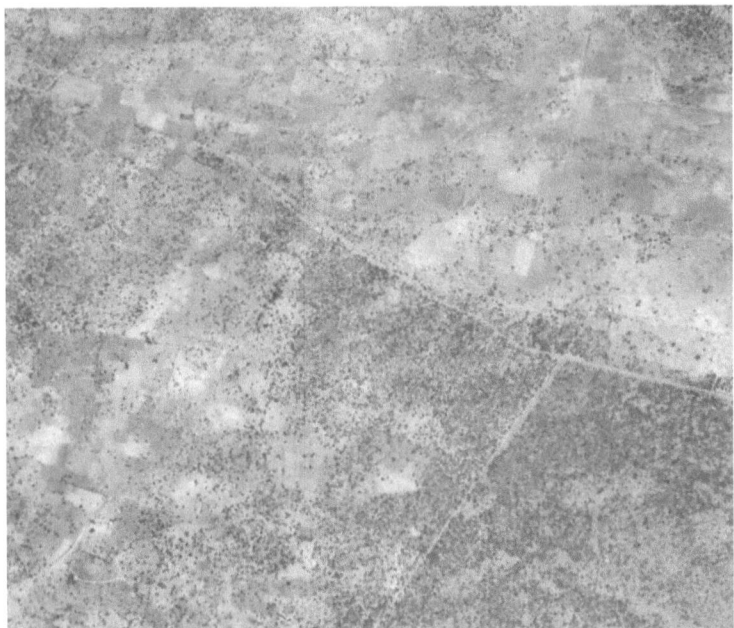

Figure 4.2 An aerial photograph of Wayisso in 1972.

Note: This photograph was taken two years prior to the communist revolution. Deforestation is visible to the bottom left and top half of the photograph

Source: Aerial photograph provided by the Ethiopian Mapping Agency.

land remains forested with little visible farmland. This changed in a photo from 1972 (Figure 4.2), where new pale patches of farming plots are visible. These photographs suggest that it was precisely at the end of Haile Selassie's reign when more people in the area began experimenting with farming. However, the small, scattered plots confirm what elders remember: that for most, this was small-scale cultivation, supplementing what were primarily pastoral livelihoods.

Socialism

Just two years after the 1972 aerial photograph was taken, a military junta overthrew Emperor Haile Selassie in the distant capital city. Formally the Provisional Military Administrative Council, the "Derg" abolished the monarchy and established a Marxist-Leninist state, led by Mengistu Haile Mariam, who formally became chairman in 1977. The period that followed is known as the Red Terror, a campaign of political repression and violence during which tens of thousands of potential political opponents were imprisoned, tortured, and executed without trial. One direct consequence of this revolution and its violent methods was the first major international emigration of Ethiopians. Hundreds of thousands of political refugees sought asylum elsewhere, introducing for the first time an Ethiopian diaspora overseas.

Nobody from Wayisso fled abroad, even if all would be affected by the political upheavals occurring in the capital city. One elderly woman described Haile Selassie, or "Janhoy" (His Majesty) as she called him, as a more symbolic figure than a real presence in their lives. They were aware that unrest was happening when he was overthrown, but the news was anecdotal. "We heard rumors from others—that he had died, that he hadn't, that he was in prison. We weren't exactly sure." Few in Wayisso had seen a revolution coming, and once the revolution arrived in Wayisso, its consequences were far different in nature than what was experienced in the capital city.

In narratives of Ethiopian history, the Derg is a bloody chapter. Yet, as Prunier suggests, the violence through which the regime wielded power often overshadows the social nature of the revolution.[23] I was surprised to find that in Wayisso, many remember the Derg with some degree of fondness—as a time when the government prioritized *rural* development. One village elder listed what he saw as the major changes the Derg brought to Wayisso:

> *First, the Derg was the first one to open schools in rural areas.... Second, the Derg showed us how to plow the land. There were some young ones who were trained in farming systems. They came here to the rural areas and taught us how to plow, how to sow, how to irrigate, and how to use fertilizers, to be more productive than before. Third, we formed a union, with ten kebeles together, represented by a chief, and this union gave us fertilizer and other things. Finally, we had a meeting twice a year. This was a time set to meet with the government representatives and talk about our problems.... I personally think that when the Derg came to power, it was good. It tried to make the life of rural areas better.*

It was under the Derg's rule that Wayisso became more fully integrated into a modern state apparatus. And this political integration ushered in a new chapter of relative immobility: settling down into agricultural lives within newly formed *kebeles*, or peasant associations. Rural-rural movement for marriage persisted, as well as some degree of long-distance cattle grazing, but for most households in Wayisso, the 1970s and 1980s entailed a transition into more settled, farming lifestyles, where households claimed, cultivated, and lived from their allocated land and cattle. This settling coincided with new forms of mobility introduced by the state: conscription to meet labor and military shortages, migration for education for a select few, and migration for government work.

A sweeping land reform was one of the first major changes implemented by the Derg. As Marina and David Ottaway explain, the land reform "was unequivocally radical, even in Soviet and Chinese terms. It nationalized all rural land, abolished tenancy and put peasants in charge of enforcing the whole scheme."[24] The purpose of the 1975 Proclamation to Provide for the Public Ownership of Rural Lands (No. 31) was to, as its preamble stated, "alter the existing agrarian relations so that the Ethiopian peasant masses which have paid so much in sweat as in blood to maintain an extravagant feudal class may be liberated from age-old feudal oppression, injustice, poverty, and disease, and in order to lay the basis upon which all Ethiopians may henceforth live in equality, freedom, and fraternity."[25] The conditions of serfdom that galvanized this proclamation were only present in some areas of the empire, however. Tenancy varied greatly across Ethiopia, and owner cultivation was also common.[26] The proclamation's preamble, railing against an age-old feudal oppression, did not describe the reality in Wayisso, where cultivation was a relatively new phenomenon and most persisted in pastoral livelihoods.

To carry out the provisions of the proclamation, the government parceled *woredas*, the large administrative districts established under Haile Selassie, into smaller *kebeles*, or peasant associations. The peasant association was designed to be a unit of some three hundred or four hundred households (or some eight hundred hectares) within which land distribution, land directives, judicial tribunals, cooperatives, schools, health services, and villagization programs, among other government directives and services, would be established. Groups of four or more *kebeles* were organized into an *agargelot* (roughly translating to "service"), to organize the distribution of basic goods and social services to their respective *kebeles*. The Derg left room for different kinds of relations with nomadic peoples, like the Afar, and while the Wayisso area was categorized as grazing lands under Haile Selassie, it was recategorized as an agrarian kebele under the Derg. Thus, in 1975, the *Weyiso Macho kebele* was formally established.[27]

To gain access to material resources within an *agargelot* required registration within a peasant association. There were clear advantages to doing so. As the then chairman of Wayisso's *agargelot* explained: "Each *agargelot* had a big warehouse that kept things like sugar, salt, oil, tea . . . everything to be given to the kebeles. Everything you buy now in shops . . . even roofs, firewood—everything people needed. . . . And people didn't pay anything. Most farmers were very poor. Even though the government was at war [with Eritrea] during that time, they facilitated a lot of things for people."

The reality of land distribution in Wayisso differed from what the new constitution envisioned, however. In writing, the government allowed all individuals to claim land, setting a maximum limit of ten hectares per household. In practice, people requested land from the chairman of the peasant association and no upward limit was enforced. As one elder who served as a chairman during the time of the Derg recalls:

During the Derg, you got land if you asked for it. If you ask for it, they [the chairman] would give it to you. But you are only going to ask for it if you are active, if you are aware that more land will give you more. Otherwise, the lazy ones, if they have four plots, they think, "It's quite enough for me. What am I going to do with more?" But those who received a lot of land, they are still giving their land to their children.

Initially, when the Derg first came to power, those who served in any form of government position associated with Haile Selassie lost their land and positions and were replaced by others without a connection to the imperial regime.[28] After some time, however, these new leaders of the *Weyiso Macho kebele* began demanding higher taxes from households and pocketing a portion of them. As a neighboring *kebele*'s chairman remembers:

Those who were balabat *during the period of Haile Selassie, when the Derg came, they were thrown out of power and the younger ones were given the chance to lead. They started taking revenge on those who were in power before. They started to steal the money of the government. When the government became aware of this, they changed the rules again: everything should be by election. So, the people selected the sons of the* balabats. *Because if it is by election, the* balabats *were to some extent literate then. They know how to lead. They know how to have a leadership position. So, people elected the* balabat's *sons.*

In this way, members of the same families with greater political power during the time of Haile Selassie ended up leading the peasant association in the latter years of the socialist government's rule. Given the constraints of the political regime, they could not accumulate as much land as before, but they still continued to acquire more land than other households. They were more "active," as the elder put it, "aware that more land will give you more." For this reason, those who claimed the most land under Haile Selassie continued to hold the most land by the end of the Derg.

In short, the power inequalities that characterized the transition from communal to family landholding during the time of Haile Selassie continued under the Derg, though in a more limited fashion. Those with the foresight to claim more land "than they needed" gave more land to their children, establishing a base for income inequalities in the generations to come—inequalities with migration consequences. Those with more land could more easily generate the extra income needed to support the movement of their children to town for further schooling or for work. By the end of the Derg, as it was under Haile Selassie, families in Lineage 1 (the Hadumana of the Habernoosa) had the greatest landholdings in Wayisso. Their children also showed some of the highest rates of out-migration after the fall of the Derg.

***

Formal education took two forms under the Derg. The first was a nationwide education campaign, formally titled the Development through Cooperation, Enlightenment and Work Campaign. Shortly after it assumed power, the Derg mandated that all students and teachers in university or the last two years of high school were required to leave for the countryside to educate the peasants. The Amharic word for the campaign was *zemecha*. The sweeping land reform had already won the support of the students, and many enrolled enthusiastically as "*zemachs*" in the movement that promised to bring modernization to the masses.[29]

The reaction of rural peoples to the *zemachs* varied across regions and classes.[30] In the northern highlands, the response among rural peasants was rather indifferent, while in the southern regions, particularly those conquered territories where northern soldiers (*neftenya*, or "gun men") had been given land, peasants readily united with the *zemachs* to hunt out landlords. In other places, the arriving students offended locals with their patronizing attitude, a mix of, as the anthropologist Donald Donham put it, the "superiority born of modern education" and a Marxist contempt for traditional religious and social systems.[31] This led to violent confrontations between *zemachs* and local peoples in some areas.

In Wayisso, the experience with the *zemecha* campaign was more mundane yet still significant. Three men named Melaku, Tilahun, and Habtamu held trainings at the newly established Woransa school to teach people how to farm. In the beginning, they had a difficult time. No one showed up for trainings. "We did not see the benefits of farming," one elder explained. Years of drought were particularly difficult for these teachers. After failed rainy seasons, farmers found that they lost more than they gained. Many returned to pastoralism, which they considered more productive and better suited to an irregular climate. However, over time, more people learned to use fertilizer and were given better seeds, and production increased.

More profound than the *zemecha* campaign, however, was the establishment of formal schooling in rural areas. The expansion of formal education began in Ethiopia under Haile Selassie but only reached Wayisso during the time of the Derg. One of the first services to be provided to an *agargelot* was elementary education. Wayisso's first school was located in the Andolla kebele, ten kilometers away. In the beginning, it was mostly young and adult men who went to school. Many recall that the quality of education during the time of the Derg was better than today. "It was the first state that really tried to build roads, schools, clinics for the rural people," one older man shared. "It was during the Derg that education really started in the rural areas. They announced that every child from the farmers should have to go to school. And the quality was good." He contrasted education under the Derg with the quality of schooling today, which he described as "fake."

Despite the Derg's emphasis on expanding education to rural areas, a relatively small percentage of the population attended. At the time of the 1984 census, 24 percent of the Ethiopian population ages five years and older were attending regular school, university, or other forms of adult education, and just 8.8 percent had attended school in the past. There was a strong rural-urban divide: 53.8 percent of the population five years and older in urban areas attended school versus 18.9 percent of the population in rural areas, where the vast majority of the population lived.[32] In rural areas of the *Arsi* and Shewa (Wayisso lies near the border of these two regions), primary school enrollment ratios were 15.1 and 11.1 percent, respectively, and dropped to less than 2 percent for secondary school.[33]

Despite these low enrollment rates, the gradual impact of formal education on the social imaginations and migration behavior of people in Wayisso was so consequential that it is treated in much greater depth in Chapter 6. More relevant here is the way in which formal schooling became a key instrument of nation building. The Derg envisioned a united Ethiopia. As one government worker from that time shared, "The Derg tried to make one country. And to feel that all people are one.... We were creating awareness that Ethiopia is one, and everyone has to respect each other. And not to differentiate or neglect each other depending on their tribe."

Part of building this common identity was selecting a national language. Primary schools, as they spread throughout the country, taught in Amharic, the selected national language; local languages, including Afaan Oromo, were not allowed. This introduced a stronger disjuncture between "traditional" and "national" culture than under Haile Selassie. People needed to speak a different language to participate in the new political system and formal public sphere.

Further, through formal schooling, individuals could access new forms of salaried work within the government administration—as development agents, as *kebele* workers, as teachers. A few individuals from Wayisso and surrounding regions became part of this new political-economic structure, thus introducing a new form of work, paid employment, into the social imaginary. Salaries under the Derg were not high—just 347 Ethiopian birr per month for government workers and 180 birr for teachers, according to one government worker—but this was a distinctly different *kind* of work: salaried work. It also introduced ideas of meritocracy and social and economic mobility. As one elder put it, "In the period of Haile Selassie, if you want a position, it depends on your family.... But the Derg completely changed this." Whether the Derg *completely* changed who "had a position" is questionable, considering the relative continuity in local leadership positions. Nevertheless, the remark signals the perception that expanding access to education widened opportunities for social and economic mobility.

The Derg most directly influenced population mobility by introducing conscription to meet military and labor shortages. Constant warfare plagued the Derg regime: with Somalia in the southeast, separatist guerrilla movements in Eritrea and Tigray, and internal opposition groups within Ethiopia. To satisfy the growing demand for low-ranking army personnel, the Derg announced the National Military Service Proclamation of May 1983, which stated that all Ethiopians between the ages of eighteen and thirty were required to train for six months and then serve for two years in the military. They were expected to remain in reserve status until age fifty. Each peasant association forwarded a list of eligible recruits to regional military commissars, who would issue calls to duty. The peasant associations were responsible for ensuring that conscripts reported for duty, and there were several men from Wayisso who left to fight in the border skirmishes with Eritrea during this period.

Eventually, the government's ambitions for rural development faltered under the weight of political opposition. The Derg lacked the resources, capacities, and peace needed to realize a sustainable socialist transformation. A terrible famine in 1983 and 1984, failed resettlement and villagization projects (see Chapter 2), and the atrocities of the Red Terror bolstered support for regional and ethnically based liberation movements[34] that continually struggled to overthrow the Derg. Their unification into the EPRDF in 1989 and 1990 was a decisive turning point. This coalition bolstered their strength against the declining regime, which struggled with discontent among its own tired and overstretched military. The Derg tried to reinvent itself as a civilian government in the last years of its reign. In September 1987, Mengistu proclaimed Ethiopia a socialist republic, officially named the People's Democratic Republic of Ethiopia, and the Derg became the Ethiopian Worker's Party. But it was too little, too late. Lacking support from the Soviet Union, which faced its own impending dissolution, the regime fell to the EPRDF in Addis Ababa on May 28, 1991.

Developmental State

In the years following communism's defeat in Ethiopia and around the globe, the writers of Ethiopia's new constitution drafted a new charter for a democratic, ethnic federalism—a rejection of the united Ethiopia as envisioned by the Derg. The Federal Democratic Republic of Ethiopia, formally established in 1995, was divided into nine ethno-linguistically based regional states and chartered cities, including Tigray, Afar, Amhara, Oromia, Somali, Benishangul-Gumuz, the Southern Nations, Nationalities, and Peoples Region (SNNPR); Gambella; and Harari, and two administrative councils—Addis Ababa and Dire Dawa. The EPRDF won the first multiparty election in 1995, and its leader, Meles Zenawi, became prime minister, serving from 1995 to 2012. He was succeeded by Hailemariam

Desalegn (2012–2018) and by Abiy Ahmed in 2018, who replaced the EPRDF coalition with a new Prosperity Party in 2019.

Meles Zenawi envisioned Ethiopia as a "democratic developmental state," and he gained international attention for resisting the neoliberal Washington Consensus of his time, which advocated free-market principles and a reduction of the state.[35] The concept of the developmental state is most closely associated with the economic success stories of East Asian countries, particularly Japan, South Korea, Taiwan, and Singapore, which during the latter half of the twentieth century achieved rapid industrialization and economic growth through active state intervention and strategic economic planning. In the 1990s, the cornerstone of Zenawi's economic strategy was the ADLI policy, which aimed to use the agricultural sector as the primary engine of economic growth and development, with the ultimate goal of transforming the country into an industrialized economy. The government invested heavily in the use of improved agricultural technologies and inputs, such as high-yield seed varieties, fertilizers, and irrigation, through subsidies, extension services, and training programs. However, ADLI faced many challenges related to resource allocation, market access, and finding the right balance between agricultural and industrial development.

By the 2000s, it was clear agriculture would hold a diminishing place in the government's vision for economic growth. Following ADLI, Ethiopia launched two major multiyear development plans, known as the Growth and Transformation Plans (GTP I 2010–2015 and GTP II 2015–2020). Under Zenawi and then Desalegn, these plans aimed to sustain rapid and broad-based economic growth, focusing on transforming Ethiopia into a middle-income country, with a greater focus on industrialization and urbanization. The government still supported small-scale agriculture, of course; because the majority of the Ethiopian population are subsistence farmers, they have to. But as detailed in the government's GTPs, the government no longer believed a primary focus on agricultural production could stimulate industrialization and spark economic growth. Thus, developing infrastructure and manufacturing centers, attracting foreign investment, and creating conditions more conducive to private enterprise and the growth of the service sector became more important objectives. When Abiy Ahmed assumed power, he rejected the developmental state model of his predecessors. Lamenting the financial mismanagement of Ethiopia's state-owned enterprises, he accelerated a process of privatization, declaring, "My model is capitalism."[36]

The relatively rapid shifts in the development thinking of the state led to relatively rapid shifts in livelihood and migration strategies in Wayisso. As the government embraced more urban- and market-oriented development policies, livelihood and migration strategies in Wayisso also became more urban and market oriented. The remainder of this chapter describes two new trends—the division and multiplication of labor and the rise of entrepreneurship—and their relationship with rural-urban migration. The following chapter focuses on international migration.

***

The division of labor is intrinsic to modern economic development. As national economies grow, work becomes more specialized. As the sociologist Emile Durkheim originally theorized, the division of labor is an economic process that has come to be accepted as normal, natural, and essential to maintain social order in complex societies. Mirroring the biological sciences—where the greater the division of functions within an organism, the higher its level of development—so too for human society. But Durkheim also questioned whether something is lost in this increasing specificity, raising moral concerns about the purpose of human life and what is lost in harnessing one's energies to an increasingly specialized function or task.[37]

In Wayisso, Adami Tulu, and Ziway, there are signs of the increasing division of labor, like the women who cut roses for hours upon hours, day after day—the factory workers of Ethiopia's growing agro-industry. New shops are sprouting up across Ziway, with shopkeepers offering specialized goods and services that were unavailable to previous generations. Development theory tends to present this process as a relatively straightforward transfer of labor out of the primary sector (i.e., agriculture) and into manufacturing and services, a process facilitated by expanding education and the development of "human capital."

What is so striking about the economic activity of everyday people from Wayisso, however, is the degree to which people managed multiple kinds of income-generating activities across sectors and between the village and the town. For women and men from Wayisso, a remarkable *multiplication* of labor precedes its specialization. As I wrote in my fieldnotes at the time, "For the most part, economic development has not led to a narrowing of work, it has meant *more* work for people. They are no longer just farmers. They are farmers AND something else: a businessman, a government worker, a student."

Under the Derg and in the 1990s and early 2000s, securing a government position had been considered the most reliable and prestigious form of professional work.[38] However, government salaries have not kept up with the rising costs of living, and today, government workers—teachers, administration personnel—struggle to make ends meet. Now it is *business* or private enterprise that offers the promise of significant social and economic mobility. As one college graduate explained to me, "For the future, we need to change our life to business. My family needs to sell their cattle and build a house to rent in the city. They need to change the cattle system they have now to a more productive system."

Income-generating opportunities beyond farming are few in the village. Women continue to sell small goods, such as butter, at the local market in Adami Tulu or buy a few goods, like sugarcane, to bring back to the village and sell there. One enterprising woman thought to prepare food to sell to Verde Beef workers, but this ended when Verde Beef began serving a lunchtime meal to avoid long midday absences. The most successful village-based business is led by a young man named Addisu, who rents a large truck and buys Wayisso farmers' maize directly from them. Previously, farmers would bring their maize to the market—which entails an additional expense if one does not own a cart and donkeys—where they would sell one quintal (one hundred kilograms) for 400 birr (18.70 USD). Addisu buys the maize for the same price from the farmers, stores it in a warehouse built in Wayisso, and sells it later in the year for a higher price. This business requires the capital to rent a truck and scale and enough cash readily available to pay farmers. Addisu accessed this capital with the help of his family and the savings of his wife, who returned from Dubai a year prior. Together, they live in Wayisso, where there is no rent to pay, to save money before they move to Ziway.

Most people in Wayisso with business ambitions now look toward urban markets, and they see greater opportunity in Ziway than Adami Tulu or Bulbulla. Ziway is the local boomtown, multiplying rapidly in population and entrepreneurship. The population grew from 20,056 at the time of the 1994 census to 43,660 by the 2007 census and was likely well over 60,000 in 2018. Ziway's main roads are lined with an ever-new array of shops: restaurants and coffee houses; stationery and corner shops; mobile phone stores and pool houses; a lawyer's office and pharmacies; clothing stores and tailors; furniture shops and film houses (most often showing football matches); butcher stands; hotels; and throngs of *bajaj* taxis—three-wheeled auto-rickshaws imported from India are the primary means of transport around Ziway. Bajaj drivers are exclusively male, often young. A common aspiration of young men from rural areas who fail to pass the national examination after tenth grade is to become a *bajaj* driver in the city. In fact, several young men from Wayisso drive *bajajs* or their larger counterpart, *damas*—minibuses that transport people and goods short distances between Ziway and Adami Tulu.

Bosha drives a *damas* between Adami Tulu and Ziway every day. When I first met Bosha in 2016, he was lounging in a mostly empty storefront along Ziway's main road. The space contained a few stacks of large, plastic-wrapped cases of bottled water. His family applied for the space as part of a government-sponsored scheme to stimulate micro-enterprise. They benefited from low, government-subsidized rent and were allowed to use the space along the main road for five years, after which, if they are successful, the government expects they will use their profits to relocate their business elsewhere. Bosha's task was to man the storefront.

Born in Wayisso, Bosha left to attend school in Adami Tulu and then Ziway. He made it to tenth grade but failed the national exam. In 2016, he was twenty-two and considering his future options. As an adolescent, he had planned to become a teacher, but this once prestigious form of work has lost its allure and social standing in recent years. Often poorly paid, government teachers work at schools wherever they are assigned, which could be a distant rural area. Bosha decided he would rather stay in Ziway. When I met Bosha two years later, he was working as a driver. With the profit his family earned from a number of small-scale business endeavors and migrant remittances, they purchased a minibus to transport people the seven kilometers between Adami Tulu and Ziway. Bosha now earns more as a driver than he ever could have as a teacher—or at least that's what he told me.

Those who succeed in getting a foothold in town often straddle rural and urban lives. Most men who leave Wayisso maintain their landholdings in the village, which provides additional revenue to supplement the earnings of their income-generating activities elsewhere. Usha, for example, is in his late twenties, newly married, and trying to build a new life in Ziway. A descendent of Bedane Tuffaa (Lineage 1), Usha farms his six plots in Wayisso, studies for an accounting degree at Oromia Regional University (previously

Public Service College Oromia), and recently began another business on the side: selling eggs from a hen farm he keeps in Wayisso.

Usha was lucky to find a room in a small housing compound in Ziway for 350 birr per month. Such compounds are walled with a single entrance gate, which opens onto a central courtyard surrounded by several or up to fifteen rooms. Each room is occupied by an individual or household. Bathrooms are shared, while each family usually has a small stove for cooking and coffee roasting within or just outside their room. Usually such a room would be 500 to 600 birr. Food for Usha and his wife and baby costs roughly 500 birr per month. Rent and food alone, for a year, requires 10,200 birr (~475 USD); the costs of clothing, transportation, house supplies, and his school fees average 940 birr per semester.

Covering the costs of urban life from farming alone is difficult, if not impossible. Usha does not have very fertile land, and in 2016, after the drought, his plots failed to produce even one quintal (or one hundred kilograms) for the market. In 2017, fortunately, the rain was more plentiful. When rain is abundant, one of his plots produces, on average, about four quintals of maize, or around twelve to fourteen quintals per hectare. The price received per quintal varies depending on when you sell it. For those who sell immediately, they get around 400 birr per quintal. For those who wait, the price increases, up to 800 birr in July or August. It even hit 1,000 birr per quintal one August. For those who can afford to wait for the supply to decrease, the profit is higher. Usha is not always able to wait, but he tries.

In 2018, the rain looked promising but stopped suddenly. His land at that time was only producing one or two quintals per plot. I asked him how he would manage the higher costs of living in Ziway. He told me about his new side business raising chickens in Wayisso to sell their eggs in Ziway. Using money sent by his cousin Ademtuu in London, Usha invested 12,000 birr in the project. He started with forty-two birds in March. Two died, leaving him with thirty-eight hens and two roosters. They started laying eggs in June, and by August, they were producing twenty-five to thirty eggs per day. To sustain these birds requires a lot. They eat fifty kilograms of feed per week, which costs 620 birr per week. Usha pays for transport twice a week to pick up the eggs and deliver them to his customers in Ziway—mostly corner shop owners. He generates, after these costs, about 400 birr per month. He wants to buy his own motorbike to reduce the costs of transportation to and from Wayisso and to enable him to carry more with him. Using the minibus taxis, he cannot bring a week's worth of eggs at once. Once this business is strong and he has made back his initial investment, he wants to expand into sheep. Usha shared that he would ideally like to live in Wayisso to tend to the business. It's just not really feasible for him to do, because there is no water or electricity there. He doesn't want to raise his family under those conditions.

Rabira, a descendent of Dakabo Bulo (Lineage 2), is another example of someone who lives in Ziway but maintains his land in Wayisso. After graduating with a bachelor's degree in law from a private institution called Rift Valley University, he worked for a nonprofit organization coordinating an education program. He lives with his wife and two young children in a two-room house on the outskirts of Ziway. They keep a goat and two chickens, and his wife grows a few vegetables in the patch of land in front of their house. During sowing season, he struggles to balance his work requirements in town and the needs of his land back in Wayisso.

One day I was visiting Rabira's family in Wayisso. His mother, Momina, prepared coffee, and I was in a conversation with his brother, Bilisuma, about Verde Beef. Bilisuma's eight children circled around us quietly. Rabira stood out from the others with his clean white button-down shirt, jeans, and white-trimmed shoes. After we finished our three cups of coffee, we turned to the fields. Since it was plowing season, Rabira offered to show me how to use a plow. He took the plow from one of the hired farm laborers working on Bilisuma's plots. Behind the cattle in his fancy white shirt, Rabira looked comical. His shoes filled with the dusty soil, and whatever goofiness he naturally exuded was magnified ten times over behind the plow. His older brother laughed and pushed him away; he would show me how it was really done. Barefoot and sure-footed, Bilisuma guided the plow through the soil in a straight line, the freshly opened earth drawing little birds to see what critters had been unearthed.

After the demonstration, Bilisuma turned to his brother and reminded him that he needed to tend to his own fields. Their conversation became quiet and serious. Bilisuma exhorted Rabira that the window for plowing was narrowing. Rabira rubbed his head and kicked the dust. He decided to stay that night in Wayisso to assemble a group of people to help plow his land the next morning.

The next day, I met Rabira in his fields. Despite his overnight efforts, he was not able to find enough manpower. Bilisuma was working at Verde Beef, and Bilisuma's hired farm workers were working other plots. Bilisuma offered his own children to help. "How much do you pay them?" I asked. "For the children?" he responded, confused. I quickly realized it was a stupid

Figure 4.3 A child driving oxen on his uncle's land

question. There were four oxen. Two were Rabira's—he rented one for 1,600 birr for the season—and two were his neighbor's. Bilisuma's oldest boy drove one pair and the smaller two switched off driving the other pair (Figure 4.3). Rabira left around noon for a work meeting in town, and when he returned later in the day, he brought a large plate of food for the children.

Rabira's example is a telling one. He would not be able to maintain farming in Wayisso as an additional revenue stream for himself and his family if he did not have family members in Wayisso to support him. Likewise, when Bilisuma's family faces times of need, particularly when the next harvest is still several months away, Rabira—because of his steadier income in the city—is able to help.

When migration is only analyzed as a rural-to-urban change in residence, it misses the degree to which rural places remain a part of a migrant's field of activity. Usha's example showed how sustaining a life in town can depend on income-generating pursuits in Wayisso. Rabira's example showed how this dynamic applies across households. Those who remain in Wayisso help tend to the land of urbanites, while those living in town often help their family members in Wayisso with the steadier incomes they earn. They support the education of nieces and nephews through schooling, for example, or help in times of need or celebration (e.g., a wedding or funeral).

Money is thus shared across households within a family group. The migration of some family members to urban areas diversifies the income available to those who stay behind, particularly when major expenses arise or economic shocks occur. This is one of the basic insights of new economics labor migration theory, first espoused by economists Oded Stark and David Bloom in the 1980s. This theory was novel for decentering the rational, individual actor and taking a wider, more collective lens to understand migration decision-making, showing that decisions are often made at the household level to diversify incomes and reduce risk, not simply maximize income. In Wayisso, however, this collective lens could be expanded further; even a household frame is limited. Risk diversification does not happen just within a household. Instead, rural-urban ties and income support are spread across households within a common family group, with those who remained in the village playing a key reciprocal role in supporting the migration projects of others who, in turn, would support their kin in the village.

And yet, there are many young people in Wayisso who fail to get a foothold in town—who aspire for urban lives but lack the capability to make a sustainable move. Without the prospect of decent employment or a successful business, how will they manage the higher costs of living in town? Borama, for example (from Lineage 3), is an ambitious teenager who aspires to be a doctor, yet he is uncertain whether his family will have the income to support the extensive education this would require. Already in his late teens, he was only in sixth grade in Wayisso. Some of his cousins had been able to achieve higher years of secondary schooling in Adami Tulu but ultimately had to move back to Wayisso because their families could not afford the costs of rent and food in town.

Lack of affordable urban housing is a pressing constraint on rural-urban migration from Wayisso. Land remains nationalized, but in practice, it is often given and inherited, sold and rented as if it is privately held. Technically, it is impossible to sell land. One can only sell whatever construction lies on top of the land. In the 1990s, land was far less expensive. In the late 1990s, for example, one man from Wayisso bought a plot of land in Adami Tulu for 875 birr, on which he built two houses. The houses were much more expensive to build. In fact, the newest one, with three rooms, a metal roof, and metal windows, cost over 100,000 birr (~4,673 USD)—half of which was funded by the remittances from one of his daughters, Jaa, who worked in Beirut.

When Jaa returned from Lebanon, she also intended to buy her own land to build a house. With her savings, she informally purchased land on the outskirts of Adami Tulu from a farmer, who divided one of his plots (fifty by fifty meters) into six sections. Jaa bought two sections for 22,000 birr, and four other individuals bought the other four sections. This was far more than the 875 birr her father paid for a much larger plot fifteen years prior. Unfortunately, when Sher Ethiopia opened its second site in Adami Tulu, Jaa lost this land. The farmer received 37,000 birr in compensation for the one plot, which was still registered to his name, of which Jaa only received 10,500 birr. "[The government] thought it was just a field, so it decreased the price," Jaa explained. "But when I bought the land, my plan was to build a house on it."

As Adami Tulu and Ziway expand, the government assumes greater control over acquiring and leasing urban land. In 2012 in Adami Tulu, for example, the government took a large area of land from what were then rural farmers, offered them compensation, parceled the land into twenty-square-meter plots, and opened the land to auction. Prospective renters estimated a price they could afford and submitted their bid to the municipality. The municipality then organized the offers from highest to lowest, offering the land to those with the highest bids downward.

Most land in Adami Tulu, however, is not available for rent or housing development. It is under a ninety-nine-year lease with Sher Ethiopia, the Ethiopian subsidiary of the Dutch-owned company Afriflora Sher. One reason the land prices are now so high in Adami Tulu and Ziway is because of the influx of low-skilled laborers working in the Sher greenhouses who need housing in Adami Tulu and Ziway. The impact of large foreign companies on local labor markets and the dynamics of in-migration are discussed further in Chapter 7.

***

Once a peripheral region of the Ethiopian Empire, Wayisso village was gradually incorporated into a modern nation-state, introducing new pressures on local livelihoods and ways of life. Power and social organization traditionally structured by the Gadaa system gave way to the administrative logic of a modern state in its new and various forms. The imperial regime introduced taxes, new political positions, and land allocation practices that led more powerful families to make personal claims on what mostly remained, in practice, communal grazing lands. Although farming was not the primary occupation of this area, a few began experimenting with supplementary cultivation. After the communist revolution, the Derg's rural development agenda accelerated a process of settling down in Wayisso. Some of the most influential policies were the nationalization of land, the creation of peasant

Table 4.1 Summary of mobility types to/from Wayisso by regime period

1880s–1960s Imperial regime	1970s–1980s Communist regime	1990s–2010s Developmental state
Types of internal mobility		
Seminomadic pastoral mobility Marriage migration	Seminomadic pastoral movement Marriage migration Migration for education Migration for government work Military or labor conscription	Marriage migration Migration for education Migration for government work Seasonal rural-urban mobility Migration for work in industry or service sector
Types of international mobility		
	Hajj	Hajj Labor migration to Middle East Migration to Europe for education and work
Types of in-migration		
		Seasonal farm workers

associations that registered people to land, and the provision of basic goods and services that required registration within a peasant association. These policies encouraged a transition into settled, farming lifestyles in the 1970s and 1980s and fundamentally reshaped the political-economic order upon which these new livelihoods were built.

The rise of rural out-migration followed this period of settlement (Table 4.1). The second mobility shift, notably a rural-urban shift in migration patterns, began under the EPRDF, from the 1990s onward. The EPRDF accelerated an urban transition through its pursuit of rapid economic growth; through its embrace of privatization, foreign capital, and market forces; and by giving up on agriculture as the cornerstone of economic development. At the same time, Wayisso became increasingly connected to urban areas through infrastructure development that reduced the time required to travel to Adami Tulu or Ziway and through the spread of formal education. These trends accelerated through the 2010s, as did a rise in international labor migration, which is discussed in the following chapter.

Although these political and migration transitions were rapid, the respective livelihood patterns each regime encouraged blur into each other. Pastoral tendencies persisted for a long time after the transition to farming; young and old still have a high regard for cattle, which remain a sign of wealth and status. Similarly, the transition out of farming and to the city does not mean people abandon agriculture entirely. Rather, individuals and families balance rural and urban lives—seeking out new forms of income generation in town while maintaining their farmlands in the village. This is one of the key insights of new economics labor migration theory, which explains that rural households often use migration to diversify their incomes and protect against risks. But rather than using rural-urban migration as a strategy to sustain and ensure their center of gravity in rural areas, households in Wayisso seek to shift their center of gravity to urban areas. And once there, they use their rural land to supplement and sustain the higher costs of an urban life.

What is distinct about the rural-urban transition is the unequal access to it. Under the Derg, "settlement" was possible for all because land was allocated to every household. No one remained "trapped" in pastoral livelihoods. Today, however, migration is only possible for those households with enough money to invest in a migration project, whether that be sending their children to school in town, leasing land, or setting up a business. Thus, households who can invest in rural-urban migration are those with access to more discretionary income. As the following chapters will show in greater detail, many young people remain involuntarily immobile in Wayisso—aspiring to move to town but lacking the capability to leave. Long-standing inequalities in access to land, first established under Haile Selassie, persisted under the Derg and influenced which families could invest in migration under the EPRDF. Inequalities are not new to this society, but what is new is the way that inequalities shape how people can and cannot move.

5
The Market

When I first met Zeynaba, she was sixteen, seven months pregnant, and unhappy with her life in Wayisso. "This is not what my husband promised me," she said in a hushed tone as she hung laundry to dry. Zeynaba married Gicho at fourteen. She knew he was not rich, but she was in love. "I don't have anything in my hand to give you," Gicho told Zeynaba as he courted her, "but I have true love for you. I have plots, I have a plow, and we will work hard to change our lives." As Zeynaba told me this, she looked back and gestured toward her home, saying, "What he said is far from the truth." Zeynaba and Gicho shared a home with Gicho's two brothers and their wives and children. Unlike other well-built and well-kept huts in Wayisso, theirs had a drooping thatched roof and holes in the mud-and-stick walls. Gicho had two plots of land and no education, and Zeynaba dropped out of school in the seventh grade. Zeynaba still believed hard work could change their lives, but she no longer believed Gicho or his plow could bring the kind of change she desired. She had a plan: after her child was born, and after the coming harvest, she would migrate to the Middle East. There were jobs for domestic workers there, she told me, and they earned far more than any job she or Gicho could ever get in Ethiopia. She knew the work would be hard and thankless—a few of her relatives and friends were abroad and they told her about the difficulties—but how else could she change anything? "If I stay here, I'm just going to get pregnant again. I don't want to have more children. Just let me change my life first."

When I met Zeynaba again in late 2018, she was sitting in front of a new cinderblock house with three rooms and a corrugated iron roof. Zeynaba realized her plan. She had migrated to Beirut. A friend gave her the phone number of a broker, who connected her with an agency that arranged everything for her. She left her infant daughter with the child's grandmother, took a bus to Addis Ababa, boarded a flight to Beirut, and met her new employers at the airport. The Lebanese family had three teenagers and one toddler, and her job was to manage the household: cooking, cleaning, laundry. She earned the standard rate, 150 USD per month. After she

Moved by Modernity. Kerilyn Schewel, Oxford University Press. © Oxford University Press (2025).
DOI: 10.1093/9780197680759.003.0006

sent the first two months' wages to her agency, she transferred the rest to her family, who began constructing this house. Her employers were kind, she said, but she worked hard—seven days a week. After one year and seven months, she returned home. Subtracting the costs of leaving and agency fees, she had earned 2,400 USD. Zeynaba promised the family in Beirut she would return, but she had no intention to do so now. She wanted to migrate again, but this time to Dubai, where she heard they pay higher wages.

I asked Zeynaba, who was then pregnant with her second child, why she wanted to leave again, having already accomplished so much. She wanted to leave, she said, because this was not enough. Her ultimate goal was to build a house in Ziway and start a business—perhaps a taxi company or a corner shop. She wanted her children to have a future in town.

Labor migration from Ethiopia to the Middle East is a relatively new and gendered migration corridor, growing in number and consequence since the late 1990s. Although data from Ethiopia's Ministry of Labor and Social Affairs is incomplete, the official number of women migrating to the Middle East has grown exponentially in recent decades, from just 1,202 in 1999 to 187,939 in 2012 and a much higher but unknown number today.[1] Irregular, or undocumented, migration is estimated to be at least double formal figures.[2]

The dominant narrative about this migration corridor in international media, academic, and policy publications is overwhelmingly negative—one of "young impressionable women"[3] facing desperate economic circumstances, misled by human traffickers into abusive working conditions, only to return to Ethiopia with broken spirits, perhaps broken bodies, and little to show for it.[4] Unlike the utility-maximizing agents assumed in most migration theories, Ethiopian women are more often portrayed as trafficked, deceived, or, as one report put it, "blinded by hope."[5]

After reading this literature, I expected to hear horrific first-hand accounts of deception, abuse, and disappointment in my interviews. Instead, I met thoughtful young women surprisingly aware of the risks they were assuming in an active pursuit of capital. I met many return migrants who had been able to significantly improve their life circumstances with the money they earned abroad. Across a variety of contexts, women mentioned migration to the Middle East as a way not only to improve their lives materially but also to gain "freedom," to "do something with my life," and to "change my life and the life of my family." To change their lives, they explained, they need *money*, and for a particular subset of young women, migration to the Middle East for domestic work is the only real opportunity they have to earn it.

To understand why more Ethiopians are migrating for work in other countries, a more fundamental question needs to be addressed: why is the profit motive such a powerful force in migration decision-making today? Or to put it another way, why are people migrating for money? These questions may seem strange to a reader living in a society where monetized and market economies have been the norm for centuries. But this isn't so in many parts of Ethiopia. Consider the migration decision-making—if we can call it that—of earlier generations of pastoralists. Their movements were directed by where they could best graze their cattle or rest for a season, by the need to trade and barter, by the rhythms of their community's political and social life, by concerns about the weather, and by conflict or peace with neighboring ethnic groups. Although markets existed, the modern "market economy" did not. The profit motive did not make sense within that social system.

This chapter examines the societal impact of market expansion to illuminate why the profit motive has become such a powerful force in migration decision-making today. Although some economics textbooks might have us believe the profit motive is somehow inherent within human nature, the desire for financial gain as an orienting incentive of livelihood strategies and migration decision-making in Wayisso is a distinctly "modern" development.

The first section examines the transformation of two social practices, conflict mediation and marriage. Ethnographic accounts reveal the increasingly central role money plays within these practices and the conspicuous inequalities this introduces within a community. These examples illustrate why, more and more, managing everyday needs, material improvement, and social and spatial mobility require money. And if the purpose of work becomes to accumulate money, there are better ways than livestock rearing or smallholder farming to get it. The second half of the chapter looks more closely at the aspirations, opportunities, and constraints that shape the migration decision-making of women who leave for the Middle East. It reveals why, because of the social and economic freedoms that money can now buy a woman in "modern" society, migration to earn a higher income abroad begins to make more sense for more women.

From Cattle to Capital

In the broadest sociological sense, "markets" refer to the social structures through which people engage in material exchange. From this perspective, markets have existed for centuries in this region of Oromia. In the early twentieth century, the main market in the region was in Boramo, a rural area north of Wayisso. People gathered there for material and social exchange, bartering goods like meat, butter, grains, and cloth, while Gadaa fathers met for negotiations. As government taxes were introduced in the mid-twentieth century, cash markets began to emerge, including cattle markets in towns along the main road, such as Meki to the north and Jido to the south, and closer by in Adami Tulu. By the 1960s, Boramo's market had moved to Adami Tulu, and many locals still refer to Adami Tulu's market day as "Boramo day."

Today, Adami Tulu's market is hardly confined to a weekly event. The market is everywhere: in the proliferation of restaurants, hotels, corner shops, film houses, house rentals, and everyday material exchanges taking place across town. There remains a "market day" on Wednesday, which draws buyers and sellers from longer distances. Yet, that weekly market is one part of a more diffuse system of monetized exchanges that spread across Adami Tulu. The town itself became the market. When people aspire to move to the town and to live and work in town, much of these aspirations are animated by the desire to participate in, and benefit materially from, this ever-expanding market.

The economic historian Karl Polanyi describes modern society as market society. In his now classic book *The Great Transformation*, Polanyi argues that historically, markets and economic relations were always subordinate to politics, religion, culture, or other social dynamics. "Never before our own time," he writes in 1944, "were markets more than accessories of economic life. As a rule, the economic system was absorbed in the social system."[6] When the economy is "embedded" within society, principles like reciprocity and redistribution can hold more sway over economic life. What is distinctive about the modern transformation, Polanyi argues, is the attempt to subordinate social relations to the demands and logic of market competition—to "disembed" the economy from society. Indeed, as governments strive to grow their economies, this often requires disembedding economic relations from traditional social systems. Politics, religion, culture, and values still matter, but as market-based strategies for economic development advance, market forces exert a growing influence on the social life of a community.

One of the most powerful ways market expansion affects social life is through a process of commodification—the transformation of goods and services into objects of monetary exchange.[7] Things, interactions, or even ideas that were previously governed by social norms and relations become monetized and subject to the logic of the market.[8] To illustrate what commodification looks like practically in this region of Ethiopia, I explore how two social practices—conflict mediation and marriage—have transformed over the last several decades. I chose these two examples because they were some of the most striking from my fieldwork and are fundamentally *social* phenomena, where we would expect economic concerns to be subordinate to shared norms, values, and cultural concerns. The following ethnographic accounts detail what the commodification of these social practices entails, as well as what anthropologists refer to as the "creolization" of Oromo and Western customs.[9] A common thread across both examples is the increasingly central place of money within these social practices and the conspicuous inequalities this introduces. Although economic inequalities have long existed, wealth used to be measured in cattle, and inequalities could stretch only as far as the size of one's herds. Further, the goods and services one could buy or barter with that wealth were limited. Today, wealth is measured in money and displayed through the consumption of an ever-growing number of goods and services. Young generations' ideas about the good life now include high expectations for the quality of their material life—far higher than anything their parents' or grandparents' generation ever experienced or expected.

***

Conflict resolution in the ancient Oromo kingdom took place through the *sirna gadaa*, or Gadaa system. As the last chapter detailed, this unique governance structure oversaw all aspects of social life: the political, economic, and cultural affairs of society, including the traditional Oromo religion (*Waaqeffannaa*), marriage law (*rakoo*), and the adoption of conquered peoples into the community (*mogassa*). Conflict resolution, or *araara*, was the practice through which Gadaa elders would negotiate between conflicting parties to create peace. *Araara* literally translates as "reconciliation," which was the goal of any negotiation.

Over the centuries, as Oromo peoples expanded across Ethiopia, internal differentiation within their kingdom increased, and the cohesive functioning of the Gadaa system diminished.[10] Then, as the Ethiopian Empire began its series of campaigns to colonize the Oromo nation in the nineteenth century, it introduced competing political systems and institutions to conquered areas. In some regions, the new state apparatus undermined the functioning of the Gadaa system, whereas in other more peripheral regions of Ethiopia, where the imperial regime was not yet strongly established, the Gadaa system remained relatively robust.

In this region of Ethiopia, the Gadaa system continued to operate well into the mid-twentieth century. This changed when the Derg came into power and the new regime made a more vigorous attempt to replace all traditional and ethnically based institutions with a common political structure built upon *kebeles*, or peasant associations. Each *kebele* had its own judicial committee, which could impose fines or even imprisonment on a guilty party. This led to a major shift in how the community managed conflict. Even in grievous events like murder, the Gadaa system would have mediated between families to create peace so that they could live together. Under Haile Selassie, and then more forcefully under the Derg, people started to go to prison.

When the Ethiopian People's Revolutionary Democratic Front took over, the new constitution established a federation of ethnic states, and in the Oromia state, the government incorporated the Gadaa system as an informal legal pathway within a framework of legal pluralism. By that time, however, the Gadaa system had been so disrupted that it no longer functioned as it once did. What remains in this region of Oromia is the Gadaa grade—five elected *Abbaa Gadaa*, or Gadaa fathers, whose primary purpose is to oversee conflict mediation in their respective areas. The Gadaa fathers now serve within the administrative boundaries set by the state: at the level of the district (*woreda*), at the level of the region, or for all of Oromia.

Although the Gadaa system wields less power today than it once did, it remains a distinctive and active pathway within the country's legal system, and its handling of conflict resolution can vary widely from the formal courts. For example, in the mid-1990s, the new government decided to reduce its holdings of the land adjacent to Wayisso—what was previously called Habernoosa Ranch—and invited proposals for collective microenterprise projects. Several men from Wayisso and its neighboring *kebeles* came together, submitted a proposal, and received the land. In reality, there was no collective endeavor. They simply divided the land among themselves. Two years later, a dispute arose among some of these individuals over the land division. When Rabuma, a young man living in Wayisso, heard about this dispute, he went at midnight to sow seeds and thereby claim four of the plots as his own. This act outraged the man who claimed this land through the micro-enterprise scheme, and he formally accused Rabuma in court. Rabuma convinced the accuser to negotiate through the Gadaa fathers, and, perhaps to avoid complications from the fact that the land was not being used as a collective micro-enterprise, the man agreed. The Gadaa fathers arrived for negotiations, and after long consultations with both parties, they eventually decided that the land should go to Rabuma. The Gadaa fathers reasoned that the accuser already had a lot of land, while Rabuma did not have any—nor did his father have much to give him. It was right, they concluded, that Rabuma should have these four plots. This kind of justification—declaring what is right given the totality of the social circumstances, not simply the practical details of the incident—is foreign to formal courts.

Normally, the parties involved in the conflict mediation process give something to the Gadaa fathers as a sign of gratitude. As one young man explained, "There is a big benefit to being a Gadaa father. For example, if I kill someone from your family, I have to give money and cattle to the Gadaa fathers; otherwise they will not create peace for me." The position is therefore coveted and pursued by the informal campaigns of individuals and families. As one elder explained, before an election, family or friends will talk highly about a particular person. "They may say, 'Oh, the next Gadaa father should be Hassan. Hassan is very bright. He can speak well and convince others.' They sing about that person." The individual will also try to distinguish himself in community meanings. "In a meeting, he will talk a lot so that someone will think, 'Oh! This person should be a Gadaa father!' They want to be selected, because they are going to get cattle and money."

In theory, the Gadaa system should be available to all Oromo as an alternative to formal court proceedings. However, eliciting the assistance of the Gadaa fathers can be costly, as informal negotiations often require a significant degree of material exchange, both to the Gadaa fathers and between the negotiating parties. Although material exchanges have always been part of Gadaa negotiations, money now occupies a larger place within the conflict mediation process. To illustrate what this looks like in practice, Box 5.1 details the reconciliation process between one man from Adama, who accidentally killed a young father in a car accident on the outskirts of Ziway, and the family of the deceased. Instead of summarizing these events, I have chosen to include selections from my fieldnotes to preserve the immediacy and detail of my observations and the evolution of my reflections at that time.

Box 5.1 The Gadaa system in practice: Fieldnotes (edited for clarity), June 9–19, 2016

June 9, 2016
Before going to Adami Tulu, we ran into Galeto, who has been busy negotiating with a family who lost a young father. A man from Adama named Bahir was driving through Ziway and popped his tire just outside the city, causing him to swerve and hit another man, killing him. It was a terrible accident. The deceased had one wife and two little girls. Galeto was called as part of the Gadaa process to help with the negotiation. Negotiations with the family include, at least, some kind of payment to the family (some 22,000 birr) and covering the expenses of the funeral (1,460 birr). If the family accepts the Gadaa process, the driver, Bahir, will reconcile according to the Gadaa fathers' negotiations. If the family does not, they can present a witness at the court proceedings in Adama, and Bahir will be prosecuted through the formal court system, which means he will most likely go to prison. If the police and court system get involved, it complicates things. We will see. On Saturday there is a meeting planned with the family of the deceased, as a way of showing solidarity and support, and I was told I can join.

June 10, 2016
We went to see Bahir at the local jail in Ziway this morning. It's quite an unimpressive scene, located on the north side of the city, off one of the side streets. The jail is a two-room building with open doors and an outside area fenced with a rather pathetic hodgepodge of barbed wire, wood, and metal. Anyone can visit and talk through the fence. It was informal and casual. Two policemen looked on lazily from the porch of their building.

Bahir was dressed well, with a collared shirt buttoned up to the top, a jacket, and a baseball cap. He was clean. He was obviously embarrassed to be there. He shrugged off my condolences and asked me about my stay,

Continued

Continued

about my research. It's been a few days that he has been in jail now. On Monday he goes to the court in Adama, and if all goes well, he can be released on bail. The Gadaa elders, including Galeto, went to the victim's family to negotiate and bring about some kind of reconciliation. But the formal courts are also part of the process now—presumably because this was not simply a land dispute or family conflict, but someone actually died.

Traffic accidents are, after malaria, the number one cause of death in Ethiopia, according to my physician friend Mitikine. He said that in Addis, around one to two people die every day from a traffic accident. And so the government has become very strict in punishment, hoping to dissuade bad driving. The normal sentence for someone in Bahir's situation is fifteen years. If you don't pay a bribe, they don't let you go, and the system does what it does: imprisonment for a very long time. Whenever you go to a government office, Mitikine said, "they expect a payment for everything." You can always justify paying a bribe, another man explained, by reminding yourself that the government doesn't pay the police enough. If they did, corruption wouldn't be necessary to them as a source of income.

Tomorrow we are going to the home of the deceased for some sort of gathering. It's part of the reconciliation process. Mootiti and Shula told me that I have to cry when I am there. That "it is our culture. If you don't cry, it's really bad. Cry even if you don't care, even if you don't feel anything. You have to fake it!" They were laughing as they were sharing this with me, because I looked somewhat incredulous. I'm actually wondering what I'm going to do tomorrow. I can't summon tears on command!

June 11, 2016

I went to a gathering for the victim of the car accident. It wasn't a funeral, because he had already been buried, but it was part of the grieving and gadaa negotiation process. This morning around fifty people gathered as part of Bahir's "group," and they hired a bus to drive us to the village where the family of the deceased lived. Someone went around with a list and wrote everyone's name down; people would give donations of 20 to 30 birr each for the family of the deceased. We waited for an hour and a half or so for everyone and the bus to arrive.

Two Gadaa fathers arrived. Old men with long beards, Muslim caps, and a white shawl over their shoulders. One had a stick. Before the Gadaa fathers would do this as a service, my friend Kidane explained, but now it is a job. Bahir paid them to negotiate with this family, and our visit today was a key part of that negotiation process. It was a way for people to show up, to show their grief, and help Bahir in his negotiation. The court date in Adama is on Monday. As long as no witnesses are produced by this family or the police in court, all should go easily and Bahir should be out on bail.

The drive was only fifteen minutes, all of us packed into a bus. When we arrived, a few trucks were already there. We got out and waited. The women all wore black shawls over their heads, a sign of mourning. Those who didn't have a black shawl wore a colored one. One woman had a white one, which I was relieved to see, because I only had a white one. The elders went first. We waited there for about ten minutes, until there was a signal to come. And then we started walking towards their home, all fifty of us together. As the home came into sight, the crying began. It was soft at first but grew quickly into wailing. It grew louder as we approached their home. A man next to me was shedding real tears and shouting to the skies with raised fists.

Maybe thirty people were already sitting under a large tree in front of the family compound. There were two square houses with metal roofs. In front of the house on the left, there were about fifteen women. Two were holding a young woman who was intermittently trying to run towards us and collapsing on the ground, weeping and shouting. She must have been his wife. To the right of the women were about twenty men: one older man crying desperately, his father I assume, and other young men who must have been his age, then children. Most just walking in circles and crying.

We came to the large tree and everyone from our party sat on the benches arranged in a circle under its shade. The crying continued, and I started to cry myself. I couldn't help but be moved by the raw display of emotion. But as soon as I started to cry, we stood up and started walking back to the bus. What? I wondered. That was it? We sat there for a maximum of two minutes. It was so short! We just walked up crying, sat down, and then left. The Gadaa fathers stayed afterwards, but all of

Continued

Continued

Bahir's party left. When I asked why later, I heard two explanations. One, the most convincing, is that we are "the enemy." They are not happy with us. We just need to show our support, our grief, and get out of there. The other explanation was that the young man died quickly in a car crash, so the ritual was quick. If it had taken him a month to die, we would have stayed longer.

I kept thinking about the widow. Women almost always come from outside when they marry. Common practice here is for widows to marry their husband's brother, so that he can take care of her, but even more importantly, so that he can take care of his brother's children. If a widow were to marry again, outside the family or ethnic group, the children may not be seen as part of that new family. If the brother marries her, however, the children are kept in the family.

June 19, 2016

Last night was the final stage of Bahir's reconciliation with the family of the deceased. The family did not send any witnesses to the court proceedings in Adama and Bahir was released on bail last Monday. At least one hundred people of the deceased's family came, mostly men, but around thirty women. Then there were around fifty people who came to support Bahir, networks of friends who had been asked to come. This meeting was held at the Sher Clubhouse, one of the nicest meeting halls in town. It began with the two groups waiting outside, standing apart. Many were watching the Sher owner's colts and camels running around a fenced area next to Clubhouse. Soon after Bahir arrived, we began.

One woman from each "side" came together and started sprinkling a fermented honey drink on the ground as they walked into the clubhouse. Others followed. It was symbolic of overcoming a very bitter obstacle. Now they were sprinkling a sweet drink upon the ground, and new life would rise.

The deceased's family went first. Then Bahir with his head covered in a white shawl. Then us. The purpose of this meeting was to conclude the negotiation process, to promise that all is reconciled, that Bahir is now a part of their family and they are a part of his, that there is no going back. Four Gadaa fathers presided over the ceremony. The four fathers were elderly men, dressed in old suits with thick, white shawls wrapped across their front and shoulders. Each of the Gadaa fathers carried a leather whip, a sign of their station as they proceeded over the ceremony.

The chairs were lined up in rows facing each other, and in the middle, on mats on the ground, sat Bahir and some of the women and children from the deceased's family. Otherwise the Gadaa fathers and other men sat on the first row on one side, and the women on the other. Although it was a ceremony to signal conclusion, one woman couldn't stop weeping. The first part was a lot of talking—now we are family; God ordains these things—and Bahir kept quiet. After some time, maybe thirty minutes, Bahir gave three blankets to the family: one for the father, one for a brother, and one for another man I couldn't identify. Then there was an exchange of some small cash gifts, which seemed to be several hundred birr each, to a few people. Then eating.

It was a massive feast: lots of injera, several different wats with meat, and fried fish; Cokes, Fantas, and Highlands to go with it. All ate, and after satiated, they came back together to listen. Everyone gathered around. Bahir then gave a large cash gift, around 20,000 birr, to the father of the deceased. Then Bahir spoke to the family. They listened to his words so quietly and attentively; it was the first time he had spoken to them, I think. He was nervous, but his words seemed heartfelt. He said that they were now family, that the children are now like his own. After he finished, a man went around with documents for the family to sign; these would go to the court, saying all was reconciled, and there was no further need for the formal court system to intervene.

This whole process made me wonder: This whole affair cost so much money. What if Bahir didn't have that money? Would they have forgiven him? And if not, he probably would have ended up in prison for fifteen years. If this is how it is, I would suspect that poor people end up in the prisons, and the rich "negotiate" their way out.

Conflict resolution through the Gadaa system remains imbued with social and cultural practices and meanings. It remains a *social* practice that cannot be reduced to its economic dimension. Yet, this example shows that money now holds a central place in the conflict mediation process, and the costs to individuals and families to participate in negotiations can be very high. To avoid imprisonment, Bahir gave cash gifts of some 25,000 birr (over 1,100 USD) to the family of the deceased, plus the costs of transportation, venue, food, and noncash gifts at various stages of the negotiation process. Further, he promised to financially support the children of the deceased. Most Ethiopians would not be able to afford such gifts or commitments. Perhaps the Gadaa fathers made Bahir pay more because he could. They would probably have asked less of a poorer man. But even Bahir was nervous that these negotiations would not be enough to deter this family from triggering formal court proceedings, leading to his imprisonment. A wronged family may be more likely to seek justice through the formal court system if the accused does not have the financial resources to persuade them otherwise.

***

The transformation of marriage practices and wedding celebrations provides another lens into the commodification of social life. Earlier generations of pastoralists met their spouses through networks of relations or when traveling with their cattle. Men and women always married outside their immediate *goosii*, or tribal group. The wedding included a ceremony rich in symbols of wealth and prosperity. The bride, for example, would be covered in butter before being given to her husband. In fact, weddings required so much butter that communities established a "butter bank" between families. Referred to as *wijjoo*, which literally means "to come together," families donated large quantities of butter to those preparing for a major occasion, such as a wedding—with the expectation that they return a butter contribution at a later date.[11] The man's family, in a practice known as *gabara*, would typically give cattle to the bride's family. In the marriage ceremony, the two families would mix milk with blood from their cattle and drink it together—a symbol that they are now sharing the blood of each other and becoming family.

Today, however, as one Wayisso elder lamented, "the times have changed completely, from blood to money." Marriage is an affair that can cost some 30,000 birr (roughly 1,400 USD) for the *gabara* alone. As a result, young men are delaying marriage to secure their livelihoods first, to be able to pay for what feels to them like the ever-increasing demands of women's families. Adam, a farmer in Wayisso, explains the *gabara* he gave to his wife's family in 2008: "For her father, I gave 10,000 birr and ten cattle. I bought a mountain bike for her elder brother. I gave six blankets and one bed. And finally, I bought four jerry cans to fetch water." When asked how he knew what or how much to give, he explained that "it is culture," and "it is the elders who decide what to give." He thinks expectations have already risen since his marriage. "At that time, I gave 10,000 birr. Today it would be 30,000 birr." Adam does not wish to have a second wife. The high cost of marriage is one reason for the widespread transition from polygamy to monogamy among younger generations.

Across this district today, weddings vary from traditional ceremonies—where a woman wears traditional Oromo dress and jewelry and perhaps puts a symbolic dab of butter on her forehead, surrounded by local friends and family—to more costly affairs, with multiple meals, multiple venues, and white wedding dresses. To illustrate the degree of change, the following two stories detail the marriages of two relatively rich men. One took place in 1970 and the other in 2016. As they demonstrate, marriage has always been an occasion to share a family's wealth in celebration with the community, yet in what terms that wealth is shared and displayed has dramatically changed.

Momina was born in a rural area called Gurbica, outside of Arsi Negele, approximately twelve hours from Wayisso on foot. Momina's childhood was like many others: playing and helping her mother to prepare meals, traveling with the men and young shepherds as they left with the cattle, learning to make jewelry and baskets. Weddings were some of her happiest childhood memories, when everyone came together to sing and eat well. When she reached sixteen, it was time for her to marry. She was particularly beautiful, and many families requested that she be married to one of their sons. "Everyone wanted me," she smiled. "But I did not know who I wanted. I simply kept quiet." One day her uncle and brothers approached her parents to suggest a man named Gemechu. Gemechu was wealthy. He had over eighty cattle. His first wife had died, and he was looking for another. Gemechu had seen Momina when grazing his cattle around their area, and he approached her brother to inquire about her. Momina's parents agreed with the proposal, and she married. Although it was a marriage "without my love, without my choice," Momina explained, refusal was not an option she ever considered.

The marriage process took two months. Elders visited the family twice to pay their respects and make necessary arrangements. Momina's family offered porridge and milk at each visit. In the second month, on the third visit, they organized the final celebration and her departure. Momina's family slaughtered a cow, and Gemechu gave ten cattle to her family. The community ate, sang, and celebrated for two days. *Caccabsa*, a traditional Oromo dish, was served in an elaborately beaded container; milk and meat were consumed in abundance. On the third day, Momina left with Gemechu. She wore jewelry on her fingers and toes and a traditional headdress, and her body was coated in butter. Her face was covered so she could not see, a common custom at the time, and Gemechu led her to Wayisso. "When my husband took me, my face was covered. I didn't know where I was, or the direction home. For the first three months here, I didn't know the way to my birthplace. I asked people, 'Which way did I come from to here? From the right or the left? Through the front or the back?' I didn't know."

The first three months were difficult for her. "I don't even want to remember those first three months here with my husband." But eventually she grew accustomed to her new life. After one year of marriage, Momina gave birth to her first child. She went on to have seven children, only three of whom survived to adulthood. Two died in their infancy, and two others died at age eight, one from drowning and the other from illness. Her eldest surviving son, Bilisuma, lives next to her in Wayisso with his wife and children. Her other son, Rabuma, lives in Ziway. Her daughter was married in her late teens, and she lives in another distant rural area of Oromia.

Some aspects of Momina's marriage process—the visit from elders, the negotiation of the *gabara*—remain common today. Likewise, some girls continue to marry the person their parents choose in their teenage years. Yet, this tends to occur within families with little to no education, or when families face significant economic hardship; in these cases, the *gabara* is one way to ease their poverty. Many young people, however, particularly those with secondary and tertiary schooling, have different expectations for marriage. Boys and young men often said they wanted to pursue their education and find "good work" before getting married. Girls and young women expressed similar aspirations—for education and for work—and only once they had secured those would they find a spouse of their own choosing. Indeed, it is increasingly common for women and men to choose each other rather than accepting the arrangements of their families. Out of respect for their families, however, many couples will still send elders to the woman's family to ask for their consent and blessing.[12]

Box 5.2 describes another wedding ceremony that spanned Ziway, Adami Tulu, and Lake Langano in a single day. In contrast to Momina's marriage several decades ago, it is what the marriage of a rich man looks like today—a mix of Oromo tradition with Western embellishments: the white wedding dress, a wedding cake, bridesmaids and groomsmen, even a camera crew. This "modern" wedding illustrates the commodification and creolization of marriage practices, as well as the important role migration plays in supporting them. This expensive wedding was funded in large part by the remittances of a few family members working as domestic workers in Beirut. I draw again on my fieldnotes to describe these events in detail.

Box 5.2 A "modern" wedding: Fieldnotes (edited for clarity), May 8, 2016

The wedding. What an affair! These new kinds of weddings—the white dresses, cutting the cake, *not* putting butter on your head—started happening in the last ten years. You still find traditional weddings in rural areas, or in places where people "are not educated," as Kedir said, but in the towns, these "modern" weddings are becoming more normal. More than one young man commented that it made the prospect of getting married very difficult. Young men can't even afford the dowry, estimated by some to be 30,000, even up to 50,000 birr.

This wedding was certainly a costly affair. It was much more extravagant than I had expected when they first invited me that hot day in Wayisso, as I sat in a little mud house, eating bread, drinking coffee, and watching sweaty men chew *khat*. Well, one of those men, the father of the groom, put on quite an impressive show. All day I was wondering, where did this money come from? I later connected the dots to his daughters and sisters working in the Middle East.

It began at the home of the groom in Ziway. Maybe ten cars and minibuses were crowded around the house. The groom came out in a white suit, big Oromo-style hair, a bouquet in hand. A group of young men were singing around him. He got in the car, and they did a song and dance around the car. He had four groomsmen wearing matching suits with red ties. They all looked sharp. I saw so many people from Wayisso there, all smartly dressed in new clothes. Kedir's mom had on a new dress. There was one couple who did not have new clothes. . . . It was strange to see Wayisso in the city.

The neighbors crowded around to watch. There was even a camera crew, three guys with matching yellow company shirts. There were about seven nice, new-looking Toyota compacts. The father joined his son in the car, and then it was time to leave. It was difficult to get all of the cars out of there, but it eventually happened. And then the honking commenced.

Continued

Continued

Before heading to Adami Tulu, we drove through Ziway. Maybe fifteen cars or more now, just honking and honking and honking. People came out of their homes to wave, one threw flower petals, others were clapping and yelling. When we arrived in Adami Tulu, it was even more crowded. The outside compound of the bride's family had been covered with a tent and their large courtyard packed with chairs. A stage was set up on one side, with flashing lights, red and white balloons, pillars with faux-silk dresses and fake flowers, and large framed photos of the couple. On the table was a selection of beverages: Coke, Miranda, Sprite, St. George's beer, bottled water, Ambo. And a heart made out of roses. As soon as we entered, everyone made a dash for the chairs.

The ceremony (the first of many) was quick and to the point. The bride and groom came out together and sat at the front, and their bridesmaids and groomsmen followed. The bride was wearing a strapless white dress with an intricately feathered bottom, and she had her hair done like a princess, with a tiara on one side hugging the curls that framed her face. Her four bridesmaids wore strapless red dresses, which matched the red ties of the groomsmen. After they were all seated, on the other side of the compound, people gathered around the two sets of families for the payment of the *gabara*. After this was finished, not even ten minutes, this first ceremony was complete. The couple got up and went to get their food. Others followed according to their seats. They had ushers to manage the crowds.

There were two large tables decked with platters of meat, shiro, stews, different fried vegetables (carrots, beets, cauliflower). There was even a cooked sheep sitting on the table, its scorched head raised and a wilted piece of lettuce hanging out of its mouth. There was injera, some normal and some dyed pink and blue. It was a madhouse just trying to get a plate.

After the meal, the groom and bride went into the house. The bride's family fed the new couple (first the groom) with *caccabsa* from a beautiful, beaded container, followed by fresh milk. Then the groom presented gifts to the bride's family, mostly large, soft blankets. He wrapped one around the father of the bride (even though it was unbearably hot in that crowded room), kissed him on both cheeks, and then did the same to the mother. Then the grandfather. Then the brother, the sister, and many other adults.

I was not sure who was who by then, but a lot of people received new blankets. Meanwhile, the camera crew was all over it. They brought a bright light for the filming, which I was grateful for, because it made my own pictures better. The power would go off intermittently, but it basically held throughout the day.

After this exchange, I went outside and noticed a large pile of gifts, mostly household items: a cupboard, sofas, pillows, pans, a mattress, chairs, a table, you name it. . . . They were loaded into the bed of a large ISUZU truck, all to be taken to the couple's new home in Ziway. I tried to get a sense of who paid for what. The groom's family pays for most of it: the food, the ceremonies and decoration, then of course the *gabara*: money, cattle, blankets, etc. The woman's family will contribute other gifts and furnishings for the new home, which were quite substantial. They also gave cattle and butter. One woman dressed in traditional Oromo attire loaded two large containers of butter onto the truck.

The next stop was Lake Langano, about a forty-minute drive away. This was where Kedir used to bring his cattle—"before it was developed," he said. When we arrived, we were one of maybe fifty minibuses waiting outside the gates of a private venue. We must have waited for close to an hour. There was some sort of hold-up, then a car accident, and then one guard at the gate refused to let anyone through because they were supposed to only enter in their cars. But there were too many cars. A mass of people began pushing and yelling at the gates, and eventually we got through.

There were at least five weddings being celebrated at the same time at Lake Langano. Our celebration consisted mostly of wandering along the beach and dipping feet in the water, listening to the live music of another wedding party, taking a lot of photos, and then watching the bride and groom cut the cake. They had fireworks, a stage, and a five-tier wedding cake. The bride and groom and their bridesmaids and groomsmen posed on the stage or waved their arms to the music, threw confetti, or sprayed colored foam. People were crowded in a circle around them, like adoring fans, all with their camera phones held high to capture the moment.

The other weddings at Lake Langano were not as extravagant. I saw one Pentecostal wedding where the bride and groom walked with a group of people behind them, most wearing gospel gowns. A man strummed

Continued

> *Continued*
>
> an acoustic guitar and sang for them as they walked. A different kind of "modern" wedding.
>
> After the cake was cut, we went to drink a Coke and then returned to the minibuses. I thought we were finished, but I was wrong. We drove through Ziway again, honking and yelling and dancing in the car. It was probably 8 pm by now. The minibus returned to the groom's house. It was now dark outside and people piled out of the cars. Crowds of neighbors gathered again, kept back by a guard with a stick who enforced a strict boundary. Again, people sang and danced around the car of the groom (I didn't see the bride) and then in front of his house. We proceeded into a large tent that had been erected on the road outside the house. The same decorations from Adami Tulu had been moved here: the nice chairs, the stage, the lights, the silk pillars.
>
> The bride and groom proceeded back to the stage. The wedding party entered behind them. A group of men began dancing and singing down the aisle and the groomsmen danced on the stage around the bride and groom. The groom stood with a traditional stick and a decorated head rest in his hand. Then one Muslim leader called everyone to attention and offered a prayer, which was met with repetitive "Amens" from the audience. Then the father said a prayer. The wife's family was Orthodox. I had been surprised by the lack of religion in the previous ceremony, but there was a little dose here. Then we ate, again. First the wedding party, then us.
>
> The spread was just as if not more bountiful than the first meal. This time they had a separate room with raw meat hanging from hooks—like the little white kiosks you see in town with ribs dangling. In addition to the *kitfo* that was on the table, you could enter this room to get some fresh, raw meat. I tried to politely decline. We all ate with our own plates and napkins. It used to be that people would eat five to ten together with one large plate. "One *wat* used to be enough," someone said.

Comparing the marriages of wealthy men in 1970 and 2016 reveals the dramatically expanded scope of consumption in wedding ceremonies. New goods (a white wedding dress, the suits and ties) and new services (transport in cars, a film crew) intermingle with older practices (the payment of the *gabara*, eating *caccabsa*, gifts of butter). As more young people come to expect modern weddings, and as certain segments of the population become wealthier, the standard for what a marriage should cost and entail is increasing. When one man remarked, "One *wat* used to be enough," this signals a shift in expectations for what weddings can and should look like. To be clear, there is nothing wrong with being able to serve multiple dishes and share multiple meals. Such generosity should be celebrated. Yet it also supports a common critique of market societies: that they perpetuate a culture of consumerism, stimulate or even encourage the feeling of never having enough, and widen inequalities between the rich and the poor.[13]

The 2016 wedding evokes the concept of "conspicuous consumption," originally introduced by American economist Thorstein Veblen to describe the behavioral characteristics of the "nouveau riche" in the late nineteenth-century United States. It carries a negative connotation and refers to the practice of publicly displaying wealth to enhance one's social standing and prestige within the community. Development economists frequently criticize this practice in poorer countries, arguing that families should direct discretionary incomes toward more productive pursuits rather than one-off events like weddings.[14] However, this perspective misses how an extravagant wedding, for instance, bolsters the local economy by providing incomes to those who provide the services for it. More fundamentally, there is an inherent contradiction in development economists lamenting the consumerism of the world's poor when the very market society so many aim to foster inherently depends on shifting attitudes toward valuing increased consumption.

These critiques aside, the phrase "conspicuous consumption" still has pertinence in another, very basic sense: the way in which wealth is displayed has become more *conspicuous* in recent decades, and this is changing younger generations' expectations for what their lives should look like. From this perspective, rural-urban migration from Wayisso can be viewed as a social practice conspicuously contingent on wealth; only those who can afford to move and sustain a more expensive urban lifestyle can migrate. As the last chapter showed, descendants of Bedane Tuffaa maintained some of the largest landholdings in Wayisso across regimes, and these wealthier families were among the first to leave Wayisso. However, this dynamic is changing. Thanks to an emerging migration industry that reduces the costs of international labor migration, migration to the Middle East has become increasingly accessible to less affluent households. This industry facilitates the movement of young women who, once abroad, can remit significant sums back to their villages. Consequently, the "nouveau riche" in Wayisso are arguably Dakabo Bulo's descendants—those families who have women working in the Middle East.

Labor Migration to the Middle East

Appreciating the gradual commodification of social life makes it easier to understand the decision-making of young women who leave for the Middle East.[15] As expectations for one's material life rise, and as more of social life may be bought and sold, money assumes an increasingly central place in people's economic reasoning. The profit motive emerges as a major force in migration decision-making.

The reason young women from Wayisso go to the Middle East—and not Italy, South Africa, or the United States, for example—is because of a consolidated and gendered migration industry linking prospective migrants in Wayisso with labor markets in Middle Eastern states. The demand for domestic workers has contributed to the "feminization" of labor migration from the country.[16] Formal and informal migration systems exist between other areas of Ethiopia and other destinations for both men and women, but in the Adami Tulu and Jido Kombocha *woreda*, the dominant migration system directs aspiring labor migrants to domestic work in the Middle East. If young women wish to leave, there is a ready network of brokers, agencies, and employers eager to facilitate and profit from their international movement. The same is not true for young men in Wayisso.

The first women from this region to go to the Middle East for work came from Adami Tulu. Leaving in the late 1990s, they were mainly women from the Wolayita ethnic group whose parents had moved to Adami Tulu as wage workers on the German-owned farm commonly called "Gerbi" (see the following chapter). The Wolayita are a population that have a longer history of moving for wage work than the Oromo do. When a few heard about new opportunities in the Middle East, they decided to try their luck. When they returned having made a significant profit, others followed.

Shitaye was the first woman from Wayisso to migrate, and she left for Beirut. The next was Hawa, the great-granddaughter of Dakabo Bulo, who also made her way to Beirut in 2010 or 2011. Hawa's first work contract was arranged by an uncle who was in Saudi Arabia for Hajj. Women remember that when Shitaye and Hawa first left, they could hardly believe it. It was "not normal" for women to move independently, "to visit different places," as one woman shared. But when Hawa returned and built a house in Adami Tulu for her family, people noticed what migration abroad could do.[17]

A decade after Shitaye's and Hawa's departure, it was no longer strange for women to migrate internationally for work. By 2016, over ten women from Wayisso, and likely hundreds more from Wayisso's surrounding villages and towns, had migration experience in the Middle East. Most women who leave are in their teens or twenties with middling levels of education, usually failing to finish secondary schooling. The decision to leave falls at an important moment of transition in their life course, as they navigate the path from childhood to adulthood. In some cases, the decision to leave is an active pursuit of capital, one worth leaving their education to pursue. In other cases, the decision to leave is made when education is no longer possible and they want to avoid the alternative—generally marriage and early motherhood. International labor migration has become a way to disrupt what young women described as an otherwise predictable, rural future.

***

The income migrant domestic workers can earn in the Middle East trumps any other economic opportunity available locally to rural men and women with low levels of education. For most Wayisso households, their primary source of income comes from the harvest they glean from their land once a year. Land access ranges from one to twenty plots per household (0.25 to 5 hectares); 75 percent of households have 2 hectares or less. Almost all households in Wayisso grow maize. Under good conditions, one plot produces some eight to twelve quintals (one hundred kilograms) of maize for the market, which is then bought for around 400 birr per quintal (roughly 19 USD in 2016), bringing a potential income gain of 3,200 to 4,800 birr (~150 to 225 USD) per plot. Of course, given farmers' dependence on rain, as irrigation is not yet viable in this area, a year of drought means some farmers may fail to produce even one quintal for the market. Farming also requires investments: in seeds, oxen, and, for those households that can afford it, fertilizer and additional manpower. For one farmer in Wayisso with one hectare, his net profit in a good year is around 14,500 birr (678 USD). However, in 2016, after a year of drought, he made only 1,320 birr (62 USD).

Beyond farming, there are development initiatives for the economic empowerment of women in the area. In Ziway, for example, microentrepreneurship is visible in the proliferation of small coffee huts (*mana bunaa*) that branch out from the main road. The government gives the space for free or a small fee, and women sell coffee, tea, and sometimes food. In rural areas, the opportunities to make an income for women are more limited. Some may, of their own initiative, sell things at the local market in Adami Tulu or buy a few goods like sugarcane to bring back to the village and sell there. Government development agents also encourage women to begin small poultry farms. Two women in Wayisso tried. They invested 3,000 birr (140 USD) to build the chicken hut and began with fifteen chickens, selling each egg for 3.50 birr (16 cents) at the local market in Adami Tulu. It began well, but they encountered problems when one husband kept asking his wife for the money she made and was "just spending it on things in town." They decided to put the business on hold.

It is in this economic context that young women and their families consider migration to the Middle East, where the profit a woman can make is more reliable and substantive than the profit to be made from rain-fed agriculture or even a small business. Women working in Beirut, for example, typically earned 150 USD per month. After expenses, another return migrant earned over 2,300 USD in her first eighteen months in Dubai.

For a young person deciding to leave, migration to the Middle East is framed as an investment, for themselves and their families. As one woman put it, "First I want to do something for my family, and the rest I will use for myself." Shiko took that approach. Born in Wayisso, she left after finishing seventh grade. The first time she worked abroad for two years, and with the money she sent back, her family built a new home in Wayisso and bought cattle. She paid the 30,000-birr *gabara* for her brother to get married. After coming home and resting for several months, she left again, but this time, her father said, "We are only listening to her voice. Now she tries to live for herself." She has her own bank account in Ziway, and the family has not received any of her earnings. "Maybe she has a boyfriend," her brother speculated. Whatever the case, it was clear the family saw the money as hers.

After helping their families, the most common aspiration women expressed was to save enough money to move to town, build a home, and open their own business. In Ziway, new corner shops, restaurants, cafes, mobile phone stores, and hairdressers are popping up along new roads laid to accommodate the housing boom. Many of these shops have some

Figure 5.1 A return migrant's store on the outskirts of Ziway

connection to migration (Figure 5.1). One woman who worked in Saudi Arabia for two years, for example, paid some 840 USD in up-front costs to open her own restaurant. "If I didn't go to Saudi Arabia, I could never have opened my own business," she said. Many women preferred living in town, not only because the lifestyle and business opportunities were better, but also because of the social distance from rural areas. As one return migrant, who owns a corner store in Ziway, expressed, "I chose Ziway because it's close enough to my family, but far enough away where they are not going to come and ask for things for free all the time."

Through the visible change remittances bring to the lives of migrants and their families, labor migration to the Middle East enters into what human geographers refer to as the "mental maps" of other young women, a possible pathway in their imagined futures.[18] Often, young women who aspired to go to the Middle East would mention a neighbor, family member, or friend who was able to "change her life" and inspired them to follow a similar route. In Wayisso, one of the most obvious signs of change is the construction of new homes. In sharp contrast to the traditional one-room thatched huts, one such migrant-funded house has reflective windows, bright paint, multiple rooms, and a corrugated iron roof—all conspicuous signs of discretionary income. On the inside, someone had painted "AMANEE BAATI BARAA 2010" across the wall. Amanee left for Beirut in 2015, and her family built this house with her remittances in 2017 (2010 in the Ethiopian calendar). Her mother was proud. "*Jabdu*," she said—her daughter is strong.

***

Migration abroad for domestic work is often not the first desired pathway to change. Most girls and young women would prefer to realize their aspirations through formal education and securing decent work in Ethiopia. In many ways, attending secondary and higher education is one way young women postpone the responsibilities of adulthood, as they strive to develop the capabilities needed to realize the adult lives they desire. When education is no longer viable, however—whether because they fail the qualifying exams or their families no longer support their schooling—adulthood is thrust upon them, often in the form of marriage or migration.

Girls in this district began to enter formal schooling in the 1990s, and since then, the rate at which they have accessed primary and secondary education has dramatically increased. In the Adami Tulu and Jido Kombolcha *woreda*, girls' school enrollment is now almost equal to that of young men, though enrollment sharply decreases for both sexes after eighth and tenth grades, when a regional and then national examination determines whether students can continue in the formal education track. If young women fail these exams—and most do; only 34 percent of pupils in the district pass the national exam, according to one government official—their future options are limited. As one mother in Wayisso explained, "After the national exam at grade ten, if they pass, they proceed to the preparatory level. If they fail, they have two opportunities: to marry someone or to fly outside to the Arab [countries]."

The government encourages those who fail the examinations to enroll in technical and vocational schooling or higher education through private institutions, but not everyone can afford to do so. "My grades were not good enough to continue to preparatory school. And to take the technical and vocational classes, it needs income, money," one young woman named Mimi explained. She left for Beirut just three months after failing the national examination. "I didn't have anything in my hand. That's why I decided to leave." Mimi left to avoid an early marriage and the gendered restrictions that can come with it: "Nobody pushed me to go. I had friends who had migrated. And it is better to do something.... If I did not migrate, I would have been married and then I would be dependent on my husband. I wouldn't have the capability to do anything without my husband's permission." With the help of her family, Mimi is building a house in Adami Tulu and plans to open a shop there after she finishes her contract.

Not all young women have the chance to take the public examinations, however. Under pressure to help alleviate the poverty of their families, some stop their schooling to marry. The *gabara* that a bride's family receives can be a significant boon to households in difficult economic circumstances. This was the situation Damitu faced when she left for Saudi Arabia at the age of fourteen. "My family was not able to send me to school. Not even a government school. They needed money to survive." Her three older brothers were in school, but as she expressed, "there is extra pressure for the girl to stop school." Her father wanted her to marry, but Damitu knew of other girls who had gone abroad and had an idea. "I convinced my father that migration would be better than getting married now. I would be able to make some money to send home; then I could return and get married. My father agreed, and he arranged for me to go." For Damitu, migration to Saudi Arabia was the best option among a poor set, but one she negotiated with her family.

As more women leave for the Middle East, it becomes easier for others to do the same. Migration, once exceptional, is increasingly normalized as a potential pathway in the life trajectory of a young woman. Further, as more women leave, prospective migrants are better able to draw on their networks to learn about opportunities, brokers, destinations, and work conditions elsewhere. Some even draw on their networks abroad to arrange their own migration, cutting out the brokers and middlemen and thereby lowering the costs of leaving. These dynamics fuel what migration theorists call the "cumulative causation" of migration—that is, as migratory experience grows within a sending community, it becomes easier and more common for other community members to leave.[19]

***

Despite the potential gains and increasing accessibility of international labor migration, the majority of young women in Wayisso and its surrounding towns still do not migrate to the Middle East. Understanding why so many do not migrate can illuminate why some do.

Many girls and young women harbor the hope that they can change their lives through achieving higher levels of education and securing decent salaried employment in Ethiopia. Women who go on to achieve tertiary levels of education rarely consider labor emigration worth the risk or sacrifice. Yet, even among young women whose futures remain severely limited by educational or economic constraints, many still do not consider the risks worth taking. The fear of working for "a bad family" outweighs the potential income gains.

As more women leave as labor migrants to the Middle East, stories of bad experiences make their way back. One woman from the district returned with a broken leg. Another never received her salary after working for a family for two years. Even if these experiences are outnumbered by those in which women remit or return with significant earnings, these stories become known in the community. Additionally, the government and international organizations have begun information campaigns to educate the Ethiopian population about the dangers of (particularly irregular) migration to the Middle East. Many women in town said they heard about the evils of "Arab migration" from watching television.

Women processed these risks differently. More highly educated women and those with few personal connections to labor emigration tended to magnify the risks. For example, one university graduate who recently returned to Ziway to help with her family's business expressed, "When women come back from the Arab countries, they are mentally disordered. OK, for some people, maybe they were lucky and are able to improve their lives, but for the majority, it's not good." However, those who aspired to leave and those who had migrants in their personal networks more often focused on what they saw with their own eyes: a neighbor or friend who had been able to materially improve her and her family's life. For those who aspired to leave or had left, these concrete results outweighed the negative narratives that are beginning to penetrate the imaginary about migration to the Middle East. As one aspiring migrant rationalized, "Most people find good families. Only a few end up with bad ones."

Of course, there are also many young women who would like to migrate to the Middle East but lack the capability to do so. The poorest families in Wayisso do not have the means to work with a reliable agency, nor the social networks to help. In this area, families reported investing between 6,000 and 12,000 birr (280 and 560 USD in 2016) in up-front costs. Local and regional brokers, who facilitate contact with agencies in Addis Ababa, make different arrangements with potential migrants depending on their desired destination and what they can afford. It is cheaper (and the earning potential lower) to go to Lebanon, for example, than Saudi Arabia or the United Arab Emirates. In some instances, a migrant may cover all the costs required to go abroad and begin earning directly. More often, families cover the costs of the passport, health checks, and transportation to and from Addis Ababa, and the agency covers the rest: the costs of the flight and visa applications, as well as its own fee, which it then deducts from the worker's first few months' salary. There is also the option to pay nothing, but it is common knowledge that this is with less trustworthy agencies, and as one woman explained, "it takes a *long* time before you start earning money."

In other cases, young women fail to secure the support of their families to leave. Many parents, aware of the risk and potential for abuse abroad, prefer that their daughters stay in Ethiopia. As one mother expressed, "Most of our daughters would like to go abroad. I think the reason is to change their life quickly. . . . But all the Arab households are not good. They may harm them. Rather than working for them, it is better if they stay here." Husbands also discouraged migration, but for more nuanced reasons. One man in Wayisso explained that he refused to let his wife leave because he did not want her to become "abnormal" and dissatisfied with a rural life. He described how a woman from a neighboring village divorced her husband upon return and married another man in town. Another husband expressed a worry that his wife might "get used to the lifestyle and facilities there [and] may not like life in the rural areas." "She may not like a rural husband," his wife jokingly chided.

***

The profit motive is a powerful force in the migration decision-making of women who leave for the Middle East. Young women now aspire for urban lives with a greater degree of social and economic freedom, education, and material consumption than their mothers' generation ever experienced or expected. It is precisely because of the commodification of so many dimensions of social life, because of the increasing power of *money* to buy social, economic, and spatial mobility, that women consider leaving and their families often support them. Thus, as the Ethiopian economy develops—as market forces become stronger, as more of social life may be bought and sold, as expectations for consumption increase, and as inequality widens within a community—migration begins to make more sense for more people. This is one of the main reasons that economic development in poorer places tends to stimulate both rural-urban and international migration.

Labor migration to the Middle East offers the prospect of capital—that is, discretionary income women can invest in a better future, for themselves and their families. The fact that women can more easily access these opportunities abroad—due to a migration industry focused on fulfilling the demand for female domestic workers in the Middle East—disrupts a gendered hierarchy where men have always been the economic providers and power holders. Men were the leaders of their pastoral herds; men were the first farmers; men were the first to go to school and access new forms of salary-based work with the government or foreign companies. Throughout these livelihood transitions in Wayisso, the realm of women remained primarily in the home. If women did work to supplement household incomes, their contributions were generally small, through selling goods, like butter, at the Adami Tulu market. Migration to the Middle East, precisely because it gives access to unprecedented incomes to rural women, is challenging entrenched gendered norms and expected life course trajectories. Within just a single generation, young, often unmarried women are now providing for the education of their siblings, funding their brothers' marriages, constructing a new house for their families in the village, or building their own house or business in town. This is unprecedented change in such a short span of time.

And yet, the gendered social, cultural, and economic constraints women leave are still there when they return. Many do not realize all that they had hoped for through their migration. One woman was frustrated to find that her family did not respect her wishes for how her remittances should be spent. Another discovered that the newfound respect she received from the community fizzled once her savings ran out. Many women feel compelled to leave again after failing to realize their aspirations for change after a single contract. Migration alone cannot alleviate the social ills women continue to confront. However, given these constraints, migration becomes one powerful social process, alongside others like expanding education, reconfiguring the place of women in Ethiopian society.

From a macro-level perspective, the massive movement of labor migrants to the Middle East is one of the clearest lenses through which to analyze the structural injustices inherent in our globalizing world, where international labor markets are bifurcated between the transnational professional elite and the informal migrant workers that undergird rich economies.[20] Yet, at the micro level, it is crucial to view migrants' decision-making from the angle of agency. Women will continue to leave Ethiopia because they are choosing what they see as the best path among a limited few to change their life circumstances. The aspiration to migrate arises in the context of a deeper transformation in the social imaginary, where young women and men alike are now looking toward the city rather than the village as the home of the good life. And a good life in the city requires capital.

6
Education

"Being a student shows me the way forward in life," Yomen explained as she prepared a fire to roast coffee, breaking corn husks over a small charcoal stove. A confident young woman, she tells me that I will have five rather than the usual three cups in exchange for an interview with her. I agree, and throughout the interview, she was playful, sometimes serious, and often a little restless. I could not help but see signs of the child she was in the process of leaving behind. Yomen had recently received news that she failed the national exam after tenth grade, barring her continuation into preparatory school. But she was not yet ready to choose between marriage or migration, the default alternatives for girls who fail out of school. Instead, she planned to spend the year with her mother in Wayisso, helping with her younger siblings and studying to retake the national exam.

I asked Yomen what her education means to her. "Education gives me the chance to distinguish between a life of darkness and a life of light," she said. "Earlier, my life was dark. I'm trying to change my life to be light now, because I am educated." Yomen compared her life to the "dark" lives of her uneducated sisters, who all married and had children at younger ages. "They didn't know anything.... They simply married according to the expectations of our family," she explains. "I have seen my sisters' lives after they married, and I don't want it. I want to improve my life first. After you get married, you have children, then you spend all your time with your children, and you can't work on achieving a better life." She still hoped to retake the qualifying exam, continue into preparatory school and then university, and become a doctor. For Yomen, like so many young people across Ethiopia, schooling is a practical way to postpone marriage and the responsibilities of adulthood while improving one's prospects for when that day comes. At a more fundamental level, education is seen as a pathway out of "backwardness" and into "modernity," out of "darkness" and into "the light."

Yomen's generation is the first to go to school on a wide scale. In Ethiopia, net enrollment rates in primary school increased dramatically from 21 to 93

Moved by Modernity. Kerilyn Schewel, Oxford University Press. © Oxford University Press (2025).
DOI: 10.1093/9780197680759.003.0007

percent between 1996 and 2014.[1] Over a quarter of the Ethiopian government's expenditure went to education in the 2010s.[2] In Ethiopia and around the world, expanding education is a universal and uncontested aim of development policy.[3] Alongside its intrinsic value, the social benefits of schooling are well known. Education tends to expand economic opportunity, promote health, and contribute to greater gender equality.[4] Yet, the impact of rising educational attainment on migration has received comparatively little attention. That may be because migration, unlike income, health, or gender equality, is often not perceived as a universal good. On the contrary, increased political interest in migration focuses on reducing the internal and international mobility of the world's poor. Governments and nongovernmental institutions alike, across a wide variety of contexts, perceive growing rural-urban migration as a challenge to rural futures and urban sustainability, and the international migration of educated citizens as a loss for national development—what is often referred to as the "brain drain."

Yet, as this chapter will show, widening access to formal education—even at just the primary and secondary levels—is one of the most important drivers of rural out-migration. In one study examining the relationship between educational attainment and the migration aspirations of Ethiopian youth, economist Sonja Fransen and I found that even just primary levels of schooling significantly increased the desire to live somewhere else.[5] One reason is structural: young people often have to leave rural areas to attend secondary or tertiary schools, and as more people become educated, they assume new kinds of work in the industrial and service sectors—sectors that tend to concentrate employment opportunities in urban places.

Another reason is more intangible but no less weighty: formal schooling is a cultural process, what the anthropologist Ulf Hannerz once described as "an organized way of giving individuals cultural shape."[6] In other words, schools are formal spaces in which young people are "socialized" and trained for work and citizenship in modern societies.[7] This socialization process accelerates deep shifts in the social imaginary. In agro-pastoral communities in southern Ethiopia, for example, Sabrina Maurus examines how the experience of going to school alters young people's imagined futures and even their experience of time. She finds that young people who have not been to school have a "cyclical notion of time that focuses on the reproduction of the agro-pastoral life world," whereas students living in town have "a linear time-reckoning, centered upon individual and national development."[8] In traditional agricultural communities, Getnet Tadele and Asrat Ayalew Gella find notably negative attitudes toward rural ways of life among young people in school. Boys and girls, they write, "come to see how backward and traditional the lives of their parents are, as a result of their education."[9]

The Rise of Formal Schooling

Historically, in Ethiopia and around the world, formal schools were the domain of religious institutions. In ancient Abyssinia, the Ethiopian Orthodox Church oversaw the training of clergy and the children of the nobility. By the turn of the twentieth century, there were a few European missionary schools and a small number of Islamic schools in the Muslim areas of the empire. In the Oromo kingdom, the Gadaa system provided a "nonformal" system of education seamlessly integrated into the political, economic, and religious affairs of society.

As Emperor Menelik II's ambitions for Ethiopia's transformation grew, he recognized that Ethiopia needed, as historian Richard Pankhurst writes, "a growing number of Ethiopian government officials with the skills required both for the preservation of the country's independence and for the all-important task of modernization."[10] He opened the first public school, Ecole Imperiale Menelik II, in October 1908 in Addis Ababa, and the same year, Ras Makonnen, the governor of Harar, opened another primary school in his city.[11] Haile Selassie opened the second modern educational institution in Addis Ababa, the Safari Makonnen School, in 1925, followed by the first school for girls, the Empress Menen School, in 1931. Although other schools gradually opened in different parts of the empire—a technical school, a teachers' training school, a school for orphans, a school of art, a boy scouts' school, and provincial schools in at least fourteen different towns[12]—the numerical reach of formal schooling remained limited. By 1935 in Ethiopia, there were only twenty public schools with some eight thousand pupils.[13] Those seeking university-level educations all left to pursue their degrees abroad.

Whatever progress had been made in expanding public education was severely halted during the Italian occupation of 1936 to 1941. Fascist educational policy in East Africa required a distinct separation in schooling for Italian children and "colonial subjects." During this time, many of Ethiopia's established public schools were requisitioned for Italian children, and new schools opened to establish a set of basic skills that better suited the Ethiopian "race" and that would serve the military and economic requirements of the Italian Empire.[14] Higher levels of education were seen as a threat to the mission of Italian occupation, and more highly educated Eritreans and Ethiopians who spoke French and English were routinely arrested or disappeared. General Guglielmo Nasi, the temporary governor of Harar, summarized the Italian view on education well. On June 5, 1938, he argued against "any ambition to extend elementary education for natives." He explained: "This is a fundamental political mistake that tends to put individuals out of class who, solely because of their education, will refuse to work in the fields, as we know by our own colonial experience and by that of other countries. They are attracted to the towns, ask for Government employment, compete with nationals in trades that should be reserved to the latter, forming a class of discontented, or even worse, rebellious people."[15] Nasi knew, in other words, that education does not simply transmit information and skills but changes the way pupils see the world and their place in it. The Italian administration accepted and enforced this expressed need for rigid control over access to education. As a result, by the time the Italians were defeated and expelled from Ethiopia, Pankhurst writes, "the country found itself largely destitute of the skilled personnel required to face the problems of independence."[16]

Upon his return as emperor, Haile Selassie continued his efforts to further access to modern educational institutions across Ethiopia, yet his efforts were restricted by teacher shortages and other resource constraints. The government recruited foreign teachers for public schools and continued to allow missionary and other private schools. By 1952, some sixty thousand students were enrolled in four hundred primary schools, eleven secondary schools, and three colleges.[17] Mostly located in larger towns and cities, new schools were financed through foreign aid or a special tax on agricultural land. Unfortunately, the rural inhabitants whose taxes supported the expansion of public education rarely saw the fruits of this new development.[18]

The country's first university, the Haile Selassie I University, was established in Addis Ababa in 1961 (it was later renamed Addis Ababa University in 1974). There was also the University of Asmara, a private university founded by Roman Catholics in 1958, although its initial enrollment was almost all Italian. Most students looking to pursue higher education continued to migrate overseas, often to the United States, France, and Canada. Many were guaranteed high positions in Haile Selassie's government upon their return.

Yet growing access to higher education had political ramifications for the stability of the Ethiopian Empire. Aware of the conditions of other postcolonial African nations and the democratic ideals espoused elsewhere, many intellectuals who had been educated abroad became critical of the inequalities and authoritarianism of Haile Selassie's empire. The most notable example is the story of the failed revolution of the Neway brothers.[19] Germame Neway, the intellectual mastermind behind the plot, was educated in Addis Ababa and later the United States and wrote his dissertation on settler land policies in Kenya. Returning to Ethiopia in 1954, he assumed a governing appointment in Jijiga. Inspired by his studies, he attempted to reform land rights for the peasants in his jurisdiction, only to be thwarted and reprimanded by the emperor. Frustrated at the inequalities and rigidity of the imperial regime, Germame and his brother, General Mengistu Neway, chief of the military division of the Royal Guard, plotted to overthrow Haile Selassie.

On Tuesday, December 13, 1960, Haile Selassie left the country for a state visit to Brazil, and the Neway brothers seized their chance. General Mengistu Neway took control of the imperial palace in Addis Ababa and, the following morning, coerced the emperor's eldest son, Prince Asfa-Wasan, to broadcast a proclamation in which the "economic backwardness" of Ethiopia was attacked, the formation of a new government proclaimed, and the start of a new era promised.[20] The movement secured the support of the university students and imperial bodyguard but failed to move the noblemen, army, and most of the townspeople of Addis Ababa. Informed of the coup d'etat, Haile Selassie quickly returned to Ethiopia, and after a brief few days of confusion and fighting, the revolution fizzled and fell. Germame Neway committed suicide. Mengestu was captured, tried, and executed a few months later. Historian Christopher Clapham argues that what made this failed revolution distinct was the desire to institute an entirely new system of government, inspired by modern, democratic principles. While intrigues and rebellions had certainly threatened Haile Selassie before, the Neway revolution sought to transform the political framework, not just replace the person in power. It foreshadowed the larger revolution to come—one that was better planned and executed and ideologically inspired by another vision for modernity: Marxism.

When the Derg military regime successfully overthrew Haile Selassie in 1974, only 10 percent of the Ethiopian population was literate. The new regime proclaimed universal education and literacy as a fundamental right of the people. In the *zemecha* campaign, tens of thousands of students and teachers left the cities to bring education and empowerment to the countryside. This effort was short-lived, however, and the greatest impact of the Derg on the education of Ethiopia's rural population came through its establishment of formal schools in rural areas. The aspirations of the government exceeded their capability to open and resource new schools, yet many remember the quality of education for the schools that did open as being very high. As one professor at Addis Ababa University recalled: "During the time of the Derg, higher education was not as widespread, but the quality was better. . . . Education was important, recognized, and invested in. The quality was on par with other European countries. Today, education is more widely available, and this is good, but the quality is worse."

After the fall of the Derg regime and the rise of the Ethiopian People's Revolutionary Democratic Front in the 1990s, access to formal education, particularly primary schooling, rapidly expanded across the country. Galvanized by the United Nations' Millennium Development Goals, today's federal government has vigorously pursued the achievement of universal primary education. It has developed ambitious policies and programs to expand the number of schools in rural areas, abolish school fees, and train new cohorts of teachers; education as a percentage of total government expenditure increased from approximately 12 percent in 1980 to 27 percent in 2015.[21] As a result of these investments, the number of primary schools increased from 9,900 in 1995 to 32,048 in 2014.[22]

Despite this remarkable progress, many challenges remain. Enrollment rates are up, yet completion rates are lower—at 70 percent for grade five and 53 percent for grade eight.[23] Likewise, enrollment rates in secondary school and tertiary-level schools have not experienced the same gains as primary enrollments, at just 40 percent and 9 percent in 2014, respectively.[24] Further, with rapid expansion come questions about declining quality, at all levels of education, related to resource constraints and teacher training.[25] Economist Tassew Woldehanna and his colleagues compared learning outcomes among two cohorts of twelve-year-olds, first in 2006 and then in 2013, and found a substantial and statistically significant decline in mathematics and reading scores between the two groups. In mathematics, for example, the percentage of correct scores declined from 54 percent to 37 percent.[26] They found that children in rural areas, attending government schools, from poorer households, and whose parents have little or no education were particularly disadvantaged. It is fair to conclude that the rapid increase in enrollment, particularly remarkable in rural areas across Ethiopia, has not been matched by improvements in learning. On the contrary, rapid expansion appears to have hastened a decline in the quality of education.

The government is aware of these challenges, but as one Ethiopian professor explained, they accept it as a price to be paid for growing access. Yet, he shared, there are also other elements at play beyond the desire to simply expand access. He gave the example of a results-based aid scheme funded by the United Kingdom, which offered the government of Ethiopia payment per student sitting and passing the grade ten examination (slightly more if they were female and/or from disadvantaged areas), with total reward payments of approximately 15.6 million pounds over a three-year pilot period. This incentivizes schools to move pupils through the system without real quality control. "People are getting degrees, but it doesn't mean much," he noted. This professor's graduate students today have worse English-language skills than his first-year undergraduate students many years ago. "The education system is a mess," he said.

Despite these shortcomings, education is still widely perceived as a key pathway to success, through which rural and urban families alike must pass to achieve a better future.[27] As a result, young people and their families increasingly invest their limited resources in schooling.[28] Diplomas and university degrees are highly prized because they allow people to pursue salaried government positions or more lucrative professional work with foreign companies. Yet, as the quality of education declines and the number of people with diplomas and degrees increases, the job prospects associated with higher educational attainment are less secure than they may have been a decade or so ago. Under these circumstances, some families decide to invest their limited resources in what many see as an alternative pathway to success: labor migration. As one young woman who aspired to migrate to the Middle East put it, and many others agreed, "Education is good, but migration is a quicker and more sure way to change my life."

Regarding international migration, low levels of overall educational attainment in Ethiopia may help explain the relatively low levels of emigration. Total educational attainment in Ethiopia is nearly 20 percent lower than other African countries at similar levels of economic development.[29] Yet, among the cohort that achieves tertiary levels, emigration is significant. For example, the emigration rate to Organisation for Economic Cooperation and Development (OECD) countries was just 0.7 percent of the total Ethiopian population in 2015–2016, but 14 percent for highly educated

Ethiopians[30]—a rise from 10 percent in 2000–2001.[31] Research suggests that one reason emigration appears to rise with development is that a greater share of the population become college graduates, the cohort with the greatest propensity to emigrate.[32] This appears to be the case in Ethiopia. However, it is also notable that rising levels of primary and secondary education also seem to increase migration propensities for some forms of labor migration. Female labor migrants in the Middle East, for example, show higher educational attainment than nonmigrants, but usually just upper primary or lower secondary levels.[33] Rising access to formal education appears to stimulate the aspiration to leave as well as the capability to do so by enhancing the knowledge, skills, and networks people need to realize a migration project.

"Learning to Leave"

"It was during the Derg that education really started in the rural areas," one Wayisso elder remembers. "They announced that every child from the farmers should go to school. And the quality was good." The first school serving Wayisso was in Andolla, a *kebele* some ten kilometers away. Wayisso's first students remember walking to and from the Woransa School through acacia forest, cautious of wild animals like lions and hyenas. They learned basic mathematics and history, and they learned to read and write in Amharic, the national language. Although universal primary education was a stated aim of the socialist government, only older boys and men attended the school, and most still did not see the value of formal education at that time. Attitudes toward education changed under the current government, as more primary schools were established in more *kebeles*, and the potential of education as a pathway to more lucrative work became clearer as some individuals from Wayisso attained higher levels.

Today, in the formal school system in the Adami Tulu and Jido Kombolcha (ATJK) *woreda*, grades one through four constitute the first cycle of primary school, and grades five through eight, the secondary cycle. Primary school is taught in the mother tongue of the region, Afaan Oromo. A regional exam in Afaan Oromo after grade eight determines whether the student moves into secondary school. Those who fail have the option to retake the exam the following year. Grades nine and ten constitute the first cycle of secondary school, where classes are taught in English. A qualifying national exam in English takes place after grade ten, which determines whether the pupil can continue into preparatory school, or grades eleven and twelve. After grade twelve, students take the national entrance exam for university, also in English.

For individuals who fail the qualifying exams after grades ten or twelve, alternative education pathways exist: technical and vocational training or other college courses, such as teacher training. Private educational institutions also flourish in the area, thanks to growing demand from young people who failed their exams but still have strong aspirations for higher education. Several young men and women from Wayisso attend college and bachelor-level courses in Ziway at Rift Valley University, the largest private university complex in Ethiopia with twenty-seven campuses around the country.

One-third of Wayisso's population never attended school. For women older than fifteen, the share is almost half (48.6 percent). Table 6.1 shows the educational levels attained by men and women born or living in Wayisso, disaggregated by age group.[34] Most of the oldest living generations, aged sixty and over, never attended school; only a few men attained some years of primary schooling. From the 40-to-59-year-old cohort, more men attained a few years of primary school, two completed secondary, and one received a university degree. No women from this cohort attended school.

Table 6.1 Educational attainment by age and gender in Wayisso

Education level	Educational attainment (%)							
	0–19*		20–39		40–59		60+	
	F	M	F	M	F	M	F	M
None	2.0	3.1	41.6	5.5	100.0	19.4	100.0	70.0
Grades 1–4	36.6	56.3	4.0	7.3	—	32.3	—	10.0
Grades 5–8	45.5	26.0	24.0	16.5	—	38.7	—	20.0
Grades 9–10	13.9	11.5	13.6	31.2	—	—	—	—
Grades 11–12	1.0	2.1	3.2	3.7	—	6.5	—	—
Diploma	1.0	1.0	12.0	22.0	—	—	—	—
Degree	—	—	1.6	13.8	—	3.2	—	—
Total	100.0	100.0	100.0	100.0	100.0	100.0	100.0	100.0
n	101	96	125	109	47	31	7	10

*Children 10 years and under who have not yet begun schooling are not included.
Source: Household survey 2016.

The first girls to go to school come from the generation of women in their twenties and thirties. Although attainment rates still lag behind men overall, almost one-quarter of women completed primary levels (24.0 percent). A notable share has some degree of secondary schooling (16.8 percent). Tertiary education at the university level or higher remains the sphere of men in this age cohort. Fourteen men hold a university degree and one man has a master's degree, compared to just one female university graduate and one female postgraduate degree holder (Ademtuu). Among young people who failed the qualifying exam for preparatory school, diplomas—through governmental or private institutions—are a popular alternative for those who can afford it. Fifteen women and twenty-four men in the 20-to-39 age cohort had some sort of diploma. Popular certifications are in teaching, accounting, business, or hotel management.

For Wayisso's youngest generation, those under the age of twenty, primary schooling is now standard. Attendance is facilitated by the fact that a primary school opened in Wayisso, as well as changing social norms about educating girls. In fact, girls under the age of twenty now show higher levels of primary schooling than boys. Boys often begin schooling at later ages or are more likely to be pulled out of school to help with the cattle or farm. In Wayisso, seventeen boys between the ages of six and ten had not yet started their schooling, compared to thirteen girls.

There is a clear generational divide in educational attainment, such that the generation in their twenties and thirties is where we might expect formal education to have the greatest impact on migration outcomes. Indeed, it is precisely this generation that first began leaving Wayisso in large numbers. As the previous chapters illustrate, this generational movement was shaped by other political, economic, and demographic changes as well, but access to formal education is a major, if often underappreciated, influence.

Disaggregated by gender, the connection between education and mobility shows similar but distinct trends (Tables 6.2 and 6.3). There is a strongly positive correlation between years of education and number of places lived. This relationship is strongest for men, followed by unmarried women, and then women more generally.[35] For both sexes, the completion of primary school after grade eight appears to be a turning point: those with secondary and higher levels of education live in urban areas, and those with little or no education live in rural areas. This distinction is particularly striking for men (Figure 6.1), but it also holds for women (Figure 6.2).

Table 6.2 Number of places lived by educational attainment, women

Educational attainment	Number of places lived (%)						Total	n
	1	2	3	4	5	6		
None	11.2	82.2	6.5	—	—	—	100.0	107
Grades 1–4	100.0	—	—	—	—	—	100.0	4
Grades 5–8	8.0	52.0	28.0	10.0	—	2.0	100.0	50
Grades 9–10	—	54.8	32.3	9.7	3.2	—	100.0	31
Grades 11–12	—	40.0	20.0	20.0	20.0	—	100.0	5
Diploma	—	25.0	31.3	18.8	12.5	12.5	100.0	16
Degree	—	—	—	—	50.0	50.0	100.0	2
Total	9.3	63.7	17.2	5.6	2.3	1.9	100.0	215

Note: For women born or living in Wayisso aged fifteen and over.
Source: Household survey 2016.

Table 6.3 Number of places lived by educational attainment, men

Educational attainment	Number of places lived (%)						Total	n
	1	2	3	4	5	6		
None	71.4	23.8	4.8	—	—	—	100.0	21
Grades 1–4	82.8	17.2	—	—	—	—	100.0	29
Grades 5–8	69.4	22.4	2.0	2.0	2.0	2.0	100.0	49
Grades 9–10	2.2	55.6	26.7	13.3	2.2	—	100.0	45
Grades 11–12	—	12.5	50.0	25.0	—	12.5	100.0	8
Diploma	—	8.3	25.0	41.7	16.7	8.3	100.0	24
Degree	—	6.3	18.8	31.3	37.5	6.3	100.0	16
Total	38.5	26.0	14.1	12.5	6.3	2.6	100.0	192

Note: For men born or living in Wayisso aged fifteen and over.
Source: Household survey 2016.

Most women with no or primary levels of education live in two rural places, reflecting the common practice of rural-rural migration for marriage. Those men with only primary or lower levels of education are more likely to have only lived in one place, Wayisso (see Table 6.3). However, for both women and men, those with secondary or higher levels of education experience greater rates of mobility. Seventy percent of men with a diploma or degree, for example, have already lived in four or more places, almost all urban areas. Two men with a diploma or degree now live in rural areas, but this is because

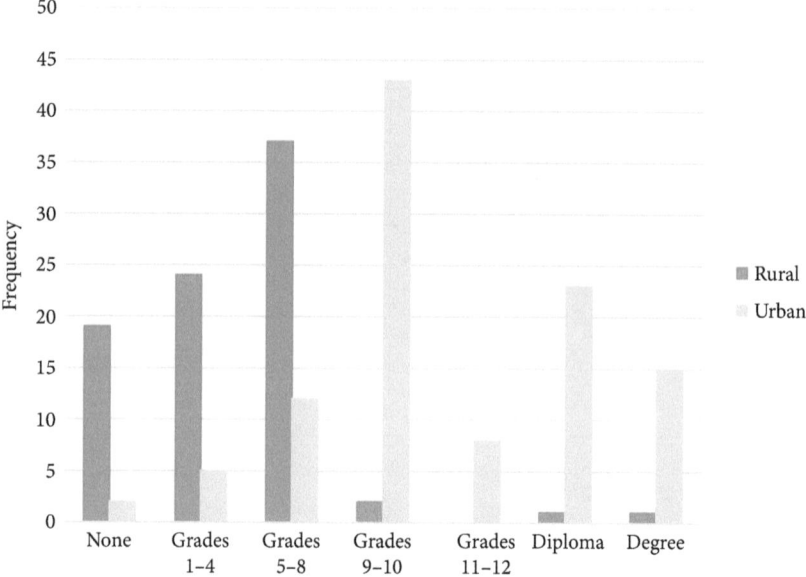

Figure 6.1 Place of current residence by educational attainment, men
Source: Household survey (for men fifteen years and older).

they obtained government positions that were assigned to rural *kebeles*. It is also interesting to note that only one out of seven women from Wayisso working in the Middle East has no formal education. The other six have similar levels: three completed grade seven, three completed grade eight, and one completed grade ten.

Thus, those with higher levels of education are not only more likely to move out of Wayisso but also more likely to move *more*. For many, this mobility occurs across short distances: from Wayisso to Adami Tulu and then to Ziway, for example. But the rising number of people living in four or more places suggests this mobility now extends beyond the district. For the cohort in their twenties and thirties, 23.8 percent of men and 21.7 percent of women have lived in four or more distinct places. The youngest generation will likely show even higher rates of mobility as they grow older.

In addition to generation and gender, family lineage has a clear impact on educational attainment and migration or immobility outcomes. The family trees in Figure 6.3 illustrate the concentration of higher educational achievement within family lineages. The family trees in Figure 6.4 detail the out-migration from Wayisso. Comparing these two sets of family trees (Figures 6.3 and 6.4) reveals that where educational attainment clusters, so too does out-migration. Table 6.4 confirms these trends and shows that they

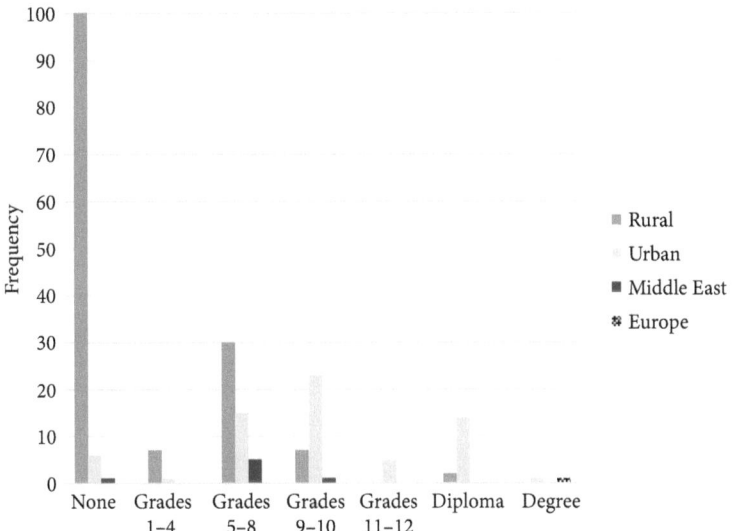

Figure 6.2 Place of current residence by educational attainment, women
Source: Household survey (for women fifteen years and older).

hold across gender as well. The average years of education are higher for men and women in Lineage 1, followed by Lineage 2, then Lineage 3. Rates of mobility follow suit.

One reason for these family differences stems from the fact that some household heads, most notably elders from Lineage 1, embraced and encouraged formal education for their children, while other elders, particularly those in Lineage 3, did not immediately see the value in it. An embrace of education meant making certain economic sacrifices to enable their children to attend formal schooling, as well as challenging social norms when it concerned educating their daughters. Hassan from Lineage 1, for example, was one of the first men in Wayisso to encourage his daughters to go to school and continue their education. His daughter, Ademtuu, is the only person from Wayisso to have left Ethiopia for Europe. Her first international move was for education: a master's degree in the Netherlands. Education was a cause and consequence of her spatial mobility, and the main reason her life came to be so drastically different from other women in her village.

Another one of Hassan's daughters, Basha, explains how her father was different from others in Wayisso. Basha married in her early thirties, after pursuing several different work opportunities: teaching in a government school, opening a shop in the city, starting a humble poultry farm to raise chickens and sell eggs. In 2017, she moved to a town on the outskirts of Addis

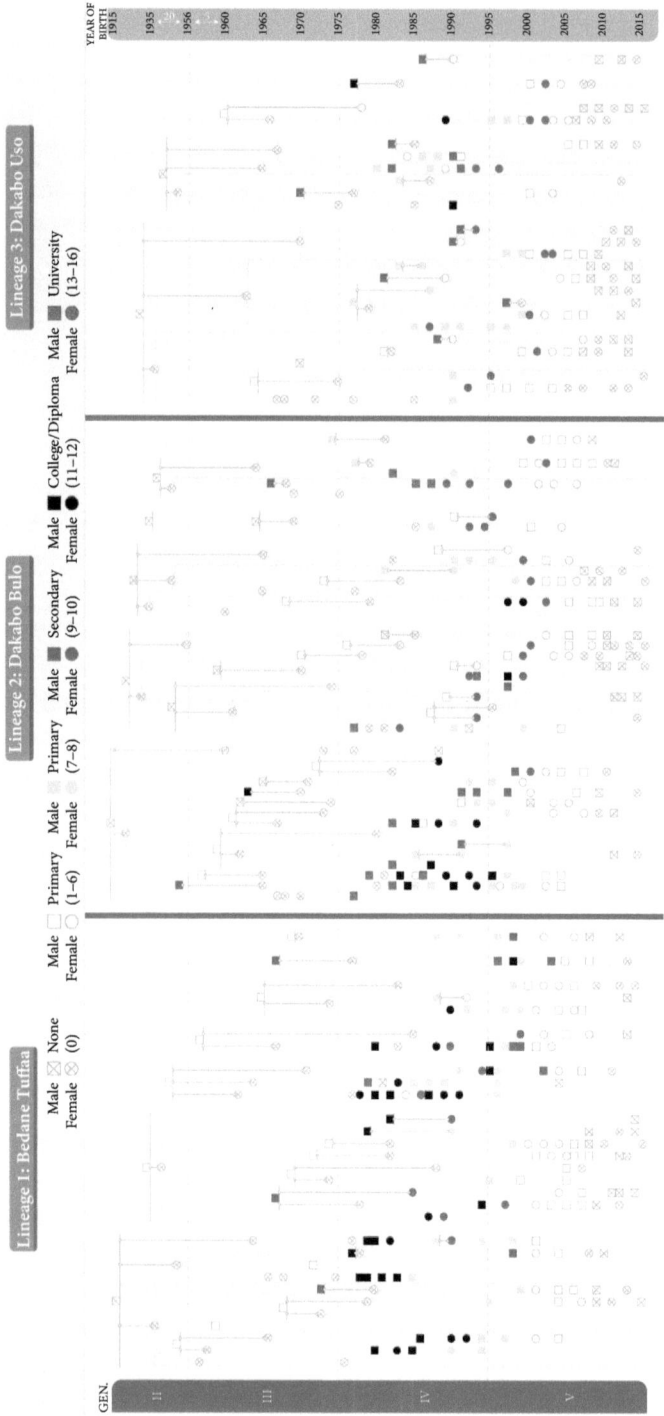

Figure 6.3 Family trees: educational attainment in 2016

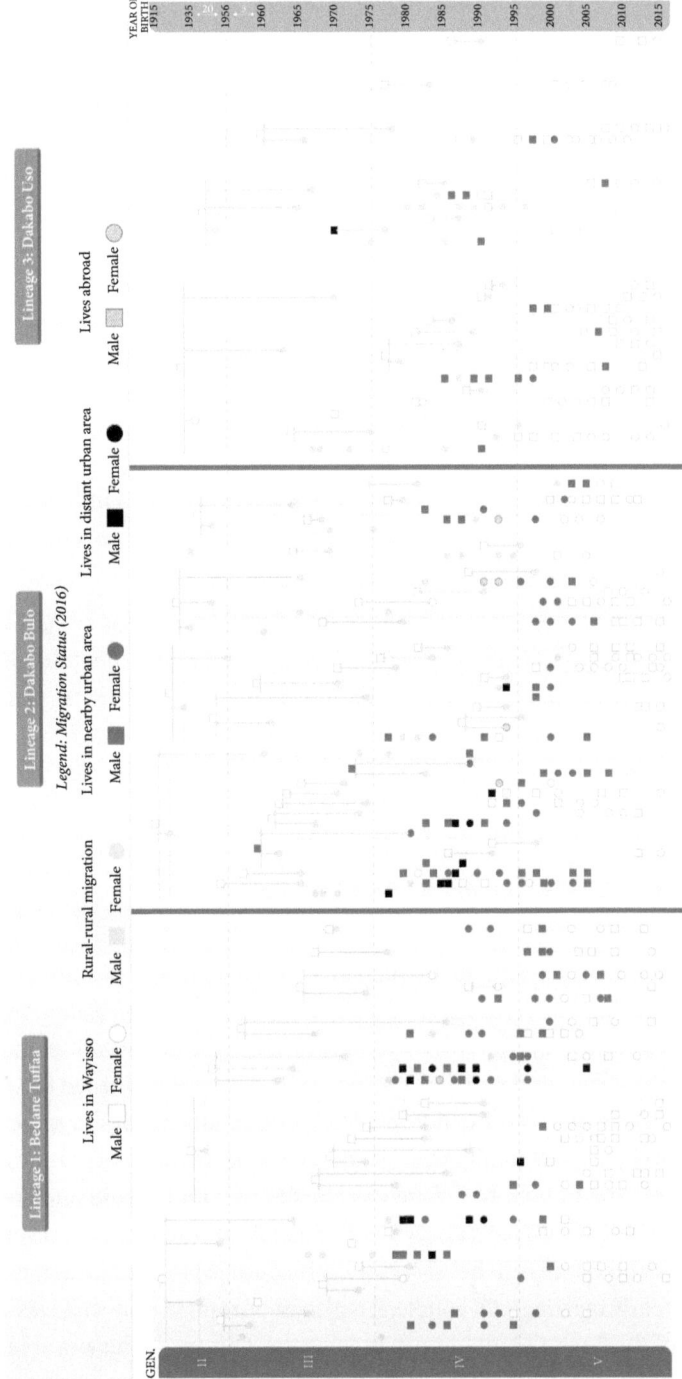

Figure 6.4 Family trees: migration status in 2016

Table 6.4 Education and mobility by family lineage for ages 20–39

	Lineage 1			Lineage 2			Lineage 3		
	F	M	Total	F	M	Total	F	M	Total
Years of education (mean)	6.9	11.2	8.6	4.9	9.7	7.4	3.8	8.6	6.2
Number of places lived (mean)	2.9	3.8	3.2	2.5	2.9	2.7	2.0	2.0	2.0
n	44	32	76	43	45	88	28	28	56

Note: For women and men born or living in Wayisso aged fifteen and over. Source: Household survey 2016.

Ababa to her new husband's home. She reflected on her father's influence on her decisions:

> My father played a great role in my life. He always told us not to marry early or very young. He encouraged us to continue our education and to be successful. No one asked me to marry before I completed grade ten. When I failed grade ten, I was very angry, and so I tried to proceed to the next level. I wasn't thinking about marriage. And my father advised me to continue with my education. He said, "You can't get knowledge after marriage. Just first get your knowledge, be qualified, and after you will find a husband as you want." This was the advice of my father.

I later learned that Hassan's first daughter with his first wife did not go to school. She married in her teenage years and moved to a rural *kebele* several days' journey from Wayisso. After a few years, her husband began working away from the village and married a second wife. He rarely returned to look after her or their two small children. "She became lonely," Basha remembered. "It was only our family who would check on her and her children. There was no one to help her." One day she fell ill with typhoid and soon thereafter passed away. Her tragedy is still difficult for the family to discuss and perhaps another reason her sisters were encouraged to pursue their education over early marriage. Of course, it is also important to note that Hassan had some of the largest landholdings in Wayisso. This meant he was able to afford to send his children, including his girls, to school in town.

This was not the case for other families, who have less land and thus less discretionary income. Yet the constraints on education were not only financial. Many household heads did not see the value of educating their children when primary schools first became available in the area. Caawaa, an elder in Lineage 3, expressed regret for not encouraging his children to go to school. "The reason so many of my children stayed in Wayisso is because I did not give them time for their education. Instead of ordering them to open their exercise book, I ordered them to farm and look after the cattle. So they missed their education. . . . They spent their time farming rather than in school." Many of his sons sat around him, laughing light-heartedly. Caawaa pointed to Wariso, who was in his early twenties. "This one, he is clever. He was a ranked student, very clever, but he became sick and dropped his education for many years. I was expecting great things from him, but then he got sick." Wariso is better now and enrolled in Wayisso's primary school. But he is also already married with three children, and it is harder to attend secondary school in town once you are married.

If young people aspire to go to school and achieve secondary or tertiary levels, they face several obstacles. The first is securing familial support for that decision. Others will have to cover their time away from the fields, cattle, or household tasks. It is not uncommon nowadays to see old men taking cattle down the road from Wayisso to drink from the Awash River, for example. This was largely the responsibility of boys in previous generations. Furthermore, for girls and young women in school, families forego or postpone the traditional *gabara* they could receive upon the marriage of their daughters to another family, a significant financial boon during times of economic hardship. Even when families wholeheartedly support their children's education, however, challenges remain. Not all families can afford the cost of sending their children to secondary school in town. Even if tuition at government schools is free, the costs associated with renting a room, paying for meals, or commuting daily can be insurmountable for poorer families.

***

There is at least one primary school in every *kebele* of the ATJK woreda—though not all schools offer the full eight years of the two cycles of primary school. Secondary schools are only located in the district's towns or cities: Ziway, Adami Tulu, Bulbulla, Oitu, and Jido. Preparatory schools and vocational schools are only available in the larger towns: Bulbulla and Ziway. Private schools also exist, but these are all likewise located in urban places.

Because secondary and higher educational institutions are only available in town, students from Wayisso usually need to move to attend them. Though this movement—what anthropologist Gina Crivello called "migration-for-education"—is common in many developing countries experiencing an educational transition, it is often overlooked in theoretical perspectives about migration. Classical migration theories tend to predict a positive relationship between education and migration, yet theories of migration decision-making describe education as a form of "human capital" that boosts the expected economic returns of the migration project, thus making the cost-benefit equation more likely to swing in the favor of leaving over staying. Although valid, this perspective assumes education is something that is attained in origin areas, shaping the migration decision-making process *before* migration occurs. This neglects the well-documented but little theorized reality that the first reason for rural-urban migration in many developing countries is to go to school.

Consider Adam's migration history, which is intimately tied to his schooling trajectory. Adam was born in Suro, a *kebele* neighboring Wayisso, in 1983. He tended to his family's cattle in his early years and first attended Suro's primary school in 1995, at the age of twelve. By 1998, he finished grade four, the last grade available. To continue to grade five, he moved to Adami Tulu, where he stayed with a relative and spent one year attending the public school. The following year, the government announced that grades five through eight would open at the Suro primary school. Adam returned to Suro for grade six, but after he finished, grades seven and eight were still not available. He then moved back to Adami Tulu to attend grade seven. At school, he met his wife and married when he was in grade eight.

Adam and his wife both passed the regional exam after primary school, but the only options for continuing into secondary school were in Ziway or a smaller town, Bulbulla. In 2003, he moved with his wife to Bulbulla, and they both attended grade nine. His wife dropped out after having their first child. Adam continued through grade ten but failed the qualifying national exam at the end of that school year. They returned to Suro. For one year, they lived with his parents and siblings, and Adam helped with farming while contemplating his next move.

Adam's father, seeing the predicament his son faced, gave Adam one hectare of land that he had acquired in Wayisso in the early 1990s. In 2007, Adam, his wife, and his two children moved to Wayisso. Although grateful to have his own land, he knew one hectare of land was not enough to achieve the kind of life he wanted to provide for his family. He decided to continue studying. He did not have enough money to move or regularly commute to take classes in Ziway, but his friend told him about a distance-learning business management course being offered in Shashemene, a large city some eighty kilometers south. For the next three years, Adam studied business management from a distance. It was not easy. He struggled to balance the demands of his everyday work with the program's requirements for self-learning. "I didn't have the chance to be a regular student. I was plowing the land, sowing the crops, and harvesting." With the money he gleaned from his crops, he financed his trips to Shashemene for occasional in-person tutorials and exams. Despite these difficulties, Adam finished and graduated.

Even with his new business management diploma, however, it has been difficult to find work. He applied for management positions with several companies in the area but never received an invitation to interview. He decided to continue studying. In 2018, in addition to farming, he was enrolled in a new weekend class in accounting at the private Rift Valley University in Ziway.

One cannot help but wonder if all the sacrifices and resources Adam has invested in his business management and accounting diplomas will, in the end, result in the professional work opportunities he desires. Good jobs are hard to find. It is likely that his aspirations will go unrealized and he will remain, like so many others in Wayisso, feeling "stuck."[36]

While Adam creatively balanced a life in the village alongside his educational pursuits, many others feel that their inability to leave Wayisso is a direct cause of their inability to pursue higher levels of education. Bilisuma, for example, was born a decade earlier than Adam, in 1972. He spent his childhood tending his father's cattle herd, which at one point numbered over one hundred. "We didn't depend on crops then. We sustained our lives with the cattle." In 1987, when he was fifteen, Bilisuma began his education at the Woransa school opened by the Derg. At the time, school was almost exclusively attended by boys and men. Although the benefits of education were not yet widely appreciated, Bilisuma's father allowed him to attend. He continued his education through grade six, which he completed in 1994 at the age of twenty-two.

Although Bilisuma wanted to continue into grade seven, his father felt it was time for Bilisuma to "start his life," to marry and to receive some land and cattle of his own. He therefore refused his son's request to continue studying. Although Bilisuma resisted marriage, even to the point where village elders had to be called, in the end, he could not deny his father. That same year, he married a young woman his father chose for him. Yet Bilisuma carried his frustration into his marriage, fighting it even after it began. The marriage did not last long, only three months, and they separated. Bilisuma returned to farming, trying but failing to find a way to continue his education, until his father convinced him to marry again. In 1996, Bilisuma married another woman, and this time he was more open and content with the decision. Looking back, he reflects on his father's priorities at that time in his life: "I think that my father didn't do it to hurt me. It is just lack of awareness and education. That's why he took me out of my education to continue my life with a woman. He was worried that if he died, there would be no one to take the cattle and protect and plow the land. He was thinking about the life of our family."

After three years of marriage, Bilisuma, then in his late twenties and the head of his own household, decided to return to school. He attended the Woransa school for grades seven and eight and passed the regional exam, which opened the possibility to proceed to secondary school. By this time, Bilisuma had four children, and the only available high schools were in neighboring towns. He looked to Bulbulla, a town south of Wayisso, which had one high school. It was too costly to move his entire family, so he rented a small room there to attend grades nine and ten. To cover the rent, he cut down acacia trees from the forest neighboring Wayisso—government land that had little oversight at that time—and sold the wood to bakeries in town. He remembers this as a time of great effort and great difficulty, with little support from his family: "My family didn't want me to learn. My mother especially didn't like it. She always told me to come back [to Wayisso] and stay with my children. She would say, 'Why are you leaving your children and your wife? What is the value of this education?'"

Bilisuma failed the national exam after grade ten, meaning the formal pathway to preparatory school and university were now closed to him, though attending vocational or technical college or receiving a diploma remained as viable alternatives. Bilisuma passed the entrance exam to attend the technical and vocational school in Ziway but could not afford to rent a room there. "I really wanted to study in college, but I didn't have the money to pay for it." He decided to ask for help from the community in Wayisso. He prepared a community gathering, offered tea and coffee, and explained his predicament to his neighbors. The community responded generously, but their contributions were not enough. "Life again was difficult for me," Bilisuma remembers. "I decided to stop thinking about my education. I decided to drop it and put education out of my mind. I came back to my family and started working."

Bilisuma continued farming his land, tending to his cattle, and selling wood to bakeries in Bulbulla. This additional revenue stream came to an end when the Verde Beef company moved into the area and cut down all the trees in the forest neighboring Wayisso. At first, Bilisuma was happy. He rented a truck to transport and sell the wood in Bulbulla, and with the money he earned, he built a new house in Wayisso for his growing family. "But after that, all the trees were gone, and I didn't have any more opportunity." Bilisuma then tried working at Verde Beef, but he found the work very difficult. It exacerbated a pre-existing injury and was not worth the low pay. He then tried working at the neighboring meat-packaging company, but in the heat of the Oromo protests in early 2016, the company shut down. Bilisuma did not continue when they reopened.

Bilisuma now has seven plots of land—less than two hectares—and eight children. When thinking about his children's future, he believes education is critical:

> *When I was a child, the backwardness of my family was a great problem. My family didn't want their children to go to school. But now, I know the benefits of education. . . . As much as I can, I'm going to struggle in my life to educate my children. Because I don't have anything to give them, except education. If they become well educated, they may change their life in the future. I don't have many plots. I don't have money. I can't give to them like my father gave to me. So the only thing I can do is to educate my children.*

Despite his good intentions, Bilisuma's children are likely to struggle like their father to access higher levels of education. Bilisuma's oldest son, for example, is already seventeen years old, yet he is only enrolled in grade six at Wayisso's primary school.

***

Education and migration have reciprocal links. Young people first leave Wayisso to go to school, but the experience of formal schooling and living in town generates new aspirations and expectations for their future that tend to stimulate further movement. Some have no choice but to return to Wayisso—like Bilisuma and Adam, neither of whom could afford to move and keep their families in town. But many others with secondary or higher levels of education strongly resist returning to the village. They choose to stay in Adami Tulu or Ziway or move elsewhere in search of better work opportunities. As the survey data shows, higher levels of education are associated with more moves. Migration for education leads to migration because of education.

"Going to school is part of the socialization process," the educator Margaret Lecompte wrote in 1978. "Schools transmit skills, aspirations, norms, and behavior patterns which assist in the assumption of specific roles." Toward this end, schools employ both a formal and "hidden curriculum." As Lecompte describes, the formal curriculum teaches students subjects like reading, writing, and mathematics. The "hidden curriculum," on the other hand, teaches norms, values, and behaviors deemed important for the socialization process.[37] In Ethiopia, one of the explicit aims of the public education system is to produce "trained manpower for the insatiable demand of the modernization process," as one exhibit at Addis Ababa University put it in 2016.[38] To achieve this aim, the school systems teach young people the knowledge and skills needed to eventually assume new kinds of jobs as factory workers, teachers, nurses, accountants, lawyers, scientists, or entrepreneurs. Yet, long before they begin specialized classes to learn these new vocations, children are taught to aspire to those kinds of jobs, and indirectly, they are taught to devalue agricultural and other rural livelihoods.

The urban bias of modern education is not unique to Ethiopia. As Michael Corbett argues in *Learning to Leave*, the contemporary school curriculums typically stand in opposition to the values, demands, and work of rural lives. Corbett reveals the "irony of schooling" in a small coastal community of Nova Scotia, where rural youth who are successful in their education come to see their communities as places to be left behind. Although halfway around the world, what Corbett describes in Nova Scotia is also occurring in Wayisso, its surrounding towns, and in rural communities across Ethiopia: the formal and hidden curriculum of modern schools deepens discontent with rural lives and teaches children that progress is something to be had in towns, cities, or countries elsewhere.[39]

For one rather blatant example from a social studies textbook for seventh graders,[40] see Figure 6.5. This exercise presents two pictures to the student: "my village home," a decrepit mud-and-stick hut with a thatched roof, and "my town home," a two-story white house, with a balcony and palm trees. The box asks the students to look at homes A and B and describe each picture

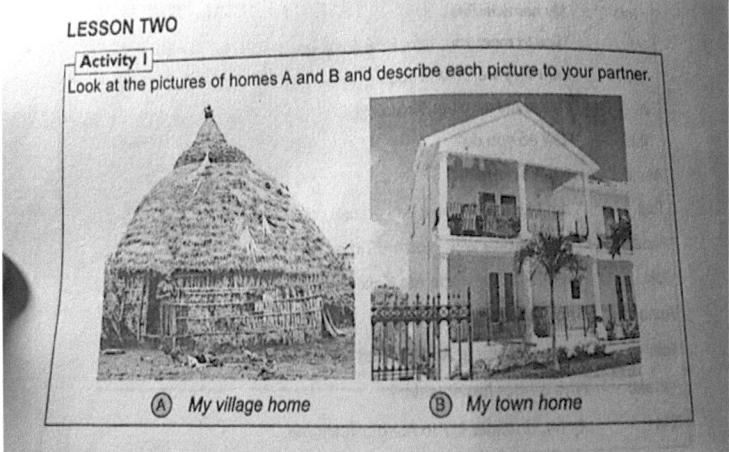

Figure 6.5 A social studies exercise for seventh graders

to their partner. On the following page, the textbook asks students to say which home they prefer and why. The village home was hardly representative of the well-kept traditional homes in Wayisso, and I had yet to see such a fancy townhouse in Ziway. Hardly hidden, this example shows how formal education can shape young people's perceptions of village and town life.[41]

Perhaps more influential than the promise of an urban, professional future that education implicitly or explicitly holds is the actual experience of living in town while studying. "It completely changes young people. Once they live in an urban area, they are completely changed," one father in Wayisso complained. Another mother explained her understanding of why:

> Initially they go to town to go to school. This is why they leave. But then they taste the life of urban places—they get pure water in front of their house, they have light, they access as many services as they like. When they come back to their birthplace, they see how we are spending our lives with the soil. We don't have time to part with this soil. Here life is based on farming. There in the city, they use a bajaj *for transportation. Here, they have to use a cart to go and fetch water from far away. They hate it.*

When young adults from Wayisso shared their life histories, the experience of moving to town for school was one of the most formative experiences of their life. What people shared about their first experience of living in town was remarkably common: the difficulty of living away from one's family; learning to prepare food independently; having to pay for *everything*; easy access to clean water and electricity; being able to study after school rather than herding cattle or doing other chores. Through these experiences, young people learned "to be an urban person," as one young man put it. They "adapted" to urban life.

Ademtuu was the first girl from Wayisso to move to Adami Tulu for school. "Ah, don't remind me," she laughed when I asked her about it. "It was hard, but I miss it. It took us three hours to walk from Wayisso to Tulu," where she lived in a rented room with her brother and cousins:

> *Tulu was a small town then. It had electricity and water—but the water was sourced from one place. You had to take your jerrycans to collect it. Not like Ziway, where everyone had water in their own compound. I remember I used to like to sleep with the light on. When we rented the room, the owner would come by to make sure we turned the light off at night. But I would keep it on, even when I slept. I would wake up if I heard him coming and yell, "I'm studying!" just to keep the light on.*

Access to running water and electricity is an important difference between rural and urban life, and it is one major reason young people prefer to live in town. They are also exposed to new forms of media and technology. Young people can watch movies or football matches in makeshift movie theaters. More and more urban youth have a smartphone and a Facebook profile, while cell phone reception remains patchy and unreliable in Wayisso.

Once they migrate to towns and cities, young people become even more connected to opportunities elsewhere. From the perspective of Wayisso, Ziway is like the "capital city," as one man described it. But once in Ziway, other urban centers further afield enter people's aspirational horizons. In our study of migration aspirations among Ethiopian youth, Sonja Fransen and I found an interesting trend in aspired futures: rural youth more often imagined moving to small towns or cities within their district, whereas urban youth looked to larger urban areas or the capital city. This hierarchy in the mental maps of young people mirrors actual internal migration patterns, where young people often go from rural areas to neighboring towns for education before making longer-distance moves to larger urban centers— what the migration literature refers to as "step-wise migration."[42] A rise in stepwise migration reflects rising opportunities for education and paid employment and is different in nature than the international migration trends described in the previous chapter—where young women unable to pursue the stepwise migration of their more privileged peers faced a choice between international labor migration or marriage.

The Aspiration-Opportunity Gap

Young and old alike believe that education enables young people to take charge of their futures, to be "a decision-maker" as one older mother put it. She explains, "When I was young, women did not go to school.... That is why I agreed to marry the person of my father's choosing. I was uneducated. I didn't have any other opportunity. Rather than losing my family, I agreed to live with someone who I didn't know. If I were educated, I would have known what to do with my future." "You would have chosen something else?" I asked her. "Yes. I would have made decisions. If I had studied, I would have been a decision-maker." Because of the high regard this mother holds for education, she treats her children differently: "Today, our children are studying.... They know what they are going to do. And we are not going to force them into something else or to interrupt their lives. That is the great difference between now and then."

This mother's sentiments echoed those of Yomen, which I shared at the beginning of this chapter, particularly her reflections on how her education distinguished her life from her sisters':

> *There is a big difference in my life compared to my older sisters.... I went to school. I know something. I have the right and I have the opportunity to look at which [way] is good and which one is bad, and I want to choose the way that I like. But they didn't do like that. They simply went the way of their family. But at my age, I am going to decide for myself. This is the difference.*

What Yomen or other women are able to decide for their futures depends, of course, on the actual opportunities available to them, as the last chapter illustrated in relation to women who migrate to the Middle East, and as Chapter 9 will show in relation to Yomen's future. But for all students, the degree to which their formal schooling prepares them for work in the real world remains a significant question. The quality of education in many government schools is low. Schools face serious resource constraints, and

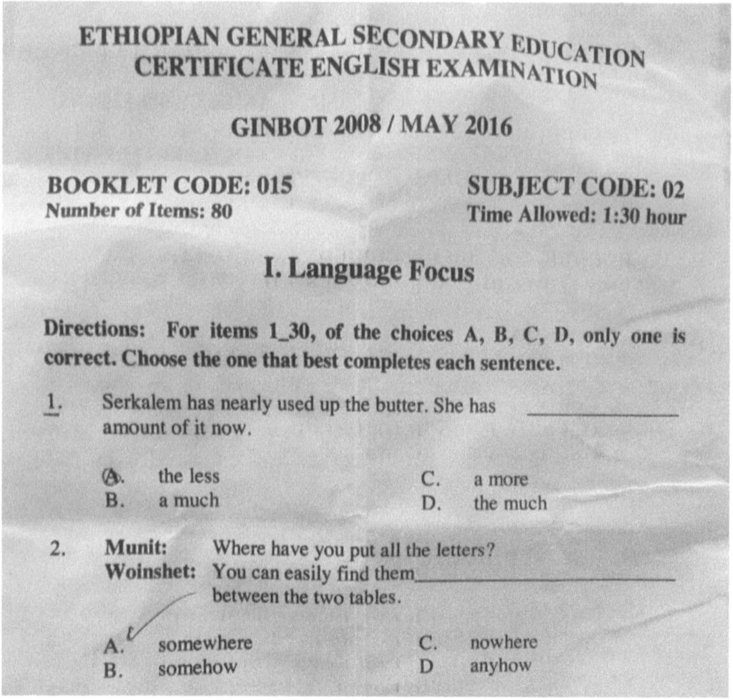

ETHIOPIAN GENERAL SECONDARY EDUCATION
CERTIFICATE ENGLISH EXAMINATION

GINBOT 2008 / MAY 2016

BOOKLET CODE: 015 — SUBJECT CODE: 02
Number of Items: 80 — Time Allowed: 1:30 hour

I. Language Focus

Directions: For items 1_30, of the choices A, B, C, D, only one is correct. Choose the one that best completes each sentence.

1. Serkalem has nearly used up the butter. She has ________ amount of it now.

   A. the less — C. a more
   B. a much — D. the much

2. **Munit:** Where have you put all the letters?
   Woinshet: You can easily find them________ between the two tables.

   A. somewhere — C. nowhere
   B. somehow — D anyhow

Figure 6.6 An English question

both students and teachers struggle to navigate the changing languages of instruction.[43] Government secondary schools often rely on what is commonly referred to as "plasma instruction"—named after the plasma display panels that televise lessons. The aim is to offer quality and equitable education for all children, and the in-class teacher supplements the lessons with an introduction and a summary at the end of the videos. But as one student complained, teachers and students often do not understand what the instructors on the television are saying. One young man told me he enjoyed going to school and "just watching television" but later failed his exam and regretted that he had not learned much.

One afternoon, a young woman sat down with me to evaluate her answers to the English section of the national exam. Her confidence in my English ability began to wane as I stared at the first question and read it several times over. "What is the correct response?" she asked impatiently. "I don't think there is one," I replied. Nevertheless, I assured her that her response, A, was most likely the best one (Figure 6.6).

Because of the low quality of education, young people who invest in education to obtain professional work often fail to develop the skills and capacities required for those professional positions. This "skills gap" is a challenge across Ethiopia, yet the ramifications go beyond skills. There are also significant consequences for young people whose aspirations and expectations for their future far exceed the actual opportunities before them. In one survey of young Ethiopians' imagined futures, youth aspired to fourteen years of education on average (a university-level degree) and professional forms of work.[44] Yet, the majority of the same youth surveyed, between the ages of seventeen and nineteen, had not made it past primary levels. For a country where over three-quarters of the population still live in rural areas, many subsisting as smallholder farmers, the overwhelmingly professional aspirations captured by that study are striking. There is clearly a disjuncture between young people's stated aspirations for the future and what many of them will realistically be able to achieve. Ethiopia's school system is not solely responsible for this aspiration-opportunity gap,[45] but it certainly contributes to widening it.

This aspiration-opportunity gap has important, tangible consequences. In one ethnographic study in Jimma, a large town about a seven-hour drive west of Wayisso, anthropologist Daniel Mains examines the struggles of young men who complete their schooling but are unable to find government positions or other professional work. These young men often prefer unemployment over available but socially undesirable work, and Mains explores the creative strategies they use to sustain their lives and dignity as they wait for the good jobs that might never come.[46] This helps explain the counterintuitive reality that unemployment rates are higher for educated Ethiopians. In 2013, unemployment was twice as common among individuals with university or graduate degrees compared to the national average, and almost three times as common for those with secondary-level schooling.[47] The simple story that there are not enough jobs for Ethiopia's young people is slightly misleading. There are jobs, just not enough jobs that match the aspirations of young people with schooling.

It was not uncommon to meet young people from Wayisso who were in similar situations to the young men Mains describes. Many were unemployed or underemployed, but they held onto aspirations for further schooling, professional work, or dreams of starting their own business. Work is available—for example, it is easy to get a job picking or packaging roses in Sher's greenhouses—but no individual from Wayisso with secondary schooling or higher levels of education would consider working there. When I asked Yomen whether she had considered working in Sher's greenhouses after she received news that she had failed the national exam, she looked at me like I was crazy. "No," she explained in no uncertain terms. "It's too tough. It's hot in the greenhouse. It's hard work and only for 800 birr.... It's not worth it."

***

For most of human history, children learned the knowledge and skills they needed to support their livelihoods "informally." Education was embedded within social systems, taught within families and communities, and passed down over generations. Today, children continue to learn informally from their families and communities, environments, and everyday experiences. However, with the rapid expansion of public schooling across the country, young people are introduced to a new educational system, organized by the state and disembedded from the community. This "formal" education takes place in classrooms and is taught by professional teachers trained in a standardized curriculum that aims to prepare pupils to be successful citizens of industrialized nation-states.

In Wayisso, there is a clear disjuncture between the values, skills, attitudes, and knowledge being taught in formal school and those required to advance rural livelihoods. As rural sociologist Ben White has argued, modern schooling "teaches young people not to want to be farmers."[48] In Wayisso, knowledge related to cultivation and livestock is transmitted through informal channels, most often the family, while formal education is exclusively a pathway *out* of agriculture and into something else. Many young people will not achieve the educational levels they wish or the alternative kinds of work they desire, and agriculture will remain an important part of their lives. Yet, the social devaluation of agricultural work means young people are increasingly dissatisfied with rural lives. There is both a structural "deskilling" of rural youth,[49] who receive an education irrelevant to rural lives, and an aspirational reorientation toward professional, urban futures, even though many will struggle to secure the kind of urban work they desire.

Changing aspirations matter. They shape how individuals come to see and evaluate their lives, and they influence how Ethiopians perceive and contribute to their society's development. More specifically, the aspirations people hold for their futures orient how they invest their limited resources. Bilisuma, for example, did not spend the money he earned from selling wood on agricultural inputs, more land, or additional livestock—all things that might have improved his economic prospects in Wayisso. He spent it on his education. He believed investing in education would get him better work and enable him to move to town. Bilisuma, Adam, and Yomen all share a vision of a good life that is impossible to achieve in Wayisso. They want to be educated. They want good, salaried work or to own their own business. They want to live in Ziway.

If we take these aspirations seriously, it is easier to see why development efforts to increase the education levels and incomes of rural households are more likely to facilitate rural out-migration than to stop it. Providing higher levels of education to rural areas may alleviate the initial need to move to town, but more likely, it will simply delay rather than reverse this general urbanward shift in migration aspirations and behavior. This is because it is not just the location of schooling that shapes migration trajectories; it is also the content of formal schooling—its formal and hidden curriculum—that orients young people's aspirations toward lives that are impossible to achieve in rural places.

This disjuncture between the aspirations cultivated by formal education and the realities of rural life in Wayisso directly contributes to the aspiration-opportunity gap that lies at the heart of this book's argument. Development, rather than simply alleviating the factors that "push" people out of rural areas, cultivates a desire for new kinds of lives—lives centered around education, professional work, and urban amenities. In essence, the very process of development, of which expanding access to education is a key component, generates new aspirations that often can only be met through leaving rural areas behind. Some will leave for towns and cities in Ethiopia; a smaller but notable number will cross international borders. Still others will remain in Wayisso, feeling stuck between the kinds of lives to which they aspire and the real opportunities available to them.

7
Foreign Investment

In 1902, Herr Götz left his native Germany to seek adventure and fortune in Ethiopia. Travelers' notes describe him as an eccentric man, with flaming red hair and beard, blue eyes, and a philosophical bent. He worked for a few years as a pioneer trader, and in 1910, he acquired a fifty-year lease on an eight-square-kilometer property southwest of Lake Ziway,[1] where he established an ostrich farm. On top of its highest hill, Götz built a large home, described by visiting travelers as "picturesque like a medieval castle," a "queer place, a bachelor hall on a hilltop with a magnificent view in all directions," and a "square, squat, impregnable roost."[2] This was the beginning of the *woreda*'s first town, Adami Tulu, which translates to "hill with fort."

Götz's hired help—and thus, Adami Tulu's first residents—were mostly Gurage peoples, a semitic-speaking ethnic group from a more mountainous and population-dense region roughly a hundred kilometers west. The local Arsi Oromo pastoralists had no interest in working for Götz or performing any other form of wage labor at that time. By 1927, Götz and his workers managed a farm with fifty ostriches and three hundred cattle, fenced in by six miles of candelabra cactus. His son Herr Zahn and a few other Germans moved to Ethiopia to work with him. They built a modern windmill by the Awash River and traveled from place to place in a Ford truck.

As Götz's enterprise prospered, relations with the local pastoralists soured. We know little about the exact grievances that led to confrontations, but conflicts between the Arsi Oromo and the Germans increased. In one instance,[3] tensions reached such heights that an investigation committee, including members from European legations, arrived from Addis Ababa. One of the Germans—"the most violent German" according to one traveler's notes—was taken to Addis Ababa for trial and eventually expelled from the country.

Götz chose to remain in Ethiopia, yet conflicts with the local pastoralists continued. In 1936, in the midst of the Italian invasion of Ethiopia, the Arsi Oromo seized the interregnum to attack, sack, and burn Götz's house. He fled, retreating to an island on Lake Ziway. The Italians established an administrative center in Adami Tulu, taking over what remained of his house. When Götz returned to the mainland, the Italians did not receive him kindly, nor did they return his house to him. They "obliged him to live in a shack below," as the naturalist David Buxton wrote in his *Travels in Ethiopia*. Buxton, who was in Ethiopia to study locusts, visited Götz in 1943, just two years after the Italians had left. He learned that, after their departure, "disorder prevailed once more. The Arussi were again on the warpath, looting and destroying. This was the last straw; Goetz withdrew to the island for good.—Hermit and philosopher by nature, he was content to life out his life there."[4] Thus, the first chapter of foreign investment in this district of Ethiopia came to a dramatic close.

***

Foreign investment is often described as a catalyst for economic development. It takes two main forms: indirect investments, where foreign investors buy stakes in domestic companies that trade on their respective stock exchanges, and direct investments, where foreign investors gain extensive or full ownership over domestic companies and assets and play an active role in their management and business trajectory. The benefits of foreign direct investment (FDI) are widely touted: FDI provides the influx of capital needed to begin new enterprises that otherwise would struggle to get off the ground, it facilitates the transfer of technology as foreign companies import modern machines, it contributes to human capital development as new companies employ and train employees, it enhances international trade integration, and the profits generated by foreign investment contribute to corporate tax revenues in the host country.[5]

FDI's benefits for local economic development, however, are neither automatic nor evenly spread. Concerns include the repatriation of profits out of host countries to foreign bank accounts; harmful environmental impacts, particularly with extractive and heavy industries; and, as one report by the Organisation for Economic Cooperation and Development (OECD) put it, a lack of "positive linkages" with local communities and "social disruptions of accelerated commercialization in less developed countries."[6] The domestic policies of host country governments are often blamed for these unfavorable outcomes, but foreign investors share equal if not greater blame, particularly when their business strategies focus on maximizing profits over environmental sustainability or contributing to the well-being of the new communities in which they operate.

An increasingly explicit goal of FDI is to reduce migration from migrant-sending countries by stimulating local job creation. As one United Nations (UN) report espousing the benefits of foreign direct investment, trade, and aid asserted in 1996, "A better way to manage economic migration is to generate rapid economic growth in the countries of origin. Broad-based and rapid development will induce potential poverty migrants to stay at home of their own free choice rather than migrate under compulsion."[7] The underlying assumption is that FDI can act as a substitute for migration; as opportunities for employment increase in one's home country, fewer people will need to leave. However, a growing body of research has uncovered the opposite effect: FDI is associated with greater net emigration from countries that receive it.[8] One study examining the links between FDI and migration in the decade following the 1996 UN report found that a 1 million dollar increase in FDI between one OECD country and another increases immigration by about sixty migrants. When the same amount is invested in a non-OECD country, immigration increases by about one thousand.[9]

***

FDI has a rocky history in Ethiopia, and in the Adami Tulu and Jido Kombolcha (ATJK) *woreda* specifically, as Götz's story attests. Haile Selassie embraced foreign investment as an important strategy for building a modern imperial state. During the last decades of his reign, Wayisso elders recalled another German who arrived after Götz and established a farm, this time focused on crop production. Farm workers arrived from the more populous highland regions to the west and south, this time largely the Hadiya and Wolayita regions. The town of Adami Tulu grew once again, and by 1967, there were 1,266 official residents.

When the Derg nationalized land and industry in the 1970s, most foreign investors across the country were either kicked out or fled voluntarily. Conscription ensured a steady labor supply to the newly state-owned farms and factories, and some of the first long-distance movements from Wayisso occurred during this period as a few men left to work on distant government farms while others were sent to fight the Derg's territorial battles with

Eritrea. After several years, facing political instability and economic stagnation, the Derg reconsidered its relationship to outside investors. In 1983, it issued a Joint Venture Proclamation, which attempted to incentivize foreign investment through tax and duty relief, tariff protections, and the ability to repatriate profits.[10] Foreign businesses, however, were not convinced. In 1989, the government revised the proclamation to allow majority foreign ownership in some sectors, but it was too little, too late. Opposition forces were making headway against the declining regime, and by 1991, the socialist government fell.

The Ethiopian People's Revolutionary Democratic Front gradually liberalized trade, privatized many industries, and made other structural adjustments to enhance the participation of private actors in the development process, including foreign investors. As a result, FDI began to return to Ethiopia in the late 1990s. Net inflows grew from just 170,000 USD in 1992 to 350 million USD in 2002 and peaked at over 4 billion USD in 2016, over 5 percent of the country's gross domestic product at that time. FDI fluctuated in the years that followed. Political unrest associated with the Oromo protests and then the Tigray War once again discouraged investment. In 2020, FDI stood at 2.4 billion USD.[11]

The ATJK *woreda* is strategically located along a main road that leads northward to the country's capital and commercial airport and southward to Kenya. In the late 2000s, three major foreign-owned companies established themselves in the district: Verde Beef, a cattle processing company immediately adjacent to Wayisso; Sher Ethiopia, a cut flower farm that now operates the largest rose farm in the world with greenhouses spanning Ziway and Adami Tulu; and Castell winery, the first privately own winery in Ethiopia, managed by the French Castell Group (see Figure 0.2 in the introduction). My research focused on the first two companies: Verde Beef because of its proximity to Wayisso and Sher because of its scale. I had many questions about how these foreign companies and new opportunities for wage-based work would affect migration patterns and development outcomes in the area. In particular, would the expansion of local job opportunities, at both Verde Beef and Sher Ethiopia, change how people thought about staying or leaving? I soon discovered that these new kinds of jobs would not act as a substitute for internal or international migration. Workers expressed frustration that their wages were only enough to help meet the needs of subsistence, not their need for change.

Verde Beef

Verde Beef Processing PLC is a cattle feedlot and processing company that occupies a 1,300-hectare farm immediately adjacent to Wayisso. Established in 2014, it quickly became the largest feedlot and beef processing business in Ethiopia, partly because there is so little competition. In 2016, it processed five thousand cattle and employed four hundred people. The business model is relatively straightforward: the company purchases one-year-old calves, fattens them to meet export standards within three to six months, and then processes them for export to the Middle East, their primary market.

Verde Beef's vision, according to their website, is to "help catalyze an industrial and agricultural revolution in Ethiopia, building upon recent infrastructure development and a decade of double-digit growth in the country's GDP and create one billion dollars of total value in our companies by 2025 for the benefit of Ethiopia and our investors."[12] The company aims to become the largest cattle feedlot operation in northern Africa, with a targeted capacity to feed, process, and export more than 130,000 carcasses per year. They promise a targeted investor return in excess of 30 percent.

Verde Beef is a project of the American company Verdant Frontiers, which recruits investors for start-up companies in Ethiopia. Verdant Frontiers chose Ethiopia because of its "progressive pro-business government," its strategic location for Middle Eastern and European markets, lack of competition, the "compelling need for jobs and economic development to alleviate poverty," and "unlimited resources in affordable labor."[13] In 2015, the private equity firm 8 Miles, which focuses exclusively on making investments in African businesses, acquired 29 percent ownership. The following year, Verde Beef received expansion financing through a loan guarantee program provided by the United States Agency for International Development (USAID).

USAID provided financing to Verde Beef, because the company was seen as a praiseworthy example of private sector development with positive social impact. The business provides incomes to the families that sell their cattle to the company; they employ hundreds of (mostly) men who might otherwise be underemployed or unemployed; and they have made philanthropic contributions to neighboring communities, like the freshwater well they built in Wayisso. A video on the USAID website features two community elders expressing their thanks to the company: "Verde Beef provided water for our community, and jobs and land for our children. They are really helping us. Verde Beef gave cattle to 550 women in our community, fattened the cattle, and let the women sell the cattle for profit, to lift these women out of poverty."[14]

On paper, this particular case of FDI looks like a win-win: it is helping the local community while also providing a large return to its investors. But what USAID's promotional video does not feature are the grievances of the surrounding communities, particularly Wayisso. Verde Beef often hired community elders as mediators to address the concerns of neighboring villages, but many in Wayisso felt the company used these elders to communicate their own concerns (e.g., telling people not to graze their cattle on Verde Beef's land) while refusing to address the issues that elders raised on behalf of the Wayisso community. With aims to return over a 30 percent profit for their investors, pressures to scale the business quickly were intense. Verde Beef's managers had little freedom to significantly adjust business strategies in light of the concerns of a relatively small neighboring community.

Some concerns from the community were difficult to address, like the distasteful stench that wafts over Wayisso when the winds blow westward. Others were impossible to reverse, like when Verde Beef cut down all of the trees that had previously forested the land in one fell swoop to plant maize for cattle feed. But the most contested issue of all was the company's decision to build an electric fence around the perimeter of its property (Figure 7.1). In the final stage of this enclosure, the fence barred the main pathway from Wayisso to the central road. This is the primary way families in Wayisso and more distant *kebeles* travel to the Awash River with their cattle or access transportation to neighboring towns. In response, Verde Beef suggested the community should create new pathways to the Awash River that go around its property.

Verde Beef could offer no alternative to a more fundamental problem created by this enclosure for Wayisso families: they can no longer use these fields as grazing pasture for their cattle. It is difficult to overstate how upset local families were about this "development." These 1,300 hectares of previously forested government land had served as collective grazing lands for decades, precisely because no one was allowed to farm it. During the Derg, as households in Wayisso began to plow the surrounding land while maintaining large herds, locals would release their cattle to graze surreptitiously at night on the neighboring government property. As Wayisso residents remember it, there was a general understanding, and guards would mostly turn a blind eye. This land continued to act as default grazing land through the 1990s and 2000s until Verde Beef received a lease on the land in 2014,

Figure 7.1 Day laborers constructing Verde Beef's electric fence: June 2016

at which point the company acted quickly to secure the borders of its new property. It erected an electric fence in the fall of 2016 and began employing locals, including several older men from Wayisso, as guards. They monitor the periphery of the property, attired in military uniforms, earning a meager income while their sons search in vain for new ways to keep their cattle alive.

Cattle make important contributions to the well-being of rural households. They provide milk and, on special occasions, meat. Many households rent their oxen to other households during the plowing season for additional income. Families will sell cattle if they encounter a period of economic hardship, if they need funds to make an investment, or to celebrate a marriage. If a family has a lot of cattle, regardless of their income, they are described by the community as wealthy.

This gives a new perspective on the local benefits of Verde Beef's business model, particularly the part where it buys young cattle from local farmers. An interview with Bruce Hamilton, the director of Verde Beef, framed the benefits of buying calves from local farmers in these terms: "we [have] created demand for young calves, allowing farmers to generate revenue earlier on their cattle investment. This also facilitates de-stocking which is vital to improving range land quality and the reproductive potential of the herds. As such, there is significant spill over effects from our investment that benefit the local community."[15] While the company is succeeding in "de-stocking" the neighboring communities, the benefits are not spilling over. With diminished grazing lands, Wayisso households are left with little option other than to sell their young cattle to Verde Beef or others for a one-time payment—if Verde Beef will even buy from them. Wayisso farmers said Verde Beef often bought better breeds from Borana, a region much further south. Rural households might have benefited from the opportunity to sell cattle to a regular buyer, but now, they can no longer maintain a regular supply.

Box 7.1 provides excerpts from my fieldnotes detailing a community gathering called by the regional government to manage tensions between the Wayisso community and Verde Beef over the fence enclosure.

Box 7.1 Verde Beef and the community road: Fieldnotes (edited for clarity), April 8, 2016

Kedir and I stumbled upon a gathering called by the regional government to hear the community's thoughts about Verde Beef closing the road that runs through the property the government gave them (Figure 7.2). The road is a central pathway for not only Wayisso but many *kebeles* (Suro, Andolla) that use it to take their cattle to the Awash River. The road is a major and decades-, perhaps centuries-worn transit way that to the west leads all the way to the Sudan, and to the east, all the way to Somalia. The government workers informed the community that Verde Beef does not want to leave the path open, because they would have to build a long fence on either side—an electric fence—and this would cost them 2 billion birr, they said.

Figure 7.2 A meeting with government officials in Wayisso

This is what I managed to write down about the conversation that ensued between the community and the government workers:

Continued

Continued

Man 1: This path was here long before even Haile Selassie. We have had this land for years. Why is the government now going to give it away? Everyone has seen what has happened. The government gave them this land, and they destroyed all the trees, and then we had a drought.

Man 2: Yes, we benefit from the water they created for us. [Verde Beef built a well in Wayisso.] But this is truly an imposition. Where will the cattle go? ... Verde Beef is destroying us. Why? Why not leave it? He [Verde Beef] has another road. Why not leave this one for us? The government is supposed to protect us. The government says they are building the way. But you are closing this one. Why? There were many organizations before Verde Beef that were here and left the road to us. Why does this one need to take it? We gave him fertile land, but he is not content.... Before we didn't know. But now we know. Please, I ask the government to keep it open for us.

Woman 1: They gave us water. We are grateful for this. But there are problems. Many of our cattle have died and the government has not said anything about it. They cut down all the trees and now we do not have wood for fire. Now I collect husks for the fire. We are very worried. He has cut down all the trees. Everyone knows. There was rain before. Then he came and this year we don't have any rain. We don't need it, this company. It's not helping us.

Man 3: We are told that if we cut down one tree, we have to pay a penalty of 500 birr. But he is an investor, who cut down ALL of the trees, and how much did he pay? I see what the government does for me. We are poor, and so we are nothing. They are rich, and they are respected. The government only looks after this one. If I cut trees, you punish me.

Government representative: The government thinks for the investors. The dollar is increasing, investors pay in dollars, and we need this currency. Now we are not representatives of anything. What the people say here, I accept.... Maybe Verde Beef sent this one, the farenji [he points to me], to see what we are saying.... He submitted to our office a request for 800 hectares to plow. Before he said it was 750. Now he said 800. He didn't say he would cut the trees. When we gave the ground for plowing, we thought he would keep the trees. He said he would plow. He didn't say he would cut the trees.

Man 4: When the investor came, he promised many things. To create jobs for us. To bring water and electricity. To build a school. He said many things about how it will benefit the kebele. But did he do it? Who is following that? This path has been here for so long, and it is used by so many people. If you block the way, what do you think will happen? If we blocked the main highway from Addis Ababa to Kenya, how would you feel? It is the same for us.

Man 5: Before, he promised to give work to the jobless. The managers, he calls for workers, but when we go, they don't need us. The supervision, all easy work and good work is taken by Amhara people. We are just guards. The youth have no work. Ask him, all the workers there come from other places.

Woman 2: I come from very far away. If this road closes, what am I to do? The sun is too strong, and we walk on foot. We don't have another way to go. We need a way we can go by foot.

Government representative: In the Oromo culture, we do not hate other people. We can learn from the investors. In one and a half or two years, the cattle they raise are so fat and big, they are ready for slaughter. Even here in Ethiopia, their cows after just one year are ready to send to Europe. For a local farmer it takes at least four years. How can we change our experience? How can we learn from him, and how can he learn from us? You can learn good things for yourself.

The meeting closed with prayers, led by two of the Muslim elders from Wayisso. They quickly said some prayers, and people mumbled Amen repetitively in reply. I did not follow everything, but it ended with: "God has sent an agreement for us. If the investor does good things for us, he stays. If not, remove him for us!" Everyone cheered.

It seemed to me that the government representatives were trying to show their support to the local people. One of them, who approached me afterwards, eager to know if I was there on behalf of Verde Beef, seemed relieved and less interested when I told him I was a sociologist. He told me the investors bring new technology. It takes the people here four years to fatten cattle; it takes them only two, he repeated. They bring different breeds, strong breeds from Borana. They bring new technology. But, he continued, "the land is ancient. And there is a problem with the natural resources." This was, he said, a "social mismatch."

"We are praying to God," Caawaa, an elder in Wayisso, told me one summer afternoon. "We are calling on God to remove him, to fire him from this place." He was referring to a Dutch man named Arnold, Verde Beef's manager who had overseen the company's everyday functioning for several years. "A man who wants to be a good neighbor should have a good relationship with his neighbors," Caawaa said. "He has not had a good relationship with [us].... He is closing the mouths of our cattle."

I asked Caawaa how much land he would need to maintain four or five cattle, and he estimated about five plots—one and a quarter hectare. I then asked what the Wayisso community would do if the government decided to give Verde Beef's land to them. His response surprised me. "If the government gave the land to the people, we would kill each other to plow it. We would not use it as grazing land." Caawaa's response was revealing. Verde Beef has accelerated the decline of cattle husbandry in the area through its acquisition and fencing of this land, but they are not the only reason for this decline. How households relate to land has fundamentally changed as well. Although hyperbolic, Caawaa's statement that "we would kill each other to plow it" reveals, relative to previous generations, a significant shift in the social imaginary. Land is now the property of households, an object of competition rather than cooperation, and its value lies in the income it can generate. Today, farming a relatively small portion of land brings a greater income than trying to sustain cattle upon it.

Just a few days after talking to Caawaa, a farmer from Wayisso checked in to the hospital in Ziway. He was struggling with "tension," his daughter told me. "He is anxious about his cattle." He still has a dozen or so, but he is farming all his land. "Since Verde Beef built the fence," his daughter explained, "the cattle have nowhere to graze." His daughter met him at the hospital and gave him some advice: "Sell your cattle. Just keep three or so. And with that money, buy a place in town that you can rent to others." He said it was a good idea, but it was new for him. "I don't know about these things," he said. "I will help you," she answered.

***

In June 2016, I met a research team from a company called 8 Miles conducting surveys and focus groups in Wayisso. The group of consultants were international and interdisciplinary: an old English botanist, a young Canadian anthropologist, a Swiss public health specialist, and a tough Egyptian team lead with expertise in impact assessments. These consultants were tasked with collecting baseline data on incomes, nutrition, and other aspects of life in Wayisso to be able to assess what impact Verde Beef's rapid expansion would have on neighboring communities in the future. One of the consultants explained that impact assessments like these are required to show that the company and its impact on the local community is compliant with international regulations. Such evidence is often a prerequisite to receive funding from major international funding agencies.

I met the team for dinner at a hotel in Ziway to learn more about their work and to raise some of the concerns I had heard from the Wayisso community, about the stench, the road closure, and the lack of grazing lands, and from the workers at Verde Beef, regarding the low pay, the difficult working conditions, and the perception that the better-paying administrative or managerial positions were all given to professionals from other regions. The team nodded along, acknowledging the challenges, and then the Canadian anthropologist quipped, "Ah, but the misery of being exploited by capitalists is nothing compared to the misery of not being exploited at all." He was quoting a line from *Economic Philosophy*, a book written in 1962 by the British economist Joan Robinson. Though his comment was cloaked in jest, the basic argument is a powerful one: some work is better than no work, even if wages are low and conditions are exploitative.

Many men from Wayisso had tried working at Verde Beef. One man told me he earned 660 birr every two weeks—more than workers make in Sher's greenhouses. He worked five and half days per week. He began working the land, but after an injury, he was moved to waste disposal. When I asked what he thought about the company, he had mixed feelings. The company brought work opportunities, but the work is difficult. He was grateful they built a well for the community, but he struggles to sustain his cattle now that they no longer have grazing pastures. Overall, he felt "the developers could be a good thing, if they paid people well. But the work is difficult, and the pay is not enough." When I visited him again two years later, he was no longer working there.

Workers who came from *kebeles* and *woredas* further away told a similar story. They work for a time and then move on when they grow tired or hear about better-paid work elsewhere. I spoke with one young man who came from a small village from a more remote part of the *woreda*. He was paid 50 birr per day to help construct the slaughterhouse next to Verde Beef. "The people talk like, oh it is the *farenjis*,[16] the work must be nice," he explained. "But when you go there, the work is very difficult and the pay was very little." He stayed only a few weeks and then returned to subsistence farming in his village. These are not unusual stories. I met many young men in Wayisso and elsewhere who choose to remain formally unemployed—or technically "underemployed" if they have fields to farm—rather than work at Verde Beef, Sher Ethiopia, or other foreign companies. Upending the words of Joan Robinson, they preferred the misery of unemployment to the misery of being exploited by capitalists.

Sher Ethiopia

Despite initially appearing to be a promising example of the benefits of private sector development, Verde Beef was not significantly improving the lives of Wayisso households, nor did it offer desirable or sustainable employment opportunities to the local community. Wayisso's poorest would pick up work when their situation was particularly difficult, and their situations were becoming more dire as fewer households could maintain livestock to supplement farming incomes. But this was not the kind of work that could act as a substitute for migration. This was the kind of work that people took when they fell into a particularly hard place. No one would choose to stay in Wayisso to work at Verde Beef. Anyone with the means to leave would go.

Sher Ethiopia PLC is the Ethiopian subsidiary of the Dutch-owned flower company Afriflora Sher. It . . . is a much larger and more established company than Verde Beef, and it has made significant investments in the local community. It built the best hospital in the *woreda* and established a well-respected school with free tuition for the children of its employees. The business is also very successful; it is the biggest producer of Fairtrade roses in the world, exporting three to four million roses to the Netherlands daily.[17] As one celebratory article from 2018 reposted on Afriflora Sher's website notes, "When the business started in the quiet region of Ziway in 2005, nothing else was there—there was no infrastructure, development, or obvious future for the small rose company or the area it was located in. However, just two years later, the social enterprise revolutionized the region, industry, and community." This statement reveals much about how foreign investors see sites for development: as blank slates. In the minds of foreign investors looking at Ziway, *nothing else was there.*

By 2016, Sher Ethiopia's greenhouses were as large as Ziway itself (Figure 7.3). The Ziway greenhouses and the company's secondary sites at Adami

Figure 7.3 Ziway town and the Afriflora Sher greenhouses in 2017
Source: Satellite Image from Google, Digital Globe.

Tulu and Koka use 650 hectares, the equivalent of 1,300 football fields. Their business model involves thousands of greenhouse workers planting, tending, and harvesting millions of roses each day. After the flowers are cut, sorted, bundled, and wrapped in protective sleeves, they are placed in cold storage for the evening. Before six o'clock the next morning, the roses are packed into lorries for transport to Bole Airport in Addis Ababa, where they then take a seven-hour flight to Liege, Belgium. They are transferred to another cooled lorry, which makes a three-hour drive to Aalsmeer, home of the largest flower auction in the world. After they are sold, the flowers make their way to stores and supermarkets across Europe.

Sher Ethiopia is a massive operation, which requires a workforce about as large as the population of Adami Tulu. At the time of my research, it employed some 8,000 workers, and by 2022, that number had grown to 12,500. Unlike Verde Beef, which predominantly employed men, many workers at Sher Ethiopia are young women. They come from more distant rural areas of Oromia or the southern regions. They share the same hopes as those who choose to go abroad as labor migrants: to earn enough money to return home and "change my life." There is a saying that when young women from these rural areas consider migrating, they choose between "Ziway or Dubai."

When I met Fayine in 2016, she was a new worker at Sher Ethiopia. She arrived in Ziway to escape an early marriage. The youngest of four children, she is the only girl with an education in her family. Her two older sisters married young. They were, as Fayine put it, "sold like cattle to a husband." Fayine did well in school. She even passed the formidable regional exam after eighth grade, allowing her to proceed into secondary school. But after she completed ninth grade, her father suddenly passed away. This was a devastating blow to a family of subsistence farmers. Fayine's mother felt it was time for her daughter to marry. She was no longer confident she could support Fayine in school, and the *gabara* from her marriage might alleviate some of the worst of the family's impending impoverishment.

Fayine fled. "I made a call to my family," she told me. "I said, from now on, you are not going to see me. Sell your cattle as you like, but I am a human being. You are not going to sell me!" She told her mother not to come looking for her—that she was in a place where she could get what she needed. That place was Ziway, where she moved in with a friend who was already working at Sher Ethiopia. Her friend helped Fayine get a job as well, and within twenty-four hours of arriving in town, she began her first shift cutting flowers in the greenhouses.

Fayine had only been working at Sher Ethiopia for three weeks. She worked twelve-hour days, six days a week. The work is difficult, she told me. The greenhouses are hot, and the thorns prick her hands. She was told she would earn 900 birr per month, though she had not been paid yet. She already owes 175 birr for the room she shares and 500 birr for food for that first month. She is reconsidering her decision to work at Sher, recognizing that what she would earn from her hard work barely covers her costs of living in town. I asked her about her next steps and plans for the future. "I need to go home, make up with my family, and then leave Ethiopia for an Arab country," she said. "Why do you want to go there?" I asked. She replied, "I want to change my life. Rather than burning here at Sher, it is better for me to leave Ethiopia and work in Arab country. And after I have some money, I want to come back and build my own home. After I have my own money, it is better to get married then."

Later that week I met Fayine's friend, Lentu, who had been working at Sher Ethiopia for almost a year. She arrived there after a difficult experience as a domestic worker in Saudi Arabia. After failing the national exam—a common experience she blamed on the sudden shift from learning in Afaan Oromo to English—she convinced her family to send her abroad. With the help of a broker—"they are everywhere," she told me—she secured a contract and moved to Riyadh. While the woman she worked for was kind, the man was verbally abusive and frequently failed to pay her on time. At one point, he demanded she shave her head, a request Lentu refused, stating, "I know my rights."

After a few months, Lentu fell ill, and rather than provide medical treatment, the man sent her back to Ethiopia—abandoning her at the airport in Riyadh. A week later, after securing assistance for "voluntary repatriation," she returned home, disillusioned with international migration but still determined to "change her life." She found work at Sher hoping it would be easier than what she had endured abroad, but after a year of grueling hours and low wages, she was again considering returning to the Middle East. I asked Lentu about her future plans. "I want to work and change my life," she said. "What kind of work?" I asked. She replied, "It does not matter what kind. I just want work that changes my life." "Do you think you will stay at Sher for a while longer?" I asked. She replied, "No. The work is from 6 to 6. It's too difficult. It hurts humans. I don't want to stay at Sher." She is thinking of returning to the Middle East, where she had earned the equivalent of 3,500 birr per month. "Not all families are the same," she told me. This time, she may "get a good one."

***

The young women I interviewed were mostly day workers in the greenhouses, cutting or packing flowers. Most of them work six days a week, and a normal day ranges between eight and twelve hours, with one hour for lunch. In 2016, they reported earning between 700 and 900 birr per month (32 to 42 USD). A typical rented room in Ziway is around 200 birr per month, with food costs alone approximately 400 to 500 birr per month. Another study of flower farm workers at Sher found that workers spent 85 percent of their wages on food and housing alone.[18] Moving and living in town to access work at Sher dramatically increased their costs of living, which meant that saving, and remitting, was a struggle.

Sher Ethiopia pays above the minimum wage, but that does not mean much. The minimum wage for governmental personnel in Ethiopia in 2016 was 420 birr per month, less than 20 USD. Few could afford to live in Ziway on a minimum wage, nor can people live well on the slightly higher wages from Sher. One independent assessment estimates that a living wage in Ziway would be 2.5 to 3 times higher than the prevailing wages for flower farm workers at Sher.[19] I interviewed several women who had worked for a time at Sher but left to eke out an existence through daily labor opportunities wherever they could find them in Ziway—peeling onions, washing clothes, or stuffing mattresses. The fact that they chose those forms of work over Sher speaks for itself.

One afternoon, I invited five young women working at Sher for coffee. They came from rural villages further south, and they had learned about work at the company through their friendship networks. I asked them whether they would encourage other young women from their home regions to come work at Sher too. Their responses were mixed. Some mentioned the benefit of doing something: "Don't just sit there and bother your family. Come work and do something. . . . Even if I can buy just one pair of shoes, it's better than what I had before." Others were more skeptical: "I'd tell them not to come. I've been working at Sher and there is no benefit. How can we change ourselves? If it's possible, go abroad to the Arab countries."

No one from Wayisso worked at Sher, except for one man who worked as a guard. Why workers from elsewhere continued to arrive for these jobs, while people from Wayisso did not, was puzzling. One possibility is that workers coming from elsewhere are even poorer and more desperate for work than those in Wayisso. Yet, poverty runs deep for many Wayisso families. Many households struggled to meet their basic needs and relied on food assistance for themselves and their children, particularly during a year of drought. An extra income would certainly help them. Moreover, workers from Wayisso would have an easier time accessing work at Sher's Adami Tulu complex than those coming from farther away, who would have to pay higher costs for transport and housing in town.

Another possibility is that hope can more easily flourish at a distance. The fact that this work for a foreign company is somewhere else can make the possibility for meaningful change seem greater than if this work is right in front of you. This helps explain why young women who come to work at Sher often reorient their aspirations to the Middle East, once they realize the prospects for change are dim and learn more about how much they might earn abroad.

Whatever the reason, rural and urban locals in Wayisso and Adami Tulu often disparage the work at Sher, citing concerns about working conditions—the heat, the pesticides, the low pay. Some expressed resentment toward the southern workers for coming and taking such low-paying jobs, arguing that if they wouldn't, Sher would be forced to pay higher wages. Turnover is high, however, even among southern workers. Many young women do indeed leave for the Middle East—a point of frustration for Sher's managers who invest in training their employees, only to see them move on shortly thereafter.[20]

Local Labor Markets

Foreign companies like Verde Beef and Sher Ethiopia profoundly impact local labor markets in the ATJK *woreda*, but these impacts extend far beyond the jobs they directly create. Their presence changes local economies in unforeseen and sometimes disadvantageous ways. One of the clearest examples is the labor market for agricultural work in Wayisso.

During the time of the Derg, after Wayisso households had begun farming their land, Wolayita and Hadiya men began migrating seasonally to this region seeking agricultural work. Usually, they came once or twice a year, in between the sowing and harvest times of their own fields. Most lived with the families that employed them, working their land for a share of the harvest. The need for migrant farm labor in Wayisso was due, in part, to rising levels of school attendance. Initially, households in Wayisso helped each other with their fields, in a labor organization called *debo*, where ten to twenty households helped plow each other's land and shared oxen.[21] However, as more children and young adults attended school, it became increasingly difficult just to cover the labor requirements for their own land.[22] Thus, over time, as formal education expanded in the ATJK *woreda*, the need for migrant farm labor increased. Today, seasonal work continues, where Wolayita or Hadiya laborers live and work with Wayisso families for a season. However, it is increasingly common to find day laborers who are paid per diem or per plot worked (Figure 7.4). These wages are rising as local farmers now compete with Sher and Verde Beef for the same workers.

Two migrant workers, Abreham and Belete, found work in Wayisso by first coming to Ziway. They met Bekur, a Wayisso farmer, on a well-known corner next to the telecommunications shop where agricultural laborers hang out, waiting for work. There, Bekur proposed that they work for two families in Wayisso for 500 birr (~23 USD) per month. Abreham, aged thirty, came from a rural *kebele* in the Areka *woreda* in southern Ethiopia. He has a

178   MOVED BY MODERNITY

Figure 7.4 A father and son: seasonal farm workers from Ethiopia's southern regions working in Wayisso, 2016

third-grade education, only one plot of land, and three children. It is impossible for him to grow crops for profit; he can only grow enough to feed his family, if that. "We leave our birthplace for the sake of money," he explained. "We go wherever there is money. Wherever it is, if we hear that there is money there, we will travel there."

Before arriving in Wayisso, Abreham worked in a sugar cane factory as far north as Afar. The pay was better—500 to 600 birr every two weeks—but the working conditions were too difficult, and the cost of transport to and from his home was high. He decided to try his luck elsewhere. "Now I am employed for 500 birr per month and we live here [in Wayisso].... But here, for only 500 birr, we are working thirty days. Everyday there is plowing. Everyday there is work." He and Belete planned to leave at the end of the month. The work is too difficult, and the pay is too little. That complaint was becoming familiar.

I asked Abreham about his next steps. He said, "We want to work at Verde Beef. We've been told that there is work at Verde Beef. We are going to rent a house near the road and work there." They heard that you get paid 800 or 900 birr per month as day laborers. I asked Abreham whether he might actually make more money here in Wayisso. Working in Wayisso, they get 500 birr, but they do not have to pay for housing and food. If they work at Verde Beef, they make 900 birr, or perhaps even more, but they would have to subtract the costs of housing, food, and potentially transport, depending on where they found a room to rent. Abreham's friend, Belete, interjected, "Yeah, it seems like that. It seems better. But here we don't have *any* time to take a rest. We always, early morning, go to the land and plow. They haven't given us even one day of rest. They are using our labor." He was optimistic work at Verde Beef might be different: "But at Verde Beef, at least they give time off. The work is not too hard.... Even if it is difficult, it is not more difficult than this one. This is the most difficult work that you can find. So that's why we've decided to leave this place." Belete's long-term goal is to become a merchant—to work and save enough money to open a business in a town close to his home and family.

Abreham and Belete's frustration with the low pay and difficult work conditions in Wayisso echoes the common refrain of workers across the *woreda*. Their decision to leave and seek work at Verde Beef reveals the degree to which labor markets for agricultural work are increasingly shaped by foreign companies.

Some weeks later, I was not surprised to hear Bekur mention that his hired help had left. I told Bekur he should have given the workers more rest—at least one day off per week. He defended himself by explaining that they only worked in the mornings, just two hours per day! This was quite a different tale from the one Abreham and Belete told me and did not match the work I saw them doing throughout the day when I visited Bekur's family. Nevertheless, Bekur felt Abreham exaggerated his plight, and our friend Basha agreed. "They may do two hard hours of work and feel like they have worked the whole day!"

While having this conversation, we passed another group of five Wolayita men uprooting the weeds that grew around young corn stalks. These men were day laborers working for 150 birr (about 7 USD) per plot. They live together in Adami Tulu and share the payment between them. Four were young, and one was old. None wore shoes.

After speaking with these men for a time, Bekur, Basha, and I continued walking to Wayisso. "150 birr per plot!" Bekur exclaimed. "Just four or five years ago it was only 20 birr," Basha added. "Then it rose to 50. Then 120, and last year, to 150." I asked why the costs were rising so quickly. "Before there was no Sher or Verde Beef," Bekur said. "After Sher, there is less labor and the price for work has increased."

"The Pay Is Too Little"

The work is too difficult, and the pay is too little. Whether speaking with workers at Verde Beef or Sher Ethiopia—or even the agricultural laborers employed by Wayisso families—this is the new refrain of Ethiopia's wage workers. Jobs like these will not act as a deterrent for further internal or international migration. The main reason is the inability to earn and save enough money to meaningfully change one's material and social conditions. Work at the flower farm, on the cattle feedlot, or tending Wayisso's fields relieves some of the pressures of economic insecurity, but it is not enough to "change your life." It is work for subsistence.

Similar dynamics are playing out across Ethiopia where opportunities for employment are increasing exponentially as foreign companies establish large industrial complexes. Further south, for example, is Hawassa Industrial Park, one of the largest industrial parks in the country. It housed twenty textile companies in 2018, most of which were based out of Asia and manufactured garments for international brands like Levi's and H&M. The industrial park employed twenty-five thousand workers by its second year, 90 percent of whom were women.[23] Most came from rural areas and small towns surrounding Hawassa. Government recruitment agents visited villages across the region to tout the benefits of factory work and to encourage women to apply for the new jobs.

Although it was initially hailed as one of the most effective models in creating jobs in the garment and textile sector in Africa, anthropologists Robel Mulat and Daniel Mains find a very different reality. Working conditions and wages are far below the expectations of newly arrived workers, while the costs of living in Hawassa are far higher. Workers face severe challenges meeting their basic needs for food and shelter. A 2019 report on the Hawassa Industrial Park by the New York University's Stern Center for Business and Human Rights writes that "the government's eagerness to attract foreign investment led it to promote the lowest base wage in any garment-producing country—now set at the equivalent of $26 a month. On that amount, workers, most of them young women from poor farming families, cannot afford decent housing, food, and transportation."[24] Sometimes even subsistence is not guaranteed.

Foreign companies appear to be stimulating greater internal and international migration rather than reducing it. Their very establishment stimulates internal migration, particularly rural-urban migration—reflected in the rapid population growth of Hawassa, Adami Tulu, and Ziway. Internal migration for wage work is not new to Ethiopia. There are many workers from the more population-dense southern regions who have a long history of moving seasonally or permanently for wage-based employment. But the scale of agro-industrial and industrial employment is increasing quickly, and particularly in cases where the workers are predominantly women, like Sher Ethiopia or Hawassa Industrial Park, labor migration is a new phenomenon. When these women move for work at a foreign company, they uproot themselves from the traditional life path that would have led them to marry and settle in another rural area. They then realize that the quality of their new life and their prospects for change are far lower than they had hoped, and onward migration for work that *does* pay—like domestic work in the Middle East—becomes an attractive strategy for those who can afford it and know how to do it. This is likely one reason that previous migration for work is often associated with greater desires to migrate again.[25]

The fact that expanding employment opportunities at Sher or Verde Beef does little to stop migration from Wayisso reveals how profoundly Ethiopia's development is reshaping the aspirations of its youngest generations. The measure of good work is now the promise of *change*, not simply having employment or meeting basic needs. As a result of their schooling and the increasingly transactional nature of work, young men and women alike have come to regard both agricultural livelihoods and wage work with foreign companies with disdain—too difficult, too little reward, no hope for change. When they cannot access the better-paid work or entrepreneurial opportunities they desire, wage-based employment in a globalized labor market makes even more sense.

Would things be different if these companies paid higher wages? Would rates of retention be higher, and onward migration decline? Unfortunately, we do not have good counterfactuals for comparison, and as long as the Ethiopian government advertises some of the world's lowest wages to attract foreign investors, we will not know. We are left with the hypothetical raised by one Wayisso farmer: "The developers could be a good thing, if they paid people well." But for now, "the work is difficult, and the pay is too little."

8
Land and Climate

The environment sets the context for human society. The earth's varying land and climatic conditions gave rise to remarkable differentiation in the livelihoods and cultures of the world's diverse peoples. Then the technological marvels of modernity brought the promise of transcending nature, harnessing it for human ends and sheltering humanity from its vicissitudes. We built sparkling skyscrapers in the Arabian desert. We drained swampy, inhospitable wetlands to build apartment buildings and parking lots. We tapped into geothermal energy to grow bananas in Iceland. In the process, modernization introduced new political, economic, and cultural landscapes that became far more consequential for lives, livelihoods, and societal configurations than the environmental context—and far more forceful determinants of how, where, and whether people migrate.

Yet, as humanity now confronts the specter of living in an age of climate change, development scholars and practitioners are forced to think anew about man's relationship to the environment. It is increasingly clear that the pursuit of modernization—of harnessing and transcending nature for material gain—has rendered many communities around the world *more* vulnerable to environmental change. This is particularly the case for farming families like those in Wayisso, who were taught to use modern, monocropping methods and chemical fertilizers, only to find that the fertility of their soils is gradually declining, at the same time that rainfall seems more erratic than ever before.

Climate models for Ethiopia predict warming temperatures, more irregular rainfall, prolonged drought, and a gradual desertification of the country's lowlands.[1] Concerns about climate change are amplified by soil degradation, land tenure insecurity, and insufficient government support for the backbone of the rural economy: smallholder farmers.[2] In this foreboding environmental and institutional landscape, many are concerned about the impacts climate change might have on rural communities, particularly climate-induced displacement.

Dominant narratives about climate change and migration tend to frame climate impacts as push factors displacing populations that are otherwise immobile. By examining how migration patterns in Wayisso responded to a period of severe drought in 2015 and 2016, this chapter challenges that narrative in two ways. First, it shows why, rather than driving migration, drought often constrains it, depriving many households of the resources needed to support a migration project and trapping them in even more precarious and vulnerable positions. As research and policy interest in addressing the challenges of climate-induced displacement grows, this chapter discusses why climate-related *immobility* is just as urgent a humanitarian and development concern. Second, to understand how climate change will impact patterns of migration for a given community or society, we must understand historical and present-day patterns of migration and immobility and their underlying drivers. In other words, climate impacts do not operate in isolation; they act on existing migration systems.

To help illustrate these two points, consider three mobility outcomes in Wayisso that followed a year of "failed rains":

> One young man, who was living and attending secondary school in Adami Tulu, returned to Wayisso because his family, which farms six plots (1.5 hectares), could no longer support the costs of his rent, food, and education in town. For farming families who rely on rainfed agriculture, severe drought deprives households of their expected incomes from that year's harvest. This income shock forces households to make do with less and adapt their plans. The young man dropped out of school and hoped for a better harvest next year so he could continue his studies.
>
> A second young woman, disillusioned with school and seeking an opportunity to change her life quickly, decided to leave for Lebanon. During a period of drought, her family was not immediately able to support the up-front costs of her migration, nor were they supportive of her desire to end her education. She asked a cousin working in Beirut to arrange a contract with friends of her employer's family. Her cousin agreed and offered to cover the travel and visa costs from her own salary. Within just a few months after having the first real intention to migrate, this young woman was on a plane to Beirut.
>
> A third young man was involuntarily immobile in Wayisso. He has felt this way for a while—believing a better future is in town but unable

to get there. This year, he was planning to marry, first bringing his wife to Wayisso and later, hopefully, moving together to Ziway. But the drought meant he had to postpone his wedding. He could not afford the costs of the expected bride price: cattle and blankets, among other gifts. He continued to tend the two plots of land he had been given informally by his father and hoped that next year's harvest would allow him to wed and, somehow in the future, find a way to move to town.

To explain these divergent mobility outcomes from the same village experiencing the same environmental stress, we must engage other dimensions of the social realm. For the first man, we cannot understand why drought led to a *return* to Wayisso unless we also appreciate the relatively high costs of access to secondary school in town. We cannot understand why the second woman left for the Middle East without an understanding of gendered labor markets and migrant networks, which *facilitate* international migration even in a context of drought-induced resource deprivation. And for the third man, we cannot understand the degree to which drought *deepens* involuntary immobility in the village without an understanding of how spatial immobility is tied up with other kinds of social and economic immobility. This man has struggled to move to town for quite some time; drought undermined that prospect even further, at the same time that it deprived him of the opportunity to marry and establish his own family. For many smallholder farming families, drought does not just constrain migration. It constrains a whole host of other life aspirations.

***

Wayisso village lies within the East African Rift, which runs from the Dankali depression in Afar; down through Lakes Koka, Ziway, Langano, Abjata, and Shala; southward past Lake Turkana in Kenya; and onto the great equatorial lakes. It is framed by distant highlands to the east and west, where richer soils and more predictable biannual rainfalls supported early agriculture and settlement. The drier lowlands, forested with acacia trees and savanna vegetation and closer to freshwater lakes, suited more mobile, pastoral livelihoods.

Due to less frequent rainfall and the heightened exposure to malaria that comes with being sedentary, agriculture is riskier in the central lowlands. The seminomadic movements of generations of Oromo pastoralists thus gravitated toward the lakes in the dry season and away from them in the wet. Political and cultural factors—territorial boundaries with other ethnic groups, movements to attend marriage celebrations or Gadaa gatherings—also shaped the direction of these movements, of course. But finding conditions appropriate for grazing their cattle was a consistent priority. Wayisso elder Haji Tefo, born in 1914 (he claims it was when Emperor Iyasu reigned), describes a childhood moving between regular grazing pastures. "We spent time in Rapee around the border with the Silt'e, but sometimes, for two months or so, we would spend time in Hora Qalo. If there was no grass, we were going to go there. If there was grass, we could stay here." How long they stayed in each place, he said, "depended on the weather."

In his adulthood, Haji Tefo lived through dramatic societal changes that exerted a far greater influence on mobility patterns than the "weather." And yet, much still depends on the weather. In fact, the sedentarization of Wayisso residents, combined with a newfound reliance on rainfed agriculture, renders households *more* exposed and vulnerable to irregularities in the weather than previous generations of pastoralists who used their mobility to adapt—who could bring their livelihoods with them to seek water and better pastures elsewhere. The vulnerability that comes with being immobile was particularly clear while doing fieldwork in Wayisso after failed rains in 2015.

The Drought

One lazy afternoon in Ziway in March 2016, I joined Kedir to watch music videos on the Oromia Broadcasting Network. After an endearing video where a young man with traditional Oromo hairstyle sang about his love for his cattle, the president of the Oromia region, Mutaar Kadiir, appeared on the screen. He had been absent since the Oromo protests broke out in late 2015, and we wondered if he would make a comment on the current political situation. Instead, he had a message for Ethiopia's farmers. Enough crops had been produced for the market, Mutaar Kadiir said. Now is the time to share our harvests with the communities that had been hit hardest by that year's drought.

Failed rains in 2015 and an El Niño–induced drought led to acute food insecurity across Ethiopia in 2016. Wayisso was designated by the government as a priority *woreda* requiring assistance,[3] and local precipitation data confirms farmer perceptions that 2015 was a particularly dire year

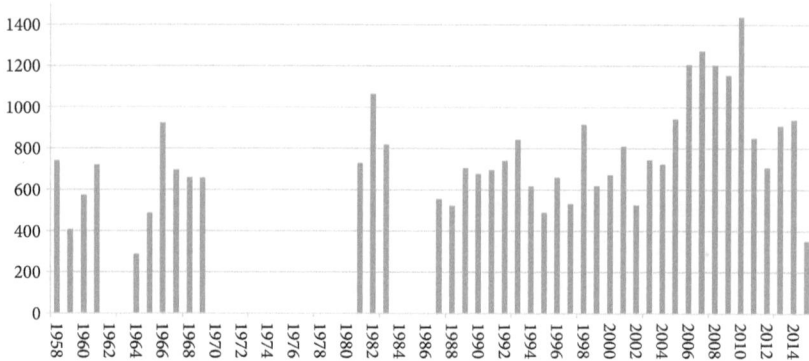

Figure 8.1 Total rainfall for Adami Tulu, 1958–2015 (millimeters per year)
Source: Meteorologist Office in Adami Tulu and Meteorologist Center in Addis Ababa.

(Figures 8.1 and 8.2). The last comparable year with recorded rainfall data was in 1964 during the time of Haile Selassie. Unfortunately, precipitation data was not collected during the early 1970s, when a severe drought struck Ethiopia and led to famine and starvation in other regions of Ethiopia, notably the country's northern and eastern regions. Nor do we have data for the historic drought that took place under the Derg's rule in 1984.[4] Thus, we know years of low rainfall and periodic droughts are a recurring phenomenon in this region, but as Figure 8.1 shows, we also know that the drought of 2015 was the worst one since at least 1987, after which local rainfall data was collected on an annual basis.

Local explanations for the drought were many. Some blamed deforestation practices in Wayisso. "It began from individuals cutting trees to make charcoal," one man explained. "When individuals cut trees to make money, then climate change comes." Others blamed the sweeping deforestation of hundreds of acres neighboring Wayisso, when Verde Beef moved in. Immediately after this devastation to the landscape, a drought followed, and in many people's minds, it was Verde Beef's fault. As one woman expressed in a community gathering, "We are very worried. [Verde Beef] has cut down all the trees. Everyone knows. There was rain before. Then he came and this year we don't have any rain."

Anxiety about the drought is compounded by concerns over the declining fertility of their land. "The land has been plowed for many years. It is impossible to get the same harvest we had in earlier times," a village elder complained. "The land is finishing its fertility. Maybe the government tries

Figure 8.2 Wayisso community pond: February 2016

to tell people otherwise, to motivate people—in the media the government talks blah blah blah about production—but nothing changes. It is science that the land becomes less fertile when you plow yearly." Many farmers blame the never-ending government-led push to increase yields through subsidized fertilizers, pesticides, higher-yield seeds, and monocropping for their problems. A government development agent working at the Agricultural Research Institute in Adami Tulu shared what he hears as the most common concerns of farmers:

> *They tell me, "20 years or 15 years or 30 years ago, we had maybe 500 or more cattle, and we were harvesting more. Even though we didn't use any chemical fertilizer or any other input, we were harvesting more. And we were getting more money both from animals and from crops. We were living a better life! ... Because you forced us to use chemical fertilizers and inorganic things, and even though production doubled or increased a bit, we still prefer the situation before there was absolute change, climate change." This is what is in the mind of the producers.*

In these narratives, the threat of climate change is interwoven with the threat of modern, intensive agriculture: both undermine the long-term productivity of the soil and the sustainability of smallholder farming livelihoods.

Regardless of how accurate farmer perceptions are about the degree of climate change occurring in this region, the relative declines in soil fertility, or their causes, these perceptions about changing land and climate are important indicators of how farmers understand their local conditions and prospects. After all, people's *perceptions* of environmental change matter more than any objective measure when it comes to their migration decision-making.

In this light, farmers clearly question whether agricultural livelihoods are sustainable and desirable, and the fear of climate change and more frequent and severe drought only magnifies these concerns. Yet, instead of directly forcing people off their land, narratives about climate change bolster an already-shifting social imaginary away from rural agriculture toward urban, nonfarm futures. In fact, in 2002, Daniel Hailu, a master's student from Addis Ababa University, conducted research in Wayisso during a year that also experienced relatively low rainfall and found that ensuing drought was "fan[ning] an already high fervor" to invest in formal education over agricultural livelihoods.[5] Thus, over the longer term, the threat of drought becomes one reason among many others for the social and economic devaluation of farming.

To understand how an environmental stress like drought impacts migration patterns, it is essential to appreciate existing mobility systems and their determinants. Only then can we explain why migration patterns during years of relatively high rainfall in the late 2000s and 2010s do not conform to what a simple push-factor narrative would suggest—that years of higher rainfall would be associated with less migration, because farmers are better able to support their livelihoods and stay in place when their harvests are more abundant. On the contrary, these years of relatively high rainfall overlap with a new phase in Wayisso mobility transition when *more* people began leaving the village. As Chapter 3 details, beginning in the 2000s, young people migrated in ever-larger numbers to Adami Tulu and Ziway. A smaller subset experimented with labor migration to more distant Ethiopian cities and the Middle East. Good harvests gave them the resources they needed to invest in these new migration projects. At the most basic level, the timing of this mobility transition—that is, more people began leaving Wayisso during years of higher average rainfall—suggests a more complicated story than "drought drives migration." On the contrary, in Wayisso, the most direct and dire effects of the drought came in the form of deepening involuntary immobility.

"Displaced in Place"

Most Wayisso households grow one cash crop per year, generally maize. For those who have no other sources of income, the sale of their harvest sustains the household for that year. One farmer in Wayisso explained that in the best possible year, his three plots could produce 1,200 kilograms for the market. The year he was married—"a good year"—he harvested 700 kilograms of maize. In these good years, farmers can earn enough to support activities, consumption, or investments beyond subsistence—like a wedding or a child's education. After the failed rains in 2015, however, this farmer harvested just 20 kilograms of maize, the equivalent of just 3.50 USD. In bad years like this, household livelihood strategies are reduced to what the climate literature refers to as "coping"—finding ways to endure through a difficult period.

Despite significant hardships following a period of drought, the poorest households in Wayisso did not consider moving away. Most already felt that they lacked the resources to migrate before the drought struck; they could not afford a room to rent or the higher costs of food in town. The drought only reduced their migration capabilities even further. Moving under those conditions, they shared, would only increase their vulnerability, not reduce it. The most impoverished households relied on their neighbors and periodic food aid to make it through the most difficult periods, and at least in the village, they have the dignity of their home and land, their networks of social support, and emergency food stores if they had them.

Thus, for households that relied on rainfed agriculture to subsist—many of whom already felt involuntarily immobile in the village—a period of drought further eroded any prospect of migrating. At the same time, it eroded the capability to stay. The idea that drought reduces the capability to stay of those who remain in the village is admittedly not intuitive, yet it is essential to show why someone who stays in place may still be considered "displaced." Individuals, families, and communities have the capability to stay when they have the resources, freedoms, and opportunities to "lead the lives they have reason to value,"[6] as Amartya Sen put it, *where they live*. Thus, staying in place does not mean someone has the "capability to stay," as I am using the term. To use a rather coarse example, someone who stays in place while slowly starving is deprived of the capability to stay. Integrating the capability to stay into the aspiration-capability framework can help us see how a period of severe drought deepens involuntary immobility among the most impoverished households to the point where some become "displaced in place."

The phrase "displaced in place" was introduced by anthropologist Stephen Lubkemann to describe households that were immobilized by civil conflict in Mozambique.[7] Labor migration played an important role in the social and economic life of many drought-prone communities before a fifteen-year civil war began. The conflict disrupted many of these mobility systems, and the most disadvantaged were those who were trapped by surrounding conflict, unable to flee their villages. These new constraints on mobility-based livelihood strategies had devastating effects, deepening poverty and insecurity. Lubkemann questions whether the disruption and disempowerment we associate with wartime movement are in fact greater for those who are immobilized in conflict settings. The displaced in place, he claims, are "theoretically invisible" in migration and refugee studies because of the implicit conflation of displacement with spatial movement. In a similar vein, we might ask whether those who are displaced in place by drought (or other climate hazards) too often remain invisible in research and policy on climate-related migration and displacement.

***

Just as I was struck by the degree to which drought deepens involuntary immobility and constrains migration from Wayisso, I was equally struck by instances in which, despite the drought, migration continued from households with access to nonfarm incomes—whether a business in town, salaried work, or migrant networks that could give or lend money. These are all sources of migration capability that allow migration and other life projects to continue, even during a major economic shock.

Consider the young woman mentioned earlier in the chapter who left for Lebanon. She was able to draw on her migrant networks to overcome her migration constraints. Yet, it is also important to note that she did not migrate *because* of the drought; in fact, the drought was a distant consideration in her decision-making. In this instance, she had a heated political argument with a teacher that prompted a rather rash decision to leave. Another man who migrated around the same time had been offered a salaried government position managing a government warehouse in another district. A third young woman moved from Wayisso to Ziway to attend college. Her family (Lineage 2) runs a number of small businesses in town and was still able to cover her school fees that year.

Because households with access to greater economic and social resources are less reliant on rainfed agriculture for their livelihoods, their aspirations for migration were also less likely to be *primarily* for drought-related reasons. Thus, drought concerns intersect with other anxieties and life aspirations—for education, independence, meaningful work outside the farming sector, urban lifestyles—many of which are driven by and associated with Ethiopia's development.

This divergence in migration and immobility experiences during the drought raises an important development concern. The drought's most direct effect on migration trends from Wayisso came in the form of deepening involuntary immobility among the most vulnerable households that rely on rainfed agriculture as their primary source of livelihood. For households whose livelihoods rely less on farming, and thus are more resilient to the economic shock a severe drought brings, the effects of the drought on migration were more indirect. The migration and other life projects of the more privileged families continue, while the poorest fall into ever more precarious positions. Drought thus threatens to widen existing inequalities between the poorest and wealthiest households in the village, and much of that inequality stems from access to migration and migrant networks. In this light, it is easier to see why we might wish to be cautious about characterizing all migration from drought-stricken regions as "displacement" or "climate migration." In fact, those who moved were the least affected by the drought; the most disadvantaged remained immobile in the village.

Of course, there were many households in Wayisso that fell between these two extremes. Even those who had been able to move to town in previous years were not sheltered from the drought's impacts. Small businesses faltered as the drought reduced the purchasing power of the local community. Plans for migration to the Middle East were put on hold until a better harvest when young women or their networks could help cover the upfront costs. Families who had relied on hired help to work their farmlands as they pursued education or business adventures in town could no longer afford to hire workers for the next planting season. When I wanted to ask one family in town who would do the farm work that year, my translator Tilah suggested I not ask the question—to spare them the embarrassment of having to explain that they would be the ones working in their fields that year.

Migration as Adaptation

The migration and immobility experiences in Wayisso do not fit neatly with research from other areas of Ethiopia, like the highlands to the north or the south, where temporary migration for wage-based employment is a common household coping strategy during a period of drought.[8] In many contexts where environmental change threatens local livelihoods, households will strategically send one or several members to work in other destinations to diversify incomes, reduce risk, and enhance resilience to climate shocks or stresses.[9] In a meta-analysis on adaptation covering sixty-three studies and 9,700 rural households in sub-Saharan African drylands, one-quarter of rural households relied on migration as an adaptation strategy.[10] Such findings have given rise to growing scholarly and policy interest on the idea of "migration as adaptation."[11]

Research in this area finds that migration and the subsequent transfer of financial remittances, knowledge, and social networks from destination to origin communities can indeed enhance the adaptive capacity of smallholder farming households.[12] However, the impacts are highly context dependent. Whether and how households use migration as an adaptation strategy, and its impacts on climate resilience, depend significantly on a household's resources, knowledge, and networks and the severity of climate impacts they face. More socioeconomically advantaged households will have greater capabilities to invest in both in situ adaptation and migration as a proactive adaptation strategy, while disadvantaged populations face a more constrained set of adaptation and coping options.[13] Some of the poorest households may fail to adapt at all and fall into ever more precarious circumstances.[14] A key insight from research on migration as adaptation is that households with greater *choice* in decisions to migrate or to stay tend to experience greater climate resilience than those whose mobility or immobility feels involuntary.[15]

There are clearly many dimensions of Wayisso's experience that resonate with the existing literature on migration as adaptation. Households with family members working elsewhere, particularly those that received remittances from the Middle East, were more resilient during a period of drought. More fundamentally, households with greater *choice* in decisions to migrate or to stay tended to experience enhanced climate resilience, because greater choice correlates with greater capabilities.

And yet, there were other ways in which experiences in Wayisso did not resonate with existing literature on migration as adaptation. For example, it is notable that migration was never once described by households as a strategy to cope with or adapt to the drought. Further, the remittances farming families received were rarely invested in the farm or allocated toward farm-level adaptation. If anything, they prioritized hiring farm workers so they could pursue other kinds of work. During the 2015 planting season, before the rains failed, only 40 percent of Wayisso households used fertilizer and just 4 percent used pesticides. By contrast, 53 percent of Wayisso households had hired farm help.

A key discrepancy between the reality in Wayisso and the discourse on migration as adaptation stems from basic assumptions about the aspirations of rural households. Adaptation research tends to see migration either as a last resort and sign of adaptation failure or as a household income diversification strategy to support voluntary immobility at origin. In other words, households desire to stay in place, despite an environmental threat, and will strategically send one, two, or more members of a household to work in other areas. The remittances they send home thus contribute to the diversification of a household's income, reducing risk and enhancing a household's capability to stay in place over the longer term. This reality has been well documented in places like Morocco, where, as early as the 1970s, researchers identified migration as a strategy to "*partir pour rester*"—to leave in order to stay.[16] Similarly, in Senegal, the migration and remittances of some household members enabled others to stay at home and continue agricultural lifestyles, what they perceive as the good life.[17] There are many places around the world where communities still perceive the "good life" as being where they are, and households will strategically use migration to enhance their long-term capability to stay in place.

But this is not the reality in Wayisso, and Wayisso is not unique in this regard. There are also many rural places where households, particularly those headed by younger generations and those with some degree of formal education, no longer aspire to a future in farming. As these places face environmental stress, migration as adaptation takes on a different character. To understand migration motivations in these contexts, it will be essential to integrate research at the climate-migration nexus with research at the migration-development nexus, which will likely reveal that, in places like Wayisso, migration as adaptation is rarely a *climate* adaptation strategy and is instead a *development* strategy of households navigating changing societal and environmental conditions.

Access to Land

Whenever I asked in casual conversations why people are leaving rural areas, farmers, students, and government and development workers often gave the same answers: climate change, land scarcity, and population pressure—three interrelated, highly structural explanations that make the very question of why people move seem obvious. The underlying narrative is that young people are forced out of agricultural livelihoods by environmental and demographic pressures. The previous section complicates this push-factor narrative by showing how climate stress like drought can constrain development-driven migration. In this last section, I briefly address the other two points: land scarcity and population growth. I treat these together because they work in tandem. As rural populations grow, younger generations have less land to inherit, and as one village elder bluntly put it: "Whether they are educated or uneducated, if they are in the rural area, they don't do anything if they don't have land. That's why they migrate."

The ability to farm or keep cattle clearly depends on access to land. Grazing lands diminished with the rise of farming, and farming lands diminished as rural populations continued to grow. As one farmer explains, when people first switched to farming, "people might farm one plot, half a plot, two plots.... It was really fifteen years ago that they started to farm *all* their land. Before, they divided up the land, but they still kept some as pasture." He then gave the example of a man who has twenty to twenty-five plots: "If he divides this among five children, the children have much less. They don't have enough land to care for their cattle, and so they farm. But they have less, so they farm all their land." With each generation, grazing land and farmland dwindle in tandem, putting significant strain on traditional methods of rearing livestock. To keep cattle in the same place for a year or longer "makes them weak, skinny," one elder told me. Through the 1990s and early 2000s, families would send someone with the cattle to visit kin in distant villages that might still have more grazing pastures, though this is uncommon today. "Everything is farmland," he told me. "Where would you go?" Cattle too are now "stuck" in the village.

Figures 8.3 and 8.4 illustrate how families in *ganda Bedane*, between 2008 and 2016, converted land surrounding their households into farmland, thereby maximizing all available land for agriculture. The lighter patches of land in Figure 8.3 are unfarmed, kept for living and livestock grazing. These reduced significantly just eight years later (Figure 8.4). The large square of land in the bottom right corner is land owned by Verde Beef. It served as grazing land in 2008, but the trees were uprooted as the land was prepared for maize by 2016.

Ethiopia's constitution formally guarantees youth access to land if they wish to farm it, but in practice, local administrations often fail to find available land to allocate, leading most young adults to rely on inheriting land from their parents. Traditionally, sons inherit land from their fathers after marriage, though some now informally receive and work plots before they wed.[18] Although a few women have their own land in Wayisso—for example, the widow of Nageso (Lineage 2) or a daughter of forward-thinking Dessie (Lineage 1)—this remains rare.

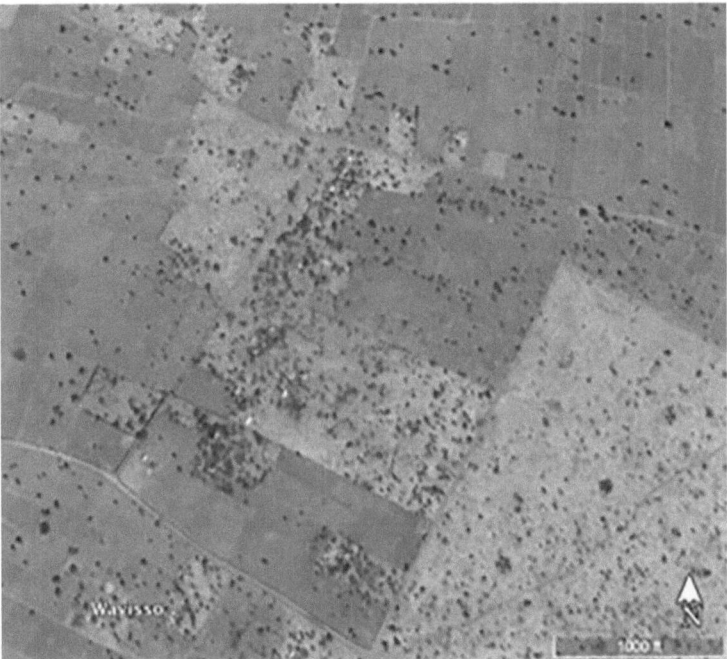

Figure 8.3 Aerial view of Wayisso households in 2008 (lighter patches are unfarmed land)
Source: Satellite image from Google, Digital Globe.

Figure 8.4 Aerial view of Wayisso households in 2016
Source: Satellite image from Google, Digital Globe.

Access to land within families varies greatly as well, from one plot (a quarter hectare) among a few young households to twenty plots (5 hectares) among a few older families. The average is six or eight plots, or 1.5 to 2 hectares.[19] Although land scarcity is a very real and urgent constraint on rural livelihoods, there was no clear or significant correlation in my household survey data between landholding and migration outcomes. Households respond to relative land scarcity in different ways, and even within the same family lineage, households may show greater or lesser rates of rural out-migration.[20]

Because landholding is a source of wealth in Wayisso, having more land could in theory support both the capability to migrate and the capability to stay. As younger generations increasingly aspire to urban futures, those whose families have greater landholdings are more likely to realize their aspirations for education and urban work, while those with limited landholdings tend to have fewer resources to make a sustainable move to town.

Thus, in Wayisso today, having little land to farm can fuel migration aspirations at the same time that it reduces migration capabilities.

However, other factors beyond land or even wealth can have a greater impact on whether or how people move. In Lineage 3, for example, some elders with significant landholdings still saw higher rates of immobility among their descendants, one important reason being that they did not prioritize sending their children to school (see Chapter 6). Further, some individuals from households with relatively little landholdings are able to leave Wayisso if they have family or migrant networks to finance or otherwise facilitate their migration projects for them. It was not uncommon, for example, for children from Wayisso to live with an uncle, aunt, or cousin in town while they attended secondary school. The child helps with household chores, and her parents avoid the otherwise insurmountable cost of renting accommodations for their child. Thus, family networks can facilitate the movement of some individuals who would otherwise have insufficient resources to make a move.

Because of these mediating factors, population "pressure" on rural livelihoods in the form of diminished landholding does not have a direct or deterministic link with rural out-migration. Educational attainment is a far better predictor of who lives outside the village.

Beyond Wayisso, it is also worth noting how land scarcity is associated with very different *kinds* of migration across social and geographic contexts. For example, in the Wolayita region in the South Ethiopian Regional State, 95 percent of households cultivate less than one plot of land. In fact, in a report on agrarian reform in Ethiopia from 1984, development researcher Dessalegn Rahmato already noted the problem of land scarcity for the Wolayita, whose primary livelihoods were agricultural. Today, this region has some of the highest rates of rural out-migration.[21] It is primarily the Wolayita who come to Wayisso for seasonal farm work and to Adami Tulu and Ziway for wage work in Sher's greenhouses.

Balquo, for example, is a seasonal farm worker from the Wolayita region working for a family in Wayisso. He explained his motivations for moving: "The great problem for the Wolayita is land. We can't find land to plow.... They have so many plots here! If there were so many plots in Wolayita, we would be rich." Though the land size might be greater per household in Wayisso, the soil is less fertile, and there is only one annual harvest, not two like in the more population-dense highlands. Despite these differences, people compared land issues in Wayisso to those of the Wolayita a generation ago. One Wayisso farmer expressed his worry: "What is happening is like what happened to the Wolayita. Our land is minimizing. Scarcity. Lack of land. It's happening."

Like the Wolayita, diminished landholding puts pressure on rural livelihoods in Wayisso and becomes yet one more reason young generations cannot envision a future in agriculture. Yet, unlike the Wolayita, Wayisso farmers are not willing to migrate for seasonal or agricultural work elsewhere. The *kinds* of migration occurring from Wayisso are different in nature and direction than the *kinds* of migration occurring among the Wolayita. When I asked why, many explained that the Oromo "hate farming"; it is not a deep-seated tradition like it is for the Wolayita. It's hard work, something the Oromo in this region came into (relatively) recently, and something they are quite happy to leave behind.

The common practice in Wayisso of hiring migrant farm labor raises another important question: why, if people do not have enough land to farm, do so many households employ daily or seasonal laborers from the south? There is enough—arguably too much—labor power among the young men born in Wayisso to tend the land, yet more than half of Wayisso households employed seasonal or daily migrant workers to assist with some aspects of farming. As mentioned, more households paid for farm help than for fertilizer in the 2015 planting season.

The fact that most households paid for some form of farm help signals that young men and women are busy pursuing alternative, nonagrarian livelihoods. For example, Caalaa, one of Dakabo Bulo's descendants, works for a nonprofit in a more distant urban city. When he is away, his brothers oversee the tilling and maintenance of his land. They employ seasonal labor migrants on his behalf, and Caalaa helps pay for their labor on his brothers' land in return. A share of the profits from the land supplements Caalaa's income from his salaried employment.

Of course, not all households can afford to do this—even those that can afford to migrate. Marki, one of Bedane Tuffaa's descendants, is a young man pursuing his bachelor's degree at Rift Valley University in Ziway. He has two plots in Wayisso, and during the farming season, he works the land himself, sometimes missing his classes. Yet the income from his harvest is essential to help sustain his continued pursuit of higher education in town.

Once in town, some sell their land when their urban pursuits seem promising enough or the maintenance of the land becomes too great an expense and effort to be worth it. In this way, rural households can expand their landholding. Others pass down their land to their children as one way of passing wealth along to later generations. But it is clear their aspirations for their children are not for them to become farmers, even if they farm a few plots of land on the side.

As Wayisso's population grows, landholding decreases with each generation, meaning that livelihoods based on agriculture alone are not sustainable in their current form for future generations. For it to become so, there needs to be a fundamental shift in farming practices—for example, toward irrigation or more regenerative farming practices that can restore the soil. However, there are no signs of this occurring. Most families choose to invest their discretionary income in other livelihood strategies—in education, migration, and other business pursuits—instead of agricultural innovation or adaptation. Why? They "hate farming." There are far more reasons than lack of land fueling desires to leave.

***

Despite rapid social change in recent decades, Ethiopia remains a country of smallholder farmers. Farming families like those in Wayisso produce 95 percent of the country's agricultural outputs while relying primarily on rain-fed agriculture and a "low input, low output" subsistence production system.[22] The country's reliance on rainfed agriculture as the backbone of the rural economy renders the country especially vulnerable to the effects of climate change. In this context, climate-induced displacement is understandably an urgent concern. However, this chapter offers two important cautions. First, some of the gravest effects of climate change may be borne by those who *cannot* move in the face of severe environmental stress or threat.[23] Just as climate change will displace some populations, it will immobilize others, leading the most vulnerable to become "displaced in place."

Second, and relatedly, many people who do move away from climate-stressed contexts are not necessarily those who are most vulnerable to climate change, nor are they always moving primarily for climate-related reasons. Households with greater resources, knowledge, and networks—also those households that already show higher degrees of mobility for education, work, or other reasons—can draw on other sources of migration capability (e.g., nonfarm incomes, social networks, and migrant remittances) to maintain their migration projects. Because these households do not rely solely on rainfed agriculture for their livelihoods, drought rarely becomes a dominating factor in their migration decision-making. Over the longer term, then, drought compounds the causes of poverty and immobility among the poorest households. It risks widening inequalities between those who have access to migrant remittances and nonfarm incomes and those who do not.

Future research will benefit from moving beyond push-factor narratives toward more dynamic systems thinking. In other words, rather than assume environmental stress (or demographic "pressure") will push otherwise happily immobile populations out of rural livelihoods, it is more realistic to assume that many people are already moving, or aspiring to move, for all sorts of reasons. From this starting point, the task is then to understand existing mobility systems, their social determinants, and how environmental changes intersect with these social determinants. This approach will enable researchers to better explain why the same environmental stress can lead to very different kinds of migration and immobility outcomes within and across social and geographic contexts. It may also allow policy makers to anticipate the development challenges that reduced migration might bring.

9
The Good Life

Social transformation entails a twofold process of change: in the structural dimensions of our material lives and in our collective social imaginaries—both of which have implications for, among many other things, the ways in which we move and settle. While previous chapters have considered structural and aspirational change in tandem, this last analytical chapter gives focused attention to the social imaginary. Individual migration aspirations are rooted in a social imaginary that orients values and visions of the good. From this perspective, I suggest urbanization is not only a demographic, economic, or political process. It also entails an urbanization of the social imaginary, the gradual displacement of values, norms, and attitudes that sustained rural ways of living with values, norms, and attitudes that support the social and economic systems of urban, industrial society.

Charting transformations in the social imaginary is a challenging endeavor. While the previous chapters anchored arguments in a mix of qualitative and other data (e.g., survey responses, aerial photographs, or rainfall records), gauging shifts in mindset, values, and aspirations necessarily relies on methods that center the narratives and perspectives of those living through change. Here, I draw almost exclusively on in-depth interviews and ethnographic observations to explore how people think about and describe a "good life." Through thematic and narrative analyses—examining the language, metaphors, and recurring themes people use when describing their understandings of the past, present, and future—I explore how a community's collective sense of what constitutes a good life has changed in patterned ways over time.

This chapter unfolds in three parts. The first section narrates the most common stories told about the good life and its transformation, showing how it has shifted from a rural, pastoral ideal toward an urban ideal centered on heightened material well-being, economic mobility, and personal freedom. While almost all agree the good life is no longer a rural one, I also explore diverging perspectives based on generation, education, gender, and social hierarchies, reminding us that there is no singular or static conception of "the good." Further, although a good life is no longer seen as attainable in Wayisso, not everyone has the means to leave. The second section explores how people adapt their aspirations and plans in light of the capability constraints they face. The final section shifts perspective to consider the impact of migration on the social imaginary. While previous chapters focused primarily on how different dimensions of social transformation give rise to migration aspirations, here I focus on how the practice of migration—as people leave, remit, and return—actively influences ideas about the good life.

Stories about the "Good Life"

How the past, present, and future are described, desired, or disdained reveals important facets of an operating social imaginary. This section considers how people describe their pasts; how they see themselves now—sometimes "stuck" between their present realities and idealized futures; and the strands that constitute the imagined "good life" toward which they strive.

For earlier generations, nearly everyone agreed, a rural life was the good life. "Earlier, our families lived a rich life—they simply drank milk and ate butter. Their way of life was good," one elder shared. The tropes of milk, butter, and honey are everywhere in people's imaginations of the past. Their ancestors were strong, wealthy, and happy. "During the time of my great-grandfather, our lives were based on the cattle. We lived by drinking milk, by eating butter. We slaughtered the cattle and drank their blood. When you compare these people to the people today, they were stronger, because they drank milk, ate butter, and drank blood," one middle-aged farmer shared.

Naturally, some degree of romanticization is inherent in people's recollections of the past. "At that time, there were no thieves. There was no killing anyone... without a reason. You loved everyone," another elder reminisced. Whatever you needed was available. Money was not an issue: "We didn't use much money. There was no place for money. At that time, one cow was 1 birr. One birr was so much money!"

The symbolic and material center of the good life was cattle. The number of cattle people had was the measuring stick of wealth, and how they ate and drank was another clearly related one. Meat, milk, and butter all came from their livestock. When strangers were received or when marriage rites were held, wealth was shared in cattle, milk, butter, and meat. One elder described a special meal called *Tuma Nyaata*, made from red meat that had been dried in the sun, ground with mortar and pestle, and then mixed with butter, milk, and blood. "That was the meal for the wealthiest people.... It was considered that whoever eats *Tuma Nyaata* is respected and given recognition. He is wealthy and strong enough to do anything."

In addition to the number of cattle he owned, a man's social position was determined by his position within the Gadaa system (see Chapter 4). While only a select few became Gadaa fathers, the advantages this afforded were in the currencies of respect, prestige, and power. For some, it also meant more cattle, as they negotiated disputes. And the more cattle and respect a man had, "the more wives he was given," as one woman put it. Thus, another measuring stick of wealth and status was the number of wives and children a man had.

At this time, the good life—with abundant cattle, good grazing lands, a large family, and a firm position within the established social system—could only be sustained or even envisioned in rural areas. Towns were places for the poor, and even as Adami Tulu and Ziway grew in the mid-twentieth century, wealthy people continued to prefer a rural life. In the 1960s, even the most advantaged and wealthiest men with ties to Haile Selassie's government eschewed urban areas. As one elder explained:

> *Ashu Bentuu was one* balabat *during the time of Haile Selassie. Even he didn't have a house here in Adami Tulu. At that time, we thought that wealthy people were going to live in rural areas, and it is only the poor who are going to move to urban areas. Even Bentuu's daughters and sons did not have a house in the urban area. Because those who are wealthy, those who have many cattle, are going to be in the rural area. They didn't want to be in the urban area. It is the poor who settled those cities [Adami Tulu and Ziway].*

Just as young and old shared a belief in the wealth and prosperity of earlier generations, they shared the opinion that "the rural life has passed": "The good life is no longer in the rural areas." The same signs of wealth for previous generations were used to illustrate the decline and fall of rural lifestyles. As one older man put it, "In our age, we were drinking milk. We ate butter. We ate porridge. But now we are proceeding to [cooking] oil. I hate oil. I don't want to eat it. The life of society has changed from milk to oil, from butter to oil, from porridge to oil." Another older woman recounted,

"Now butter is too expensive, but before we could get it all the time. Now, it is difficult to even eat butter, but before, we would use it for our hair!"

Further, and as I described in Chapter 5, the material and symbolic status of cattle has largely been replaced by money. As one elder explained in relation to marriage practices:

> *Earlier, we drank blood as part of the marriage ceremony. The girl's family will bring a container of blood—if the girl's family is wealthy, they will bring two—and they mix the blood with milk. Every family member would then drink that blood to show that we are now sharing the blood of each other. And four cattle would also be given to her family. But recently, times have changed. It has changed completely from blood to money, what we call the* gabara *for the woman's family. Now, nobody drinks blood. They just give money to her family.*

The decline of rural life is captured in the movement from butter to oil, from blood to money.

Perhaps more than any objective evaluation of whether the quality of life was truly better before than it is now, these narratives show that people have come to *see themselves as poor* in Wayisso, something they were not before. Their ancestors would certainly be "poor" according to our definitions of poverty today. They would fall below the 2.15 USD per day poverty line set by the World Bank, for example, if simply because they exchanged cattle and goods more than money. They had higher mortality rates, particularly among children. And as egalitarian as the Gadaa system may have been, it was also patriarchal, with men leading the community's decision-making.[1] Yet, when people in Wayisso reminisced about the past, these negative elements were rarely mentioned. People remember that the lands were green, and their ancestors were wealthy, dignified, strong, and happy.

Today, however, the good life is nowhere to be found in rural areas. It has moved to the city. As so many people shared, both young and old, male and female, "it is much better to live in the city."[2] At the most fundamental level, people have changing expectations for the quality of their material life, and what are now seen as basic needs—easy access to clean water, electricity, toilets—are only found in town. As Chapter 6 illustrated, young people are often exposed to these facilities when they first move to town for schooling. Afterward, it is difficult to return to areas with no light or plumbing. As one young woman put it, "What can my generation do in Wayisso? We cannot meet our basic needs there."

These changing expectations go beyond basic needs. The city is also the realm of consumption and access to technology, knowledge, and, perhaps most importantly, the potential for *change*. "To change my life" is the most common reason people give for wanting to leave, and the ability to better one's socioeconomic circumstances was perceived as impossible in Wayisso. This change might manifest in many ways: in access to education and for the lucky few who make it to tertiary levels and professional jobs; in access to business opportunities such as opening a shop, driving a *bajaj* taxi, or renting houses; in the proximity of new kinds of fashion, mobile phones, foods, television, and films that become outer signs of an inner transition to a "modern" lifestyle. But the most important element is that these types of changes are only seen as being possible to realize in urban areas. "In Wayisso, you can work hard your whole life, but you do not see any change. The life of a farmer today, even if he works hard his whole life, will look the same in twenty years," one young man explained.

Old signs of social status remain, like being elected as a Gadaa father or the number of cattle one owns, but new forms of urban-based status symbols are proliferating. One day I met a teacher who had recently left his job for a management position in a beer company. He joked that he had grown fatter since I last saw him. He was doing well in his job, he told me. In fact, he boasted, he just had raw meat and beer for breakfast—a modern iteration of *Tuma Nyaata* in the city.

Men and women also adopt new forms of clothing in the city. Men often wear jeans, T-shirts, and sleek sneakers. Women wear bras, trousers instead of skirts, and even short dresses on special occasions. In Ziway, I lived for a time with several women in their late twenties and early thirties who were not yet married. One older man remembers that when some of them returned to Wayisso in their new clothes, people could not believe it. "These women are empowered!" he laughed. "They are wearing jeans!"

Because the city is perceived as a place with greater possibilities for change, it is also seen as a place with greater choice. For young women in particular, the city was described as a place of freedom. In the village, women contribute to household incomes—through assisting with farm work or selling goods at the market in Adami Tulu, for example. However, the city represents an opportunity to earn a steadier income, to play a more active part in shaping their family's economic future, or to find income-generating work that would give them more leeway to avoid an early marriage.

As Chapter 4 made clear, new forms of work in the city need not be complex. One married woman, for example, described her desire to move to the city and sell a few things from her residence. "I know we can generate an income here [in Wayisso], but in the city, you can open a small business in front of your residence. You create work around your living area.... Here, in Wayisso, women spend most of their time sitting, or going from here to there, or preparing meals, or just sitting during the winter season." Likewise, for many young men as well, the city was a place to diversify their incomes. The desire to work year-round, to earn a steadier income, signals a new conception of work and economic engagement, another "modern" element added to the social imaginary.

There are many women who cannot migrate to the city, however, because they or their families do not have the means to support the move. As Chapter 5 detailed, the aspiration to migrate internationally—most often as domestic workers to the Middle East—was driven by a desire to accumulate capital that could be invested in income-generating activities in town, such as a shop or restaurant. Thus, migration abroad is a pathway for women to access the city. Migrants shared that when they returned, they would open a shop, and with that small degree of financial independence and social distance, they would have far more freedom than they ever had in the village.

Thus, to reduce the allure of the city to capital and consumption would be too narrow; money is necessary to achieve aspired change, but the desire for change goes far beyond it. The city is also the site of education and knowledge, of technology and wider horizons. One young man in Wayisso told me that the city was the "place of modernization." When I asked what he meant by modernization, he answered, "When I say modernization, I mean education. You get good education in the city. And if you need information, you get this from urban areas—watching TV, using the internet, other things. That is what I mean by modernization." Indeed, smartphones and the internet bring unprecedented access to a wider social world. An excerpt from my fieldnotes illustrates this point:

> *That evening, we sat around the kitchen. All of us crowded in, some chopping collard greens, others chopping onions, garlic, tomatoes, squatting over their cutting boards or the bubbling pots on the electric stove on the floor.*

Everyone else was absorbed in their phones. Mootiti was dancing, mimicking the moves from a video someone played on their smartphone. Sultan, a recent migrant to the city, sat squinting at the square screen of his small Nokia phone, attempting to scroll through Facebook. Shula made fun of his small screen and he was mad in his macho, half-joking kind of way. Marki gave me his phone to play a game; the avatar runs along train tracks and tries to catch gold coins and avoid being caught by a policeman. He then asked me to help set up an email account for him. Kadija asked me to set up a Twitter account for her. Gashi stopped by the kitchen, an older man who loves his smartphone with equal vigor but nevertheless joked about technology. That everyone was on their phones. How times have changed. That sort of thing. It's the same everywhere, I thought. We were all like a bunch of teenagers in the US, sitting together with our faces glued to our screens. (May 7, 2016)

The city becomes the place of access to this wider social world. This is, practically speaking, because good access to the internet is largely limited to urban areas. Connectivity rates are low in Wayisso, and rarely could those living in rural areas afford a smartphone. The new ability to consume technology and participate in new virtual worlds is part of what geographer Wilbur Zelinsky, writing before the age of the internet, described as the "mobility of the mind":

But perhaps the greatest of the new mobilities is that of the mind. Perception and thought are no longer tethered to the living memory and to the here and now but have been stretched to virtual infinity.... This intellectual mobility is not just outward to all parts of the earth and the observable universe or backward and forward through time but is into other dimensions as well— the psychological, the esthetic, and the scientific. All these forms of motion are closely interrelated: increasing freedom of spatial movement is both cause and effect of other forms of enhanced mobility.[3]

***

Although almost everyone in Wayisso agreed that a good life is no longer possible in rural places, it was common for older generations to have mixed views about life in the city. Some were quick to condemn the foreign lifestyles of urban youth. One afternoon, the mother of one of the young women with whom I lived in Ziway came to stay with us. She would visit from time to time, to "take a rest," as she put it, and check on her children. But she said she preferred living in Wayisso. "Young people just sit around and laugh all day. They don't work," she said with a sly smile, leaning against the wall with her legs outstretched. Her daughter laughed and poured her a cup of coffee.

Other older parents in Wayisso expressed concern about the negative effects of living in the city. Urban youth could become entitled and lazy, some shared, or corrupted by *khat*, a plant commonly chewed as a stimulant. One older man living in Wayisso, Godana, lamented that young people who leave are no longer satisfied with rural lifestyles: "If they come back to the rural area, they can't get transportation. They can't get pure water. They can't access the facilities that they need. This is the great problem, why they don't come back." Young people's dissatisfaction with rural lives, he felt, is driving a wedge between families. He continued: "They are forgetting their family who are living in Wayisso. There is a gap in families now—between father and son—there is a gap. They don't want to come back and ask after their parents. They don't want to look at the condition their parents are living in. There are some people who die without their sons or daughters visiting them. Even if they come back, they immediately return to the city."

In the worst cases, he explained, young people move to the city and become addicted to alcohol and drugs: "The youth who taste the city life are completely changed.... They start chewing *khat*. They start smoking cigarettes. They start drinking alcohol.... From morning to night, they just sit somewhere and chew *khat*. They hate working and coming here.... And if they don't have money, they start stealing from others."

He went on to tell me two stories about children whose lust after money drove them to turn on their parents. In the first, one young man from a neighboring *kebele* frequently returned to his village to ask for money from his mother. At first, she supported him. She sold an ox and some of her land. "Whenever he would come, she just gave." One day, she refused. Her son threatened her, demanding the money, but she ignored him, returning to her work. The young man became so upset that he killed his own mother.

In the second story, a young man came home one day to ask his father for cattle. "I won't give you any cattle," he said, "but if you want to change, come with me, plow with me, work with me, and I'll give you cattle." His son refused and became so angry that later that afternoon, as his father was working in the fields, the son stabbed him. Others stopped the son before he took his father's life, but his father was so injured that he could no longer work. "He is simply sitting now." As for the boy, the community "gave him a good beating" and "gave the boy to the Silt'e people. They told them to just take him. 'If you like, kill him.'"

These stories did not happen in Wayisso, and I did not make any substantive attempt to verify them, because regardless of whether they *really* happened, the stories communicate a powerful narrative: young people move to the city and become corrupted by a lust for money to such a degree that they begin to value it over family and hard work, turning on and even killing their parents.

As unfair as these portrayals of corrupted youth may be, the claim that young people come to disdain rural lifestyles after living in the city is something urban youth do not deny. But younger generations were equally quick to condemn the attachment to village life that they saw in some of their elders. One young man, still living in Wayisso but with his aspirations set on Ziway, explained: "My mother lives in Suro. She doesn't want to leave her birthplace. There is backwardness around there.... My mom doesn't like to drink pump water. She still drinks the water which the cattle drink, from the lake. People stay because of backwardness."

Another young man in Wayisso shared a similar perspective but emphasized the difficulty older generations might have adapting to new ways of living and working in the city:

Young people always want change. They look forward. They think about the infrastructure they will gain in the urban area: like job opportunities, like pure water, like television ... all the facilities of the urban areas. But when it comes to the elders ... their income is based on plowing and cattle. This is the only work they know. ... They are not educated. They are not well trained. They don't have the knowledge to do urban work. The work and the life that they are familiar with is only plowing and cattle, so they prefer to live here.

Many older men and women indeed felt personally unequipped or uninspired to migrate and build an entirely new life in town. Instead, they put their hope in their children. As Caawaa, one elder in Wayisso, expressed:

The life that we had has already passed. It was good, taking everything fresh, but it has already passed. Now I am close to death. If I have the power to educate my children, I may help them. That's what I wish for those kids. They should work hard and educate themselves and start life like the others in the urban area, because life in the rural area has become too difficult. So they should learn more and change their life.

Across generations, education is always considered a good thing. Even the skeptical older man, Godana, who elaborated the many ills of urban youth, admired one aspect of urban life: access to education. "But the good part for the new generation is education. When they are educated, they create new things for society. Like infrastructure, transportation, even doctors. . . . The only ones who can create the plane, who can create the bus, who create anything are those who are literate."

The high value placed on education led to some conflicting narratives about the past, even from the same individual. For example, early in my interview with Shuko, an older woman living in Wayisso, she presented a somewhat romantic vision of the past:

Those times were incomparable to these ones. At that time, no one was poor. We drank milk. We ate porridge. Everything was easy. Just we ate, we drank, after that we would play, we would dance and sing with our friends. I didn't worry about life. It's not at all like today. Today, it is too difficult. Nothing is easy. But at that time, our family had cattle. We had milk. We prepared porridge. Just eating and playing and dancing and taking care of ourselves. It was a good childhood.

Nevertheless, later in the interview, when speaking about education, she shared: "My childhood was dark. Because at that time, there was no education. There was no school. Even when the school came, my family registered us, but then they didn't send us or allow us to learn. It was very difficult for girls to study. Girls were only allowed to stay at home." Thus, the older generation concluded that the good life is no longer in rural areas, and the past was better than the present, but education was one factor that inverted that narrative.

Navigating Constraints

Although almost everyone felt that the good life is no longer a rural one, not everyone had intentions or plans to leave. Notions of the good life shape aspirations, but these aspirations are mediated by one's capabilities, or lack thereof. As one young woman from Wayisso who was selling coffee in Ziway explained, "In Ziway, you can find work. You can find anything. You have light, water, everything is here. But you need money. If you have money and you are able to work, you can find anything in Ziway." For those without the means to make the move, they preferred to stay in the village. Two older women in Wayisso explained, "Life in the city is very good if you have something in your hand. Otherwise, we prefer the rural life. Here we find everything without money, without expense. But if you are wealthy, it is better to be in the city." Often, when I asked young people about their first impressions of city life, they mentioned the expense, the need to pay for *everything*—rent, food, even tea and coffee. In the village, everything is "free." Thus, people may all want to ideally move to the city, but as one young man explained, "people stay because they get married, or they have children, and they don't have the money to make the move."

One afternoon, I sat with two wives of one village elder, both of whom lived in Wayisso. The second wife began listing the names of all those who have left and continued:

> *Those are the people who have money, who move to Ziway. That's what I see in my area. Now their houses are empty. It is sad. . . . Money moves from the rural areas to the city. The resources are good in the city. The health is good. You get water and light from the city. Those who go to live in the city don't come back to the rural areas. Even if I went to the city, I know I would not want to come back.*

The first wife chimed in, "I would like to have a shop in the city!" The second wife continued, "Before people liked milk *too* much. Now they don't even like milk. The time for keeping animals has passed."

Thus, even though most agree that urban lives are better than rural ones, people adjust their expectations and plans for their lives continually. Consider the example of Bilisuma from Chapter 6. He tried several times to move to the city, to pursue his education and thereby secure an urban future, but because of financial constraints, he could never successfully make the move to town. Eventually, he resigned himself to a future in Wayisso. He has no plans to move again, even though he still believes that a better life is elsewhere.

This point is particularly relevant to research on migration aspirations. The Gallup World Poll survey, for example, shows just how widespread migration aspirations can be. Between 2010 and 2015, this survey found that 30 percent of the population of 157 countries around the world expressed a wish to move abroad.[4] However, over this same period, less than 1 percent migrated. In Ethiopia, if you ask someone whether they would like to migrate, many will say yes. Whether they actually plan to, and whether they have the resources to do so, is an entirely different matter.[5]

Yomen, whom I introduced in Chapter 6, provides another example of aspiration adaptation. When I first met Yomen, she was eighteen and living with her family in Wayisso. The youngest of eight children, she was the only girl in her family to go to school. "Earlier people thought that women shouldn't go to school," and her six older sisters "just simply married according to the expectations of our family." Because of her education, however, she sees her future differently: "But in my case, I am educated. I went to school. And I know something. . . . I want to choose the way that I like."

In my first conversation with Yomen, she was quick to ask me whether I could help her migrate abroad. "I would be so happy if I could leave Ethiopia," she said. "I don't want to live here." I asked her why. "In Ethiopia, it is not a good life. Even my own life, when I look back at it, I am not happy with how I've spent it. There are many problems here in Ethiopia. That's why I want to fly abroad." When asked where she would like to go, she said, "Not to the Arab countries. If I had the chance, I'd like to go to the United States, or Europe, anything except Arab." Yomen had no plans to migrate to the United States or Europe. She had not applied for the US Diversity Visa—the most accessible legal pathway to someone without migrant networks—nor did she know how she might do so.

Yomen was in a position common to many young women who have high hopes for the future and limited capabilities to realize them. She failed the national exam after grade ten and was spending the year helping her mother and studying to retake the exam. She wanted to continue on to preparatory school and then university. She did not like the typical options for women who could not continue their education. "The first option is to get married. The second is to migrate to the Arab countries. The third option is to sit with your families, like me," she laughed. She wasn't thinking about marriage yet—"I'm still thinking about improving my education level. I'm not thinking about marriage"—but she was also not eager to leave Ethiopia as a domestic worker. She was particularly influenced by what she had heard from her friends working overseas. While not necessarily victims of physical abuse, they told Yomen that "the Arab people don't respect Ethiopians."

Her neighbor went to Dubai, and "the work is difficult, they always nag her, they shout at her. That's why I'm scared [to leave]."

When I met Yomen again some six months later, her future plans had changed. She did not retake the national exam, because she missed them. She was visiting her sister in Qore, about one hundred kilometers south of Adami Tulu, and she had not been able to get transportation back in time. That is the excuse she told me, anyway. Taking stock of her options, she began an application to migrate to the Middle East as a domestic worker. Yet, she never completed it because she still had reservations: "I am afraid to go there. Maybe I won't have a good family." Her family also wanted her to stay for the same reasons. Instead, she was considering opening a *mana bunaa*, a small coffee hut in Qore. Her family would help her pay for it. Although coffee houses are an already saturated market, she reasoned it is "better to try and compete than to sit around doing nothing here." When asked if she would consider working at Sher, the flower farm down the road, Yomen quickly said no. "It's hard work and only for 800 birr. . . . It's not worth it." I wondered aloud whether she might be able to make more money at Sher than selling coffee. She responded curtly, almost offended, "Work at Sher is not a way to improve my life." For Yomen, work was about more than money; owning her own business might bring a sense of pride, while working long hours for low wages at Sher felt degrading, something to be ashamed of.

Yomen, like so many young people around the world, shifted her aspirations and strategies to achieve them continually. When speaking with Yomen again sometime later, I asked again about her future hopes. I was surprised by her response, how much her aspirations and expectations had changed since our first conversation: "Even if it is in a rural area, I want to make my life better than the others. I want the food I prepare to be good. To have a good toilet, a good bathroom. Everything that my children need should be facilitated. This is what I wish for."

When I returned to visit Yomen again two years later, her mother greeted me and threw her hands up into the air with happiness: "Yomen is married!" We went to her new home in the adjacent rural *kebele*, only to discover she had just left for the hospital to give birth to her first child.

Ideas about the "good life" set the aspirational horizons within which young people develop expectations for their lives. For most young people in Wayisso, their aspirational horizons are set on towns and cities in Ethiopia. However, to say that young people now believe "the good life is in the city" does not mean all people will migrate there. Aspirations are necessary but insufficient determinants of migration. Most young people lack the capability to realize their life aspirations and so they adapt their hopes and plans in light of the more immediate opportunities and constraints before them.

***

The preceding chapters focused primarily on how Ethiopia's pursuit of development reshaped the social structures and the social imaginary in such a way that rural-urban and international migration became more common. However, it is also important to give attention to how *migration* itself contributes to a shifting social imaginary and accelerates structural change. Migration is not just a consequence of social transformation; it is also one of its drivers.

Arjun Appadurai argues that the two strongest forces shaping imaginations of modernity are migration and the media.[6] For those living in Wayisso, migration indeed is one of the strongest forces shaping the broader life aspirations of others (to Appadurai's list, I would also add formal education). The migration of some introduces new possibilities to others. Those who leave the village and access new income-generating opportunities in town are able to change their lives and the lives of their family members in ways that others see and then come to desire. Migrants "model" new practices that others observe and then consider imitating—especially when the first exceptional migration of a few generates conspicuous positive outcomes.[7]

As migration behavior diffuses throughout a community, it becomes less exceptional and more of the norm. In some places, it eventually becomes so commonplace that a culture of migration consolidates. "People learn to migrate, and learn to desire to migrate," as the sociologist Syed Ali once put it.[8] In Wayisso, one could argue that a culture of migration exists relative to migration to town, but international migration is not yet so widespread that one would say it has become culture. Nevertheless, in a relatively short period of time—the first few women left for the Middle East in the late 1990s—this labor migration corridor is a potential pathway many young women now seriously consider. If a culture of international migration abroad were to emerge, what is occurring now in the Adami Tulu and Jido Kombolcha *woreda* illustrates what changing patterns of aspirations and behavior look like before a culture of international migration takes root.

To understand how migration reshapes the social imaginary—specifically, how migration influences the values, norms, and aspirations of both migrants and nonmigrants—I focus on two core mechanisms. First, I explore how migrant remittances produce visible inequalities in communities of origin, reshaping local perceptions and comparisons of lifestyles "here" and "there." Once people do aspire to leave, a second question emerges: why do certain destinations become more prominent in people's imagined futures than others? Why, for instance, do some women from Wayisso move to the Middle East while no men move abroad? Why are Adami Tulu and Ziway far more common destinations than Bulbulla, another neighboring urban area in the same *woreda*? While Zelinsky's general insight that migration increases with modernization may hold true, understanding the prominence of particular destinations requires examining how specific migration systems take shape.[9]

Developing Discontent

One way to approach the study of migration aspirations is to ask, what are the origins of discontent? What causes someone to be dissatisfied with their current place and conditions? The question, of course, assumes that people are sometimes satisfied with where they are. Perhaps they never are and always desire some degree of change. But we do not always see abrupt transformations in the kinds of lives people pursue and live. Long periods of relatively consistent ways of living can shift suddenly in a single generation. In Wayisso, transformations in livelihoods and lifestyles shifted from seminomadic pastoralism to farming to urban work in just four generations—and as previous chapters have argued, it would be incorrect and misguided to characterize rising rural out-migration as "forced." How and why, then, do people come to see other places and ways of living as *better*?

Some might argue that the desire for change, for continual progress, is the very essence of modernity—particularly in its capitalist form.[10] After all, discontent fuels the capitalist system. As the German sociologist Wolfgang Streeck argues, human needs are not fixed; they are "fluid and socially and historically contingent."[11] Thus, he suggests an approach to the study of contemporary capitalism that focuses on "consumption and the evolution of consumer 'needs,' or better: desires. Here in particular, dreams, promises and imagined satisfaction are not at all marginal but, on the contrary, central."[12] Streeck shows how scarcity is a taken-for-granted condition that acts as the cornerstone of contemporary political economy. But needs are dynamic, he argues, and what is seen as "necessary" for life is largely socially defined.

There are deeper questions that could be addressed about human nature and the origins of discontent, but there is one concrete way in which migration fuels a sense of discontentment among those who remain: through what social scientists call "relative deprivation," the idea that subjective evaluations of well-being or deprivation are made in relation to one's reference community rather than any absolute criteria.[13] In the 1980s, economists Oded Stark and Edward Taylor applied the concept to explain international migration dynamics from Mexico. They showed that even when controlling for absolute income gains, the probability of participating in international migration to the United States was directly related to a household's relative deprivation—that is, their income *relative* to their reference community.[14] Relative deprivation, as a motivating force in migration, suggests that individuals and families are not motivated to better their lot in absolute terms; rather, they evaluate their current conditions and seek to improve them in relation to how others in their community are doing. The implication follows that in places where incomes are universally low, migration aspirations will be lower than in areas where income inequalities are wider and more conspicuous, even if average incomes are higher overall.

In Wayisso, the remittances sent home from migrants in town or young women in the Middle East are visible to neighbors—through the construction of a new home (Figures 9.1 and 9.2), in paying the tuition fees for a sibling's private education, by moving a parent to town—fueling a sense of relative deprivation among households that do not have a migrant elsewhere. Hein de Haas found a similar reality in southern Morocco; socioeconomic divisions often exist between households with a migrant abroad and households without, what he terms the migration "haves" and "have-nots."[15] Through the visible changes remittances bring to the lives of migrants and their families, feelings of relative deprivation in the community deepen, and internal and international migration enters into what geographers have referred to as the "mental maps"[16] of others, a possible pathway in their

Figure 9.1 A traditional home in Wayisso

Figure 9.2 A new home in Wayisso, built with migrant remittances

imagined futures. Young women who aspired to go to the Middle East would often mention someone they knew who was able to "change their life," who inspired them to follow a similar route.

Mental Maps

Migration aspirations and behavior often follow the trajectories traversed by others. Many young women in Wayisso, for example, imagined their futures in Wayisso, in Adami Tulu or Ziway, or in the Middle East. Few seriously considered Addis Ababa, although they certainly knew it existed, and even fewer seriously considered Europe or America, which were considered by some the same distant place and referred to interchangeably. As mental maps expand, they do so unevenly—not in a gradual expansion from the local to the global, but with jutting nodes in sometimes unexpected places.

The act of seeing someone leave, noting where they go and what types of change that migration brings to the migrant and their families, expands the aspirational horizons of those considering their future options. When I asked young women who expressed an aspiration to migrate to the Middle East where they wanted to go, they often said a place where they knew someone else had been and had a successful migration experience. Then, if they do leave, the migration experience expands their mental maps even further.

Jaa, for example, left Wayisso for Beirut first—like almost all the other young women from Wayisso. She worked for a "nice family" for 2,500 birr per month, a higher rate than the average pay there. I met her shortly after her return to Ethiopia. She expressed the desire to leave again, but this time, she explained, she plans to go to Jeddah in Saudi Arabia. "I wish to return to an Arab country, but not Beirut. . . . In other Arab countries, the pay is better." In Jeddah, they pay around 7,000 birr per month, she told me, and for those who know Arabic, some pay 9,000 birr per month. "So I have decided to go to Jeddah. But in Jeddah, with the Muslim families, you have to cover your whole face. You only open your eyes. This would be very difficult for me!" Having already left once, Jaa is more aware of the working conditions, payments, and possibilities across potential destinations. Through her migration, her mental map expanded, and her imagined futures, aspirations, and plans shifted accordingly. Should she go to Jeddah, her migration will likewise introduce this destination into the mental maps of her social network.

Similar dynamics shape internal migration as well. For young women migrating from more distant rural areas of Oromia or Ethiopia's southern regions to work at flower farms in Ziway, the move often felt as significant as migrating abroad, and their decision-making closely mirrored that of women who chose international migration to the Middle East. Many arrived at Sher after further schooling ceased to be an option—either due to failed exams or family pressures to marry—and social networks greatly influenced their decision. As one young woman explained, "Other girls from our village had gone to work at Sher and told us that there is work there, that there is money." Because Sher is foreign owned, migrant workers expected higher wages than at Ethiopian-owned companies. These women migrated during a pivotal transition in their life course, driven by the same aspiration as those who leave the country: to earn enough money to "change my life."

Once at Sher, however, many young women turned their gaze to the Middle East. Dissatisfied with the difficult work, low pay, and high costs of living in Ziway or Adami Tulu, they were unable to save and invest in a better future—even if their earnings provided some independence and reduced acute poverty. While working at Sher, these young women encountered others who shared information about better opportunities abroad. Fayine, for example, from a rural area in southern Oromia, had worked at Sher for only a few weeks but was already planning to leave. She knew someone from her home region who went to Kuwait and "changed her and her family's life." At Sher, she also heard from others that Kuwait was a good place to go, along with practical guidance on how to leave. Sher, then, is a node where women expand their mental maps and develop new migration aspirations.

For most families in Wayisso, in the hierarchy of destinations, Ziway was at the top. As one young man in Wayisso explained, "No one is going to move to Bulbulla or Adami Tulu hoping that there will be a change. They go there for the sake of education, because there is no high school here in Wayisso. They may go for the market. But if they leave Wayisso, they prefer Ziway. Not Adami Tulu or Bulbulla." "Why?" I asked. "The capital city of Ethiopia is Addis. For the people around here, Ziway is like the capital city! They think about it like this, so they prefer Ziway." Indeed, Ziway had the largest market, the most dynamic proliferation of small businesses, and higher rates of population growth.

The mental maps of young people with higher levels of education, however, expand to include wider horizons. Most lived in Ziway for their secondary schooling, and for those who attended university, they often moved to larger urban centers like Jimma, Adama, or Addis Ababa. Once there, Ziway was no longer the "capital city." Migration aspirations were reoriented toward larger urban centers within Ethiopia. These young people

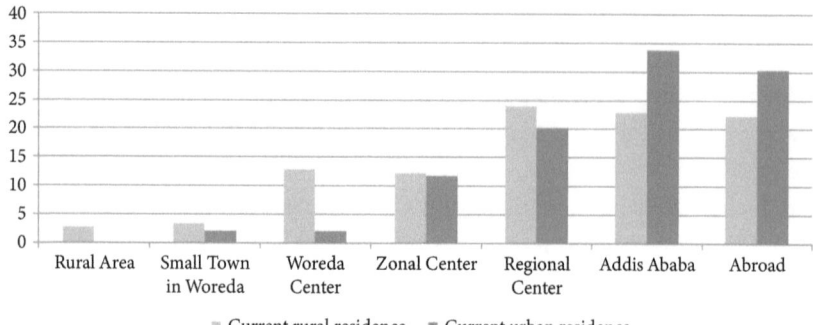

Figure 9.3 Most likely migration destination (%) by current residence

Source: Young lives study Ethiopia, fourth round, 2013–2014, older cohort (*n* = 823). Reproduced from Kerilyn Schewel and Sonja Fransen, "Formal Education and Migration Aspirations in Ethiopia," *Population and Development Review* 44, no. 3 (2018): 573.

also became more aware of distinctions in international destinations—of the risks of irregular migration to Europe, the difficult working conditions in the Middle East, or the possibility of applying for a Diversity Visa for the United States. In one study using data from the Young Lives project in Ethiopia, Sonja Fransen and I found that young people in rural areas more often imagine migrating to smaller or regional urban centers (Figure 9.3). In fact, the difference in aspired destinations between rural and urban residents is most striking for *woreda* centers, like Ziway.

***

In Wayisso, the good life used to be a rural, pastoral life. The quality of that life was measured in cattle and described in terms of abundance—of milk, butter, and honey. However, that life has passed, and the settled village is now described as a place of poverty, stagnation, and struggle. Today, the good life is in the city, and it is measured in access to material means for immaterial ends: freedom, knowledge, social mobility, and transformation. The city promises access to basic needs like clean water, electricity, and education, but more fundamentally, it promises *change* in one's material and social circumstances. Nevertheless, people tell conflicting narratives about the past and present, of rural and urban lives. Young people were more likely to see older generations as "backwards," while older generations were more likely to see urban youth as "lazy" and corrupted by the city. Women were more likely to see the past as "dark" and the future as "bright." Older men lamented the decline in the dignity of rural livelihoods.

The relocation of the good life from Wayisso to the city is not simply a story of changing tastes or preferences. This aspirational shift is driven by powerful forces of social change—political, economic, cultural, and technological. Market expansion and the commodification of social life have instilled a new understanding of agency, one tied to the acquisition of capital or professional work as the key to achieving social and spatial mobility. Formal schooling opens the possibility of professional work and fuels discontent with traditional ways of life. In this changing social landscape, spatial mobility becomes increasingly tied to other forms of mobility—social, economic, and intellectual. For those with the capability to leave, the city promises a greater degree of choice, a chance to rewrite one's future. Those without that capability can feel left behind, grappling with the disorientation of staying still while their social world is in flux.

This disjuncture between a transformed social imaginary and existing social realities has far-reaching implications. In Wayisso, the aspiration-opportunity gap is widening between generations, and between families with different levels of wealth and migrant networks. As those with greater capabilities migrate, they introduce new inequalities to the village and, through their visible success, inspire others to leave. Those without the means to move must contend with their deepening relative deprivation and find ways to manage or acquiesce to their immobility. Like Yomen, some may reorient their aspirations, striving to make the most of what feels like a less desirable life in the village, while others may find it harder to escape feelings of frustration and resentment. In places where mounting inequality, unmet aspirations, and simmering resentment converge, conditions become ripe for political movements like the Oromo protests of the late 2010s. As Tatek Abebe argues, Oromo youth were particularly active in the protests because they are both "excluded from a rural future" and excluded from "a modernist development future that unequally distributes the fruits of economic growth."[17] This exclusion finds tangible expression in the reality of involuntary immobility.

Understanding the origins of discontent, and how the practice of migration itself influences a community's social imaginary, is key to moving beyond simplistic push-factor narratives about why people leave. In Wayisso, it is not poverty or climate change alone driving rural out-migration. It is also the changing nature of progress itself. Young people now aspire for lives—filled with educational opportunity, independence, consumption, and transformation—that are unattainable in rural places.

They are moved by modernity. The desire to change one's life stems from, and is stimulated by, Ethiopia's development. What lessons this one small village offers to mobility transition theory and, more broadly, to understandings of the relationship between migration and development is the focus of the following, final chapter.

10
Lessons from Wayisso

The story of Wayisso village is a modern tale. As the Ethiopian state expanded into this once peripheral region, Indigenous forms of social organization through the Gadaa system—harmonious with age-old pastoral ways of life—gave way to the political logic of a nation-state, reconfiguring relationships to land and livelihood. This process intensified under the Marxist Derg regime in the 1970s, which turned this informal settlement into a peasant association. Collective grazing lands were nationalized, allocated to households, and turned into croplands. New political structures, economic relations, educational institutions, languages, and identities penetrated social life. Initially resistant to abandon ways of living and moving that had sustained their ancestors for generations, Wayisso households eventually settled into agricultural livelihoods. This settlement set the foundation for new forms of migration in subsequent decades.

By the new millennium, young people were leaving Wayisso to pursue new kinds of lives in neighboring towns and cities. The abandonment of rural lives coincided with rapid national development under the Ethiopian People's Revolutionary Democratic Front. This self-titled "developmental state" invested in mass public education, infrastructure expansion, and the commercialization and industrialization of agriculture. It courted foreign investment and embraced the power of the market. As a result, the thinking of smallholder farmers in Wayisso came to mirror the development thinking of the state. They too turned away from agriculture to pursue the promise of self-development, of economic gain through professional work, private entrepreneurship, and labor migration.

This final chapter offers lessons from Wayisso about the complex relationship between migration and development. It begins by arguing that Ethiopia's development has cultivated a "transformation ethic" among younger generations, a value system that prioritizes progress, social mobility, and change over stability and subsistence. It suggests the transformation ethic is a powerful, distinctly modern, and often overlooked driver of migration desires in Ethiopia and around the world that undermines push-factor

Moved by Modernity. Kerilyn Schewel, Oxford University Press. © Oxford University Press (2025).
DOI: 10.1093/9780197680759.003.0011

narratives and their associated policy recommendations. The second section looks more closely at migration transition theory and offers several suggestions from this case study for future theorizing and comparative research. The third section reflects on how to refine migration and development policies in light of mobility transition theory and the transformation ethic. The final section returns to the question of what stories we tell about why people migrate. It summarizes the complex, sometimes conflicting, and still unsettled narratives surrounding migration and development in today's world.

The Transformation Ethic

While writing this book, I led a project reviewing climate-related migration forecasting models for the United States Agency for International Development. How well can we predict climate migration, the agency wanted to know, and how might this inform their priorities and programming moving forward? Over the course of that review and in my interviews with modeling experts, I was struck by the limitations of even our most sophisticated attempts to predict future migration trends. While these models have become increasingly adept at mapping climate hazards and population vulnerability, they still struggle to produce estimates of future migration that can be confidently applied to the real world.[1] This is for many reasons, but one important one is that all migration models—regardless of whether they focus on economic, political, or environmental drivers—rely on basic assumptions about what the underlying "utility function" of prospective migrants looks like. In other words, models make claims about what people prioritize, how they weigh costs and benefits, and what ultimately motivates them to stay or leave.

A core challenge to global modeling is that the calculus of migration is not universal. There is no model of migration decision-making that can accurately capture migration decision-making in all places and at all times. What people value and how they make decisions about their lives—whether those involve livelihoods, marriage, or migration—differ significantly across societies and social groups. Worldviews, cultural norms, values, education levels, economic resources, and gendered experiences, among countless others, all shape what constitutes a cost or a benefit, and what is a "rational choice" in that context. Further, and perhaps more importantly, the development process itself can transform the very utility function researchers assume. The *logic* of migration decision-making is not static; it changes as societies transform. This is why, to understand why people are leaving Wayisso and leaving rural communities around the world, we need to understand not simply the objective costs and benefits of moving, or the factors that facilitate or constrain mobility, but the social imaginary and visions of "the good" that guide economic reasoning—and how the social transformations associated with "development" impact those.

Consider, for example, the "subsistence ethic" identified by James Scott in his study of precapitalist peasant societies in Southeast Asia in the 1970s. A subsistence ethic describes a shared set of values that prioritizes the security of a subsistence livelihood over the potential for profit or wealth accumulation. "Living close to the subsistence margin," he wrote, "the peasant household has little scope for the profit maximization calculus of neoclassical economics.... In decision-making parlance his behavior is risk-averse; he minimizes the subjective probability of the maximum loss.... It is this 'safety-first' principle which lies behind a great many of the technical, social, and moral arrangements of a precapitalist agrarian order."[2] Identifying this subsistence ethic allowed Scott to explain patterns of peasant rebellion and resistance in Southeast Asia and to challenge prevailing notions that peasants behaved irrationally. Peasants are rational, he argues, but the logic or ethic that guides their rationality is not the logic of *Homo economicus*, a self-interested individual motivated by profit maximization.

Although Scott did not focus on the migration implications of a subsistence ethic, his insights resonate with the influential new economics labor migration (NELM) theory of Oded Stark and colleagues in the 1980s.[3] NELM was the first to theorize migration as a household-level strategy to manage risk through the diversification of income sources. The remittances migrants send home serve as a form of insurance for households vulnerable to market failures or environmental shocks at origin. Household risk management thus takes precedence over individual wealth accumulation. Here, the logic of migration decision-making is fundamentally different from that of neoclassical economic theory, where individuals make migration decisions based primarily on expected wage differentials.

Research from around the world continues to affirm the relevance of NELM to explain migration patterns from communities subsisting on precarious livelihoods.[4] And yet, NELM does not explain migration decision-making universally. Sometimes migration *is* an individual decision made in the pursuit of higher incomes. It is easy to challenge neoclassical economic theory, its caricature of human nature, and all that the profit motive fails to explain. But with time, I have become increasingly bothered by how much the profit motive and wage differentials *do* explain about migration patterns. By studying the migration decision-making of people leaving Wayisso, I came to realize this says less about human nature and more about the kind of world we now live in.

Nowhere is the profit motive more striking, for example, than in the decision-making of young women who leave Wayisso for domestic work abroad. This international labor migration gives rural women access to unprecedented incomes, and despite significant risks and exploitative working conditions, they continue to leave. This is not simply for money's sake, however. It is because of what money can now buy in modern society. It is precisely because of the commodification of so many dimensions of social life, and because of the increasing power of money to disrupt an otherwise predictable, rural future, that women consider leaving. Sometimes it is for their families and sometimes it is for themselves. As the Ethiopian economy "develops"—as the forces of the market become stronger, as more of social life may be bought and sold, as expectations for consumption increase, and as inequality widens within communities—migration for money begins to make more sense for more people.

There is another ethic at work in Wayisso, though. Beneath the profit or other motives for migration lie deep-seated aspirations for *change* and *progress*—manifestations of a new and distinctly modern "transformation ethic." By transformation ethic, I mean a shared set of values that prioritizes social and economic mobility over social reproduction. Consider, for example, how one young farmer explained his motivation for migration: "[In Wayisso] a man can work hard his whole life, and in twenty years, his life will look the same." What might be seen as an achievement within an alternative ethic—stability, subsistence, social reproduction—is now a sign of failure.

Sabrina Maurus describes this transformation ethic forcefully in her research with agro-pastoral communities in southern Ethiopia. Through participation in formal schooling, she writes, "young people's concept of time shifts from a cyclical one, concentrated on the reproduction of the social world, towards a linear one, focused on personal and 'national' development."[5] This is similar to the "ideology of progress" Daniel Mains describes in *Hope Is Cut*, where he explores the aspirations and everyday lives of unemployed youth in Jimma, a large city some three hundred kilometers west of Ziway. Mains finds that migration desires are increasingly driven by aspirations for "a different life from their parents', one filled with progress and change."[6] As one of his informants explains, "Today's generation is different. In the past everyone expected to do the same work as his parents. Today everyone wants to learn and to have a better life. If someone's father is a farmer, then he wants to be a modern farmer, or else to do a different job altogether."[7]

This transformation ethic is motivating migration from rural communities around the world. In Peru, Gina Crivello explores young people's desires to "become somebody in life." For rural youth, she finds, "becoming somebody" often requires moving "someplace else." Thus, rural youth imagine their futures in the next biggest town or capital city.[8] Her work builds on the insights of Peruvian anthropologist Carlos Iván Degregori, who describes a shift away from the Myth of the Inkarri, an Indigenous myth of reconquest, to the Myth of Progress, defined by education, urbanization, and economic growth. Degregori writes, "The indigenous peasantry launched forward with an unsuspecting vitality towards the conquest of the future and of 'progress.' The school, commerce, and... salaried work, these are the principal instruments for this conquest, and migration to the cities—increasingly planned—opens up new horizons."[9]

In rural Andhra Pradesh, India, Virginia Marrow finds that widening access to formal education generates new aspirations for professional futures among children and their families. Part of this aspirational shift is a concomitant devaluation of farming, even among those who have no other livelihood option. She raises an important concern for how children evaluate their lives and self-worth: "The over-valuing of formal qualifications and the under-valuing of forms of work such as agriculture risk being internalised by children, leaving those who do not succeed feeling they are 'a waste.'"[10] In rural, agricultural communities, the emergence of a transformation ethic naturally gives rise to migration aspirations, even among those who may lack the means to move.[11]

It is difficult to disentangle the transformation ethic from a particular kind of development, one exemplified by what Karl Polanyi first termed "market societies"—a fusion of the modern market economy and the nation-state system. This model of development, with its emphasis on economic growth, bureaucratic governance, and technological advancement, profoundly affects the "work of the imagination," as Arjun Appadurai puts it.[12] Expansions of capitalist markets, formal education, mass media, and infrastructure, while undeniably material changes, simultaneously lead to immaterial shifts in our worldview. They transform how we understand ourselves, our communities, and our place in the world. This interplay between the material and the immaterial underscores why scholars like Robert Bellah define modernity not simply as a set of economic or political structures but as a "spiritual phenomenon or a kind of mentality."[13]

Although the transformation ethic has global reach, its emergence and expression are neither inevitable nor uniform. How it is channeled, resisted, or adapted depends on the societal context.[14] Countless communities around the world cultivate alternative ethics and visions of a good life, emphasizing values and practices that directly challenge mainstream development's focus on material progress—and quite likely give rise to a different logic of migration decision-making. For example, Indigenous communities in the Andes promote *Buen Vivir*, a worldview that prioritizes harmony with nature over economic growth. African social movements grounded in the Ubuntu philosophy ("I am because we are") similarly emphasize collective well-being and interdependence. From Indian ashrams to European eco-villages to global peasant movements like *La Via Campesina*—all represent diverse expressions of resistance to the materialism and individualism associated with mainstream development. These examples reveal the dynamism and diversity of human value and aspirations, highlight possibilities for reimagining development beyond narrow economic metrics, and are the source of inspiration for "postmodern" and "postdevelopment" thought.

And yet, although various groups, from Indigenous to intentional communities, actively cultivate alternative visions of the good life and social transformation, these efforts have largely been unable to curb the global spread of capitalist development. Market forces continue to profoundly influence how development is envisioned, enacted, and ultimately experienced—particularly for younger generations. This influence is only likely to intensify in an age where the very fabric of our attention is increasingly commodified and harnessed to fuel the relentless expansion of the market.

Understanding these deep shifts in the social imaginary—and their relationship to migration aspirations—complicates the hope that addressing the root cause of rural out-migration is a simple or straightforward task. Values, norms, and attitudes are already shifting in Wayisso in ways that will encourage more migration: valuing new forms of consumption, higher levels of education, and upward socioeconomic mobility; changing gendered norms that increasingly embrace the education, economic contribution, and spatial mobility of women; and new attitudes toward work that prioritize incomes, status, and the prospect of *change*. These are the hallmarks of a new ethic of transformation.

Lessons for Mobility Transition Theory

Zelinsky introduced mobility transition theory as a corollary to thinking about the demographic transition, or what he called the "vital transition"—the historical shift from a premodern state of high birth and high death rates to low birth and low death rates in societies at high "thresholds of socioeconomic development."[15] Three demographic variables—fertility, mortality, and migration—together determine whether the population of an area or country grows or declines, yet Zelinsky noticed that research largely focused on the first two, fertility and mortality. "The remarkable expansion of personal mobility has been largely overlooked, despite its rich potential for interpreting the larger phenomenon of modernization."[16]

In its simplest form, mobility transition theory posits a general increase and diversification of all forms of internal and international mobility in what Zelinsky called "early modernizing societies." The Wayisso case study offers several insights specific to current theorizing about the mobility transition in these contexts, which today are more often described as "low-income," "developing," or "industrializing" societies.

First, Wayisso's mobility history resonates with geographer Ronald Skeldon's critique of the "myth of the immobile peasant," the idea that peasant populations are relatively sedentary or static and become more mobile with modernization.[17] As Zelinsky originally put it, "The onset of modernization . . . brings with it a great shaking loose of migrants from the countryside."[18] Skeldon, on the contrary, shows how agricultural communities in preindustrial and precolonial societies showed relatively high degrees of regional mobility. The most profound transformation of the mobility transition, he argues, is in the changing nature and "spatial diffusion" of migration rather than in volumes as such.

By focusing on a historically seminomadic society, Wayisso's history further suggests that the *immobilization* of traditional mobility systems may also be intrinsic to the modern transformation. Mobile populations are difficult to control. In nation-state building, governments register people to places to know who is where, to collect taxes, to provide social services, and to enforce laws.[19] Whether communist or capitalist, the policies pursued by modern states both assume and enforce this sedentary logic, and current definitions of migration—movement from one place of residence to another, across a state-designated administrative boundary—are only viable within this sedentary frame.[20] Thus, long-standing forms of nomadic, circular, and seasonal mobility associated with traditional economic systems decline as new forms of internal and international migration emerge.[21] Yet, new constraints now determine who can and cannot migrate, introducing for some the distinctly modern experience of feeling "stuck" or "trapped" in place.

Wayisso's mobility history also shows why it is essential to examine transformations in internal and international migration together. Current research on the mobility transition focuses predominantly on explaining changing volumes and rates of international migration. This misses two important dynamics: (1) diversification in the nature, direction, and composition of international mobility and (2) the ties between rising international migration and a more profound urban transition. Regarding the first, in Ethiopia, international migration for educational, religious, or trade purposes under Haile Selassie became increasingly dominated by regional and long-distance asylum-seeking movements under the Derg. Under the current government, these migrations continue, but new forms of regular and irregular labor migration to a growing number of destinations are becoming increasingly common. In fact, the rapid rise of international labor migration is one of the most striking changes of the last few decades. As a result, the composition of international migrants today reflects a much wider swath of the Ethiopian population.

This diversification of international migration is intimately tied to changing patterns of internal migration. There is a well-established trend of "stepwise" migration in existing research, where people move from villages to towns to cities and then (perhaps) abroad.[22] This was the case for Ademtuu and many others from Wayisso who are now living in towns and cities across Ethiopia. A rise in stepwise migration reflects rising opportunities for education and paid employment. It also reflects changing labor market structures, which tend to disperse opportunities for skilled work across urban areas. The pursuit of professional work often requires a willingness to move to it.

However, the links between internal and international migration can also defy a stepwise logic. The finding that rural women are migrating to the Middle East to finance an urban future in Ethiopia highlights the contradictions of globalization. Many women migrate (sometimes several times) to the Middle East to support their or their family's move to town. They are neither the least educated nor the most educated, neither the poorest nor the richest. Unable to pursue the stepwise migration of their more privileged peers, these young women have aspirations for change, limited local opportunity, and just enough resources to participate in this emerging migration industry. International labor migration thus arises in the context of a deeper urbanization of the social imaginary, where young women and men alike are now looking toward the city rather than the village as the home of the good life. And a good life in the city needs capital.

Finally, the three core mobility shifts highlighted here—the sedentarization of traditional forms of seasonal and circular mobility, the urbanization of internal migration trajectories, and the diversification of international migration—are likely general enough to capture the big-picture shifts of mobility transitions elsewhere. But as Skeldon cautions in his reflections on mobility transition theory, "No single path of sequential change in migration or any other variable can be expected to exist, and reversals or stasis will occur."[23] Indeed, relatively little is known about the conditions of migration decision-making when migration systems decline—or the other side of the "inverted-U" first posited by Zelinsky. The theoretical framework applied here, integrating the social transformation and aspiration-capability frameworks, provides the conceptual tools to more rigorously explore variation in how the timing, sequencing, and intersectionality of social change processes stimulate different kinds of migration or staying behavior across societies over time.[24]

Juxtaposing the experiences of Wayisso and of Ethiopia with other local and national case studies is essential to better understand variations in how the mobility transition unfolds. I suspect, for example, that the extent of *involuntary* immobility in Wayisso may be an artifact of its history. Pushed into agriculture under the Derg regime, farming has only been the primary work of a few generations. There was not sufficient time for deep culture to grow around it, and this is one reason I believe migration aspirations are so ubiquitous today. Unlike Wayisso, many rural communities around the world express a stronger sense of rootedness, place attachment, and *voluntary* immobility. In the United States, Appalachian communities have been studied extensively for this very reason.[25] In the Pacific Islands, where rising sea levels and coastal degradation threaten local livelihoods, many Indigenous populations prefer to remain on their ancestral homelands for reasons that include a deep connection to land and place-based identity, knowledge, and culture. Some express a preference to die in their traditional territories rather than relocate.[26] Looking to places with a higher prevalence of voluntary immobility and place commitment provides one avenue into understanding how different social imaginaries and ideas about the good life give rise to different (often noneconomic) priorities for development.

Finally, comparative case studies would also reveal important variations in the gendered dynamics of mobility transitions. While the urbanization of internal migration and the rise of international labor migration are shared features of mobility transitions around the world, the specific composition and direction of these flows are often strongly influenced by labor markets. In Wayisso, for instance, the ready availability of brokers and agencies facilitating the movement of women into domestic work in the Middle East stands in stark contrast to the dearth of similar opportunities for men in the village. This reality highlights the powerful influence of globalizing and gendered labor markets in shaping *who* moves and *where* aspiring migrants imagine their futures. Comparing Wayisso's experience with case studies from other regions where international labor migration is dominated by men—for example, male migrants from Bangladesh working in construction in the Gulf states—would provide further insight into how gender norms, labor market demands and recruitment, and the structure of specific migration industries influence gendered mobility patterns at local and global scales.

Lessons for Migration and Development Policy

Embracing the reality of the mobility transition will be essential to meeting the demographic opportunities and challenges of the twenty-first century. Ethiopia is in the midst of demographic changes of historic proportions: rapid declines in birth and mortality rates and increasing life expectancy.[27] By 2050, the country is projected to be among the world's top ten most populous countries, joining long-standing members such as Brazil and India.[28] Beyond Ethiopia, Africa has the youngest population of any continent, with a median age of around nineteen years. The continent's demographic transition has significant implications for its social, economic, and political future. It presents both challenges and opportunities, depending on how governments and societies manage this period of change and whether they embrace or resist migration as an inevitable part of that future.

Countries across Africa, including Ethiopia, face complex challenges that stem from a rapidly growing working-age population and limited employment opportunities. Governments often struggle to scale access to education, housing, decent work, and social services at the pace demanded by young generations. This exacerbates the aspiration-opportunity gap that drives rural-urban and international migration. From a global perspective, it is striking that wealthy, industrialized nations face the opposite challenge: aging populations, a shrinking workforce, and ballooning health care and pension costs. An abundance of research highlights the economic benefits of immigration for industrialized nations—in fact, as labor economist Michael Piore originally noted, there is a structural need for immigrant labor in wealthy, aging societies that struggle to find enough workers to take on the difficult, dangerous, and thankless jobs that keep societies functioning.[29] The economic benefits of emigration are also wide-ranging for sending countries. Emigration can relieve pressure on domestic labor markets, and migrants send back money, knowledge, and networks that can contribute to the development of their home communities. Facilitating migration, many agree, is one important way to address the population and development challenges of the twenty-first century.

Many advocates of "migration for development" make their arguments in primarily economic terms. But in reality, migration is not just an economic matter, nor a demographic one. It touches deep sociocultural fears and political dynamics. Politicians and policy makers in aging societies, frantic about the economic crisis associated with low fertility rates and population decline, seem to be embracing every strategy other than publicly acknowledging the need for immigrant labor: technological innovation to address labor shortages and elderly care, raising the retirement age, and new incentives to encourage families to have more children. In a rather extreme example, Hungary's prime minister Viktor Orban offered mothers with at least four children a lifetime exemption from income tax in a bid to increase birth rates. "In all of Europe there are fewer and fewer children, and the answer of the West to this is migration," Orban said. "They want as many migrants to enter as there are missing kids, so that the numbers will add up. We Hungarians have a different way of thinking. Instead of just numbers, we want *Hungarian* children."[30]

The more societies resist the reality and requirement of migration in today's global world, the harder it is for origin and destination communities to benefit from migration. Migration policies generally tend to favor the entry of the "highly skilled" while attempting to restrict the entry of "low skilled" workers, asylum seekers, and refugees.[31] To achieve the latter goal, governments pour resources into securing their borders instead of revamping the outdated immigration systems that could, if thoughtfully designed and adequately funded, more effectively manage many different forms of migration for society's benefit. Because stronger border controls do not address the underlying reasons that people leave, nor the persistent demand for immigrant labor in advanced economies,[32] they only push many migrants into more dangerous and precarious trajectories. As the migration scholar Stephen Castles observed, "The more that states and supranational bodies do to restrict and manage migration, the less successful they seem to be."[33]

Instead of revamping outdated and underfunded immigration systems, many wealthy governments have put their hopes—and significant funding—into development aid to address the perceived root causes of migration: conflict, poverty, climate change, and poor governance. For example, the European Union Emergency Trust Fund for Africa, established in 2015, allocated over 5 billion euros "to address the root causes of instability, forced displacement, and irregular migration by promoting economic and equal opportunities, security, and development across the continent."[34] Similarly, in 2021, the US government implemented a "Root Causes Strategy," committing 4 billion USD in funds and programming to address the root causes of migration from El Salvador, Guatemala, and Honduras. The strategy had several pillars, the first of which is addressing economic insecurity and inequality in the region.[35]

What these strategies fail to recognize is that, even if successful, their economic agendas are likely to reinforce a development paradigm that, over the long term, tends to encourage migration, particularly from rural places in what the World Bank categorizes as low- and lower-middle-income countries. The historical experience of European countries, and more recent experiences of countries like Mexico, suggests that rates of international migration will eventually decline at higher levels of economic development—as countries begin to receive more migrants than they send. However, such a shift in national migration systems can take decades, even generations, to occur. In the meantime, before migration declines, we should not be surprised if it increases. (And governments would be both empirically misguided and morally remiss to make development aid contingent on its decline.)

Clearly, specific projects focused on specific aims like increasing access to education, generating local employment, teaching climate-resilient agricultural techniques to smallholder farmers, or combatting corruption are not in themselves going to drive migration. In some instances, these interventions may reduce migration for a time or for a targeted segment of the population—especially those who aspire to stay. But short- and long-term effects can differ, and all too often development interventions operate within and ultimately reinforce a development paradigm that widens the aspiration-opportunity gap for rural youth.

Consider, for example, one study by Douglas Massey and colleagues assessing the impact of local development in Nepal's Chitwan Valley on patterns of rural out-migration. They examine whether providing modern facilities and services closer to rural people's homes—including transportation, new markets, employment, schools, health clinics, and movie halls—reduces migration. The authors find that, in the short term, there are clear negative effects on out-migration: "more banks, buses, employers, markets, and government programs in the community increase local employment and earnings opportunities to reduce the odds of migration."[36] However, they also find that, over the long term, growing up in a community with more social and economic resources actually increases the odds of migrating. They argue, "In such a setting, one's parents have more opportunities to earn money and finance human capital formation, and individuals have access to more resources to invest in their own human capital."[37] For rural youth, investing in one's "human capital" usually means leaving. Although this study uses the language of increased "human and social capital" to explain its findings, one wonders what kinds of changes were occurring in the social imaginary of these rural Nepalese communities as the valley "developed"—how their visions of a good life changed.

Root cause development agendas would do well to consider the social imaginary of a given society. The hidden assumption of many root cause interventions is that receiving communities are operating within a subsistence ethic—where threats to survival, subsistence, or stability are the primary drivers of migration. Development interventions often try to alleviate these threats and assume people should no longer need to leave. But this way of thinking is doomed to fail in contexts (like Wayisso) where a transformation ethic has taken hold—where subsistence, stability, and social reproduction are no longer considered enough. When the aspirations of younger generations are oriented toward social and economic mobility, it will be essential to incorporate spatial mobility into development planning. The desire for mobility reflects a profound change in mindset: away from subsistence or stability to progress and change. In these contexts, government policy and planning will need to adapt to see migration as intrinsic to mainstream, capitalist development.

The core argument of this book—that contemporary migration patterns stem from the structure and logic of modern societies—points to the depth of transformation required to fundamentally reshape the drivers and dynamics of migration in the world today. To truly address the root causes of migration would require a paradigm shift in how we think about and pursue development, particularly in rural places.

There are good reasons to consider more radical changes to the theory and practice of development. It is striking, for example, that no so-called developed country has figured out rural flourishing. From the United States to Europe, Australia, and Japan, rural areas tend to be poorer than urban areas, with insufficient infrastructure and economic opportunity and older and declining populations.[38] Many rural areas in the world's wealthiest countries still do not have satisfactory access to quality education, health care, or the internet. In advanced capitalist economies, it is inefficient and unprofitable to provide these services to rural areas, causing states to intervene just to ensure basic needs are met. The challenges of rural communities have dire consequences. In the United States, mortality risks from drugs, alcohol, and suicide—"deaths of despair"—are positively associated with more rural places.[39] Rural counties comprise less than two-thirds of all US counties, yet one study finds that nine out of ten counties with the highest rates of food insecurity are rural.[40] Must a country's development require the hollowing out of rural places?[41] Is this the development trajectory other countries that still remain primarily rural, like Ethiopia, should aspire to follow?

The twin challenges of climate change and global inequality add further urgency to the need to rethink the basic aims and assumptions of development as a global social project. Given the centrality of urbanization to current development models, this task could be powerfully advanced by focusing on rural places. How would the values, actors, and logic of development need to change to enhance the capability to stay and flourish in rural places? Surely, no answer to this question can ignore rural and urban interconnections, but an emphasis on *rural* well-being may offer a counterbalance to the urban bias so prevalent in development thought and practice today. Discovering new pathways for rural flourishing may reveal new pathways for human flourishing.

Moved by Modernity: Conflicted Narratives, Conflicted Lives

Human beings construct narratives to understand the world—everyone from big data scientists who look for patterns of correlation and causation, to ethnographers who strive to convey the perspectives and experiences of others, to everyday folks trying to make sense of their lives. Narratives are powerful tools that social scientists wield to explain social reality, some more consciously or carefully than others.

What stories do we tell to understand why people migrate? Surely there are many depending on who is doing the telling. This book was initially written in response to one prevailing narrative that dominates discussions about migration from "developing countries" like Ethiopia: *push-factor narratives* that revolve around the adverse forces such as poverty or climate change that compel individuals to abandon their homes. These narratives can be found in public discourse, policy documents, and academic publications alike. They persist because they highlight real and pressing constraints on rural peoples and livelihoods. In Wayisso, factors like climate change, limited arable land, and poverty pose substantial challenges to the sustainability and desirability of rural livelihoods. Droughts, which compound the hardships of smallholder famers who are already struggling to subsist with dignity, are a recurring phenomenon in the region and threaten to become more frequent and severe.

And yet, even in Wayisso, attributing migration primarily to poverty, drought, or some other push factor fails to explain why migration from Wayisso looks the way it does: why the wealthiest and most educated tend to move to neighboring towns and cities, why young women with middling levels of education are moving to the Middle East, and, most importantly, why the poorest and most disadvantaged remain in the village. Push factor narratives obscure the unsettling truth that those most vulnerable to the negative impacts of poverty, climate change, or other push factors are often the least capable of migrating away from them. For Wayisso's poorest residents, these push factors act more like weights, pressing them down rather than out of the village.

Push-factor narratives also reinforce a reductive and overwhelmingly negative view of migration from "developing country" contexts. Wayisso is a poor village in what the United Nations classifies as one of the world's "least developed countries," yet people there are not defined by these push factors. Their lives are not characterized by misery and suffering, nor are those who leave Wayisso making a desperate escape from poverty. They are moving for knowledge and education, for independence, for love, and to seize new kinds of work that will allow them to, in their words, *"jiruu koo jijiruuf"*—to change their lives. In this context, push-factor narratives miss deep shifts in the social imaginary, new worlds of aspiration, expectation, and desires for transformation. By emphasizing a single dimension of force, push-factor narratives flatten the humanity of the migrant.

Few migration scholars subscribe to push-factor narratives, and many working in so-called developing country contexts advocate for an alternative narrative, one in which development drives migration. But even among those who embrace this core claim of the mobility transition, competing schools of thought tell different stories about *why* development drives migration. Consider, for example, two very different stories that could be told about the relationship between migration and development in Wayisso.

The first is a positive and optimistic one: Ethiopia's development brings rising levels of education, income, and connectivity, which in turn increases the aspirations and capabilities of growing numbers to migrate. People are leaving Wayisso to gain knowledge, skills, and opportunities for employment in a diversifying and urbanizing economy. They migrate to enhance their material prosperity and to send money back to their families so that they too may improve their lot at origin. Some, particularly women, may migrate to escape the suffocating social norms of traditional society and realize new levels of financial and social independence. From this vantage point, spatial mobility is tied to other forms of social, economic, and intellectual mobility. Migration is not a sign of poverty, nor is it a problem. Rather, it is a "natural" part of the development process. To use the language of the aspiration-capability framework, development drives migration because it increases aspirations and capabilities to migrate, and rising migration reflects a community's expanding aspirations and capabilities to live modern lives.

The second story is more critical and pessimistic. In this narrative, Ethiopia's "development" has accelerated the commodification of social life, environmental degradation, and the erosion of traditional knowledge systems and culture. In Wayisso, this story would highlight the decline in dignity and self-determination that comes with "modern" work. Is it progress that a traditional community of pastoralists are now working as wage laborers in an industrial animal processing facility owned by foreign capitalists that exports beef for Middle Eastern markets? Is it progress that young women, faced with limited economic prospects locally, have to migrate as far as Saudi Arabia to clean the homes of wealthier families, often under exploitative conditions, just to get the capital needed to return, move to town, and open a simple shop? Further, despite increased access to formal schooling, the country's current education system fails to impart relevant knowledge or skills for rural livelihoods. Economic inequalities have widened, leaving a too large segment of the population feeling stuck and increasingly vulnerable to droughts that threaten to become more frequent and severe. This second story focuses less on aspirations and capabilities to migrate and more on aspirations and capabilities to stay, and in this telling, development drives migration because it erodes a community's capability to stay and flourish in rural places.

Is it possible for both narratives to be true? There are some in Wayisso who tell versions of the first story and others who tell versions of the second. There are also certainly academics espousing these different narratives—from those working with mainstream development institutions to postdevelopment scholars advocating that we abandon the idea and project of "development" altogether. Perhaps these stories provide different lenses on the nature of social transformation in the modern period. Development can lead to empowerment in one domain and disempowerment in another. Perhaps development drives migration from rural communities because it increases aspirations and capabilities to migrate at the same time that it erodes aspirations and capabilities to stay.

Migrants too embody these tensions. Ademtuu, the first migrant from Wayisso to live in Europe, has no intention to return to Ethiopia. "I am not happy here," she said from her small flat in London, "but I know I couldn't be happy there anymore either."

In 2018, after several failed attempts, she secured a visa for her brother Lencho to join her in London. I knew Lencho well from my time in Ziway. He is an energetic young man, drawn to drawing and music, but as he told me then, "there's no space for that professionally here." He had worked for the police briefly but left after the Oromo protests became heated in 2016. He went back to school in Ziway but failed to find good work. He applied for the Diversity Visa to work in the United States but did not win that lottery. He even attempted to migrate irregularly to Kenya once, but as he told me, "my friends chickened out, and I didn't have enough money to go on my own." When he learned he could join his sister in London, he was ecstatic. This was his chance.

I met Lencho in London a year after his arrival. He and Ademtuu shared their own apartment. Ademtuu was grateful to have her brother with her, yet Lencho appeared worn and unhappy. Work, when he can find it, is difficult, he told me, and the pay is too little—a lament that echoed the complaints of workers in Sher's greenhouses and Verde Beef's feedlots. Lencho missed his family and community, the warmer weather, and Ziway's slower pace of life. Despite these hardships, he regularly sends money home to his wife and young son—money that makes a real difference to their well-being and future prospects. Like Ademtuu, Lencho is not happy in London, but he is also not willing to return to Ethiopia. And I remembered how Marshall Berman described modernity: "To be modern is to find ourselves in an environment that promises us adventure, power, joy, growth, transformation of ourselves and the world—and, at the same time, that threatens to destroy everything we have, everything we know, everything we are."[42]

Epilogue

During my time in Wayisso, rumors circulated about government plans to construct a highway that would cut through the village to better connect Addis Ababa with Hawassa. The existing two-lane road was treacherous, riddled with potholes, and ill-equipped to handle the growing volume of traffic: sputtering taxis, personal cars, lumbering buses, and large lorries ferrying goods southward toward Kenya or northward to the capital city's airport. Indeed, better roads were needed.

When a new four-lane highway linking Ziway to Addis Ababa opened in October 2021, travel times shrank dramatically. As construction pushed south, cutting through Wayisso's cornfields, local farmers began receiving compensation for their lands—a process officially dubbed "development-induced displacement." But one might ask: is "displacement" the right word when so many longed to leave anyway?

In 2023, a friend captured the shifting landscape in a poignant Instagram message to me: "Most of the youths are flowing into Zway and almost making a village here.... This road connection is continuing and passing through Woyiso and most of the people get compensation and become 'millionaires,' settling in Zway. They bought a piece of land or a house, but Woyiso is almost abandoned."

I returned to Wayisso in 2024 to see these changes for myself. Ziway had been officially renamed Baatuu—a reclaiming of its original Oromo name and a small but significant victory for the Oromo political movement of the late 2010s. Baatuu city now formally encompasses both Ziway and Adami Tulu towns. I chose to keep the name "Ziway" throughout this book and to distinguish it from Adami Tulu, as this more accurately reflects how people spoke about these places during my research.

While in Wayisso and Baatuu, I asked about the families I had surveyed in 2016—who received government compensation and what did they do with those funds? I learned about sixty-four household heads. Five had passed away and about half (thirty households) had received compensation. Amounts ranged from modest sums (31,000 birr or roughly 565 USD in 2023) for the inconvenience of construction dust on crop production to over 1.2 million birr (around 22,000 USD) for losing large parcels of land. Nearly everyone who received substantial compensation used it to build housing in Baatuu—whether for their themselves, for their children, or as a rental investment.

Among the twenty-nine households that did not receive any compensation, a striking 83 percent (twenty-four households) still remained in Wayisso. Unfortunately, very few of the Alekira families (Lineage 3)—some of the poorest and least mobile in 2016—received money. Their lands lay farther from the construction zone. Today, they remain particularly vulnerable to unpredictable rains and crop failure.

While visiting his wife in Baatuu, I called Lencho in London. Both Lencho and Ademtuu have moved into the care sector, and Lencho works ten hours a day seven days a week. He started the process of moving his family to London. As we reflected on the road construction together, he shared his worries for the rural youth in town: "We are not city people. We don't know business." Indeed, many households who received a lot of money ran through it quickly. One father of four, for instance, received 400,000 birr (approximately 7,300 USD in 2023) for the loss of a thousand-square-meter plot. He began building a house in Adami Tulu but was unable to complete it. "The money was like a dream," he said. "It was like dew on the grass in the morning sun!"

Lencho's concern was echoed by many young adults in Baatuu who had opened small shops—simple corner stores or clothing shops. One woman, thanks to the new highway, travels monthly to Addis Ababa to buy modern clothes and sell them in her shop along Baatuu's main road. But many others have similar ideas, and as competition increases, almost all struggle for economic viability. And now many no longer have their farms to supplement the costs of urban living.

The more secure shift in livelihoods seemed to be among those who had been able to build rooms to rent to workers from other rural areas moving to town—mostly to work at Sher Ethiopia. The Sher greenhouses are still bustling, employing thousands of young women and churning out millions of roses each day for European markets. Salaries for greenhouse workers have increased fivefold since my last visits—but so too has inflation. In 2016, 1 USD was equal to about 21 Ethiopian birr. By late 2024, it had risen to 120 birr.

Verde Beef shut down their operations in Ethiopia in 2021, the same year the Tigray War began. Like Herr Götz a century ago, their ambitions to transform the local economy and to "catalyze an industrial and agricultural revolution" met unforeseen challenges, and they eventually retreated in the face of internal conflict and regional unrest. Yet, Verdant Frontiers, Verde Beef's parent company, is still thriving. They boast projects across Africa: new ventures in agriculture, fintech, and real estate—all endeavors "creating flourishing communities, compelling investor returns, and life changing jobs." Their website assures potential investors that "Africa's time is now."[1]

But what about Wayisso's time? The village may soon be gone, a casualty of modernization, yet its story still speaks to enduring tensions in our age: between the relentless pursuit of economic growth and the sustainability of rural life, between aspirations for progress and the costs of leaving what we know behind. The road through Wayisso may indeed bring new possibilities and prosperity for some, but not for everyone. It is a reminder that the future we create is paved with choices—about what we value, where we invest, who gets to decide, and, just as importantly, who will move and who gets left behind.

Methodological Notes

What I refer to as "Wayisso" is situated within the Wayisso Qancerra *kebele* (peasant association), in the Adami Tulu and Jido Kombolcha (ATJK) *woreda* (district), in the Oromia state. Throughout the book, I refer to the village simply as Wayisso. This is because the Wayisso Qancerra *kebele* is today a combination of what used to be two separate *kebeles*, and my household survey and interviews focused in the "Wayisso" section of this *kebele*. Thus, it is simpler and more accurate to simply refer to "Wayisso," and it reflects how the inhabitants referred to this place. I chose one version of spelling Wayisso—not the most common one—and several alternative spellings exist in various administrative documents: *waeso*, *wayeso*, *woyisso*, *wayiso*. The Oromo language formally adopted the Latin script called *Qubee* in 1991, although various versions of a Latin-based script (as well as a Ge'ez script) had been used to codify the language before then. Today, *Afaan Oromo* is the regional language of the Oromia state, yet different dialects and spellings remain common, particularly for proper nouns.

When it concerns the history of Wayisso, many of the names detailed in the book are the true ones: like the names of the founding patriarchs, the first farmers, the local community leaders of previous generations, or the first women and pilgrims to go to the Middle East. However, in the more detailed, personal accounts, I use pseudonyms instead of actual names. When I asked for consent to record an interview, I asked informants if they would like to make up a "fake name." This was to reinforce the idea that the interview could be anonymous. Often, the pseudonym used here is the one of their choosing. However, some insisted I use their real names, a request that I honored.

I recognize that pseudonyms are hardly adequate anonymizing tools in ethnographic research. At the beginning stages of this research, and in compliance with the usual standards of research ethics, I assumed it was enough to simply anonymize all personal details I collected. However, I later realized that anyone familiar with Wayisso or the ATJK *woreda* could, if they made the effort, discern about whom I am speaking. I may use the pseudonym Ademtuu, but if only one woman has left Wayisso for Europe, everyone in Wayisso knows who that one person is. I am inclined to agree with ethnographers who suggest that, especially in our digital age, full anonymity is impossible in ethnographic research.[1] Nevertheless, there are steps researchers can take to safeguard their respondents from any potentially compromising information, even if it was voluntarily shared in the interview. I took two steps toward this end: First, when I returned in October 2018, I approached individuals whose stories I knew I would use in greater detail in this book. I shared what I hoped to include about their stories, asked follow-up questions, and confirmed again that they would be comfortable with me doing so. Second, for those individuals with whom I did not have the chance to acquire a second consent, I either cut their stories or left out any details that I thought could be potentially compromising. There are several stories and experiences related to the Oromo protests that remain untold here for this reason. Finally, I include some of my own photographs throughout the book, and in a few, individual faces are shown. I only use photographs in which subjects gave permission for me to take and use the photos for my research.

My research took place over several visits: for ten days in April 2015, from January to July 2016, for two weeks in November 2016, and return visits for two weeks in October 2018 and ten days in October 2024. In the spring of 2016, I conducted a household survey to capture basic demographic information as well as the mobility histories of individuals born in or living in Wayisso. The household survey was carried out with 73 households that lie within three family clusters within the Wayisso Qancerra *kebele*. Forty-three *kebeles* make up the ATJK *woreda*, the next administrative tier. The entire Wayisso Qancerra *kebele* had some 441 households in 2010 (the last official census round).

Rather than randomly selecting some households within somewhat arbitrary government-set boundaries of the *kebele*, I decided to focus on and survey all households within one particular area of the *kebele*, where three family lineages cluster into what I refer to in this book as "Wayisso." This allowed me to follow the mobility histories of larger family groups after the transition to settlement. Bedane Tuffaa was one of the first to settle and populate the area with his wives and children. This growing cluster of family compounds was and still is referred to as *ganda Bedane*, who is part of the Hadumana sub-branch of the Habernoosa *gosi* (roughly, tribe) of the Arsi Oromo. Just half a kilometer away, another *ganda*, or family cluster, founded by a man named Dakabo Bulo, is part of the Abayii *gosi* of the Arsi Oromo. Finally, a third family cluster is part of the Alekira, another sub-group of the Habernoosa *gosi*. A fourth cluster of families fell within this relatively small geographic area, who together were part of the Qoma *gosi* of the Arsi Oromo. I did not include them in this survey because they arrived in Wayisso later and were settled by several different households at once. In total, I surveyed seventy-three households, gathering information about 657 individuals.

For the survey, I defined a household through the men. Because many families are polygamous, one household may include several wives and their children. A new Wayisso household formed when one of the sons married and remained in Wayisso. Marriage is an important marker in the life course. After marriage, a man is expected to build his own home, receive his own land and cattle, and begin having children. The size of a household varied from two people (e.g., a newly married couple) to over thirty (e.g., an older man with three wives, each with many children). I only encountered one household where the husband had died and the wife became the de facto household head. More often, and according to tradition, a widow would marry one of her deceased husband's brothers. One reason for this tradition, one woman explained, is that the children of the deceased would remain within their father's family.

The survey was divided into two parts: the first assessed the economic characteristics of the household and the second captured the demographic and mobility characteristics of each individual within the household. The first part assessed a number of indicators: how many houses they have; the features of those houses that require investment (e.g., an iron roof); whether they have a house in town and their means of transportation to town; how many plots of land they have; whether they used fertilizer or hired help last season; the number of cattle and animals they own; and whether the household head has a mobile phone, a smartphone, or a radio. Together, these indicators signal the relative wealth and economic conditions of the household.

The second part focused on the details of each individual within the household, including the father, mother(s), and children. This section asked about basic demographic information, schooling, income-generating activities, and current and previous places of residence. If one of the children married and became a new household head in Wayisso, a follow-up survey was conducted with that household. If a son or daughter left Wayisso and began a family elsewhere, these new households were not surveyed—however, their individual details are still captured in the survey because of their relation to their parents who remain in Wayisso. In this way, I was able to trace the mobility histories of each of these households back to the founding patriarch, which are depicted in the family trees presented in Chapters 3 and 6.[2]

The household survey provided a snapshot of mobility trajectories to and from Wayisso village. To understand how and why (im)mobility patterns changed over time, I needed to hear the stories of people's lives, how they narrate the social transformations that shaped their region and history, how they understand the good life and how it has changed, and why they moved or stayed. My interviews were structured to capture first and foremost people's own narratives about their lives and history before asking more specific questions about migration. I wanted to hear what social transformations were important for them and how (im)mobility directly or indirectly figured into these changes before explicitly asking about migration.

Of course, arriving at a single story about social change in Wayisso was a challenging if not impossible task. People often do not remember history in the same way. Thus, it was important for me to compare these stories with other historical sources. For example, it was particularly difficult to discern in what years people began farming land in Wayisso based on my interviews alone. Therefore, it was helpful to examine aerial photographs of the area from the 1960s and 1970s from the Ethiopian Mapping Agency, which revealed when more people began to use the land for cultivation (see Chapter 4).

The in-depth interviews had roughly four components. The first focused on the *life history* of the individual, to understand the major experiences, phases, and turning points across the individual's life course; while not asking about migration directly, these stories revealed the important moments of transition within their lives and the degree to which (im)mobility experiences shaped their life trajectories and decision-making. The second component of the interview focused on *imagined futures* to understand each individual's aspirations, for themselves and their families. Again, I was particularly interested in understanding the place of (im)mobility in their imagined futures, without asking directly about it. If needed, the third stage of the interview asked more explicitly about migration aspirations, why people migrate or stay, the factors and forces that give rise to migration aspirations, and some of its consequences on their lives and society. Finally, I might also ask more specific questions of interest related to the history, present, or future of Wayisso, Adami Tulu, or Ziway. Formal interviews ranged widely in length: from twenty minutes with one uninterested farmer to four meetings, each averaging two hours, with one elder and key informant.

I carried out eighty-four formal interviews, seventeen of which were in the scoping stage and sixty-four once my research question and methodology were finalized. Fifty-three of these formal interviews were with individuals who were born in or had moved to Wayisso, including six of the ten women from Wayisso who had migration experience in the Middle East. I conducted interviews with six additional return migrants from the Middle East from other areas of the *woreda*, three phone interviews with women working abroad, fourteen interviews with current or previous workers at the Sher Ethiopia flower farms, and seven interviews with community leaders or government workers. Interviewees gave verbal consent to participate in these formal interviews, the vast majority of which were recorded and personally transcribed. There were only a few instances in which it seemed inappropriate to record the interview.

In addition to these formal interviews, I held three formal focus groups, had innumerable informal conversations, and used more general ethnographic approaches: "hanging out" with families in the village, workers in the field, young people at school, or women in the market. I lived with four young women who had moved to Ziway from Wayisso and another village, Macafara. I learned as much if not more from informal, everyday interactions with people in Wayisso, Adami Tulu, and Ziway as I did from my formal interviews.

When I was a graduate student, I was taught that the ethnographer immerses herself in a group, observing patterns of behavior, listening with a curious and critical ear to everyday conversations, and asking questions about issues of interest. "Immersion" gives the impression that the ethnographer eventually becomes so embedded in her research context that she is able to observe "realistic" behaviors, unaffected by her presence. Despite my attempts at immersion—living with people from Wayisso, following young men and women to their work in the fields or in town, filling long afternoons with cups of coffee and lazy conversations, trying to speak the local language—my positionality as a white woman was unavoidably overt. I attracted attention, eliciting everything from warm hospitality to skepticism. It took time for me to build trust with potential interviewees, and when I had the opportunity to interview some people multiple times, I realized how little is often shared in a first interview with a stranger. I realized that "hanging out" was not a separate research strategy from my formal interviews; it was a key part of it. By taking the time to socialize, I gained access to informants that might have otherwise been reluctant to participate. Further, I could evaluate to what degree everyday actions matched what young people told me in their interviews. I tried to use my foreignness to my advantage, as an opportunity for people to teach me, to explain to me "how things are," and for me to ask "stupid questions." Nevertheless, there are many opinions or behaviors I likely never observed simply because of my presence in the room.

Because existing research on this region of Ethiopia is limited, I gathered as much data as possible from government offices for Ziway town and the ATJK *woreda*. To understand how farming practices and production had changed over time, I visited the Office of Agriculture, the Office of Rural Affairs, the ATJK Livestock Office, and the Office of Rural Land and Environmental Protection. I met several times with researchers at the Adami Tulu Agricultural Research Center and Oromia Agricultural Research Institute. There, I learned a great deal from my many conversations with Shimelis Gizachew Desalegn about the concerns of local farmers and the government's strategies to address them.

To understand the growth and transformation of Ziway town, I collected statistics from the Ziway Municipality Office. The Offices of Education for Ziway and ATJK provided statistics on the expansion of formal schools, enrollment, and educational attainment. To ask questions about access to electricity across Ziway and the ATJK *woreda*, I visited the Ethiopian Electric Utility (Ziway Branch). To appreciate how the drought in 2015–2016 compared to previous years, I gathered rainfall data from the Meteorologist Office in Adami Tulu and the Meteorologist Center in Addis Ababa. To know more about the presence of foreign investors in the *woreda*, I spoke with government workers at the ATJK Woreda Investment Office and spoke informally with the manager of Verde Beef at a funeral in Wayisso.

In Addis Ababa, I visited the Central Statistical Bureau to collect and inquire about national census data; the Ethiopian Mapping Agency to obtain satellite images of

Wayisso, Adami Tulu, and Ziway from 1967 and 1972; and the Oromo Cultural Center to ask questions about Oromo history and practice. However, I spent most of my time in the capital city at Addis Ababa University, speaking with academics and reading dissertations. The master's and doctoral dissertations on Ethiopia's history—particularly those from the 1990s and 2000s—are exceptional. These manuscripts provided essential background information on Oromo history, development policy, and the evolution of land relations and farming practices in the region.

A Note on Local Networks and Research Assistants

One reason I chose the ATJK *woreda* as my fieldwork location was because of a network of contacts with the Bahá'í community in this area. As a member of the Bahá'í Faith, I was welcomed by this community with touching hospitality and warmth, and they sustained me emotionally and spiritually over the course of my fieldwork. They also provided invaluable local knowledge and research advice. For example, I consulted the Bahá'í's local assembly, or local governing body, to seek their advice about what is fair compensation for research assistance, comparing this to what was suggested by my university contacts.

Aware of the potential limitations of working through the Bahá'ís, I was attentive to how this minority religious group was perceived in the area. Many people in Ziway had never heard of the Bahá'í Faith, as it is still a relatively small religious community. In Wayisso, people knew of the Bahá'ís, as some households had converted to the new religion in the three decades previously. In the 1990s, there were tensions between some newly converted households and the existing Muslim community, but these were resolved through local conflict mediation. In the decades since, some prejudices still lingered, but there were generally good relations between the Bahá'í and Muslim households in Wayisso.

To avoid a sampling bias in my interviews, I remained conscious at the outset of nurturing relationships with those who are not Bahá'ís. My translator was an English teacher I met when visiting a secondary school in Ziway. Another translator with whom I worked briefly was met at a local coffee stand—another teacher who had set up a language school in Ziway. Likewise, I made sure that I did not oversample for interviews from my Bahá'í networks. Carrying out the household survey was one way of identifying participants and establishing initial relationships with the families. In the end, twelve out of my eighty-four interviews were with Bahá'ís.

Although English is the most widely spoken foreign language and the medium for secondary school and higher education, it was clear on my initial visit that fluency in English was only common among the highly educated. There are over ninety local languages in Ethiopia, with Amharic and Oromo being the most common. Amharic is the national language, but slightly more people in Ethiopia actually speak Oromo as their native tongue (approximately one-third of the country), and in the rural areas outside Ziway, such as Wayisso, many young people did not speak Amharic well. Thus, I decided to focus my energies on learning *Afaan Oromo*. Nevertheless, mastering the language required time beyond what was available to me, and I relied upon research assistance. I had hoped to find both a man and a woman to translate for me, but I was unable to find a woman with sufficient English proficiency in Ziway (nor could I afford to pay for a professional translator's stay in Ziway for several months). Secondary school English teachers were overwhelmingly men, and even among those who teach English, their fluency in the language was often insufficient for my purposes. I finally met one secondary school teacher,

Tilah Alemayehu, who taught English, worked as a translator for Sher Ethiopia, and was fluent in both *Afaan Oromo* and Amharic. He was born in a city further north, Adama, and I found this an advantage with doing interviews in Wayisso. Although Tilah was an outsider to Wayisso, he was an Oromo, and informants appeared willing to share things they might not have shared if it was with someone from their own community. Tilah also has a very easygoing personality and a manner that puts people at ease, for which I was very thankful.

Kedir Gemechu was my second research assistant, and he worked with me to carry out the household survey in Wayisso. Unlike my translator, I met Kedir through the Baháʼí community. Kedir grew up in Wayisso but moved to Ziway and had recently received a bacherlors in law from Rift Valley University. He was smart, amiable, and knew every household in Wayisso. Having Kedir assist with the survey in Wayisso was invaluable, particularly because he could vouch for me during a politically precarious time. While I was in Ethiopia, the Oromo protests, which had been on and off again since 2014, began to pick up steam. Discontent had been simmering for years, yet November 2015 was a turning point when peaceful and violent protests broke out across the Oromia state. The protests were initially to contest the federal government's Addis Ababa Master Plan, which proposed to expand the boundaries of the capital city into surrounding Oromia farmland. Protests were met by a brutal government crackdown, and over the subsequent four months, hundreds were killed and thousands arrested. This unrest emerged from long-standing discontent among the Oromo people with the government's development trajectory—particularly the acquisition of Oromo land for foreign investors—and lack of meaningful political participation in a government that many felt was unfairly controlled by a Tigray elite.

Ziway was not a central site for the protests. In this region of Oromia, the more violent clashes were in university towns, such as Jimma, and particularly in Shashemene, a large junction town ninety kilometers south of Ziway. In these areas, protests led to confrontations with the police, and protestors were frequently shot and killed. Protestors attacked and burned protestant churches, foreign companies, and other embodiments of "foreign influences." Closer to Ziway, in the two small towns some fifteen minutes north and south of Ziway (Bulbulla and Meki), several eighteen-wheeler trucks had been overwhelmed and torched. Because the protests were primarily aimed at the government, I was not at great risk. However, it was possible that if some people saw me, a white *farenji* (foreigner), they might assume that I worked for one of the foreign investors, and I could have been a target. Thus, I listened to the advice of local friends who suggested that I not move around too much when the protests were hot. Furthermore, everyone would be on edge and reluctant to participate in my research anyway.

Had I needed to rely upon government agencies, which were by default associated with the ruling coalition, or university contacts, who had little connection to this particular place, my research would likely have faced significant obstacles. For example, one day during my scoping research, I was planning to go with a development agent—a government worker who oversees the socioeconomic development of peasant associations—to one rural village. However, I was told by friends in Ziway that this would be a bad idea. It was likely that I would be seen as a spy if I went through the government workers, and my personal interviews would be much less welcome. In Wayisso, however, because my association was first through Kedir, rather than the government officials, community members more easily gave their trust. This would have taken much more time to build in another setting without the same level of personal contacts to vouch for me. Kedir's presence and knowledge of the community were crucial, especially during a time of heightened political sensitivity, and it was only because of his assistance that no household refused to participate in the survey.

This research is inevitably shaped by my own positionality, experiences, and relationships in Wayisso, Adami Tulu, and Ziway. The stories I've chosen to tell and those I've left untold reflect the opportunities and constraints I encountered as a researcher during a period of rapid social change. Recognizing these limitations underscores the collaborative nature of ethnographic research. The knowledge presented in this book emerges from the dialogue and trust built with the people of Wayisso, whose generosity and insights have enriched my understanding of their lives and the changing world we all inhabit.

Notes

Introduction

1. See, for example, Markos Ezra and Gebre-Egziabher Kiros, "Rural Out-Migration in the Drought Prone Areas of Ethiopia: A Multilevel Analysis," *International Migration Review* 35, no. 3 (2001): 749–771; Birhan Asmame Miheretu, *Causes and Consequences of Rural-Urban Migration: The Case of Woldiya Town, North Ethiopia* (Department of Geography, University of South Africa, 2011); and Sosina Bezu and Stein Holden, "Are Rural Youth in Ethiopia Abandoning Agriculture?," *World Development* 64 (2014): 259–272.
2. Ademtuu is not her real name. Throughout the book, I often use pseudonyms in personal stories. See the methodological notes in the appendix for more details on my approach to anonymization.
3. The Oromo are the largest ethnic group in Ethiopia, constituting over one-third of the national population. Arsi Oromo is one subgroup of the Oromo.
4. When I speak of "pastoralism" in my research area, I refer to the seasonal movement of livestock between familiar grazing pastures, also known as "transhumance." This contrasts with fully nomadic pastoralists, some of whom can follow a more irregular pattern of movement over longer distances in search of grazing lands.
5. This book is based on research that occurred between 2015 and 2018, with a follow-up visit in 2024. As of 2024, Ziway was officially renamed Baatuu—a reclaiming of its original Oromo name and a small but significant victory for the Oromo political movement of the late 2010s. Baatuu city now formally encompasses both Ziway and Adami Tulu towns. Throughout the book, I continue to refer to this city as "Ziway" and distinguish it from Adami Tulu, as it more accurately reflects how people spoke about these places during my research. See also the Epilogue for further reflections on how Wayisso, Adami Tulu, and Ziway have changed in recent years.
6. Wilbur Zelinsky, "The Hypothesis of the Mobility Transition," *Geographical Review* 61, no. 2 (1971): 221–222.
7. Robert Woods et al., "Classics in Human Geography Revisited," *Progress in Human Geography* 17, no. 2 (1993): 213–219.
8. Ronald Skeldon has been one of the most vocal advocates for retaining and refining mobility transition theory. Based on fieldwork in Peru and later Papua New Guinea, his work corrected some empirical fallacies in Zelinsky's original model, one important one being the "myth of the immobile peasant." Skeldon found that traditional societies were already very mobile; what changes with "development" is an increase in the complexity and distance of migration, rather than the volume of migration as such. In the decades since, Skeldon continued to champion mobility transition theory, urging researchers to further test, refine, and expand the theory to better link transformations in mobility systems to wider processes of socioeconomic change. This is necessary not only to prove that the idea of a "mobility transition" is still valid but also to move beyond the determinism of Zelinsky's original model. Without more detailed case studies from around the world, it is hard to understand why we see significant variation in how the mobility transition unfolds across societies. For more, see his books, *Population Mobility in Developing Countries: A Reinterpretation* (Belhaven Press, 1990) and *Migration and Development: A Global Perspective* (Longman, 1997).
9. In one study, development economist Michael Clemens describes the "average experience of economic development" from 1960 to 2020 as one in which, as poor countries develop toward US$10,000 per capita at purchasing power parity, a 100 percent increase in real GDP per capita is associated with a 35 percent rise in emigration. If you look at emigration only to high-income destination countries, this figure reaches 74 percent. This trend eventually slows and reverses after countries reach US$10,000 per capita. Geographer Hein de Haas explored

this relationship using Human Development Index indicators and found the same general pattern. For more on this, see Michael Clemens, "The Emigration Life Cycle: How Development Shapes Emigration from Poor Countries," Working Paper Series No. 540 (Center for Global Development, 2020); Hein de Haas, "Migration and Development: A Theoretical Perspective," *International Migration Review* 44, no. 1 (2010): 227–264; Thu Hien Dao et al., "Migration and Development: Dissecting the Anatomy of the Mobility Transition," *Journal of Development Economics* 132 (2018): 88–101.
10. For a review, see Hein de Haas, "Turning the Tide? Why Development Will Not Stop Migration," *Development and Change* 38, no. 5 (2007): 819–841.
11. See Dao et al., "Migration and Development."
12. See Immanuel Wallerstein, *The Capitalist World-Economy*, vol. 2 (Cambridge: Cambridge University Press, 1979) and Fraser Sugden et al., "Migration, Environmental Change and Agrarian Transition in Upland Regions: Learning from Ethiopia, Kenya and Nepal," *The Journal of Peasant Studies* 49, no. 5 (2021): 1101–1131.
13. See Kerilyn Schewel and Asmamaw Legass Bahir, "Migration and Development in Ethiopia: Exploring the Mechanisms Behind an Emerging Mobility Transition," *Migration Studies* 9, no. 4 (2021): 1673–1707.
14. See Assefaw Bariagaber, "Political Violence and the Uprooted in the Horn of Africa: A Study of Refugee Flows from Ethiopia," *Journal of Black Studies* 28, no. 1 (1997): 26–42 and Aaron Terrazas, "Beyond Regional Circularity: The Emergence of an Ethiopian Diaspora," *Migration Information Source*, 2007, https://www.migrationpolicy.org/article/beyond-regional-circularity-emergence-ethiopian-diaspora.
15. United Nations, Trends in International Migrant Stock: Migrants by Destination and Origin [Database], United Nations Department of Economic and Social Affairs, Population Division, 2019.
16. United Nations, Trends in International Migrant Stock; Fassil Demissie, "Ethiopian Female Domestic Workers in the Middle East and Gulf States," *African and Black Diaspora: An International Journal* 11, no. 1 (2018): 1–5; Katie Kuschminder et al., "Profiling Ethiopian Migration: A Comparison of Characteristics of Ethiopian Migrants to Africa, the Middle East, and the North," in *Crossing African borders: Migration and Mobility*, ed. Cristina Udelsmann Rodrigues (Center of African Studies, University Institute of Lisbon, 2012).
17. Schewel and Bahir, "Migration and Development in Ethiopia."
18. See Ronald Skeldon, "Migration Transitions Revisited: Their Continued Relevance for the Development of Migration Theory," *Population, Space and Place* 18 (2012): 154–166.
19. Throughout this book, I refer to the village simply as "Wayisso." This is because *Wayiso Qancaara kebele*, or peasant association, is today a combination of what used to be two separate kebeles. My household survey and interviews focused on the "Wayisso" section of this kebele. Thus, it is simpler and more accurate to simply refer to "Wayisso," and it reflects how the inhabitants referred to their area. I chose one version of spelling Wayisso, although several alternatives exist across administrative documents: *waeso, wayeso, woyisso, wayiso*. The local Oromo language formally adopted the Latin script called Qubee in 1991, although various versions of a Latin-based script had been used to codify the language before then. Today, Afaan Oromo is the regional language of the Oromia state, yet different dialects and spellings remain common, particularly for proper nouns.
20. This fact is well noted by the African Development Bank in their 2016 report: *African Economic Outlook 2016: Sustainable Cities and Structural Transformation* (African Development Bank, 2016).
21. Schewel and Bahir, "Migration and Development in Ethiopia."
22. Taking a long-term perspective, the meaning of migration changes in relation to the ease and norms of movement. It may be no coincidence that the first migration scholars looked at internal migration; moving across a country or from a rural village to a city, during a time of limited means of transportation and communication, meant a more dramatic departure from home and change in life circumstances than it does today. To achieve the same degree of "departure" today, at least within the materially developed world, often requires further distances, and the bulk of migration scholarship today focuses on international movement. This is what many geographers allude to when they speak of the "time-space compression" of modernity. But there is a tendency to overemphasize the time-space compression of modernity; distances still matter, and in some parts of the world, those distances might be quite small.

23. "Stepwise migration" describes "a process of human spatial behavior in which individuals or families embark on a migration path of acculturation which gradually takes them, by way of intermediate steps, from a traditional-rural environment to the modern-urban environment." See Dennis Conway, "Step-Wise Migration: Toward a Clarification of the Mechanism," *International Migration Review* 14, no. 1 (1980): 3–14; see also Anju Mary Paul, "Stepwise International Migration: A Multistage Migration Pattern for the Aspiring Migrant," *American Journal of Sociology* 116, no. 6 (2011): 1842–1886 and Russell King and Ronald Skeldon, "'Mind the Gap!' Integrating Approaches to Internal and International Migration," *Journal of Ethnic and Migration Studies* 36, no. 10 (2010): 1619–1646.
24. My thanks to Jørgen Carling for first convincing me of this point.
25. See Hein de Haas et al., *Social Transformation*, IMI Working Paper 166 (International Migration Institute, 2020).
26. Arturo Escobar, *Encountering Development: The Making and Unmaking of the Third World*, vol. 1 (Princeton University Press, 2011).
27. James Ferguson, *Expectations of Modernity: Myths and Meanings of Urban Life on the Zambian Copperbelt* (University of California Press, 1999), 13.

Chapter 1

1. John Robert McNeill and William Hardy McNeill, *The Human Web: A Bird's-Eye View of World History* (W. W. Norton & Company, 2003), 12.
2. McNeill and McNeill, *The Human Web*.
3. United Nations Population Division, *2018 Revision of World Urbanization Prospects* (Department of Economic and Social Affairs of the United Nations, 2018), https://population.un.org/wup/.
4. Scholars tend to examine "migration transitions" from the perspective of states or regions. I apply the concept here to speak in very broad strokes about shifts in humanity's mobility patterns. For more on migration transitions, see Ronald Skeldon, "Migration Transitions Revisited: Their Continued Relevance for the Development of Migration Theory," *Population, Space and Place* 18 (2012): 154–166.
5. See Hein de Haas et al., *Social Transformation*, IMI Working Paper 166 (Amsterdam: International Migration Institute, 2020).
6. David Held et al., *Global Transformations: Politics, Economics and Culture* (Polity, 1999), 2.
7. Helene Thiollet, "Migration as Diplomacy: Labor Migrants, Refugees, and Arab Regional Politics in the Oil-Rich Countries," *International Labor and Working-Class History* 79 (2011): 103–121.
8. Migration Policy Institute tabulation of data from the United Nations Department of Economic and Social Affairs, *International Migrant Stock 2020: Destination and Origin*, United Nations database, POP/DB/MIG/Stock/Rev.2020.
9. For a review of "migration systems" thinking in migration studies, see Oliver Bakewell, "Relaunching Migration Systems," *Migration Studies* 2, no. 3 (2014): 300–318.
10. See Ronald Inglehart, *Modernization and Postmodernization: Cultural, Economic, and Political Change in 43 Societies* (Princeton University Press, 1997); Anthony Giddens and Christopher Pierson, *Conversations with Anthony Giddens: Making Sense of Modernity* (Stanford University Press, 1998).
11. Robert N. Bellah, *Beyond Belief: Essays on Religion in a Post-Traditional World* (University of California Press, 1991), 66.
12. Marshall Berman, *All That Is Solid Melts into Air: The Experience of Modernity* (Simon & Schuster, 1983), 15.
13. "List of LDCs," Office of the High Representative for the Least Developed Countries, Landlocked Developing Countries and Small Island Developing States, United Nations, accessed November 28, 2024, https://www.un.org/ohrlls/content/list-ldcs.
14. Walt W. Rostow, *The Stages of Economic Growth: A Non-communist Manifesto.* (Cambridge University Press, 1960).
15. Joseph E. Stiglitz, *Globalization and Its Discontents* (W. W. Norton & Company, 2002).
16. Michael P. Todaro, "A Model of Labor Migration and Urban Unemployment in Less Developed Countries," *American Economic Review* 59, no. 1 (1969): 138–148.
17. Immanuel Wallerstein, *The Capitalist World-Economy* (Cambridge University Press, 1979).

18. Gunnar Myrdal, *Economic Theory and Under-Developed Regions* (Gerald Duckworth & Co., 1957); see also Douglas S. Massey, "Social Structure, Household Strategies, and the Cumulative Causation of Migration," *Population Index* 56, no. 1 (1990): 3–26.
19. Hein de Haas, "A Theory of Migration: The Aspirations-Capabilities Framework," *Comparative Migration Studies* 9, no. 1 (2021): 1–35.
20. Stephen Castles, "Understanding Global Migration: A Social Transformation Perspective," *Journal of Ethnic and Migration Studies* 36, no. 10 (2010): 1565–1586, 1576; see also Stephen Castles et al., *Social Transformation and Migration: National and Local Experiences in South Korea, Turkey, Mexico and Australia* (Springer, 2015).
21. de Haas et al., *Social Transformation*.
22. de Haas et al., *Social Transformation*.
23. de Haas et al., *Social Transformation*.
24. See also de Haas, "A Theory of Migration."
25. Jørgen Carling, "Migration in the Age of Involuntary Immobility: Theoretical Reflections and Cape Verdean Experiences," *Journal of Ethnic and Migration Studies* 28, no. 1 (2002): 5–42.
26. Amartya Sen, *Development as Freedom* (Knopf, 1999).
27. de Haas, "A Theory of Migration."
28. See Hein de Haas, *Migration and Development in Southern Morocco: The Disparate Socio-Economic Impact of Out-Migration on the Todgha Oasis Valley* (University of Amsterdam Press, 2003).
29. Sen, *Development as Freedom*; see also de Haas, "A Theory of Migration."
30. Sen, *Development as Freedom*, 293, and Ingrid Robeyns, "The Capability Approach: A Theoretical Survey," *Journal of Human Development and Capabilities* 6, no. 1 (2005): 93–114.
31. de Haas, "A Theory of Migration."
32. David Bacon, *The Right to Stay Home: How US Policy Drives Mexican Migration* (Boston: Beacon Press, 2014), 8.
33. Michael J. Piore, *Birds of Passage: Migrant Workers and Industrial Society*. (Cambridge University Press, 1979).
34. Charles Taylor, *Modern Social Imaginaries* (Duke University Press, 2002), 106; see also Charles Taylor, *A Secular Age* (Belknap Press of Harvard University Press, 2007).
35. Taylor, *A Secular Age*, 172; Taylor emphasizes the ways in which our social imaginary shapes interactions between people in relation to his interest in clarifying the "moral order." Taylor shows how certain social forms that characterize Western modernity—the market economy, the public sphere, and democratic self-governance—are only possible through an often taken-for-granted shift in our social imaginary. He explores the contours of "premodern societies," which tended to be organized hierarchically, with limited social mobility. He contrasts this with the modern view of equality, grounded in individual rights, and society conceptualized as the exchange of services among people. See Taylor, *Modern Social Imaginaries*.
36. Arjun Appadurai, "The Capacity to Aspire: Culture and the Terms of Recognition," in *Culture and Public Action*, ed. Vijayendra Rao and Michael Walton (Stanford: Stanford University Press, 2004), 67–68.
37. See Jørgen Carling and Francis Collins, "Aspiration, Desire and Drivers of Migration," *Journal of Ethnic and Migration Studies* 44, no. 6 (2018): 909–926, and Kerilyn Schewel and Sonja Fransen, "Formal Education and Migration Aspirations in Ethiopia," *Population and Development Review* 44, no. 3 (2018): 555–587.
38. Appadurai, "The Capacity to Aspire," 68.
39. As Appadurai writes: "This last, most immediate, visible inventory of wants has often led students of consumption and of poverty to lose sight of the intermediate and higher order normative contexts within which these wants are gestated and brought into view. And thus decontextualized, they are usually downloaded to the individual and offloaded to the science of calculation and market-economics" (Appadurai, "The Capacity to Aspire," 67–68).
40. For a review of surveys on "migration aspirations" see Jorgen Carling and Kerilyn Schewel, "Revisiting Aspiration and Ability in International Migration," *Journal of Ethnic and Migration Studies* 44, no. 6 (2018): 945–963.
41. See Dipankar Ray, "Aspirations, Poverty and Economic Change," in *Understanding Poverty*, ed. Abhijit V. Banerjee et al. (Oxford: Oxford University Press, 2006), 409–422; Carling and Collins, "Aspiration, Desire and Drivers of Migration."
42. To be clear, there is nothing inherently wrong with the logic of a cost-benefit analysis when we consider migration decision-making. Problems arise when "costs" and "benefits" are defined within a narrow economic frame or when the social context and value systems within which

that cost-benefit analysis occurs are ignored. Economists recognize that noneconomic factors also play a role in decision-making and that cost-benefit analyses are always made to maximize overall "utility," not just income. But in practice, noneconomic considerations are generally not regarded as key factors. (See Sonja Haug, "Migration Networks and Migration Decision-Making," *Journal of Ethnic and Migration Studies* 34, no. 4 [2008]: 585–605.) "Utility" remains a vague concept, roughly corresponding with happiness, that is still overwhelmingly measured in terms of income and employment. More work is needed to understand the forces that shape, and change, evaluations of utility over time. That is one goal of the Wayisso case study—to show how Ethiopia's "development" has fundamentally reshaped the *logic* of migration decision-making over time (see, in particular, Chapter 5 on the rise of the profit motive in migration decision-making).

43. Sabina Alkire, "Why the Capability Approach?," *Journal of Human Development* 6, no. 1 (2005): 115–135; Amartya Sen, "Development as Capability Expansion," in *The Community Development Reader*, ed. Irene Diamond and Gloria Feman Orazem (Intermediate Technology Publications, 1990), 41–58.
44. Naiara Rodriguez Peña, *Emigration from "Destination": The Unfulfilled Migration Aspirations of the Precariat in the "Global North"* (PhD diss., School of English, University of Kent, 2023).
45. The concept of internal and external capabilities also resonates and builds on how de Haas theorizes positive and negative liberties. He writes, "The absence of external constraint (negative liberty) is not a sufficient condition for people to exert migratory agency, because they need a certain degree of 'positive liberty' that will enable them to enjoy genuine mobility freedom—which implies a real choice about where to live. For instance, governments may grant nominal freedom of movement, but poor people may still lack positive liberty in the form of capabilities and access to resources that would enable them to actually use such negative liberty" (de Haas, "A Theory of Migration," 24).
46. Richard Black et al., "The Effect of Environmental Change on Human Migration," *Global Environmental Change* 21(2011): S3–S11.
47. Mohsin Hamid, "In the 21st century, we are all migrants," *National Geographic*, August 2019. Available from: https://www.nationalgeographic.com/magazine/article/we-all-are-migrants-in-the-21st-century.

Chapter 2

1. Liberia is the only other state that was not formally colonized in Africa. Although Ethiopia was occupied by the Italian Kingdom from 1936 to 1941, it never established formal colonial control over the country.
2. Shiferaw Bekele, "Monarchical Restoration and Territorial Expansion: The Ethiopian State in the Second Half of the Nineteenth Century," in *Understanding Contemporary Ethiopia: Monarchy, Revolution and the Legacy of Meles Zenawi*, ed. Gérard Prunier and Éloi Ficquet (C. Hurst & Co., 2015), 159–182.
3. Richard Pankhurst, *The Ethiopians: A History* (Blackwell, 2001).
4. Bekele, "Monarchical Restoration and Territorial Expansion."
5. Pankhurst, *The Ethiopians*.
6. Pankhurst, *The Ethiopians*.
7. Significant road expansion in Ethiopia occurred under Emperor Menelik II in the late nineteenth and early twentieth century. In fact, Emperor Menelik is said to have participated himself in constructing roads, so vital were they to his modernization and integration ambitions (Pankhurst, *The Ethiopians*).
8. Robert Steele, "Two Kings of Kings: Iran-Ethiopia Relations under Mohammad Reza Pahlavi and Haile Selassie," *International History Review* 43, no. 6 (2021): 1375–1392.
9. Mulatu Wubneh, "The Economy," in *Ethiopia: A Country Study*, ed. Thomas P. Ofcansky and LaVerle Berry (Federal Research Division, Library of Congress, 1991), 143–205.
10. Christopher Clapham, "The Era of Haile Selassie," in *Understanding Contemporary Ethiopia: Monarchy, Revolution and the Legacy of Meles Zenawi*, ed. Gérard Prunier and Éloi Ficquet (C. Hurst & Co., 2015), 183–208.
11. Gérard Prunier, "The Meles Zenawi Era: From Revolutionary Marxism to State Developmentalism," in *Understanding Contemporary Ethiopia: Monarchy, Revolution and the Legacy of Meles Zenawi*, ed. Gérard Prunier and Éloi Ficquet (C. Hurst & Co., 2015), 212.
12. "Memorandum from the President's Assistant for National Security Affairs (Kissinger) to President Nixon," in *Foreign Relations of the United States, 1969–1976*, vol. E–5, pt. 1, *Documents*

on Sub-Saharan Africa, 1969-1972, accessed November 14, 2023, https://history.state.gov/historicaldocuments/frus1969-76ve05p1/d273.
13. Gérard Prunier and Éloi Ficquet, eds., *Understanding Contemporary Ethiopia* (C. Hurst & Co., 2015), 1.
14. Prunier, "The Meles Zenawi Era," 226; Richard Pankhurst, *The Ethiopians*.
15. Assefaw Bariagaber, "Political Violence and the Uprooted in the Horn of Africa: A Study of Refugee Flows from Ethiopia," *Journal of Black Studies* 28, no. 1 (1997): 26–42.
16. United Nations, Department of Economic and Social Affairs, Population Division, *International Migrant Stock 2020* (United Nations database, POP/DB/MIG/Stock/Rev.2020, 2020).
17. Peter Gill, *Famine and Foreigners: Ethiopia Since Live Aid* (Oxford University Press, 2010).
18. François Piguet and Alula Pankhurst, "Migration, Resettlement & Displacement in Ethiopia," in *Moving People in Ethiopia: Development, Displacement and the State*, ed. Alula Pankhurst and François Piguet (Boydell & Brewer, 2009), 9.
19. Piguet and Pankhurst, "Migration, Resettlement & Displacement in Ethiopia," 9, citing Adrian Wood, "Population Redistribution and Agricultural Settlement Schemes in Ethiopia 1958–80," in *Population and Development Projects in Africa*, ed. John Clark et al. (Cambridge University Press, 1985), 92.
20. Piguet and Pankhurst, "Migration, Resettlement & Displacement in Ethiopia," 10; see also Giordano Sivini, "Famine and the Resettlement Program in Ethiopia," *Africa: Rivista trimestrale di studi e documentazione dell'Istituto italiano per l'Africa e l'Oriente* 41, no. 2 (1986): 211–242; Dessalegn Rahmato, *Resettlement in Ethiopia: The Tragedy of Population Relocation in the 1980s*, Discussion Paper No. 11 (Forum for Social Studies, 2003).
21. Piguet and Pankhurst, "Migration, Resettlement & Displacement in Ethiopia," 9; Gebru Woldemeskel, "The Consequences of Resettlement in Ethiopia," *African Affairs* 88, no. 352 (1989): 359–374.
22. Piguet and Pankhurst, "Migration, Resettlement & Displacement in Ethiopia," 9; Sivini, "Famine and the Resettlement Program in Ethiopia"; Woldemeskel, "The Consequences of Resettlement." Resettlement remains a common development and humanitarian strategy. From 2003 to 2005, for example, a plan of the New Coalition for Food Security resettled over half a million people across Oromia, Amhara, Tigray, and the former Southern Nations, Nationalities, and Peoples' Region. These efforts also faced significant obstacles, namely lack of adequate housing, water, or other resources for the resettled populations and lack of consideration for the rights of pastoralists in areas of resettlement, exacerbating conflicts over environmental resources. See World Bank, *Ethiopia–Urban Labor Markets: Challenges and Prospects*, vol. 2, *Background Paper*, 2007, accessed November 14, 2023, https://openknowledge.worldbank.org/handle/10986/7994.
23. Interview with Negaso Gidada in "Ethiopia's Constitution: Can It Stand the Test of Time?," *Addis Standard*, March 11, 2016, https://addisstandard.com/ethiopias-constitution-can-it-stand-the-test-of-time/.
24. Alex de Waal, "The Theory and Practice of Meles Zenawi," *African Affairs* 112, no. 446 (2013): 148–155.
25. See Meles Zenawi, "State and Markets: Neoliberal Limitations and the Case for a Developmental State," in *Good Growth and Governance in Africa: Rethinking Development Strategies*, ed. Akbar Noman et al. (Oxford University Press, 2012), 140–174; Christopher Clapham, "The Ethiopian Developmental State," *Third World Quarterly* 39, no. 6 (2017): 1131–1147.
26. Clapham, "The Era of Haile Selassie," 364; René Lefort, "The Ethiopian Economy: The Developmental State vs. the Free Market," in *Understanding Contemporary Ethiopia*, ed. Gérard Prunier and Éloi Ficquet (C. Hurst & Co., 2015), 357–394.
27. Clapham, "The Era of Haile Selassie."
28. Clapham, "The Era of Haile Selassie," 365.
29. Lefort, "The Ethiopian Economy."
30. World Bank, *World Development Indicators 2019* (World Bank, 2019).
31. World Bank, *World Development Indicators 2019*.
32. Piguet and Pankhurst, "Migration, Resettlement & Displacement in Ethiopia"; Kerilyn Schewel, *Ziway or Dubai: Can Flower Farms in Ethiopia Reduce Migration to the Middle East?*, IOM Migration Research Series no. 55 (International Organization for Migration, 2018).
33. Infrastructure development has been key to the government's development agenda. In 1997, the EPRDF established the Road Sector Development Program, which expanded Ethiopia's

road network from 26,550 kilometers, of which just 3,708 were paved, to 49,000 kilometers. Foreign companies, primarily Chinese firms, are playing a key role in road construction in recent years. By 2015, the road network had doubled to over 100,000 kilometers.

34. Paul Dorosh and Emily Schmidt, *The Rural-Urban Transformation in Ethiopia*, ESSP Working Paper 2 (International Food Policy Research Institute and Ethiopian Development Research Institute, 2010).
35. Steve Johnson, "Ethiopia Seizes Crown as Fastest-Growing Country in the 2010s," *Financial Times*, December 23, 2019, https://www.ft.com/content/c71cd2e5-7e32-4675-9680-e94bfd7f055d.
36. "News: TPLF says Ethiopia's recent Eritrea, economy related decisions have "fundamental flaws"; calls for emergency meeting of the ruling EPRDF executive, council committee," *Addis Standard*, June 13, 2019, https://addisstandard.com/news-tplf-says-ethiopias-recent-eritrea-economy-related-decisions-havefundamental-flaws-calls-for-emergency-meeting-of-the-ruling-eprdf-executive-council-committee/.
37. Internal Displacement Monitoring Centre, *Global Report on Internal Displacement (GRID) 2021* (IDMC, 2021); Jacky Habib, "Ethiopia Set a World Record for Displacements in a Single Year: 5.1 Million in 2021," NPR, May 28, 2022, https://www.npr.org/sections/goatsandsoda/2022/05/28/1100469734/ethiopia-set-a-world-record-for-displacements-in-a-single-year-5-1-million-in-20.
38. See Bariagaber, "Political Violence and the Uprooted"; Aaron Terrazas, "Beyond Regional Circularity: The Emergence of an Ethiopian Diaspora," *Migration Information Source*, June 2007, https://www.migrationpolicy.org/article/beyond-regional-circularity-emergence-ethiopian-diaspora.
39. The remainder of this chapter draws on material previously published in Kerilyn Schewel and Asmamaw Legass Bahir, "Migration and Development in Ethiopia: Exploring the Mechanisms behind an Emerging Mobility Transition," *Migration Studies* 9, no. 4 (2021): 1673–1707.
40. Prunier and Ficquet, eds., *Understanding Contemporary Ethiopia*, 4; J. Spencer Trimingham, *Islam in Ethiopia* (Geoffrey Cumberlege, 1951).
41. Donald N. Levine, *Greater Ethiopia: The Evolution of a Multiethnic Society*, 2nd ed. (University of Chicago Press, 2000).
42. Levine, *Greater Ethiopia*, 38.
43. The 1984 census, for example, covered about 81 percent of the Ethiopian population, omitting lowland areas with nomadic populations. The 1994 census did not cover the nomadic populations of Afar and Somali regions where pastoralists are dominant. See Sara Randall, "Where Have All the Nomads Gone? Fifty Years of Statistical and Demographic Invisibilities of African Mobile Pastoralists," *Pastoralism* 5, no. 1 (2015): 1–22.
44. *Kilil* Planning Bureaux. Data cited in John Markakis, *Ethiopia: The Last Two Frontiers* (Boydell & Brewer, 2011), 28.
45. Randall, "Where Have All the Nomads Gone?"
46. Central Statistical Agency (CSA), *The 2007 Population and Housing Census of Ethiopia: Results for Country Level. Statistical Report*, vol. 1 (Central Statistical Agency, 2010).
47. See, for example, Claudia J. Carr, *Pastoralism in Crisis: The Dasanetch and Their Ethiopian Lands*, Research Paper no. 180 (University of Chicago, Department of Geography, 1977); Stephen Devereux, *Vulnerable Livelihoods in Somali Region, Ethiopia* (Institute of Development Studies, 2006); Sarah Rettberg, "Contested Narratives of Pastoral Vulnerability and Risk in Ethiopia's Afar Region," *Pastoralism* 1, no. 2 (2010): 248–273. See also Sue Lautze et al., "Why Do Famines Persist in the Horn of Africa? Ethiopia 1999–2003," in *The "New Famines": Why Famines Persist in an Era of Globalization*, ed. Stephen Devereux (Routledge, 2006), 222–244; Tobias Hagmann and Alemmaya Mulugeta, "Pastoral Conflicts and State-Building in the Ethiopian Lowlands," *Africa Spectrum* 43, no. 1 (2008): 19–37; Piguet and Pankhurst, "Migration, Resettlement & Displacement in Ethiopia."
48. Piguet and Pankhurst, "Migration, Resettlement & Displacement in Ethiopia."
49. Sabrina Maurus, "Times of Continuity and Development. Visions of the Future among Agro-Pastoral Children and Young People in Southern Ethiopia," *AnthropoChildren* 6 (2016): 1–24.
50. Pankhurst, *The Ethiopians*, 195.
51. Central Statistical Office (CSO), *Survey of Major Towns in Ethiopia. Statistical Bulletin 1* (Imperial Ethiopian Government Central Statistical Office, 1968).

52. Markos Ezra, "Demographic Responses to Environmental Stress in the Drought- and Famine-Prone Areas of Northern Ethiopia," *International Journal of Population Geography* 7, no. 4 (2001): 259–279.
53. Cf. Wilbur Zelinsky, "The Hypothesis of the Mobility Transition," *Geographical Review* 61, no. 2 (1971): 219–249.
54. World Bank, *Ethiopia–Urban Labor Markets*.
55. Piguet and Pankhurst, "Migration, Resettlement & Displacement"; Ezra, "Demographic Responses to Environmental Stress."
56. Pankhurst, *The Ethiopians*; Blunch and Laderchi, "The Winner Takes It All: Internal Migration, Education and Wages in Ethiopia," *Migration Studies* 3, no. 3 (2015): 417–437.
57. Piguet and Pankhurst, "Migration, Resettlement & Displacement."
58. Abbas Gnamo, *Conquest and Resistance in the Ethiopian Empire, 1880–1974: The Case of the Arsi Oromo* (Brill, 2014).
59. Chris McDowell and Arjan de Haan, *Migration and Sustainable Livelihoods: A Critical Review of the Literature*, IDS Working Paper 65 (Institute of Development Studies, 1997).
60. Alula Pankhurst, Philippa Bevan, Catherine Dom, Agazi Tiumelissan, and Sarah Vaughan, eds., *Changing Rural Ethiopia: Community Transformations* (Tsehai Publishers, 2018).
61. Catherine Dom, "Migrating for Work from Rural Communities (2010–2013)," in *Changing Rural Ethiopia*, ed. Alula Pankhurst et al. (Tsehai Publishers, 2018): 431–463.
62. Niels-Hugo Blunch and Catarina R. Laderchi, "The Winner Takes It All: Internal Migration, Education and Wages in Ethiopia," *Migration Studies* 3, no. 3 (2015): 417–437.
63. Annabel S. Erulkar et al., "Migration and Vulnerability among Adolescents in Slum Areas of Addis Ababa, Ethiopia," *Journal of Youth Studies* 9, no. 3 (2006): 361–374; Kerilyn Schewel and Sonja Fransen, "Formal Education and Migration Aspirations in Ethiopia," *Population and Development Review* 44, no. 3 (2018): 555–587.
64. See Getnet Tadele and Asrat Ayalew Gella, "'A Last Resort and Often Not an Option at All': Farming and Young People in Ethiopia," *IDS Bulletin* 43, no. 6 (2012): 33–43; Ben White, "Agriculture and the Generation Problem: Rural Youth, Employment and the Future of Farming," *IDS Bulletin* 43, no. 6 (2012): 9–19; Daniel Mains, *Hope Is Cut: Youth, Unemployment, and the Future in Urban Ethiopia* (Temple University Press, 2013).
65. Blunch and Laderchi, "The Winner Takes It All."
66. Claudio Montenegro and Harry Patrinos, *Comparable Estimates of Returns to Schooling Around the World*, World Bank Policy Research Working Paper 7020 (World Bank Group, 2014).
67. Schewel and Fransen, "Formal Education and Migration Aspirations."
68. Michael A. Clemens, *The Emigration Life Cycle: How Development Shapes Emigration from Poor Countries*, Center for Global Development Working Paper 540 (Center for Global Development, 2020).
69. Terrazas, "Beyond Regional Circularity"; Donald N. Levine, *Wax & Gold: Tradition and Innovation in Ethiopian Culture* (University of Chicago Press, 1965); Teferi Mergo, "The Effects of International Migration on Migrant-Source Households: Evidence from Ethiopian Diversity-Visa Lottery Migrants," *World Development* 84 (2016): 69–81.
70. United Nations, Department of Economic and Social Affairs, Population Division, *Trends in International Migrant Stock: The 2019 Revision* (United Nations database, POP/DB/MIG/Stock/Rev.2019, 2019).
71. Terrazas, "Beyond Regional Circularity."
72. Clemens, *The Emigration Life Cycle*; Hein de Haas, *Migration Transitions: A Theoretical and Empirical Inquiry into the Developmental Drivers of International Migration*, IMI Working Paper Series No. 24 (International Migration Institute, 2010).
73. Mergo, "The Effects of International Migration."
74. United Nations, Department of Economic and Social Affairs, Population Division, *Trends in International Migrant Stock: The 2019 Revision*.
75. Bina Fernandez, "Household Help? Ethiopian Women Domestic Workers' Labor Migration to the Gulf Countries," *Asian and Pacific Migration Journal* 20, no. 3–4 (2011): 433–457; see also Asnake Kefale and Zerihun Mohammed, *Ethiopian Labour Migration to the Gulf and South Africa* (Forum for Social Studies, 2015).
76. Fassil Demissie, "Ethiopian Female Domestic Workers in the Middle East and Gulf States: An Introduction," *African and Black Diaspora: An International Journal* 11, no. 1 (2018): 1–5.

77. Ethiopian Statistics Service (ESS), *Labour and Migration Survey Key Findings* (Ethiopian Statistics Service [Ethiopia], 2021).
78. Bina Fernandez and Marina de Regt, eds., *Migrant Domestic Workers in the Middle East: The Home and the World* (Palgrave Macmillan, 2014); Marina de Regt, "Ways to Come, Ways to Leave: Gender, Mobility, and Il/legality among Ethiopian Domestic Workers in Yemen," *Gender & Society* 24, no. 2 (2010): 237–260; Kerilyn Schewel, "Aspiring for Change: Ethiopian Women's Labor Migration to the Middle East," *Social Forces* 100, no. 4 (2021): 1619–1641.
79. See Pankhurst, *The Ethiopians*.
80. Teshale Tibebu, "Ethiopia in the Nineteenth Century," in *Oxford Research Encyclopedia of African History* (Oxford University Press, 2018), https://doi.org/10.1093/acrefore/9780190277734.013.279.
81. See Pankhurst, *The Ethiopians*; and Richard Pankhurst, "The Trade of the Gulf of Aden Ports of Africa in the Nineteenth and Early Twentieth Centuries," *Journal of Ethiopian Studies* 3, no. 1 (1965): 36–81.

Chapter 3

1. The Habernoosa have five "doors" (*balbaala*)—the Hadumana, the Godemena, the Alekira, the Afemena, and the Mujemena—each being what might be referred to as subtribes of the Habernoosa. Bedane Tuffaa was of the Hadumana *balbaala*. Dakabo Uso was of the Alekira *balbaala*. The third, Dakabo Bulo, was Abayii, another *goosii* of the Arsi Oromo. He gave some of his daughters in marriage to the sons of Dadi Tashité, a Habernoosa of the Godemena *balbaala*.
2. Seminomadic peoples are distinguished from fully nomadic peoples by having a home base at which some crops may be cultivated. The movements of fully nomadic peoples tend to have a less fixed pattern of movement, and they typically do not cultivate crops.
3. See also Hein de Haas et al., *The Age of Migration: International Population Movements in the Modern World*, 6th ed. (Guilford Press, 2019).
4. Jørgen Carling. "Involuntary Immobility: Theoretical Reflections and Empirical Illustrations," *Journal of Ethnic and Migration Studies* 28, no. 1 (2002): 69–85.
5. Unfortunately, the daughters of these founding patriarchs are not depicted in Generation 2 because there was not sufficient historical memory of who they were and when they were born. It was said all married and moved elsewhere. Only a few from this generation are now deceased; most are still living. Similarly, I do not have reliable information about the wives of the first generation, and so they are not depicted in the family trees.
6. In total, seven women from the household survey were living in the Middle East. Two were distant relatives of Lineage 2, whose family members moved into Wayisso at a later date. Because they were not direct descendants of Dakabo Bulo (or wives of his descendants), they are not depicted in the family trees.
7. For the purpose of the survey and family trees, one's "place of residence" refers to where the individual spent the majority of the year.
8. Abbas Haji Gnamo, "Islam, the Orthodox Church and Oromo Nationalism," *Cahiers d'Études africaines* 165, no. XLII-1 (2002): 99–120.
9. Among the Habernoosa *goosii* in the region, Haji Gemeda of the Mujemena and Hajiti Hawi Irbemo were the first to leave Ethiopia in 1967 (1960 Ethiopian Calendar). After them, Haji Gelato Leta of the Hadumana and Hajiti Shunqaa Daraarso left for the Hajj in 1971 (1964 Ethiopian Calendar).
10. See Marina de Regt, "Ways to Come, Ways to Leave: Gender, Mobility, and Il/legality Among Ethiopian Domestic Workers in Yemen," *Gender & Society* 24, no. 2 (2010): 237–260.

Chapter 4

1. A. Hoben, *Social Soundness of Agrarian Reform in Ethiopia*, Unpublished Report for the U.S. AID Mission to Ethiopia, 1976.
2. See René Lefort, "The Ethiopian Economy: The Developmental State vs. the Free Market," in *Understanding Contemporary Ethiopia*, ed. Gérard Prunier and Éloi Ficquet (C. Hurst & Co., 2015), 357–394.
3. Torsten Hägerstrand, "Migration and Area," in *Migration in Sweden: A Symposium*, ed. David Hannerberg et al. (C. W. K. Gleerup Publishers, 1957), 27–158.

4. See also Ronald Skeldon, "Migration Transitions Revisited: Their Continued Relevance for the Development of Migration Theory," *Population, Space and Place* 18 (2012): 154–166; Ronald Skeldon, "The Evolution of Migration Patterns during Urbanization in Peru," *Geographical Review* 67, no. 4 (1977): 394–411.
5. Mohammed Hassen, *The Oromo of Ethiopia: A History, 1570–1860* (Cambridge University Press, 1990).
6. See Hassen, *The Oromo of Ethiopia*, which details a history of the Oromo from 1570 to 1860, with a particular focus on the Oromo in the Gibe region. He draws on Asarom Legass's work, *Gada: Three Approaches*, to explain the general functioning the Gada system during this period.
7. Hassen, *The Oromo of Ethiopia*, 14.
8. Mohammed Hassen, "A Short History of Oromo Colonial Experience: Part Two," *Journal of Oromo Studies* 7, nos. 1 & 2 (2000): 117.
9. Éloi Ficquet and Dereje Feyissa, "Ethiopians in the Twenty-First Century: The Structure and Transformation of the Population," in *Understanding Contemporary Ethiopia: Monarchy, Revolution and the Legacy of Meles Zenawi*, ed. Gérard Prunier and Éloi Ficquet (C. Hurst & Co., 2015), 15.
10. Ficquet and Feyissa, "Ethiopians in the Twenty-First Century."
11. Ketebo Abdiyo, "A Historical Survey of the Arsi Oromo" (MA thesis, Addis Ababa University, Department of History, 1999).
12. Abdiyo, "A Historical Survey of the Arsi Oromo."
13. As cited in C. F. Buckingham and G. W. B. Huntingford, eds. and trans., *Some Records of Ethiopia 1593–1646* (Hakluyt Society, 1954).
14. Abdiyo, "A Historical Survey of the Arsi Oromo," 16.
15. Abdiyo, "A Historical Survey of the Arsi Oromo," 21.
16. John M. Cohen, "Ethiopia after Haile Selassie: The Government Land Factor," *African Affairs* 72, no. 289 (1973): 365–382.
17. Abdiyo, "A Historical Survey of the Arsi Oromo."
18. Abbas Gnamo, *Conquest and Resistance in the Ethiopian Empire, 1880–1974: The Case of the Arsi Oromo* (Brill, 2014).
19. For example, one of my informants, Haji Tefo, was serving as *cicarsum* of the Habernoosa sometime in the 1960s. The *balabat* at the time was Balambaras Edo Dinsa. "He wasn't selected by Haile Selassie to serve in this position, because in the period of Iyasu, his father had been a *balabat*," Haji Tefo explains. "At that time, it was expected that the chief's son is going to take his position." Balambaras Edo lived around Jido.
20. The Amharic title *Balambaras* was designated for the lowest rank of *balabat*; few reached higher ranks such as *Qagnazmatch* and *Grazmatch*. (See Gnamo, *Conquest and Resistance in the Ethiopian Empire, 1880–1974*.)
21. Wayisso's "founding fathers" living in the early twentieth century remained seminomadic pastoralists, and according to elders' memories, they would go to a place called Chefe Jila in Arsi to participate in the Gadaa elections every five years. They would elect a Gadaa father for each of the Luba: Robele, Bultuma, Birmeja, Horeta, and Bahara. By this time, *luba* referred to different family-based Gadaa systems. These *luba* did not follow clear spatial or tribal divides; rather, certain families were tied to each other in a *luba* system. When they required a Gadaa father's assistance, they went to the Gadaa father of their *luba*. While the generation after the founding fathers continued to go to Gadaa elections in Chefe Jila, their children slowly stopped participating. The Gadaa system still existed, but subsequent generations began to invest less in it as other forms of political-economic organization replaced them.
22. Soybeans were first introduced to Ethiopia in 1950. According to William Shurttleff and Akiko Aoyagi, *History of Soybeans and Soyfoods in Africa (1857–2009): Extensively Annotated Bibliography and Sourcebook* (Soyinfo Center, 2009), the government issued a growers' manual in Amharic and began the first trials to grow soybeans in the 1950s. These were discontinued because of low yields, until the late 1960s, when trials began again. It seems these farmers in the Adami Tulu and Jido Kombolcha *woreda* were part of the second stage of soybean trials.
23. Gérard Prunier, "The Meles Zenawi Era: From Revolutionary Marxism to State Developmentalism," in *Understanding Contemporary Ethiopia: Monarchy, Revolution and the Legacy of Meles Zenawi*, ed. Gérard Prunier and Éloi Ficquet (C. Hurst & Co., 2015): 415–438.
24. Marina Ottaway and David Ottaway, *Ethiopia: Empire in Revolution* (Africana, 1978), 67.

25. The proclamation further asserted that all rural lands shall be the collective property of the Ethiopian people, that no person or business organization or any other organization shall hold rural land in private ownership, that any person who is willing to personally cultivate land shall be allotted rural land sufficient for his maintenance and that of his family, and that the size of land to be allotted to any farming family shall at no time exceed ten hectares (one-quarter of a *gasha*).
26. Dessalegn Rahmato, *Agrarian Reform in Ethiopia* (Scandinavian Institute of African Studies, 1984).
27. According to key informants, the Weyiso Macho kebele was embedded within an *agargelot* of ten *kebeles*: Suro, Repi Woransa, Chebi Kecha, Kertefa, Alemburchure, Korme Nega, Andolla, Weyiso Macho, Kenchera, and Kudusa Reji. Ziway was separated into two *kebeles* at the time, serviced by two *agargelots*. Adami Tulu was one *kebele* and one *agargelot*. The land neighboring Wayisso remained government land. It was originally taken by Haile Selassie in 1952 and remained a state farm during the time of the Derg.
28. Haji Tefo, who had been a *cicarsum* of the Habernoosa *goosii* (from Lineage 1) during the last years of Haile Selassie's reign, described that moment of transition: "Then Haile Selassie fell and the Derg took the stage. The Derg announced, 'Land to the Tillers.' At that time, they were doing very bad things to the representatives of Haile Selassie's government, like the *balabat* and the *cicarsum*. They killed the chiefs.... Because I was a chief for Haile Selassie, I feared for my soul!"
29. See Donald L. Donham, *Marxist Modern: An Ethnographic History of the Ethiopian Revolution* (James Currey, 1999) for a comprehensive and compelling account of the Marxist revolution, the power of modernist ideas, and their impact on the Maale people in southern Ethiopia.
30. Donham, *Marxist Modern*, 31.
31. Donham, *Marxist Modern*, 33.
32. Central Statistical Authority, *The 1984 Population and Housing Census of Ethiopia: Analytical Report at National Level* (Transitional Government of Ethiopia, Office of the Population and Housing Census Commission, 1991).
33. Central Statistical Authority, *The 1984 Population and Housing Census of Ethiopia*, 120–121.
34. The Tigray People's Liberation Front, the Afar Liberation Front, the Oromo Liberation Front, the Somali Abo Liberation Front, and the Eritrean People's Liberation Front.
35. Alex de Waal, "The Theory and Practice of Meles Zenawi," *African Affairs* 112, no. 446 (2013): 148–155.
36. Debretsion Gebremichael, "'My Model Is Capitalism': Ethiopia's Prime Minister Plans Telecoms Privatization," *Financial Times*, February 24, 2019, https://www.ft.com/content/433dfa88-36d0-11e9-bb0c-42459962a812.
37. While Durkheim saw the division of labor as a potential source of social cohesion (organic solidarity) in society, he was also concerned about its potential negative consequences, particularly anomie. Anomie refers to a state of normlessness or deregulation, where individuals may feel disconnected from society's values and a sense of purpose due to excessive specialization and a lack of moral guidance. He worried that individuals might lose a sense of the larger social purpose of their work and become isolated in their narrow tasks, leading to a decline in social solidarity and individual well-being. See Émile Durkheim, *The Division of Labor in Society*, (The Free Press, 1893).
38. See also Daniel Mains, *Hope Is Cut: Youth, Unemployment, and the Future in Urban Ethiopia* (Temple University Press, 2013).

Chapter 5

1. Figures reported for the 2011–2012 year; Bina Fernandez, "Household Help? Ethiopian Women Domestic Workers' Labor Migration to the Gulf Countries," *Asian and Pacific Migration Journal* 20, nos. 3–4 (2011): 433–457; Bina Fernandez, *Ethiopian Migrant Domestic Workers: Migrant Agency and Social Change*, Mobility & Politics (Palgrave Macmillan, 2020); Asnake Kefale and Zerihun Mohammed, *Ethiopian Labour Migration to the Gulf and South Africa* (Forum for Social Studies, 2015).
2. All women who left Wayisso during my fieldwork were technically irregular migrants. Although many signed contracts with their employers, most were underage and all left during a formal ban of labor migration to the Middle East, put in place by the government between 2013 and 2018. The Foreign Affairs spokesman justified the ban at the time as a protection

from human traffickers: "This exodus, being pushed by illegal human traffickers, has created immense problems for the people of the nation. . . . It is affecting a lot of youngsters who are pushed out, deceived by the human traffickers, that has created an immense socioeconomic problem." Al Jazeera, "Ethiopia Bans Domestic Workers from Travelling to Middle East," June 13, 2013, as cited in Katie Kuschminder, *Shattered Dreams and Return of Vulnerability: Challenges of Ethiopian Female Migration to the Middle East*, IS Academy Policy Brief No. 18 (Maastricht Graduate School of Governance, 2014).
3. Teferi Mergo, "The Effects of International Migration on Migrant-Source Households: Evidence from Ethiopian Diversity-Visa Lottery Migrants," *World Development* 84 (2016): 69–81, 71.
4. See, for example, Fassil Demissie, "Ethiopian Female Domestic Workers in the Middle East and Gulf States: An Introduction," *African and Black Diaspora: An International Journal* 11, no. 1 (2018): 1–5; Faiz Omar Mohammad Jamie and Anwar Hassan Tsega, "Ethiopian Female Labor Migration to the Gulf States: The Case of Kuwait," *African and Black Diaspora: An International Journal* 9, no. 2 (2016): 214–227; Khaled Ali Beydoun, "The Trafficking of Ethiopian Domestic Workers into Lebanon: Navigating through a Novel Passage of the International Maid Trade," *Berkeley Journal of International Law* 24 (2006): 1009; Asefach Haileselassie Reda, "An Investigation into the Experiences of Female Victims of Trafficking in Ethiopia," *African and Black Diaspora: An International Journal* 11, no. 1 (2018): 87–102; and Abebaw Minaye, "Trafficked to the Gulf States: The Experiences of Ethiopian Returnee Women," *Journal of Community Practice* 20, nos. 1–2 (2012): 112–133.
5. Bram Frouws, *Blinded by Hope: Knowledge, Attitudes and Practices of Ethiopian Migrants*, Mixed Migration Research Series (Regional Mixed Migration Secretariat, 2014).
6. Karl Polyani, *The Great Transformation* (Rinehart, 1944), 71.
7. Arjun Appadurai, "Definitions: Commodity and Commodification," in *Rethinking Commodification: Cases and Readings in Law and Culture*, ed. Martha Ertman and Joan C. Williams (New York University Press, 2005).
8. Consider, for example, the nannies and daycare centers working families pay to watch their children rather than relying on the goodwill of grandparents, older siblings, or neighbors. Commodification is not always harmful or soulless; access to paid childcare, for example, has revolutionized women's ability to pursue meaningful work and contributions to society beyond childrearing and homemaking. But as commodification progresses in a given society, it means that reaping the fruits of that society increasingly requires money. To extend the childcare example, there are also many mothers and fathers who would prefer to spend more time with their children but feel compelled to take on multiple jobs or meaningless work to cover the ever-growing costs of providing for them. Whether good or bad, the point is that the gradual commodification of social life transforms the social fabric of society, requiring people to develop new ways of thinking, working, and living in that society. As this chapter highlights, it bolsters the profit motive in livelihood and migration decision-making.
9. See Ulf Hannerz, "The World in Creolisation," *Africa: Journal of the International African Institute* 57, no. 4 (1987): 546–559.
10. Mohammed Hassen, *The Oromo of Ethiopia: A History, 1570–1860* (Cambridge University Press, 1990).
11. Daniel Hailu, "Implications of Formal Education for Rural Communities in Ethiopia: The Case of Woyisso-Qancaara Kebele, Oromia Region" (MA Thesis, Department of Sociology and Social Anthropology, Addis Ababa University, 2007).
12. There are also other marriage practices that are fading in frequency but mentioned as part of "Oromo culture." *Butii*, for example, roughly translates to "abduction." A man would simply take the girl or woman without her consent and then send elders to her family to negotiate the details. This was frequent enough that parents would be worried to send their daughters to the river for water after a certain age—but it is no longer permitted. *Walgara* refers to the practice of brothers exchanging their sisters as wives. *Gutuu* refers to the promise parents make of their children to one another. *Asennaa* refers to the situation in which a woman takes the initiative to choose a man. (One informant, Abreham, shared that if multiple young women want to marry a man, they go to his home and the first one to throw a stick and hit his home gets to marry him. He then joked that stick throwing has been replaced by texting.) *Sabbatmarii* refers to a situation in which a young man suffers from some handicap, deformity, or low social standing, such that he is unable to find a wife. Together with a group of men, he goes to the home of one

woman and begins calling, over and over, appealing to the parents to give their daughter, in the name of Waqa, who created marriage. Finally, there is *Hawatta*: when the man and woman choose each other and get married without the prior knowledge or approval of their families. Sometimes a woman may do this if she is expected to marry someone she does not want to marry.

13. See Wolfgang Streeck, "How to Study Contemporary Capitalism?," *European Journal of Sociology/Archives Européennes de Sociologie* 53, no. 1 (2012): 1–28.
14. O. Moav and Z. Neeman, "Saving Rates and Poverty: The Role of Conspicuous Consumption and Human Capital," *Economic Journal* 122, no. 563 (2012): 933–956; R. Linssen, L. van Kempen, and G. Kraaykamp, "Subjective Well-Being in Rural India: The Curse of Conspicuous Consumption," *Social Indicators Research* 101, no. 1 (2011): 57–72.
15. The following section of this chapter draws from material previously published in Kerilyn Schewel, "Aspiring for Change: Ethiopian Women's Labor Migration to the Middle East," *Social Forces* 100, no. 4 (2022): 1619–1641.
16. For extensive research on this migration corridor, see Fernandez, *Ethiopian Migrant Domestic Workers*.
17. Family differences are important to explain these trends. The five women who were abroad as domestic workers at the time of the survey in 2016 were all from Dakabo Bulo's family group. Hawa first embarked upon this new kind of migration, and her sisters, cousins, nieces, and grand-nieces followed. It is notable that women in other family groups did not pursue this migration trajectory. Zooming in on women between the ages of twenty and thirty-nine, no women from Bedane's or Dakabo Uso's family groups had left for the Middle East. Significantly more women from Bedane's family were in Ziway or other urban areas of Ethiopia, while women from Dakabo Uso's family group were far more likely to remain in Wayisso. Over 92 percent of women from Dakabo Uso's family group remained in Wayisso or lived in another rural area.
18. Gary Fuller and Murray Chapman, "On the Role of Mental Maps in Migration Research," *International Migration Review* 8, no. 4 (1974): 491–506.
19. See Elizabeth Fussell, "The Cumulative Causation of International Migration in Latin America," *Annals of the American Academy of Political and Social Science* 630, no. 1 (2010): 162–177.
20. See Rhacel Salazar Parreñas, *Servants of Globalization: Women, Migration and Domestic Work* (Stanford University Press, 2001) and Saskia Sassen, *Globalization and Its Discontents: Essays on the New Mobility of People and Money* (New Press, 1998).

Chapter 6

1. United Nations, *Millenium Development Goals Report 2014: Ethiopia* (2014), http://www.et.undp.org/content/ethiopia/en/home/library/mdg/EthiopiaMDG2014.html.
2. World Development Indicators, "Government Expenditure on Education (% of Government Expenditure), 2010–2018," accessed December 7, 2021, https://datatopics.worldbank.org/world-development-indicators/.
3. The last several decades ushered in dramatic shifts in access to schooling in low-income countries, particularly at the primary and secondary level. Gross enrollment ratios in primary school in low-income countries grew from 46 percent in 1970 to over 100 percent in 2015. (Gross enrollment rates can be over 100 percent, because children who leave school can re-enroll over the course of the year.)
4. Aaron Benavot et al., *Global Educational Expansion: Historical Legacies and Political Obstacles* (American Academy of Arts and Sciences, 2006).
5. Kerilyn Schewel and Sonja Fransen, "Formal Education and Migration Aspirations in Ethiopia," *Population and Development Review* 44, no. 3 (2018): 555–587.
6. Ulf Hannerz, "The World in Creolisation," *Africa: Journal of the International African Institute* 57, no. 4 (1987): 546–559, 553.
7. Margaret LeCompte, "Learning to Work: The Hidden Curriculum of the Classroom," *Anthropology & Education Quarterly* 9, no. 1 (1978): 22–37; Emile Durkheim, *Education and Sociology* (Free Press, 1956).
8. Sabrina Maurus, "Times of Continuity and Development. Visions of the Future among Agro-Pastoral Children and Young People in Southern Ethiopia," *AnthropoChildren* 6 (2016): 1–24, 2–3.

9. Getnet Tadele and Asrat Ayalew Gella, "'A Last Resort and Often Not an Option at All': Farming and Young People in Ethiopia," *IDS Bulletin* 43, no. 6 (2012): 33–43, 37.
10. Richard Pankhurst, "Education in Ethiopia During the Italian Fascist Occupation (1936–1941)," *International Journal of African Historical Studies* 5, no. 3 (1972): 361–396, 362.
11. Pankhurst, "Education in Ethiopia During the Italian Fascist Occupation (1936–1941)."
12. These towns included Dessie, Gore, Jijiga, Lekempti, Harar, Asba Tafar, Ambo, Jimma, Gondar, Debra Markos, Adowa, Makable, and Selale; see Pankhurst, "Education in Ethiopia During the Italian Fascist Occupation (1936–1941)," 361.
13. Damtew Teferra and Philip G. Altbach, eds., *African Higher Education: An International Reference Handbook* (Indiana University Press, 2003).
14. Pankhurst, "Education in Ethiopia During the Italian Fascist Occupation (1936–1941)."
15. As cited in Pankhurst, "Education in Ethiopia During the Italian Fascist Occupation (1936–1941)," 383.
16. Pankhurst, "Education in Ethiopia During the Italian Fascist Occupation (1936–1941)," 396.
17. In addition, by the 1960s, 310 mission and privately operated schools with an enrollment of 52,000 pupils. See Teferra and Altbach, eds., *African Higher Education*.
18. Teferra and Altbach, eds., *African Higher Education: An International Reference Handbook*.
19. See Christopher Clapham, "The Ethiopian Coup D'etat of December 1960," *Journal of Modern African Studies* 6, no. 4 (1968): 495–507.
20. Clapham, "The Ethiopian Coup D'etat of December 1960," 496.
21. World Development Indicators, "Government Expenditure on Education." See also World Bank, *World Bank Education Statistics* (2017), http://databank.worldbank.org/data/reports.aspx?source=Education-Statistics-~-All-Indicators; UNESCO, *Global Monitoring Report* (UNESCO, 2011); World Bank/UNICEF, *Abolishing School Fees in Africa: Lessons from Ethiopia, Ghana, Kenya, Malawi, and Mozambique* (World Bank Publications, 2009).
22. United Nations, *Millenium Development Goals Report 2014: Ethiopia*.
23. United Nations, *Millenium Development Goals Report 2014: Ethiopia*.
24. Federal Democratic Republic of Ethiopia (FDRE), *Growth and Transformation Plan II* (National Planning Commission, 2016).
25. Girmaw Abebe Akalu, "Higher Education in Ethiopia: Expansion, Quality Assurance and Institutional Autonomy," *Higher Education Quarterly* 68, no. 4 (2014): 394–415.
26. In mathematics, for example, the percentage of correct scores declined from 54.42 percent in 2006 to 37.17 percent in 2013 ($p < 0.01$). See Tassew Woldehanna et al., "Assessing Children's Learning Outcomes: A Comparison of Two Cohorts from Young Lives Ethiopia," *Ethiopian Journal of Education* 36, no. 1 (2018): 149–187.
27. See Daniel Mains, *Hope Is Cut: Youth, Unemployment, and the Future in Urban Ethiopia* (Temple University Press, 2013).
28. Getnet Tadele and Asrat Ayalew Gella, "Becoming a Young Farmer in Ethiopia: Processes and Challenges," Working Paper No. 83 (Future Agricultures Consortium, 2014).
29. Zachary Donnenfeld et al., *Ethiopia Development Trends Assessment* (United States Agency for International Development, 2017).
30. Rohen d'Aiglepierre et al., "A Global Profile of Emigrants to OECD Countries: Younger and More Skilled Migrants from More Diverse Countries," OECD Social, Employment, and Migration Working Papers No. 239 (OECD Publishing, 2020).
31. C. Arslan et al., "A New Profile of Migrants in the Aftermath of the Recent Economic Crisis," OECD Social, Employment, and Migration Working Paper No. 160 (OECD Publishing, 2014).
32. Thu Hien Dao et al., "Migration and Development: Dissecting the Anatomy of the Mobility Transition," *Journal of Development Economics* 132 (2018): 88–101; see also Frederic Docquier et al., "The Cross-Country Determinants of Potential and Actual Migration," *International Migration Review* 48 (Fall 2014): S37–S99, https://doi.org/10.1111/imre.12137.
33. Katie Kuschminder and Melissa Siegel, *Migration & Development: A World in Motion Ethiopia Country Report* (Maastricht Graduate School of Governance, 2014); Bina Fernandez, *Ethiopian Migrant Domestic Workers: Migrant Agency and Social Change* (Palgrave Macmillan, 2020); Kerilyn Schewel, "Aspiring for Change: Ethiopian Women's Labor Migration to the Middle East," *Social Forces* 100, no. 4 (2022): 1619–1641.
34. This includes women born elsewhere who then moved into Wayisso when they married.

35. The relationship between years of education and numbers of places lived is strong for men ($r = 0.74$, $p < 0.01$, $n = 274$). For women, the relationship is more modest ($r = 0.48$, $p < 0.01$, $n = 280$), because women already move once for marriage, and most do not attend school. If we exclude married women, the correlation is stronger ($r = 0.70$, $p < 0.01$, $n = 114$). Source: Household survey data.
36. When I returned to Wayisso in 2024, Adam was still living in Wayisso. He was unable to find work that matched his new qualifications. Wariso was also still living in Wayisso, now father to seven children. His wife was pregnant and told me that after that child was born, she hoped to migrate to the Middle East.
37. LeCompte, "Learning to Work," 22. See also Margaret Frye, "Bright Futures in Malawi's New Dawn: Educational Aspirations as Assertions of Identity," *American Journal of Sociology* 117, no. 6 (2012): 1565–1624.
38. In the Education and Training Policy devised in 1994 as the new government took power, it described the purpose of education in this way: "Education enables individuals and society to make all-rounded participation in the development process by acquiring knowledge, ability, skills and attitudes." Source: Federal Democratic Republic of Ethiopia, *Analytical Report on the 2013 National Labor Force Survey* (Central Statistical Agency, 2014).
39. See also Frye, "Bright Futures in Malawi's New Dawn," where she details how education campaigns in rural Malawi lead young people to develop educational and occupational aspirations "as models for self-transformation; individuals fashion their present selves to cohere with an idealized future" (1567). The assertion of high—even unrealistic—aspirations for the future is less about "rational" plans for the future than it is about asserting an identity as "one who aspires" (Frye, "Bright Futures in Malawi's New Dawn"). For another excellent qualitative account in Uganda, see Stephen Murphy, *Educating to Leave: The Migration-Education Nexus & Transformation of Rural Livelihoods in Jinja, Uganda* (PhD diss., School of Politics and International Studies, University of Leeds, 2024).
40. Used at the Sher Ethiopia school in Ziway.
41. See also Maurus, "Times of Continuity and Development," 17–19, for similar examples.
42. See, for example, Karina Nilsson, "Moving into the City and Moving out Again: Swedish Evidence from the Cohort Born in 1968," *Urban Studies* 40, no. 7 (2003): 1243–1258; R. King and R. Skeldon, "'Mind the Gap!' Integrating Approaches to Internal and International Migration," *Journal of Ethnic and Migration Studies* 36, no. 10 (2010): 1619–1646.
43. Primary school is held in the local language, Afaan Oromo, but after grade eight, secondary school switches to English. Students are expected to master English to such a degree that they can not only follow lessons in English but also take the national exam in English after only two years of English-language instruction. Furthermore, teachers themselves are not always proficient in the language. It was not uncommon to encounter secondary school teachers who were supposed to teach in English yet had difficulty having an extended conversation with me.
44. Schewel and Fransen, "Formal Education and Migration Aspirations in Ethiopia."
45. The phrase "aspiration-opportunity gap" has been used in early sociological literature, particularly as it relates to education and employment. For example, Nelsen and Frost (1971) explore the gap between aspirations for education and the quality of public schools in rural Appalachia. Chowdhury (1976) used the phrase to examine the aspirations of young people in nonformal education and actual employment opportunities in Kenya, Nigeria, and Colombia. Hart Nelsen and Eleanor Frost, "Residence, Anomie, and Receptivity to Education among Southern Appalachian Presbyterians," *Rural Sociology*, 36 no. 4 (1971): 521–532; Shamsul Alam Chowdhury, *Non-formal Education and Employment: A Comparative Study* (PhD Diss, The University of Manchester, 1976).
46. Mains, *Hope Is Cut*.
47. World Development Indicators, "Government Expenditure on Education." Unemployment with intermediate education (percentage of total labor force with intermediate education) was 7.98 percent, unemployment with advanced education (percentage of total labor force with advanced education) was 5.48 percent, total unemployment (percentage of total labor force) was 2.25 percent, and unemployment with basic education (percentage of total labor force with basic education) was 3.2 percent in 2013.
48. Ben White, "Agriculture and the Generation Problem: Rural Youth, Employment and the Future of Farming," *IDS Bulletin* 43, no. 6 (2012): 9–19, 12.

49. For a powerful ethnography on the "deskilling" of young people, see Cindi Katz, *Growing Up Global* (University of Minnesota Press, 2004).

Chapter 7

1. 3 square miles or 7.77 square kilometers.
2. Götz welcomed foreign guests traveling through the region, many of whom were hunters, like the American MacCreagh and his wife who met Götz in 1928. "Small is this man and scrubby as to lurid hair and beard," MacCreagh wrote. "He reads Kant and Blavatsky; and he embarks upon no venture without first consulting a Galla witch doctor on the omens.... He was waiting for us. A witch woman had cast the stones for him and told him that white men were coming and—unguessable event—a white woman. So he had a great bowl of curdled milk ready as a thirst-quencher for the guests" (Travelers' notes from an American hunter named MacCreagh as cited in Bernhard Lindahl, *Local History in Ethiopia* [Nordic Africa Institute, 2005], 81–82).
3. A. B. Svensson (Stockholm, 1930), as cited in Lindahl, *Local History in Ethiopia*.
4. D. Buxton, *Travels in Ethiopia* (London, [1949] 1957), as cited in Lindahl, *Local History in Ethiopia*.
5. Prakash Loungani and Assaf Razin, "How Beneficial Is Foreign Direct Investment for Developing Countries?," *Finance and Development* 38, no. 2 (2001), https://www.imf.org/external/pubs/ft/fandd/2001/06/loungani.htm.
6. OECD, *Foreign Direct Investment for Development: Maximising Benefits, Minimising Costs* (OECD, 2006), 6.
7. UN Trade and Development, "Foreign Direct Investment, Trade and Aid: An Alternative to Migration," press release, November 19, 1996, https://unctad.org/press-material/foreign-direct-investment-trade-and-aid-alternative-migration.
8. Similarly, Sanderson and Kentor examine the effect of FDI on the level of emigration from twenty-five less developed countries between 1985 and 2000. The findings indicate that the stock of FDI increases net emigration over time. Matthew R. Sanderson and Jeffrey Kentor, "Foreign Direct Investment and International Migration: A Cross-National Analysis of Less-Developed Countries, 1985–2000," *International Sociology* 23, no. 4 (2008): 514–539. See also Xu Xu and Kevin Sylwester, "The Effects of Foreign Direct Investment on Emigration: The Roles of FDI Source Country, Education, and Gender," *Economic Modelling* 55 (2016): 401–409.
9. James Bang and Raymond MacDermott, "Does FDI Attract Immigrants? An Empirical Gravity Model Approach," *International Migration Review* 53, no. 1 (2018): 237–253.
10. Meskerem Daniel Menamo, "Impact of Foreign Direct Investment on Economic Growth of Ethiopia" (master's thesis, Department of Economics, University of Oslo, 2014).
11. World Development Indicators, "Foreign Direct Investment, Net (BoP, Current US$)," https://data.worldbank.org/.
12. "We invest our own capital in each project, offer preferred returns to investors and believe that in order to do long-term good in Ethiopia we must establish highly-profitable and highly-scalable companies which are good neighbors to their community. The funding needs vary for each deal and range from $1M to $10M in capital depending on the opportunity and stage of growth with a targeted investor return in excess of a 30% IRR." Scott Friesen, CEO/CFO, on Verdant Frontiers website, accessed April 10, 2016, https://www.verdantfrontiers.com/. The website no longer has this language.
13. Verdant Frontiers website, accessed April 10, 2016, https://www.verdantfrontiers.com/. The website has since changed.
14. https://www.youtube.com/watch?v=ZdEetyHp0Mw. The video was last accessed in January 2025.
15. An interview with Bruce Hamilton, director of Verde Beef Processing PLC, European Union Business Forum Ethiopia, https://www.eubfe.eu/index.php/en/interviews/66-an-interview-with-bruce-hamilton-director-of-verde-beef-processing-plc.
16. *Farenji* is a common term for white foreigners.
17. In 2013, the company reported total revenue of 81 million euros and a net profit of 17 million euros; Market Screener, June 4, 2014, https://www.marketscreener.com/quote/stock/KKR-CO-INC-44486777/news/Sher-Ethiopia-PLC-announced-that-it-has-received-200-million-in-funding-from-KKR-Co-L-P—38697349/.

18. Tizita Abate Beyene, "Implications of Cut Flower Industries in Ethiopia: The Case of Flower Farms in the Rift Valley and Sebeta" (master's thesis, Department for International Environment and Development Studies, Norwegian University of Life Sciences, 2014).
19. Ayelech Tiruwha Melese, *Living Wage Report for Non-Metropolitan Urban Ethiopia with Focus on Ziway Flower Farm Cluster* (Global Living Wage Coalition, 2017).
20. Beyene, "Implications of Cut Flower Industries in Ethiopia."
21. Daniel Hailu, "Implications of Formal Education for Rural Communities in Ethiopia: The Case of Woyisso-Qancaara Kebele, Oromia Region" (master's thesis, Department of Sociology and Social Anthropology, Addis Ababa University, 2007).
22. Hailu, "Implications of Formal Education for Rural Communities in Ethiopia," 87.
23. Daniel Mains and Robel Mulat, "The Ethiopian Developmental State and Struggles Over the Reproduction of Young Migrant Women's Labor at the Hawassa Industrial Park," *Journal of Eastern African Studies* 15, no. 3 (2021): 359–377, DOI: 10.1080/17531055.2021.1949118.
24. Paul M. Barrett and Dorothée Baumann-Pauly, "Made in Ethiopia: Challenges in the Garment Industry's New Frontier" (NYU Stern Center for Business and Human Rights, 2019), https://issuu.com/nyusterncenterforbusinessandhumanri/docs/nyu_ethiopia_final_online?e=31640827/69644612.
25. Kerilyn Schewel and Sonja Fransen, "Formal Education and Migration Aspirations in Ethiopia," *Population and Development Review* 44, no. 3 (2018): 555–587.

Chapter 8

1. Kanta Kumari Rigaud et al., *Groundswell: Preparing for Internal Climate Migration* (World Bank, 2018).
2. Kathleen Hermans and Robert McLeman, "Climate Change, Drought, Land Degradation and Migration: Exploring the Linkages," *Current Opinion in Environmental Sustainability* 50 (2021): 236–244.
3. Government of Ethiopia and UN Office for the Coordination of Humanitarian Affairs, "Ethiopia: Drought Response Situation Report No. 04 (as of 31 August 2016)," accessed March 1, 2023, https://reliefweb.int/report/ethiopia/ethiopia-drought-response-situation-report-no-04-31-august-2016.
4. This chart shows rainfall data in mm/year for the Adami Tulu meteorologist office—the closest station to Wayisso. For some missing months, rainfall data from Ziway was substituted as a proxy for Adami Tulu. Even still, some years are missing, particularly a large gap in the 1970s, when rainfall data was not collected.
5. Daniel Hailu, "Implications of Formal Education for Rural Communities in Ethiopia: The Case of Woyisso-Qancaara Kebele, Oromia Region" (master's thesis, Department of Sociology and Social Anthropology, Addis Ababa University, 2007).
6. Amartya Sen, *Development as Freedom* (Knopf, 1999), 293.
7. Stephen Lubkemann, "Involuntary Immobility: On a Theoretical Invisibility in Forced Migration Studies," *Journal of Refugee Studies* 21, no. 4 (2008): 454–475.
8. Clark Gray and Valerie Mueller, "Drought and Population Mobility in Rural Ethiopia," *World Development* 40, no. 1 (2012): 134–145.
9. See Richard E. Bilsborrow, "Population Growth, Internal Migration, and Environmental Degradation in Rural Areas of Developing Countries," *European Journal of Population/Revue européenne de Démographie* 8, no. 2 (1992): 125–148; Richard Black et al., "The Effect of Environmental Change on Human Migration," *Global Environmental Change* 21 (2011): S3–11, https://doi.org/10.1016/j.gloenvcha.2011.10.001; Caroline Zickgraf, "Keeping People in Place: Political Factors of (Im)mobility and Climate Change," *Social Sciences* 8, no. 8 (2019): 228.
10. Charlotte Wiederkehr et al., "Environmental Change, Adaptation Strategies and the Relevance of Migration in Sub-Saharan Drylands," *Environmental Research Letters* 13, no. 11 (2018): 113003.
11. Richard Black et al., "Migration as Adaptation," *Nature* 478, no. 7370 (2011): 447–449.
12. Chandan Kumar Jha et al., "Migration as Adaptation Strategy to Cope with Climate Change: A Study of Farmers' Migration in Rural India," *International Journal of Climate Change Strategies and Management* 10, no. 1 (2017): 122–141; Robert McLeman, "Conclusion: Migration

as Adaptation: Conceptual Origins, Recent Developments, and Future Directions," in *Migration, Risk Management and Climate Change: Evidence and Policy Responses*, ed. A. Milan et al. (Springer International Publishing, 2016), 213–229.
13. Muluken Elias Adamseged and Sindu Workneh Kebede, "Are Farmers' Climate Change Adaptation Strategies Understated? Evidence from Two Communities in Northern Ethiopian Highlands," *Climate Services* 30 (2023): 100369; Dula Etana et al., "Climate Change, In-Situ Adaptation, and Migration Decisions of Smallholder Farmers in Central Ethiopia," *Migration and Development* 11, no. 3 (2022): 737–761; D. Tebboth et al., "Mobility Endowment and Entitlements Mediate Resilience in Rural Livelihood Systems," *Global Environmental Change* 54 (2019): 172–183.
14. Chandi Singh et al., "Risks and Responses in Rural India: Implications for Local Climate Change Adaptation Action," *Climate Risk Management* 21 (2018): 52–68, https://doi.org/ https://doi.org/10.1016/j.crm.2018.06.001.
15. See Tebboth et al., "Mobility Endowment."
16. Heinemeijer et al., *Partir pour Rester: Incidences de l'Emigration Ouvrière à la Campagne Marocaine La Haye*, SGI/REMPLOD (1977) as cited in Hein de Haas, "Migration and Development in Southern Morocco: The Disparate Socio-Economic Impacts of Out-Migration on the Todgha Oasis Valley" (PhD diss., Radboud University Nijmegen, 2003), 99.
17. Marie A. Diatta and Ndiaga Mbow, "Releasing the Development Potential of Return Migration: The Case of Senegal," *International Migration* 37, no. 1 (1999): 243–266.
18. As marriages are delayed by education, lack of cattle or capital for the *gabara* (dowry), and changing social norms, young men increasingly work their own plots of land before they are married.
19. The average landholding in Wayisso is relatively large compared to other areas of Ethiopia—though it should be noted that Wayisso households only farm their land once per year, versus twice a year in the surrounding rain-dense highlands. One survey of land access in Oromia and the southern regions finds an average farm size of 0.86 hectares, with half of all households having only half a hectare (two plots) or less, compared to a national average of 1.22 hectares. Farm sizes were greater in the districts surveyed in Oromia than the former Southern Nations, Nationalities, and Peoples' Region, and they note particularly low levels of land access in the Wolayita region, where 95 percent of households cultivated less than one plot of land. Sosina Bezu and Stein Holden, "Are Rural Youth in Ethiopia Abandoning Agriculture?," *World Development* 64 (2014): 259–272.
20. For example, Dessie (Lineage 1) once had 16 hectares, which he allocated unevenly to his six sons, giving 6.25 hectares to his first born and 1 hectare to his last son. None of Dessie's six sons left Wayisso. By contrast, his brother, Haji Tefo, had fifteen sons. From his 20 hectares, he gave 4 hectares each to his four sons from his first wife. All stayed in Wayisso. Migration is a much more common strategy among the eleven sons of Haji Tefo's second and third wives (see the family trees from Chapter 3). Eight of these eleven sons have left, and those who stayed have relatively little land (one has 1.5 hectares and the other two have none). Those who left were born later (1970s and '80s) and were the first to attain tertiary education. Generation and educational attainment have a clearer relationship to rural out-migration than access to (or lack of) land. Families in Lineage 3 also show higher rates of immobility despite some having relatively large amounts of land and others very little. The first born of Caawaa's second wife has the largest amount of land among all of Caawaa's sons: nineteen plots, or 4.75 hectares. Yet, he already has eight sons from his first wife and two from his second—a number that is likely to increase. With that much land, he could have more easily financed the migration of his children to town for education or work, yet they all have stayed in Wayisso. Other sons who received just two plots, or 0.5 hectares, have also stayed in Wayisso. As Chapter 6 details, variations in the mobility of younger generations largely reflect whether their parents valued and invested in formal education. Caawaa, by his own admission and now with some regret, did not.
21. Bezu and Holden, "Are Rural Youth in Ethiopia Abandoning Agriculture?"
22. Israel Tessema and Belay Simane, "Vulnerability Analysis of Smallholder Farmers to Climate Variability and Change: An Agro-Ecological System-Based Approach in the Fincha'a Sub-Basin of the Upper Blue Nile Basin of Ethiopia," *Ecological Processes* 8, no. 1 (2019): 1–18.
23. Caroline Zickgraf, "Immobility," in *Routledge Handbook of Environmental Displacement and Migration*, ed. Robert McLeman and Francois Gemenne (Routledge, 2018), 71–84.

Chapter 9

1. For more in-depth consideration of the changing place of women in the Gadaa system, see Gutema Imana, "The Muka-Laafaa: The Image of Oromo Women under the Gadaa System and Its Implications for Peace," *East African Journal of Social Sciences and Humanities* 7, no. 1 (2022): 69–84; Tadesse J. Jirata, "Contesting Images of Womanhood: The Narrative Construction of Gender Relations in Ethiopia," *African Studies Quarterly* 18, no. 3 (2019): 1–14.
2. Although technically Adami Tulu and Ziway are more likely to be categorized as "towns" rather than cities (their populations are below one hundred thousand people), they are "cities" in the imaginations of those who live in the rural areas surrounding them—particularly Ziway.
3. Wilbur Zelinsky, "The Hypothesis of the Mobility Transition," *Geographical Review* 61, no. 2 (1971): 219–249, 225.
4. Simone Migali and Marco Scipioni, *A Global Analysis of Intentions to Migrate*, Joint Research Center Technical Reports (European Commission, 2018).
5. Jørgen Carling and Kerilyn Schewel, "Revisiting Aspiration and Ability in International Migration," *Journal of Ethnic and Migration Studies* 44, no. 6 (2018): 945–963.
6. Arjun Appadurai, *Modernity at Large: Cultural Dimensions of Globalization* (University of Minnesota Press, 1996).
7. Learning and modeling others' behavior also explains other important transitions: the emergence of farming or going to school, for example. As detailed in Chapter 5, the practice of small, supplemental farming spread across the *woreda* within a relatively short period of time, sometime between 1967 and 1972, before any government intervention pushed them in that direction. Likewise for education: initially not everyone believed in the merits or benefits of formal education, but the government jobs and steady forms of income to which it gave access showed the potential of education as a pathway into another kind of future. Eventually, more people began to enroll their children, even girls, introducing a wide jump in educational attainment from one generation to the next (see Chapter 6).
8. Syed Ali, "'Go West Young Man': The Culture of Migration among Muslims in Hyderabad, India," *Journal of Ethnic and Migration Studies* 33, no. 1 (2007): 37–58; William Kandel and Douglas Massey, "The Culture of Mexican Migration: A Theoretical and Empirical Analysis," *Social Forces* 80, no. 3 (2002): 981–1004; Robin Cohen and Gísli Pálsson, *Migration and Culture* (Edward Elgar, 2011).
9. Akin L. Mabogunje, "Systems Approach to a Theory of Rural-Urban Migration," *Geographical Analysis* 2, no. 1 (1970): 1–18.
10. See Marshall Berman, *All That Is Solid Melts into Air: The Experience of Modernity* (Verso, 1983).
11. Wolfgang Streeck, "How to Study Contemporary Capitalism?," *European Journal of Sociology/Archives Européennes de Sociologie* 53, no. 1 (2012): 1–28, 10.
12. Streeck, "How to Study Contemporary Capitalism?," 10.
13. Paul F. Lazarsfeld, "The American Soldier—An Expository Review," *Public Opinion Quarterly* 13, no. 3 (1949): 377–404; Samuel A. Stouffer et al., *The American Soldier: Adjustment During Army Life*, vol. 1 (Princeton University Press, 1949).
14. Oded Stark and J. Edward Taylor, "Relative Deprivation and International Migration," *Demography* 26, no. 1 (1989): 1–14.
15. Hein de Haas, *Migration and Development in Southern Morocco: The Disparate Socio-Economic Impacts of Out-Migration on the Todgha Oasis Valley* (PhD diss., Radboud University, 2003).
16. Gary Fuller and Murray Chapman, "On the Role of Mental Maps in Migration Research," *International Migration Review* 8, no. 4 (1974): 491–506.
17. Tatek Abebe, "Lost Futures? Educated Youth Precarity and Protests in the Oromia Region, Ethiopia," *Children's Geographies* 18, no. 6 (2020): 584–600.

Chapter 10

1. Kerilyn Schewel et al., *Evaluating Climate-Related Migration Forecasting Models* (Research Technical Assistance Center, 2022). See also Kerilyn Schewel et al., "How Well Can We Predict Climate Migration? A Review of Forecasting Models," *Frontiers in Climate* 5 (2024): 1189125.
2. James C. Scott, *The Moral Economy of the Peasant: Rebellion and Subsistence in Southeast Asia* (Yale University Press, 1977).

3. Oded Stark and David Levhari, "On Migration and Risk in LDCs," *Economic Development and Cultural Change* 31, no. 1 (1982): 191–196; Oded Stark and David E. Bloom, "The New Economics of Labor Migration," *American Economic Review* 75 (1985): 173–178.
4. See, for example, Fassil Eshetu et al., "Impact of Rural Out-Migration on Vulnerability to Rural Multidimensional Poverty in Southern Ethiopia," *Journal of International Migration and Integration* 24, no. 3 (2023): 1175–1209; Mariama Zaami, "Conceptualising Migration and Livelihoods: Perspectives from the Global South," in *The Routledge Handbook on Livelihoods in the Global South*, ed. Fiona Nunan et al. (Routledge, 2022), 359–367.
5. Sabrina Maurus, "Times of Continuity and Development. Visions of the Future among Agro-Pastoral Children and Young People in Southern Ethiopia," *AnthropoChildren* 6 (2016): 1–24; see also Getnet Tadele and Asrat Ayalew Gella, "'A Last Resort and Often Not an Option at All': Farming and Young People in Ethiopia," *IDS Bulletin* 43, no. 6 (2012): 33–43; James Sumberg et al., "Introduction: The Young People and Agriculture 'Problem' in Africa," *IDS Bulletin* 43, no. 6 (2012): 1–7; Laura Camfield, "'From School to Adulthood': Young People's Pathways through Schooling in Urban Ethiopia," *European Journal of Development Research* 23, no. 5 (2011): 679–694; Tatek Abebe, "Trapped between Disparate Worlds? The Livelihoods, Socialisation and School Contexts of Rural Children in Ethiopia," *Childhoods Today* 2, no. 1 (2008): 1–29.
6. Daniel Mains, *Hope Is Cut* (Temple University Press, 2013), 71.
7. Mains, *Hope Is Cut*, 76. In Ethiopia, the "ideology of progress" Mains identifies finds expression in different "narratives of success," or pathways through which people imagine a better life can be achieved. Murugan and Abebaw suggest that Ethiopians increasingly view migration as an established pathway to success—a "short-cut" through which individuals and families, facing significant opportunity constraints locally, can achieve their aspirations for a better and more prestigious life. In their study of the factors motivating human trafficking from Ethiopia, they argue that modern capitalist expansion creates a "a disjunction between socially expected ends/goals and the ways/means of achieving those goals" (78). Faced with high aspirations for modern notions of success and severe constraints on achieving them locally, many Ethiopians see migration as the only means to achieve their desired ends and sometimes put themselves in precarious conditions to achieve it. See Padmanabhan Murugan and Biniam Abebaw, "Factors Contributing to Human Trafficking, Contexts of Vulnerability and Patterns of Victimization: The Case of Stranded Victims in Metema, Ethiopia," *Ethiopian Journal of the Social Sciences and Humanities* 10, no. 2 (2014): 75–102.
8. Gina Crivello, "'Becoming Somebody': Youth Transitions through Education and Migration in Peru," *Journal of Youth Studies* 14, no. 4 (2011): 37–41; Gina Crivello, "'There's No Future Here': The Time and Place of Children's Migration Aspirations in Peru," *Geoforum* 62 (2015): 38–46.
9. Carlos Iván Degregori, *Del Mito de Inkarri al Mito del Progreso: Poblaciones Andinas, Cultura e Identidad Nacional* (Instituto Constructor, 2007): 6, as translated by and cited in Crivello, "'There's No Future Here,'" 38. 'Principle' was changed to 'principal' for the translation used here.
10. Virginia Morrow, "Whose Values? Young People's Aspirations and Experiences of Schooling in Andhra Pradesh, India," *Children & Society* 27, no. 4 (2013): 258–269 (abstract).
11. The Nigerian geographer Akin Mabogunje, the founder of migration systems theory, was one of the first to seriously incorporate changing aspirations into migration theory. He writes that economic development generally brings with it "greater social and cultural integration of rural and urban areas such that levels of expectations in both areas begin to converge towards a recognizable national norm of what is the 'good life'" (4). The growing interconnectedness of rural and urban areas "sharpens the awareness and desire of villagers for the ever increasing range of goods and services which the urban centers have to offer" (4). Decades later but making a similar claim, sociologists Peggy Levitt and Deepak Lamba-Nieves note the emergence of "consumption-oriented strategies of upward mobility and new aspirations among youth" (6) as one important consequence of development. Migrants accelerate these changing aspirations at origin by sending back social remittances—new ideas, behaviors, and identities—that can in turn cultivate desires to migrate among youth who remain. See Akin L. Mabogunje, "Systems Approach to a Theory of Rural-Urban Migration," *Geographical Analysis* 2, no. 1 (1970): 1–18; Peggy Levitt, "Social Remittances: Migration Driven Local-Level Forms of Cultural Diffusion," *International Migration Review* 32, no. 4 (1998): 926–948; Peggy Levitt and Deepak

Lamba-Nieves, "Social Remittances Revisited," *Journal of Ethnic and Migration Studies* 37, no. 1 (2011): 1–22.

12. Arjun Appadurai, *Modernity at Large: Cultural Dimensions of Globalization* (University of Minnesota Press, 1996).
13. Robert N. Bellah, *Beyond Belief: Essays on Religion in a Post-Traditional World* (University of California Press, 1991), 66.
14. Further, any comparison of values and visions of the good across generations, communities, and societies inevitably reveals diverse manifestations of how "local" and "global" cultural forces interact, synthesize, and transform each other. Cultural anthropologists use the term "creolization" to conceptualize how local peoples shape and are shaped by the "intercontinental traffic in meaning" in our global age. Local social structures provide the matrices through which global flows of culture refract, giving rise to distinct cultural syntheses and expressions, such as the marriage and conflict mediation rites described in Chapter 5. See Ulf Hannerz, "The World in Creolisation," *Africa: Journal of the International African Institute* 57, no. 4 (1987): 546–559, 547–548.
15. Wilbur Zelinsky, "The Hypothesis of the Mobility Transition," *Geographical Review* 61, no. 2 (1971): 219.
16. Zelinsky, "The Hypothesis of the Mobility Transition," 223.
17. Ronald Skeldon, *Population Mobility in Developing Countries: A Reinterpretation* (Belhaven Press, 1990).
18. Zelinsky, "The Hypothesis of the Mobility Transition," 236.
19. See, for example, Ronald Skeldon, *Population Mobility in Developing Countries* on Peru: "The patterns of pre-Columbian migration were progressively and profoundly altered by the Spanish colonial administration. A mobile population is difficult to control and from the late sixteenth century, the Spanish introduced a policy to 'reduce' the dispersed population into centrally planned villages, the *reducciones*. The transition to living in these villages took some time and occurred against the background of a population in rapid decline resulting primarily from the introduction of disease by the Spanish conquerors" (51).
20. Hein de Haas et al., *The Age of Migration: International Population Movements in the Modern World* (Bloomsbury Publishing, 2019).
21. Oliver Bakewell, "'Keeping Them in Their Place': The Ambivalent Relationship between Development and Migration in Africa," *Third World Quarterly* 29, no. 7 (2008): 1341–1358.
22. Dennis Conway, "Step-Wise Migration: Toward a Clarification of the Mechanism," *International Migration Review* 14, no. 1 (1980): 3–14; see also Anju Mary Paul, "Stepwise International Migration: A Multistage Migration Pattern for the Aspiring Migrant," *American Journal of Sociology* 116, no. 6 (2011): 1842–1886.
23. Ronald Skeldon, "Migration Transitions Revisited: Their Continued Relevance for the Development of Migration Theory," *Population, Space and Place* 18 (2012): 154–166, 164.
24. This comparative analysis was the goal of the Migration as Development project, led by Hein de Haas, of which this research was a part (European Research Council Consolidator Grant project, H2020/2015-2020, Grant Agreement 648, 496).
25. For example, sociologist Peter Uhlenberg explained unexpectedly high rates of immobility in southern Appalachia between 1930 and 1960 by arguing that tightly knit community dynamics countered classical push factors like high rates of poverty and unemployment. More recently, geographers Holly Barcus and Stanley Brunn, examined the dynamics of place attachment in eastern Kentucky. They distinguish those who are "rooted in place" by choice from those who are "tied to place" because they lack the capability to leave. The rooted in place "were born, raised, and will likely die and be buried, in the same location" (38)—and happily so. Those who are rooted in place are more likely to describe their home country with adjectives like "close knit," "family oriented," "quiet," "peaceful," "safe," and "wonderful," (38) while those who are tied to place use words like "underprivileged," "uneducated," "unsophisticated," "illiterate," "backwards," and "broke" (42). This finding resonates with Simona Vezzoli's work in a small Brazilian town, where despite significant economic decline, she finds many aspire to stay because of feelings of what she calls "relative endowment," juxtaposing the idea of relative deprivation as a motivation for migration. Those who aspire to stay describe a good life in terms of proximity to family, the natural environment, tranquility, and peacefulness—notably noneconomic factors. Peter Uhlenberg, "Non-Economic Determinants of Non-Migration: Sociological Considerations for Migration Theory," *Rural Sociology*

38, no. 3 (1973): 297–311; Holly R. Barcus and Stanley D. Brunn, "Towards a Typology of Mobility and Place Attachment in Rural America," *Journal of Appalachian Studies* (2009): 26–48; Simona Vezzoli, "Understanding Aspirations to Stay: Relative Endowment within a Time–Space Perspective," *Migration Studies* 11, no. 2 (2023): 259–285.
26. See Carol Farbotko, "Voluntary Immobility: Indigenous Voices in the Pacific," *Forced Migration Review* 57 (2018): 81–83; Carol Farbotko et al., "Relocation Planning Must Address Voluntary Immobility," *Nature Climate Change* 10, no. 8 (2020): 702–704.
27. Assefa Hailemariam, "Ethiopia's Changing Demography," in *The Oxford Handbook of the Ethiopian Economy*, ed. F. Cheru et al. (Oxford University Press, 2019).
28. Jennifer D. Sciubba, *8 Billion and Counting: How Sex, Death, and Migration Shape Our World* (W. W. Norton & Company, 2022).
29. Michael Piore, *Birds of Passage: Migrant Workers and Industrial Society* (Cambridge University Press, 1979).
30. Emphasis added. Tim Hume, "Prime Minister Makes Offer to Hungarian Women: Have 4 Kids and Never Pay Income Tax," Vice, February 11, 2009, https://www.vice.com/en/article/gyayzb/prime-minister-makes-pitch-to-hungarian-women.
31. Stephen Castles, "The Forces Driving Global Migration," *Journal of Intercultural Studies* 34, no. 2 (2007): 122–140; see also David FitzGerald, *Refuge beyond Reach: How Rich Democracies Repel Asylum Seekers* (Oxford University Press, 2019).
32. See Hein de Haas, *How Migration Really Works: A Factful Guide to the Most Divisive Issue in Politics* (Random House, 2023).
33. Stephen Castles, "Why Migration Policies Fail," *Ethnic and Racial Studies* 27, no. 2 (2004): 205–227, 205.
34. European Commission, "European Trust Fund for Africa," accessed January 10, 2024, https://trust-fund-for-africa.europa.eu/.
35. These are examples of part of a broader trend in what political economist Sarah Bermeo describes as "targeted development." Industrialized states, unable to isolate themselves from the impact of events in developing countries, have responded with a strategy of targeted development: pursuing development abroad when and where it serves their own self-interest. In this case, the aim is to reduce migration. Sarah Bermeo, *Targeted Development: Industrialized Country Strategy in a Globalizing World* (Oxford University Press, 2018).
36. Douglas S. Massey et al., "Community Services and Out-Migration," *International Migration* 48, no. 3 (2010): 1–41, 31.
37. Massey et al., "Community Services and Out-Migration," 31.
38. Domenico Marino and Domenico Tebala, "Rural Areas and Well-Being in EU Countries + UK: A Taxonomy and a Cluster Analysis," *Sustainability* 14, no. 22 (2022): 15213.
39. Jong Hyung Lee et al., "Rural Disparities in Deaths of Despair: A County-Level Analysis 2004–2016 in the U.S.," *American Journal of Preventive Medicine* 64, no. 2 (2023): 149–156.
40. Feeding America, "Rural Hunger Facts," accessed January 11, 2024, https://www.feedingamerica.org/hunger-in-america/rural-hunger-facts; Feeding America, *Map the Meal Gap 2019* (Feeding America, 2019), accessed January 11, 2024, https://www.feedingamerica.org/sites/default/files/2019-05/2017-map-the-meal-gap-full.pdf
41. Patrick J. Carr and Maria J. Kefalas, *Hollowing Out the Middle: The Rural Brain Drain and What It Means for America* (Beacon Press, 2009).
42. Berman, *All That Is Solid Melts into Air*, 15.

Epilogue

1. https://www.verdantfrontiers.com/.

Methodological Notes

1. See, for example, Geoffrey Walford, "The Impossibility of Anonymity in Ethnographic Research," *Qualitative Research* 18, no. 5 (2018): 516–525 and Will van den Hoonaard, "Is Anonymity an Artifact in Ethnographic Research?" *Journal of Academic Ethics* 1, no. 2 (2003): 141–151.
2. A few households, which were part of the Abayii survey group, could not trace their lineage back to Dakabo Bulo but had moved there later and were considered part of the Abayii group. For this reason, they are not captured in the family trees. For the family trees, I included only kin descended from one of the three original patriarchs.

Index

For the benefit of digital users, indexed terms that span two pages (e.g., 52–53) may, on occasion, appear on only one of those pages.

Tables, figures, and boxes are indicated by an italic *t*, *f*, or *b*.

acquiescent immobility, 27–28
Adami Tulu, 12*f*, 65*t*, 66*f*, 68*t*, 93–99, 105, 160–162
Addis Ababa, 37–38, 45, 65*t*, 67*f*, 220*f*
ADLI, 41–42, 76, 91
agency *see* aspiration–capability framework
agricultural Development-Led Industrialization *see* ADLI
agricultural labor, 177, 181–182, 186–188, 194, 198–199
agriculture, transformation of, 38–39, 42, 164, 185, 186–187
Appadurai, Arjun, 32–33, 214, 227–228
Arsi Oromo, 58–59, 78–79, 160–161
aspiration–capability framework, 21, 25–36, 189–190, 231, 238
aspirations
    adaptation of, 30, 158–159, 192–194, 211–213, 220–221, 237–238
    aspiration for transformation, 215–216, 237–238
    aspiration–opportunity gap, 30, 128–129, 155–159, 175–176, 210–211, 232–233, 234–235
    socially shaped nature of, 21, 30–32, 215–216, 218–220, 235–236 *see also* good life; social imaginary
    youth aspirations, 151–152, 153–155, 157–159, 202, 226–227

Bacon, David, 28–29
balabat mirt, 79–80, 86
Bedane Tuffaa (family lineage), 58–59, 62*f*, 64–65, 68*t*, 144*f*, 145*f*
Bellah, Robert, 20, 227–228
Berman, Marshall, 20, 240
Bulbulla, 66*f*, 67*f*, 147

capability
    capability approach, 25–29, 31*f*, 33–35, 98, 128–129, 137–138, 192, 196–197 *see also* de Haas, Hein; Sen, Amartya
    capability to stay, 28, 189–190, 193, 196–197, 236, 238–239 *see also* aspiration–capability framework; displaced in place; relative deprivation; subsistence ethic
    capability to migrate, 27, 27*f*, 28–29, 33–35, 196–197, 210–213, 238–239
capitalism, 23, 91, 216
Carling, Jørgen, 25–27
cattle, 4–5, 114, 166–170, 194, 202–204 *see also* Verde Beef
conflict and displacement, 38, 40–41, 43–44, 190
conflict mediation *see* Gadaa system
conspicuous consumption, 122
constraints on mobility *see* aspiration–opportunity gap
creolization, 106, 116–117
Crivello, Gina, 148, 227
cumulative causation, 23, 127

Dakabo Bulo (family lineage), 58–59, 63*f*, 65, 68*t*, 144*f*, 145*f*
Dakabo Uso (family lineage), 58–59, 64*f*, 68*t*, 144*f*, 145*f*
de Haas, Hein, 23, 25–29, 216–217
Derg regime, 39–41, 51–54, 75, 83–90, 101, 135–136, 138, 162–163
development paradigm
    application in Ethiopian policies and discourse, 37–39, 41–43, 90–92, 223 *see also* foreign investment
    concepts of development and progress, 14–15, 23, 92, 161–162 *see also* migration and development;

development paradigm (*Continued*)
  modernization theory; push-factor narrative
  critiques of, 22–23, 29, 39, 43, 221–222, 228, 236, 238–240
  produces discontent, 215–217, 221–222, 238–240
diaspora, Ethiopian in United States, 8, 51–55, 71
displaced in place, 189–191, 199
diversification of international migration, 11, 56, 71–74, 230–231
drought, 183, 185–188, 189–193, 237

education
  access and inequality, 136–137, 142–143, 147, 183
  gendered effects, 140–142, 147, 155–158
  historical development, 87–89, 133–138, 141*t*, 142*f*, 143*f*, 144*f*, 145*f*
  impact on migration, 48–57, 131–132, 137–138, 140–142, 148–152, 197, 219–220
  symbolic and social role, 131–133, 151–153, 155–159, 209–210, 219–220, 226–227
empire, Ethiopian, 4, 37–38, 79–83, 107 *see also* Selassie, Haile; Menelik II
environment *see* land, and climate
EPRDF *see* Revolutionary Democratic Front
Ethiopian state formation, 75–78, 89–91, 99–100
ethnic federalism, 41, 90–91

family lineage, 64*f*, 142–146, 146*t*, 147 *see also* Bedane Tuffaa; Dakabo Bulo; Dakabo Uso
foreign direct investment (FDI) *see* foreign investment
foreign investment, 38–39, 42–43, 161–163 *see also* Verde Beef; Sher Ethiopia
Fransen, Sonja, 47–48, 49*t*, 50*t*, 132, 154–155, 219–220, 220*f*

Gadaa system, 71, 75, 77–78, 106–109, 109*b*, 133
Ganda Bedane, 4–5, 58–59
gender
  and education *see* education, gendered effects
  and labor/employment, 102–103, 173–174, 180–181 *see also* Sher Ethiopia
  and migration, 61–62, 65, 66–67, 102–104, 116–117, 122–130, 173–175, 183–184, 232
  and shifting roles/power, 102–104, 129–130, 155, 205–206

globalization, 13, 19–20, 130, 230–232
good life
  as culturally embedded and socially variable, 32
  generational differences in perceptions of, 106, 207–210, 220–222
  historical definition (cattle, family, status), 202–204
  as imagined ideals that shape aspirations, 30–32, 106
  modern definition, 204–207
  redefinition of, from rural/pastoral to urban/modern, 201–202, 220–221
  unachievable in Wayisso, perception of as, 221–222 *see also* aspiration–capability framework; social imaginary
Götz, Herr, 160–161
Gurage, 44, 160

Hawassa Industrial Park, 180–181

immobility *see* acquiescent immobility; involuntary immobility; voluntary immobility
intergenerational change, 207–210, 220, 226–227
involuntary immobility
  contrast with voluntary immobility and seasonal migration, 188, 231–232
  displacement in place and aspiration constraints, 25, 27*f*, 60, 65, 184, 189–190
  drivers: drought, lack of capabilities, exclusion from futures, 183–184, 191, 221, 231–232
Italian occupation, 37–38, 133–134, 160–161

labor market, 30, 92–94, 97–98, 101, 122–130, 157–158, 163, 171–172, 173–179, 181, 225–226, 230, 232 *see also* Verde Beef; Sher Ethiopia
land
  and climate, 1–2, 13, 34, 182, 224, 237
  cultivation of, 81–83, 99–100, 158, 197
  degradation and use transformation, 182–184, 185–188, 199–200
  reform, 75, 79, 85–87
  tenure, 47, 79–80, 86–87
legal pluralism, 107–109 *see also* Gadaa system
Legass Bahir, Asmamaw, 9, 43–44

Mains, Daniel, 157, 180, 226–227
market economy

conceptualized through Polanyi's "market society", 105–106
emergence and expansion from weekly market to town-wide system, 105
generating inequality and new standards of consumption, 120–121
leading to commodification of social life, 106
linked to commodification of rural life and mobility, 226
shaping aspirations for urban life and migration, 105
marriage practices, 114–122, 204
marxist regime *see* Derg regime
Maurus, Sabrina, 132–133, 226–227
Menelik II, 37–38, 45, 133 *see also* empire, Ethiopian
mental maps, 125–126, 154–155, 216–217, 218–222
migration
adaptation to environmental or structural change, 192–194
decision-making processes, 25–26, 97–98, 104
environmental drivers of migration, 185–190, 191–192
generational migration patterns, 60
internal migration, 47–48, 49*t*, 56–57, 74, 154–155
irregular migration, 33–34, 55, 128, 220
migrant remittances, 93, 98, 125–126, 130, 192–193, 199–200, 216–217, 225
migration for domestic work, *see* gender, and migration
migration for education, *see* education, impact on migration
migration transition curve, 7*f*
narratives and representations, 25–26, 192–194, 214–215, 237–239
religious dimensions of migration, 71
root causes of migration, 16, 21, 234, 236
rural–urban migration, 47–48, 56–57, 61–62, 66*f*, 88, 98, 100–101, 121–122, 129, 148, 180–181, 214
stepwise migration patterns, 13, 71, 154–155, 180–181, 230–231
theoretical approaches, 22, 25–26, 30, 225–226

migration and development
interconnected processes, 6–8, 21–23, 223–224, 234–235
policy debates and agendas, 232–236
theoretical approaches, 21, 23–26, 29–30, 216 *see also* aspiration–capability framework; development paradigm; push-factor narrative; social transformation framework
migration to Middle East
characteristics and outcomes, 66–67, 103–104, 122–123, 124–130
motivations and aspirations for, 71, 102–103, 124, 126–127, 174–176, 218–219 *see also* gender, and migration
mobility transition
in Ethiopia/Wayisso, 8, 44–57, 59, 188, 229–232
theory of, 6–8, 229–232
modernity
critique of development's double-edged effects, 238–240
divergent models: imperial, socialist, developmentalist, 37–43
stimulates aspirations and mobility, 221–222
structural and existential dimensions, 20–21, 227–228
tension between agency and alienation, 240
modernization theory, 6, 22–25, 227–228

NELM *see* new economics of labor migration
neocolonialism *see* foreign investment
New Economics of Labor Migration (NELM), 225–226
nomadic and seminomadic populations, 44–45, 57, 59, 67–69, 100*t*, 184–185, 215

Oromo, 76–79, 106–107, 133 *see also* Arsi Oromo; Gadaa system; Oromo protests
Oromo protests, 43, 163, 185, 221, 239

Pankhurst, Richard, 133–134
pastoralism, 44–45, 58–59, 81–83, 184–185, 215 *see also* cattle; Gadaa system
peasant associations (kebele), 4–5, 84–87, 89–90, 107, 138, 147
Piore, Michael, 30, 232–233
Polanyi, Karl, 105–106, 227–228

process of commodification, 106, 114, 116–117, 122, 129, 221, 226
profit motive, 104, 122–127, 129, 225–226
push-factor narrative
  contrasted with aspiration–capability framework, 25–26, 238
  contrasted with transformation ethic and social imaginary, 16, 21, 238
  distorts development–migration link, 2, 188, 200, 237
  dominance in policy and discourse, 1–2, 223–224, 237
  neglects aspiration and transformation, 2, 20–21, 188, 237–238
  overlooks stratified (im)mobility, 2, 4–5, 12–13, 237
  shapes policy and marginalizes migrant voice, 223–224
  structural bias and neglect of agency, 2, 6, 237

relative deprivation, 216–217, 221
resettlement, 40–41
Revolutionary Democratic Front (EPRDF), 41–43, 53*f*, 76, 90–91
rural flourishing, 236

Saudi Arabia, 19–20, 52*t*, 55–56, 71
Scott, James, 225
sedentarization of traditional mobility
  customary mobility patterns and seasonal movements, erosion of, 81–83
  development and environmental change, linked to, 184–185
  nomadic and semi-nomadic livelihoods among Oromo, transition from, 44–45
  pastoral sustainability and land use, consequences for, 184–185
  rural livelihood transformation, 44–45, 92, 155–158, 182, 184–185
Selassie, Haile, 38–40, 81–84, 133–134, 160–163 *see also* empire, Ethiopian
Sen, Amartya, 26, 29, 189–190
Sher Ethiopia, 163, 172–177, 218–219
Silt'e, 58, 81

Sirna Gadaa, *see* Gadaa system
Skeldon, Ronald, 6–7, 229–231
social imaginary
  concept of social imaginary, 30–32, 214, 225
  migration, relationship with, 57, 201–202, 214–215, 235–236
  urbanization of, 21, 57, 130, 181, 188, 201–208, 230–231
social transformation framework, 21, 23–25, 28–30, 31*f*, 34, 35–36, 224–225, 231
socialism *see* Derg regime
Stark, Oded, 97–98, 216, 225
subsistence ethic, 225, 235–236

transformation ethic, 16, 223–228, 235–236

urbanization
  aspirations for, *see* social imaginary, urbanization of
  as a development process, 18–19, 22, 42–43, 45, 56–57
  of internal migration, 9, 47–50, 49*t*, 74, 180–181, 218–219, 231–232

Verde Beef, 151, 163, 164–172
voluntary immobility
  associated with rootedness, place attachment and place-based identity, 231–232
  linked to aspiration–capability framework, 25–28 *see also* aspiration–capability framework
  linked to good life and capability to stay, 193 *see also* capability to stay; migrant remittances

wage labor, 9, 19, 30, 45, 56, 160, 180–181, 192, 197, 238–239
Wayisso, *as ethnographic field site*, 117*b*, 167*b*, 243–249
Wolayita, 77, 122, 177–179, 197–198

Zelinsky, Wilbur, 6–7, 207, 215, 229–232
zemecha campaign, 88, 136
Zenawi, Meles, 41–42, 76, 90–91
Ziway, 11, 12*f*, 62–63, 65–67, 65*t*, 66*f*, 68*t*, 72*f*, 73*f*, 219–220

www.ingramcontent.com/pod-product-compliance
Ingram Content Group UK Ltd.
Pitfield, Milton Keynes, MK11 3LW, UK
UKHW041135230426
470302UK00016B/92